THE WORK -AT- HOME SOURCEBOOK

Sixth Edition

LIVE OAK

Lynie Arden

Live Oak Publications
Boulder, Colorado

Distributed by Publishers Group West

© 1996, 1994, 1992, 1990, 1988, 1987 by Lynie Arden

All rights reserved. No part of this book may be reproduced or transmitted in any form or by arv means, electronic or mechanical, including photocopying, recording or by any information storage and retrieval system without written permission from the publisher.

Publisher's Cataloging-in-Publication
(Prepared by *Quality Books Inc.*)

Arden, Lynie, 1949-
The work-at-home sourcebook/ Lynie Arden. --6th ed.
p. cm.
Includes indexes.
ISBN 0-911781-14-5 (paper) : $19.95

1. Home labor--United States--Directories. 2. Home-based enterprises--United States--Directories. 3. Business enterprises--United States--Directories. I. Title.
HD2336.U5A73 1996 338.7'4'02573
QBI96-20071

Live Oak Publications
P.O. Box 2193
Boulder, CO 80306

Disclaimer

Every attempt has been made to make this book as accurate and complete as possible. There may be mistakes of content or typography, however, and the author and publisher make no guarantees, warranties, or representations of any kind. This book is designed as a general guide to the subject. The reader is urged to investigate and verify information and its applicability under any particular situation or circumstances.

The author and publisher shall have no liability or responsibility to anyone with respect to contacts, negotiations, or agreements that may result from information in this book, or for any loss or damage caused or alleged to have been caused directly or indirectly by such information. If legal advice or other expert assistance is required, the services of a competent professional person should be sought.

Table of Contents

Table of Contents

WORKING AT HOME

How To Go To Work From Your Home

"This is our lifestyle; it's called freedom."
—Janice Katz, Sacramento Professional Typists Network

Personnel manager Pat Mahy wasn't looking for a job at home, but when Escrow Overload asked her to give it a try a couple of years ago, she said okay.

"Starting out I had my doubts. I couldn't imagine being without the stimulation of other people at work. It had some appeal, though. I figured my time might be better spent if I wasn't wasting it commuting. Well, I was thrilled within a week!"

Pat is one of the 40 million Americans who currently work at home, a number that is currently growing at a rate of almost 20% a year. Some government studies have indicated that as much as 75% of the work done in this country could eventually be moved home.

Not everyone would be happy working at home, of course, and many people are simply not interested in moving their work home. Still, more and more people are having the same experience as Pat Mahy, who says "I'm still finding more hidden benefits to working at home the longer I do it."

Using This Book

If you want to give working at home at try, this book can be a good place to start. It won't teach you how to start a home business from scratch and it won't duplicate certain other work-at-home topics that are well covered in other books.* As far as we know, though, nowhere else can you find as many specific opportunities for working at home—involving so many diverse options—already assembled for you into one neat package.

** For an unusually good selection of home-business books see the free catalog available from The New Careers Center, listed in the Resource Guide of this book (page 329).*

A Wide Range of Possibilities

You'll quickly notice that there are a variety of work styles represented in this book. Once you leave the confines of the traditional nine-to-five centralized work mode, a colorful rainbow of employment options appear. There is freelancing, independent contracting, working on commission, salaried positions, co-oping, and various combinations of these and other ways of working. You can get paid by the hour, by the piece, by the sale, by the project, or by the year.

You'll want to consider your needs carefully. Do you need the security of a salary? If so, freelancing is not for you. Have you always wished you could get paid for what you produce because you do it faster and better than almost everybody else? Then you may be able to boost your income by opting for piece rates. Alternately, you might want to be able to depend on a set salary, yet have lots of opportunities for earning more than the base rate by earning commissions, bonuses or other incentives. Telemarketing and market research positions, for example, often offer this type of compensation package.

One other point needs to be made about salaries. In comparing the salaries (and other forms of compensation) offered for working at home to those of conventional employment, be sure to take into consideration the many savings you'll enjoy by working at home. The money you'll save on clothing, commuting, parking, lunches and other items may make it worthwhile for you to take a home-based job that, on the surface at least, offers less money than you would make going into an office every day.

Opportunities Everywhere

You'll find over 1,000 companies in this book which have work-at-home arrangements, but it's important to keep in mind that these listings represent only a small sample of the work-at-home opportunities actually available today. This book will be most valuable to you if you use it as an idea generator.

Suppose, for example, that in skimming through the company listings you notice there are a number of typesetting jobs at home. You had a job setting type for a publishing company for several years and feel confident you could do the work, but for one reason or another none of the specific jobs in the listings are exactly right for your situation.

By all means don't be discouraged. Study the job listings carefully, noting the names of the companies, their pay structure, how many home workers they employ and other pertinent information. Then go talk to each publishing company in your town. They may never have considered hiring home workers before but if you can explain how other publishing companies have organized their home work programs—and the benefits they are getting from their programs—you'll have a good chance at getting exactly the work you want.

Some of the benefits you'll want to mention are the following (and they're not limited to publishing companies):

Increased Productivity

A 20% increase in productivity is average, with some employers reporting substantially more than that. Some dedicated telecommuters have reported up to an 80% increase over their office-bound counterparts.

Lower Turnover

Once settled into a home-based job, would you give it up? Turnover among home-working employees is so low, some companies have waiting lists up to a year long for new applicants.

Near Zero Absenteeism

Flexiplace usually means flexitime, too. Work schedules can be manipulated to accomodate child-care needs, fevers and sniffles, and yes, an occasional case of playing hookey on a beautiful spring day. As long as the work gets done within the overall time limits of the job, everyone's happy.

Improved Recruiting

In areas with low unemployment, flexiplace is often used as an added inducement to potential employees. This is especially true for fields like computer programming where demand for highly qualified workers often exceeds supply. Several years ago, Continental Illinois Bank had a problem finding qualified secretaries in the Chicago area. They reasoned that many competent women were at home with children and were therefore unable to participate in the job market. The bank started Project HomeWork to solve the problem.

Lower Costs

Many companies start home work programs when they run out of room for expansion and don't want to tie up additional capital in office space. Insurance, utilities, training, maintenance and other costs often go down when workers go home.

HOME WORK AND THE LAW

There are two areas of the law that directly affect home workers; labor laws and zoning ordinances.

Labor Laws

Only a handful of states have labor laws specifically regarding working at home. In each case, their purpose is to govern "industrial home work" (work which would normally be done in a factory such as product assembly). Industrial home work is usually low skilled, low pay work in which there has been a history of worker exploitation. The purpose of the state labor laws is to insure worker safety and insure that minimum wage requirements are met.

States without labor laws specifically relating to home work fall under the jurisdiction of the U.S. Dept. of Labor and its Fair Labor Standards Act of 1938 (FLSA).

The FLSA initially prohibited seven industries from using home workers. In 1938, this was a good idea since sweatshop conditions were the established norm. In December, 1984, after years of see-sawing through the courts, the ban on knitted outerwear was lifted. The remaining prohibited industries were: gloves and mittens, belts and buckles, jewelry, women's apparel, embroidery, and handkerchiefs.

Senator Orrin Hatch introduced the Freedom of the Workplace bill (S.665) soon after the ban on knitted outerwear was lifted. It calls for the complete reversal of the FLSA restrictions on home work. As written, workers' rights would be protected by the same certification process that is required for home knitters.

Congresswoman Olympia Snowe of Maine introduced a similar bill, the Home Employment Enterprise Act (HR2815) in the House of Representatives. It was virtually the House twin of Hatch's bill. Congresswoman Snowe told the House, "Cottage industries play a vital role in the economy of the state of Maine, large parts of New England, and other areas of the nation. The independent nature of home work and the unavailability of alternative employment opportunities make working at home ideal. It is time to safeguard the freedom to choose to work at home."

Before either bill came up for a vote, prohibitions on industrial home work in five of the six industries were lifted by the U.S. Dept. of Labor, effective January 9, 1989. New, tougher enforcement requirements went into effect at the same time.

Ann McLaughlin, Secretary of Labor, said "Workforce flexibility is a critical element of our effort to create jobs, enhance the quality of worklife for American workers and improve our competitive edge in world markets. The changing workforce demographics demand that we provide employment opportunities that allow workers the freedom to choose flexible alternatives including the ability to work in one's own home. Women, for example, have entered the workforce by the millions; home work adds a measure of worker flexibility and economic freedom.

"At a time when flexibility is an operatonal imperative to our competitive advantage, government should enhance, not impede, workers' choices," McLaughlin added.

There is only one industry the FLSA still prohibits from using home workers — women's apparel. This omission was apparently an attempt on behalf of the DOL to avoid direct confrontation with its most active opponent in this action, The International Ladies Garment Workers Union. Aside from the prohibition mentioned here, there are no other occupations covered by labor laws. Furthermore, these laws only pertain to employees, not independent contractors, independent business people, or otherwise self-employed workers.

Zoning

Before working at home in any capacity, you should find out what your local zoning ordinance has to say about it. If you live in a rural area, chances are good that you have nothing to worry about. In populated areas, however, there are often specific provisions in the zoning laws pertaining to home occupations.

Zoning laws tend to focus on the impact of a given activity. Sometimes called "nuisance laws," they are designed to protect neighborhoods from disruptive noise, traffic, odors, etc.

Chicago is an extreme example. Within the city limits, it is illegal to use electrical equipment in a home occupation. That means no calculators, no typewriters, no computers. The laws are outdated in Chicago and are too often outdated elsewhere around the country. The city council in Chicago is working on a new ordinance that will be more accomodating to home work, and it's possible for you to initiate zoning changes in your city, too.

Zoning boards are made up of your neighbors and local business people, and it is likely they are unaware of problems caused by outdated zoning ordinances. If you are frustrated by your city's zoning code, get to know these people, attend some meetings, and propose that the laws be changed.

Independent Contractor Status and Tax Savings

More often than not, home workers are paid as independent contractors. In essence, this means you are totally responsible for your own work. While different government agencies don't necessarily agree on the definition of independent contractor, generally speaking, there are two major factors affecting how home workers are classified. They are the "degree of control which the employer exercises over the manner in which the work is performed," and "opportunities for profit and loss."

It should be noted that no government agency will take you on your word that you are an independent contractor. Even if you have a written contract with a company declaring that you both agree to an employer/independent contractor relationship, the legitimacy of that relationship must be proven.

The issue here is not whether being an employee is better or worse than being an independent contractor. There are advantages and disadvantages in every situation. Rather, the issue is whether the term "independent contractor" is being applied consistantly and correctly. If you meet all I.R.S. criteria for independent contractor status, you'll be responsible for your own taxes, most notably Social Security tax, which is renamed "Self-Employment Tax" for this purpose.

Business expenses will help you at tax time, so you need to keep records right from the start of any and all expenditures. Business expenses generally fall into two categories: direct and indirect.

Direct expenses are those which occur in the day-to-day operation of your business. Costs for office supplies, phone service, advertising, bookkeeping, equipment, books, trade publications and seminars related to your work, and insurance are all examples of direct, fully deductible expenses.

You shouldn't forget the more subtle types of deductions, either. Entertainment in the course of your work, whether in your own home or not, is ordinarily deductible if you discuss or conduct business while you're entertaining and keep a record of what went on and with whom.

The same thing is true for vacations. You can generally write off a portion of your vacation expenses if you spend some time along the way looking for new business. Remember, the government expects you to try to expand your business.

Indirect expenses are those that are a part of your usual domestic bills—utilities, rent or mortgage payments, maintenance and housecleaning, property insurance, etc. Indirect expenses come under the heading of the Home Office Deduction.

The Home Office Deduction is the most common and significant way for home workers to reduce their federal tax. In order to claim the deduction, you must show that your home work space is used regularly and exclusively as your principal place of business and meeting place. (If you are a salaried employee, you may also be eligible if you can prove that your employer requires you to keep a home office as a condition of employment. In this case, you should consult an expert to determine if you meet the requirements.)

Home office expenses are deductible at the rate of whatever percentage of square footage your work space takes up. If your home is 1,000 square feet and you use 200 square feet exclusively for work space, you can normally deduct 20% of those receipts. A word of caution: if you use your work space for any other purpose than work, you can not deduct any of these expenses. Therefore, working on the kitchen table is a bad idea unless you really don't have any choice.

At last count, there were some 23 possible deductions for a home office. To make sure you don't miss any, get a copy of I.R.S. Publication 587, "Business Use of the Home." It is available free from any I.R.S. office and is updated annually.

Making the Most of Working at Home

If you perservere in your efforts to land a home job, in time you're likely to succeed. Your home work space is where you will be spending a large portion of your life—in fact, you will most likely spend more time there than any other place. The consideration you give to its design could have a tremendous impact on the success of your home work experience.

Wouldn't it be wonderful to have a work place all your own, some private space free from distractions? A beautiful office maybe, with a separate entrance, big windows facing out onto a garden, with elegant furniture and the latest equipment modern technology has to offer. Fortunately, dreaming is free.

You may have to start out on the kitchen table or in a corner of the living room. Millions have started the same way and that's okay—for a while. To make the most out of working at home, though, you'll need to begin planning ways to make your working space more comfortable, efficient and permanent.

Five elements directly affect mental attitude and productivity in every work space: light, sound, furniture, air quality, and color.

Proper lighting is essential to the good health of any worker. It has been conclusively demonstrated that improper or inadequate light has varying degrees of negative effects on people. At the very least, it can cause significant decreases in productivity. Some people have more serious reactions, including long term bouts with depression.

Adequate overall lighting is not necessarily optimal lighting. Care should be taken to reduce glare from both direct and indirect sources. Whether light is reflected from a bright window or from a video display terminal (VDT), glare can cause eyestrain and headaches. You can usually solve glare problems by moving your furniture around, changing the type and strength of your lightbulbs, or installing screens over windows and VDTs.

Sound doesn't usually have the same impact on the work place as light, but it is an important factor to consider. Noise can come from traffic, children and lawnmowers outside and appliances, children, pets and your own work equipment inside, causing distraction and lower productivity. You can install sound absorbing material to reduce noise or you can attempt to mask the noise with neutral sounds (white noise) or with music. Most electronics stores sell white noise generators.

The right furniture can also make a difference in your work performance and satisfaction. The type of work surface you need depends on the type of work you're doing, but in any case it doesn't have to be fancy or expensive. What is important is that the surface be large enough to suit the task, that the height is right for you, and that it is sturdy enough to hold your equipment without wobbling.

A good chair is definitely worth the investment. It should provide ample back support, thereby reducing fatigue and backaches. Features such as adjustable back tension, an easily-adjusted height mechanism and rollers will make your life easier, too. If you work with a keyboard, even for short periods of time, don't get a chair with armrests. Armrests can prevent you from getting close enough to the edge, with resulting aches and pains in your back, neck and shoulders.

Air quality and temperature can also have a major impact on your physical comfort. Ideally, you want fresh, clean air no warmer than 75 degrees or cooler than 68 degrees. Indoor pollution can be caused by lack of ventilation, especially with highly weatherized homes. Pollution sources include carpets, upholstery, stoves, aerosols and cleaning fluids, to name only a few. In addition, there are few jobs that don't involve their own polluting substances. Correction fluid, hobby and craft supplies, paint, glue and lint are examples.

The best way to clean up your indoor air is with ventilation. Plants help, too. Certain common houseplants, such as Spider Plants, gobble up indoor toxins. Electric air filters can help, too. They cost more than plants, but require less care. Negative ion generators are especially helpful in the presence of electronic equipment such as computers.

Color is the final factor which you should consider. It can set the overall tone of your work space and make it a place you want to be—or a place you'd rather avoid.

White and very light colors aren't stimulating, but do reflect the most light, making a space appear larger than it is. Blacks, browns, and greys make a space appear smaller than it is, absorbing light and creating feelings of fatigue. Blues and greens are relaxing, feel cool, and reduce blood pressure. Reds, oranges, and yellows are bright, stimulating, cheerful and warm. In too strong a contrast, however, they can cause irritability and increased blood pressure.

Carefully choosing the color scheme and other aspects of your work space can make a big difference in your productivity as well as how you feel about your work. It's usually not necessary to spend a lot of money to make your

work place pleasant; just use some imagination and take the time to think through how you can make the most of the space that's available to you.

HOME BUSINESS OPPORTUNITIES

BUSINESS OWNERSHIP: THE FINAL STEP TO INDEPENDENCE

It wasn't long ago that starting a new business was beyond the reach of many. Starting a business from scratch required a large investment, usually over $100,000 for a storefront operation. Keeping the business going with the high overhead took a great deal of time and effort. For those of us interested in adding more freedom and flexibility to our lives, business ownership was a fate worse than a job.

Times change. There are now a growing number of ways to go into business without the heavy burdens of the past. You can start a business at home without the huge investment and with much of the risk removed. By buying into a proven business system, you can take advantage of the knowledge and experience of a successful business. For as little as a few hundred dollars, you can have independence and security — an unbeatable combination.

This section is not about starting a business on your own. Instead, it contains over 450 opportunities to buy into a proven business system. Some are franchises, some are not. All offer some level of training and support and all give you a better chance of success than going it alone.

A franchise is a successful business formula that essentially sells a clone of itself to a franchisee for a license fee, and then collects royalties on the revenues. Franchising is a preferred way for a business to expand its operations. The franchisee gets a business plan, financial planning and marketing strategies, a trademark, advertising help, training and ongoing technical and business support. The franchisee has the satisfaction of running his or her own business, but still has the security and support of being associated with a large organization. There is a price to be paid for the security—in the form of royalties and also in being obligated to do things according to the company's policies and guidelines.

For those with more independent leanings, there are many stand-alone business systems that offer a basic package similar to a franchise, but without the ongoing obligations. You can buy a turnkey system that provides you with everything you need to get started—from a business plan to paper clips. But an independent turnkey business system is generally less expensive than a franchise because they don't offer ongoing support, use of the company name, or national advertising. And, while franchises often grant territorial exclusivity, independent business opportunities generally offer no such protection against local competition. But—in addition to lower upfront costs—they don't charge ongoing royalties or advertising fees. Some independent business systems do offer ongoing support or consultation services for a set period of time, usually a year, so there is plenty of time to get valuable answers to questions about your new business.

Not all independent business systems are turnkey. You'll see, as you read through some of the listings, that there is a wide range of services offered. With many, you can decide for yourself how complete your package should be. You may want, for example, to obtain training at home through the use of video tapes if you can't afford to get away for a week to attend training classes at company headquarters. With many companies, you have that choice. Other options might include office equipment, a computer system and/or software, a start-up tool kit, advertising materials, or consulting services.

No matter which type of business opportunity you opt for, you are to be congratulated for having the courage to take the final step to independence. In addition to having more control over your life, business ownership is a great way to insure yourself of optimal income potential. For anyone who is serious about making money at home, the listings in this section offer a real opportunity for success.

AUTOMOTIVE

Automotive services, particularly in the after-market, have always comprised a huge industry. That hasn't changed. What has changed is the need to have all automotive services performed at centralized locations. More and more opportunities are opening up to homebased entrepreneurs, mostly through mobile services.

In this section you will find a variety of opportunities to make a good income taking care of cars. Auto detailing, one of the most popular business opportunities, is now a $2.5 billion industry. It's popularity among new entrepreneurs is based on the assumption that anyone can clean a car, even if this is the ultimate car wash. And it's true. Furthermore, it's a business that can be started for under $1,000 and profits can go into six figures annually.

The next step up from detailing is restoration. Restoration services include paint chip repair; paintless dent repair; repair and recoloring of vinyl, leather, and plastic parts.

A long, long time ago we were able to get our car's oil changed at our friendly neighborhood service station. The word "service" was changed to "gas" and quick lube shops took over the oil and lube responsibilities. Today, you don't even have to leave home to get an oil change. Mobile services will come to you, wherever you are, so all you have to do is make a phone call. This business is more expensive to get into because there is the need for a properly outfitted van, but there is a tremendous opportunity for repeat business that's very appealing.

And finally, glass repair is still growing fast, saving customers time and money over the replacement alternative.

APPEARANCE PLUS, INC., 4100 N. Powerline Rd., #B-5, Pompano Beach, FL 33073; (954)969-0888.
Franchise: No.
Description: Auto detailing, mobile washing, and waxing of cars, boats, aircraft and RVs.
Requirements: Start as low as $2,000 or go as high as $15,000.
Provisions: Products, equipment, marketing material, the right to use the name as an authorized dealer, ongoing company support, and full training program at corporate office.
Profit Potential: $50,000 to $100,000 per year.

AUTOMOTIVE REFERRAL SERVICES, Crozer Mills Enterprise Center, 600 Upland Ave., Suite 101, Upland, PA 19015. (215)499-7484.
Franchise: No.
Description: Auto buying service. You act as an independent buying agent for your customer, saving them up to $2,000 and earning you a broker fee of between $250 and $300 per vehicle. The customer takes delivery of the vehicle at a dealership and gets a full warranty as usual.
Requirements: $695 total fee.

Provisions: Manual emphasizing low cost ways to acquire customers, how to establish working relationship with dealers, how to negotiate, getting paid, and adding potential profit centers.
Profit Potential: Four sales per week should amount to $1,000 profit.
Comments: Can be started part-time.

CHIPS AWAY, 1536 Saw Mill Run Blvd., Pittsburgh, PA 15210; (800)837-CHIP.
Franchise: No.
Description: A mobile service that provides paint chip repair quickly and easily. Since the Patent Pending process only adheres to primer paint, no masking is necessary. Paint colors are easily matched exactly for a flawless finish. Send for video if you're interested in this opportunity.
Requirements: The system starts are $5,995 and there is financing available for up to 48 months.
Provisions: The fee buys complete training and all tools, equipment, and supplies necessary to start the business.
Profit Potential: It is possible to make a six figure income.

COLOR NOUVEAU, 2711 Via Cases Loma, San Clemente, CA 92672. (800)283-0233.
Franchise: Yes.
Description: Color Nouveau provides an economical alternative which has become popular throughout the industry and which makes it easy and inexpensive to touch up all exterior finishes of cars, trucks, vans, and buses, restoring them to like-new condition. Start with a mobile touch-up service which takes the shop to the auto rather than the auto to the shop. Add small quantity color matching and quick and easy color application and you have the formula for success.
Requirements: The start-up fee is $9,995 plus a maintenance fee of $50 per month. Financing is available.
Provisions: Supplied are all the training and materials necessary and everything you need to get started: air brush, power compressor, overspray remover, touch-up brushes, and enough paint toners to do over 600 cars. You also receive a set of color matching formulas contained in a 115-page manual containing over ten thousand formulas.

THE CURTIS SYSTEM, Mountain Road, Box 250, Stowe, VT 05672 (800)334-3395.
Franchise: No.
Description: Auto detailing, which is the ultimate car cleaning and polishing service.
Requirements: Package costs $1,500 complete. No experience is necessary.
Provisions: Learn at home with an illustrated manual and 95 minute training video. Also included are tools, sales and business techniques, supplies, and ongoing support with a toll-free hotline and newsletter. In addition to learning how to detail cars, you will learn how to build and run a business, how to advertise, how to get and keep customers, and how to build repeat business. The sales promotion kit provides ads, brochures, etc.
Profit Potential: Some detailers report earning $100 to $200 per car and up for about 3 - 4 hours of work.
Comments: Gross sales from auto detailing is expected to reach $2.5 billion by 1995. This business can be run part-time while staying at your present job or you can run it as an absentee owner by hiring a crew to do the work for you.

CUSTOM AUTO RESTORATION SYSTEMS, INC., 479 Interstate Ct., Sarasota,

FL 34240; (800)736-1307.
Franchise: No.
Description: Company offers a full business start-up for mobile paint touch-up, velour and vinyl repair, paintless dent repair, windshield repair, and odor removal systems.
Requirements: Prices range from $500 to $8,000.
Provisions: Depending on the size of your investment, you can receive equipment, supplies, training (business and technical), and hands-on training at headquarters.
Profit Potential: $100,000 per year.

DENT BUSTERS, INC., 2838 N.W. 39th, Oklahoma City, OK 73112; (800)880-338.
Franchise: No.
Description: The service includes "paintless" auto dent repair, i.e.: repair hail damage and door dents without paint or fillers being used.
Requirements: Total cost is $5,250.
Provisions: Cost includes a complete set of custom designed tools, five full days of hands-on training, and all information needed to start the business.
Profit Potential: $3,000 to $10,000 per month.

FITZGERALD'S, 221 North American St., Stockton, CA 95202; (800)441-3326.
Franchise: No.
Description: Automotive interior restoration including the repair and recoloring of vinyl, leather, velour, and plastic parts on the side of vehicles. The typical job takes less then an hour and the work is done on-site right out of the licensee's vehicle.
Requirements: $10,000 for complete package of all four subjects (vinyl, leather, velour, and plastic) or $2,900 for one subject.
Provisions: All licensees receive all of the necessary equipment and chemicals. Five days of training is followed up by a bi-monthly newsletter and unlimited consultation.
Profit Potential: Approximately $1,000 per week or more.
Comments: Fitzgerald's has over 700 homebased licensees.

GEO SYSTEMS, P.O. Box 8163, Clearwater, FL 34618-8163; (800)237-0363.
Franchise: No.
Description: Professional auto detailing. Optional add-ons services include teflon protective coating, building and fleet power washing, steam cleaning, window tinting, alarm systems, and windshield repair.
Requirements: Several options are available starting with a "Level I" start-up package costing $1,595. Total cost for a top-of-the-line, self-contained van unit is $17,950 plus a van lease.
Provisions: The systems include training and all equipment, tools, and supplies necessary to go into business full-time. Training includes physical hands-on training at corporate headquarters, manuals, videos, newsletters, marketing seminars, and toll-free phone consultation. Training and support covers technical and product training, management training, marketing and sales training, and financial training.
Profit Potential: Working part time, detailing three cars per week, your yearly profit would be about $18,000. Working full-time, detailing three cars per day, your profit would be over $90,000 per year.
Comments: The potential looks good for someone without experience and little start-up capital.

GLASS MECHANIX, INC., 10170 N.W. 47th St., Sunrise, FL 33351; (800)826-8523.

Franchise: No
Description: Windshield repair service.
Requirements: $1,298.
Provisions: The fee covers training, machines, and enough materials to repair 500 windshields.
Profit Potential: A windshield takes about 15 minutes to repair, and the average charge is $35. The cost is about 50 cents so it is possible to earn up to $300 a day in this business.
Comments: This company was started in a two-bedroom condominium in 1982. It now grosses over $500,000 a year.

GLASS TECHNOLOGY, INC., 434 Turner Drive, Durango, CO 81301; (303)247-9374.
Franchise: No.
Description: Windshield repair.
Requirements: Total cost is $2,455.
Provisions: Glass Technology offers a complete windshield repair business including everything needed to get started: equipment, supplies, training, and ongoing support. Training covers not only the technical aspects of the business, but business management as well.
Profit Potential: Profit per repair is about $34 for 15 minutes of work. Performing nine repairs per day would yield $80,000 per year.
Comments: This can be a good business if you take advantage of the market by approaching insurance companies, fleet accounts, and car dealers. How to get these accounts is included in the training.

GLAS-WELD SYSTEMS, 20578 Empire Blvd,. Bend, OR 97701; (800)321-2597.
Franchise: No
Description: Glass repair service.
Requirements: $595.
Provisions: The investment includes equipment and enough materials to make 125 repairs and earn over $4,000 in revenue. A set of six training tapes are also included. Training topics include business start-up, generating sales, expansion, customer relations, advertising and promotion, and time management. Video training and field training are available options.
Profit Potential: Up to $75,000 a year.

LIQUID RESINS INTERNATIONAL, Box 549, Olney, IL 62450; (800)458-2098.
Franchise: No.
Description: Glass repair is one of the fastest growing parts of the automotive industry. Most mobile windshield repair technicians travel from one business location to another, show samples of the work that can be done and request permission to inspect the business vehicles on a regular basis. Upon finding breaks in the windshield a repair is quickly performed and the bill is sent to the owner's insurance company which in turn normally pays for the total cost of the repair.
Requirements: $898 for Mobile Repair Kit and training which varies in price depending on the method you choose.
Provisions: The entrepreneur receives a complete repair kit with all the tools necessary to perform repairs on any type of break or crack. There is enough resins in the kit to provide the purchaser with $8,000 to $12,000 income. The average price per repair, across the country, is $40. The purchase can have his/her choice of manual, video,

classroom or on-the-job training which is priced separately.
Profit Potential: Three repairs per day at $40 each equals $31,200 per year; nine repairs per day at $40 each equals $93,600 per year.

LOCATIONLUBE, P.O. Box 700, E. Sandwich, MA 02537; (508)888-5000.
Franchise: No.
Description: Mobile oil change van servicing vehicles at customer's location.
Requirements: The total cost is $33,000; financing is available with $3,000 down.
Provisions: New van, equipment and training.

THE LUBE WAGON, 9430 Mission Blvd., Riverside CA 92509; (714)685-8570.
Franchise: No.
Description: Mobile lube service.
Requirements: Cost for exclusive rights to a city is $12,000; for a state $24,000. A Lube Wagon operator must build one of the company's patented trailers which takes about 100 hours and costs $2,000. The cost of the two-week training is $500.
Provisions: Names of suppliers are provided (company does not sell supplies.)
Profit Potential: The profit from one oil change is $19.50.

NATIONAL DETAIL SYSTEMS, 801 Mitchell Rd., Suite 108, Thousand Oaks, CA 91320. (800-356-9485.
Franchise: No.
Description: Mobile auto detailing service.
Requirements: No experience is necessary. The starter package costs $895.
Provisions: All dealers are given complete instructions from start to finish through our exclusive step-by-step training and operations manuals, full color 90-minute video tape and companion audio-cassette training tapes. You can work part-time with extremely flexible business hours. Included is an initial supply of products enough to complete 30 to 40 vehicles. You will also receive upscale promotional material and camera-ready artwork for business cards, gift certificates, referral cards, business forms, brochures, yellow page and newspaper ads, direct mail coupons and much more.
Profit Potential: The company claims that you will earn approximately $30 to $60 per hour. Your typical cost of cleaning/polishing products to complete an average detail is only $3.50. You should be able to generate approximately $3,000 worth of business from your initial order of supplies.

NOVUS, 10425 Hampshire Ave., South, Minneapolis, MN 55438; (612)944-8000.
Franchise: Yes.
Description: NOVUS offers a windshield repair and scratch removal business.
Requirements: The franchise fee starts at $2,900. There is a training fee of $990 plus $2,100 for equipment, supplies and materials.

NVS CORPORATION, 48 Springvale Ave., Lynn, MA 01904; (617)595-6224.
Franchise: No
Description: Windshield repair.
Requirements: The cost of a complete system is $1,999.
Provisions: The system includes equipment, enough materials to make 1,000 repairs, and detailed illustrated instructions.
Profit Potential: Up to $80,000 a year.

OIL CAN VAN, INC., One Flagler Ave., Stuart, FL 34994, (800)545-9626.

Franchise: No.
Description: Mobil oil change service.
Requirements: $39,900 including van or $14,900 without.
Provisions: Turnkey package includes equipment, computer, custom designed software for tracking and billing, media kit, and two weeks of training at your home location.
Profit Potential: Based on the average service of ten vehicles per day, five days per week, and a per vehicle service cost of $21.95, the gross annual sales would be $57,070 with a profit of $30,570. After gaining experience and efficiency that profit can go up to $74,640.

THE PAINT BULL, 3407 Bay Rd., Saginaw, MI 48603; (800)800-5725.
Franchise: No.
Description: Automotive paint touch-up and minor repair of chips, scratches, rust, scuffs, door dings, and more. Operators work a mobile service to car lots, fleets and retail customers.
Requirements: Investments from $2,995 to $7,995 for complete system.
Provisions: Complete equipment package, training and support.
Profit Potential: Up to $150 per car and more.

ULTRA BOND, 3696 Beatty Dr., Riverside, CA 92506; (800)347-2820.
Franchise: No
Description: Glass repair service.
Requirements: The combination repair kit costs $1,750. To buy exclusive rights to a protected territory, the initial total is $3,250 plus a $100 monthly supply order is required.
Provisions: Your investment covers all equipment and supplies, two days of training in California, a training video, monthly newsletter, business start-up assistance, and ongoing support.
Profit Potential: Over $50 an hour.

BUSINESS SERVICES

Business services include any business whose customers are business owners and/or managers. This area covers quite a range, and so this section will describe opportunities in advertising, payroll services, business consulting, bookkeeping and accounting, tax preparation, management training, financial management, various office support services, business products, pre-employment screening, and an assortment of miscellaneous services that cater to niche markets.

As you can see by viewing these services as a group, an incredible number of dollars is being spent by businesses. There are thirteen million companies that require bookkeeping, accounting, and tax preparation services. These businesses spend $135 billion annually on business products such as office supplies, furniture, printing, and business forms. That amount alone comprises over 3% of the GNP. Advertising takes a minimum 5% of any company's budget. The cooperative direct mail industry, which has grown 80% in just the last five years, is now a $100 million a year business. Corporations, more concerned than ever about how productivity is affecting the bottom line, spend $30 billion on management training each year.

Clearly, there is a lot of money to be made in business services. This is not, however, safe ground for amateurs. It is quite different from dealing with the public. Whereas a consumer may be willing to take a chance on an unknown product or an unfamiliar company, a business owner will not be so willing to take chances when it may affect the health of the business. Business owners are also more knowledgeable than the general public about the products and services they need. They trust only those who understand their business needs and who are willing to take the time to nurture a lasting business relationship. This takes time, but those with patience will be rewarded.

Those most likely to succeed in business services have assertive personalities and business experience. They are used to dealing with business owners and have some contacts within the business community. Working from a home office need not be a hindrance, but it is especially important to project a professional image.

ADVANCED TELECOM SERVICES, 996 Old Eagle School Rd., Wayne, PA 19087; (610)688-6000.
Franchise: No.
Description: 900# programs for businesses and entrepreneurs.
Requirements: No equipment is needed. Initial investment begins at $1,500.
Provisions: Complete turn-key program for a 900 number, marketing support, and advice.

ADVANTAGE PAYROLL SERVICES, 800 Center St., Auburn, ME 04210; (207)783-2068.
Franchise: Yes.

Description: Complete payroll and payroll tax reporting services for small businesses.
Requirements: The franchise fee is $10,000 with no royalties. Another $5,000 will be needed for start-up expenses. Sales experience is also required.
Provisions: The franchise fee buys a territory with a minimum of 5,000 businesses plus software to connect with the company. Financing for half of the fee is available at 10% interest over four years.
Profit Potential: Not available.
Comments: The company has about two dozen franchisees.

AFTE BUSINESS ANALYST, 2180 North Loop West, Ste 300, Houston, TX 77018; (713)957-1592.
Franchise: Yes.
Description: Standardized bookkeeping and tax services to small businesses.
Requirements: The franchise fee is $4,000. You will also need $500 for initial supplies, $990 for the customized software package, and an IBM-computable computer system. No experience is required. Royalties are 7% of gross receipts.
Provisions: Complete training is provided starting with two weeks of marketing at corporate headquarters. There is financing available from the company.
Profit Potential: Not available.
Comments: This is a well established company offering an inexpensive way to get into a computer based business.

AIR BROOK LIMOUSINE, P.O. Box 123, Rochelle Park, NJ 07662; (201)843-6100.
Franchise: Yes.
Description: Limousine service to transport business owners and managers between office and airport.
Requirements: The franchise fee ranges from $7,500 to $12,500. A refundable deposit of $2,000 is required for start-up. Royalties range from 35% to 40%.
Provisions: The fee buys a 10-year franchise license and training. Financing is available from the company with no interest.
Profit Potential: Not available.
Comments: This company has been around since 1969 and has over 125 franchise operators.

ALTERNATIVE UTILITY SERVICES, 845 Chicago Ave., Ste 2, Evanston, IL 60202; (708)869-8345.
Franchise: No.
Description: Service provides wholesale electricity and energy to businesses.
Requirements: $1,900 to $15,000.
Provisions: You will receive training, support, and residual income.
Profit Potential: $20,000 to $100,000 per year.

AM MARKETING, 694 Center St., Chicopee, MA 01013; (413)733-7659.
Franchise: No.
Description: Full color printing of photo business cards as well as brochures, sell sheets, and related materials.
Requirements: $325.
Provisions: The fee includes a distributors training manual, a full color catalog, 300 samples, order forms, flyers and other promotional material, and toll-free on-going support. The initial fee will be refunded after your orders total $10,000 gross.
Profit Potential: Up to $1,000 per week.

AMERICAN BUSINESS ASSOCIATES, 475 Park Ave. S., 16th Floor, New York, NY 10016; (212)689-2834.
Franchise: Yes.
Description: A formalized networking organization intended to generate sales leads and marketing information for business owners.
Requirements: The franchise fee is $25,000. You'll also need about $10,000 for home office equipment and start-up costs. Royalties are 10% of gross receipts and the advertising fee is 2%.
Provisions: The fee buys two weeks of training - one at company headquarters and one in the field, business forms, a newsletter, and ongoing support.
Profit Potential: With a good territory, you should be able to gross over $100,000 by your second year with less than 25% expenses. No-interest financing is available with $10,000 down.
Comments: This is a great franchise opportunity, particularly for women.

AMERICAN INSTITUTE OF SMALL BUSINESS, 7515 Wayzata Blvd., Suite 201, Minneapolis, MN 55426; (612)545-7001.
Franchise: Yes.
Description: AISB is a publisher of training manuals and courses on the subject of small business. All services are based on a two-volume publication titled "How to Set Up a Small Business". This publication has been endorsed by the U.S. Small business Administration, Dun and Bradstreet, and many local Chambers of Commerce. Franchisees market the materials primarily through seminars.
Requirements: There is no franchise fee or royalties. The company's profits come from sales of the training manuals and other materials. New franchisees are required to purchase $1,500 worth of start-up inventory. This includes twelve sets of manuals, ten business plan kits, and an assortment of other materials to be used for seminars.
Provisions: AISB promises to provide referrals from national advertising and other promotions to local franchisees.

AMERICAN INSTITUTE, American Institute Bldg., First Floor, 7326 S.W. 48th Street, Miami, FL 33155. (800)US-AUDIT.
Franchise: No.
Description: Business services including utility bill auditing, freight bill auditing, telephone bill auditing, lease auditing, and ARM's mortgage auditing. For example, almost every item sold in America at one time or another is moved by either truck, train or a combination of both. For any business dependent on freight, even a small 1% or 2% mistake could cost thousands or tens of thousands of dollars every year in overpayments. This business teaches you how to be a freight bill auditor and save your clients all that money. There are three reasons why overpayments occur in freight bills: the complexity of the bills, the sheer volume involved in freight shipping, and the immediacy or urgency involved in freight shipping. It can even be run like a mail order business. All you need is a telephone answering machine and calculator.
Requirements: Fees range from $3,900 to $6,900.
Provisions: Complete training to set up home business immediately.
Profit Potential: $80,000 from home.

ANSWERING SPECIALISTS, 119 West Doty Ave., Summerville, SC 29483; (803)724-6300.
Franchise: Yes.
Description: Franchisees offer an answering service with more individualized per-

sonal attention than the traditional answering service. It can be operated with only 500 square feet.
Requirements: The franchise fee starts at $18,500. If you have an existing business, you can buy a conversion franchise for $8,500. An additional $20,000 for equipment is required.
Provisions: There is a five day training course at headquarters for the franchisee and one employee. After that a company representatives gives on-site training for two days during the first month of operation. Proven sample advertising and marketing methods are also given.

AUDITEL MARKETING SYSTEMS, 111 Westport Plaza, Suite 1021, St. Louis, MO 63146. (800)622-2940.
Franchise: No
Description: As a consultant, you would find where companies have been overcharged on their telephone and utility bills. You would then get refunds or credits for your clients and receive a percentage of the savings.
Requirements: The one-time affiliation fee is $9,900. There are no royalties or additional percentages paid to the company.
Provisions: The fee includes two days of training at company headquarters, four manuals, over 100 different forms to be used in your business, a copy of the monthly newsletter, and six months of unlimited training and consultation.
Profit Potential: The president of the company consistently netted over $100,000 a year working at this part-time.

BANKS, BENTLEY & CROSS, 1500 Quail St., Ste 550, Newport Beach, CA 92660; (714)455-3929.
Franchise: No.
Description: Business arbitration and debt negotiation.
Requirements: $195 for the start-up manual plus $150 for start-up costs.
Provisions: Complete business plan and consultation.
Profit Potential: Six figures annually.

BASCO, 9351 De Soto Ave., Chatsworth, CA 91311-4948; (818)718-1506.
Franchise: No.
Description: Business advertising specialties based on the BASCO imprinting machine.
Requirements: The membership fee is $249.95.
Provisions: The BASCO starter kit, sales literature, complete information, and catalogs.
Profit Potential: 50% to 70% profit range.

BFD PRODUCTIONS, INC., 1221 S. Casino Center, Las Vegas, NV 89104; (701)382-3200.
Franchise: No.
Description: BFD Productions is a full featured telecommunications service bureau specializing in assisting software and hardware companies with their customer and technical support as well as their marketing needs. BFD offers 1-800/1-900 number applications, domestic and Canadian pay-per-call, pre-paid calling cards, automatic credit card verification, transcription, fulfillment, and production services.
Requirements: Minimum of $1,500 per 1-900 number.

BINEX-AUTOMATED BUSINESS SYSTEMS, INC., 6324 Marshall Dr., Sacramento, CA 95842. (916)483-8080.
Franchise: Yes.
Description: Financial management consulting, including a broad range of computerized services (financial statements, payroll, taxes, accounting, accounts receivable) for small businesses.
Requirements: The ability to use computers and some knowledge of business management is required. Although this is technically a franchise, there is no franchise fee, only a license renewal fee of $1,000 per year after five years. Start-up costs are around $8,500.
Provisions: The start-up costs include the license fee for the first five years, training, advertising and promotion, software and software training.
Profit Potential: Not available.

CLOSEUP: Bluejay Systems

At the low price of only $289, Bluejay Systems can be a great deal for the money. That may be why over 3,500 entrepreneurs in all 50 states plus 13 foreign countries have chosen Bluejay to help them become billing service professionals.

It is a complete system with the usual manuals, forms, and marketing materials and of course, the heart of the system is the billing software. But the most valuable part of the package is the full year of free support from the home office. Having that support to lean on in the first year is an absolute necessity to ensure success, getting it for this low price is a great bonus.

It was about two years ago when Ed Lissack of Toronto, Canada, got tired of working for someone else. He says, "I explored a few things and thought maybe I could provide a variety of different services like bookkeeping, billing, and some computer related services." He looked at Bluejay, thought the fee was quite reasonable and decided to give it a try. With that, he started Computer Age Service Enterprises.

Ed was happy to find that the manual is written in plain English, the invoices are easy to understand, and the software is easy to use. "This was the easiest billing package I have ever seen. What I really like is that as you generate an invoice, the appropriate dollar amounts automatically drop into the receivables, tax records, and so on. There is not much other software out there that does that."

Ed was not interested in building up a part-time business. He found Bluejay had some good marketing advice and followed their suggested sales strategies. Jumping in with both feet, he offered account tracking to business clients which includes receivables, invoice generating, check writing, trial balance, and financial statements. He drew from his experience as a software trouble shooter to add software and hardware installation, training, and consulting to the same clients. With referrals and just by word-of-mouth, it quickly became a full-time business with Ed happily working from 40 to 50 hours a week.

"I never want to go back to the way things used to be," he insists. "Being in business for myself is very rewarding. I have found I can be more effective and the clients tend to respect me more, too. I can give the marketplace what it really needs."

BLUEJAY SYSTEMS, 3 Meca Way, Norcross, GA 30093 (770) 564-5592
Description: Professional billing service that provides small businesses with invoice preparation and receivables management.
Requirements: $289 complete.
Provisions: Included are software, detailed marketing plans, various forms, and ongoing support. Additional quantities of marketing materials and prospect lists for any area are available.
Profit Potential: $1100-$2000 per month working part-time only 8 hours per week; $5,000 full time. The typical account is worth $100 per month which makes average income range from $25 to $65 per hour.
Comments: This is a very good buy for anyone starting out in this business. It is rare to find a complete business opportunity package for such a low cost; to also receive ongoing support is unheard of.

BOTTOM LINE MANAGEMENT, INC., 1150 Lake Hearn Drive, N.E., Suite 200, Atlanta, GA 30342; (404)847-0103.
Franchise: No.
Description: This business offers a complete line of business consulting services including debt negotiation, business brokerage, mystery shopping, lease negotiation, mediation and arbitration, and other services. The business was founded by Loren Schmerler, a well known consultant who has been a speaker for Inc. magazine for five years. Mr. Schmerler continues to oversee all training and support.
Requirements: The fee is $8,900. For a person to be successful in this field, "people

skills" are very important.
Provisions: Complete training at headquarters is provided in all areas of business consulting. Also provided are manuals, marketing training and materials, and ongoing support. Training at corporate headquarters includes actual performance of customer service, employee honesty, and competitor evaluations. The manuals include forms, sample reports, client letters, contracts, policies, employment agreements and other tools.

CLOSEUP: Bottom Line Management

For Loren Schmerler, president of Bottom Line Management, business consulting is an exciting business with both challenges and rewards. Over the past 15 years Loren has helped businesses in 160 industries solve their problems and increase the bottom line. Now he is training new consultants the tricks of the trade.

Bottom Line Management's training actually covers many skills that a consultant may be called upon to perform. Business consulting itself is a term that simply means identifying a problem and offering a solution. "Typically, a business owner may not even have a clear view of what the problem is," says Loren. "A consultant needs to be prepared to offer whatever services are required. That's what makes it so interesting. You never know what you're going to be asked to do."

For instance, a business owner might think he has a cash flow problem when in reality the root of the problem is employee morale. The result is high turnover and pilfering of inventory. "To solve a problem like this, you have to get the employees to be honest with you, the way they can't be with the boss. That's a challenge."

Another business owner may think he wants to call it quits and calls you in to help sell his business, but after learning that you can solve his headaches, decides to keep the business. "That's when it is really rewarding," says Loren.

Rewards are also financial. Typical fees for consulting start at $75 to $125 per hour and can reach $2,000 a day. It's a high price that business owners are more than willing to pay. One of Schmerler's clients saved more than $900,000 as a result of a lease negotiation and another saved $10,000 a month in expense reductions for two years.

You can be successful at this even if you don't enjoy numbers. "Mostly this requires someone who enjoys helping people," Loren points out. "You don't need an MBA. It's possible to be a consultant without ever looking at a spread sheet. It almost always comes down to people issues."

It takes about six months to become completely comfortable in this business. By that time you should be working full-time. Until that time and beyond, the company offers a lot of hand-holding. "We are highly interactive with our trainees and want to be there for them when they need us."

BUTLER LEARNING SYSTEMS, 1325 West Dorothy Lane, Dayton, OH 45409; (513)298-7462.
Franchise: Yes.
Description: This company produces and publishes management training programs in the areas of human resources development and sales marketing.
Requirements: There are no franchise fees, but there is a contractual agreement that states the consultants will market and use the Butler products in the way they were intended to be used. The materials are then purchased wholesale, and the consultants make a profit from the markup.
Provisions: Complete training is provided.

COMBINED RESOURCE TECHNOLOGY, INC., THE OH-5 SYSTEM, 1669 Lobdell Ave., Suite E, Baton Rouge, LA 70806. (800)962-0177.
Franchise: No.
Description: Cost reduction services for businesses including phone bill auditing, freight bill auditing, property tax consulting, mortgage auditing, medical bill auditing, utility bill auditing and other related auditing fields. The company has trained over 2,000 entrepreneurs in the U.S., Canada, Australia, Puerto Rico, and Great Britain.
Requirements: The start-up fee is $8,900.
Provisions: During a 4-day training workshop you will be field-trained through the use of practical case studies drawn from case files. You will learn the basic technical aspects plus how to successfully market your consulting business quickly in order to minimize the start-up time. You will take home technical and reference manuals, a video and receive a year of ongoing support.

CLOSEUP: Combined Resource Technology, Inc.

"For true security, you need to be self-employed and not depend on other people for your income," advises Jeff Huff, of Birmingham, Alabama. That's why Jeff went looking for something new, something completely different from his construction business. "I just got tired of depending on undependable people." After researching the business opportunity market carefully, Jeff found what he was looking for. Combined Resource Technology offered an opportunity to audit phone and utility bills for business customers. They trained independent entrepreneurs to find errors in billing and select the proper rate schedules to give customers the most savings.

"I chose CRT because they were very professional, had been in business for a number of years, and offered references when very few others did." As an experienced business owner, Jeff knew the most important point was that they had the most experience in the field. "During the training sessions, they were teaching from actual case studies, not just making up hypothetical cases."

At the end of four days of training, Jeff paid his $8,900 for the system and went home to Alabama to start Cost Reduction Services. "After four days,

I was out there, and I had my first check in my hands seven days after that. There was absolutely no competition." In his first month of business Jeff took in over $19,000, half of which he got to keep. Jeff had paid for his investment in one month. "Needless to say I was a happy man!"

Although Combined Resource Technology offers training in six different areas of auditing, Jeff's company focuses exclusively on phone and utility bill auditing and further specializes in hospitals, universities, and hotels. Doing so gives him more than enough business to keep him busy. Because this service can be provided from anywhere by using a phone and a fax machine, Jeff was able to expand easily. "I've got hotels in over 10 states, hospitals in three states, and universities in a couple of states. I've got hotels in North Dakota that I haven't ever seen."

Any savings or refunds that Jeff finds for his customers is split 50/50. "One university had over $200,000 in refunds and right now I have a hospital that is looking like $700,000 in refunds." With those kinds of savings, it's easy to see why he is able to earn easily in the six figures.

COMPREHENSIVE BUSINESS SERVICES, 1925 Palomar Oaks Way, Suite 105, Carlsbad, CA 92008; (619)431-2150.
Franchise: Yes.
Description: Comprehensive provides monthly accounting, bookkeeping, business consultation, and tax services to business owners.
Requirements: The franchise fee is $17,500. Start-up costs will require $10,000, office equipment will be about $12,000, and working capital of at least $5,000 will also be needed. Royalties for the first year are 4% of gross paid monthly and the advertising

fee is 1% of gross. To be considered, you need a four-year degree in accounting or its equivalent in experience, good credit, and a net worth of $100,000.
Provisions: Franchisees receive two weeks of training at corporate headquarters, a variety of continuing training programs, software, field support, and a professional direct mail program designed to provide you with prospects and appointments from the first week you are in business.
Comments: This is a well-established company that started in 1965.

E.K. WILLIAMS & CO., 2021 S. Platte River Dr., Denver, CO 80223.
Franchise: Yes.
Description: Information and management consulting services for small business. The company is also a software services company and is one of the largest publisher of business recordkeeping systems in the world.
Provisions: Once in business, franchisees attend mandatory training courses at least once a year.
Profit Potential: Not available.
Comments: This company has been in business since 1935 and was named the number one business service franchise by Entrepreneur Magazine in 1990.

ELECTRONIC VOICE SERVICES, INC., 5816 Covehaven Dr., Dallas, TX 75252; (800)713-8353.
Franchise: No.
Description: Business offering computerized touchtone services ("Info Hotline - U*S*A*") such as information and entertainment hotlines, talking time and temperature, etc.
Requirements: Info Hotline $2,495; Talking Time and Temperature $995. You will also need a 386 or 486 computer.
Provisions: Telecommunications boards, software, manuals, and technical support.
Profit Potential: Hundreds to thousands of dollars monthly.

ENERGY AUTOMATION SYSTEMS, INC., 114 Canfield, Bldg. A-8, Hendersonville, TN 37075; (615)822-7250.
Franchise: No.
Description: Dealers sell energy automations systems to businesses. Customers receive a detailed energy survey and comprehensive analysis of electrical usage, a set of recommendations to reduce the electrical bill, a projection and a guarantee of savings, and a return on investment higher then 50% a year. Products include occupancy sensors, fluorescent light controllers, transient surge protectors, etc. The company produces the actual report for you and local contractors of your choice perform installations.
Requirements: An entry level dealership costs $12,500. There are no ongoing fees. You can attend a free, one day orientation in Nashville with no obligation.
Provisions: Complete training.
Profit Potential: The average gross profit for each sale is between $15,000 and $20,000.

EXPENSE REDUCTION MARKETING SYSTEMS, 111 West Port Plaza, Suite 1021, St. Louis, MO 63146. (800)782-1050.
Franchise: No.
Description: It's been estimated that American businesses spend tens of billions of dollars each year on simple, everyday business needs. In this business you would concentrate on those areas where overcharges are common and where it's easiest to demon-

strate substantial savings. These areas include office products, printing, cleaning and maintenance, office equipment, insurance, advertising specialties, computer supplies, and express delivery service. The goal is to realize at least a $5,000 first-year savings for most of the companies who sign contracts as clients.
Requirements: The start-up fee is $9,900.
Provisions: The fee covers two days of intensive training plus six months of ongoing training.
Profit Potential: You will be trained to take only those projects that yield a minimum of $5,000 in savings to a client, which produces a $2,500 fee for you. Some associates do two or three of these a month part-time while others do as many as ten or more per month full-time.

EXPRESS LABELS..., 223 McCormick, Ave., Sweetwater, NJ 08037; (800)477-5345.
Franchise: No.
Description: Express label service offering labels to be shipped within 24 hours to any business. There are hundreds of combinations to choose from: mailing labels, product labels, computer labels, video and audio cassette labels, diskette labels, bumper stickers, etc. There are also software compatible forms such as bank checks, envelopes, index cards, invoices, mailers, purchase orders, sales orders, statements, etc. There is an unconditional guarantee on all products.
Requirements: $295.
Provisions: The fee gives you a business manual, 100 product catalogs, and telephone support.
Profit Potential: Individual effort determines the amount of income. The potential is a five to six figure income.

FIESTA CARTOON MAPS, 1033 E. Watson Dr., Tempe, AZ 85283; (800)541-4963.
Franchise: No.
Description: Dealers sell cartoon maps of area, usually as a fund raising project for local organizations. Licensees can grow as large as desired. Maps are updated each year resulting in an annual money making venture.
Requirements: The one-time fee for a territory large enough for a 100 ad map is $6,495. Additional territories are $1,500 each. No experience is necessary.
Provisions: The fee covers hotel and round trip airfare to Phoenix for three days of training, operations manual, sales manual, 100 maps for samples, invoices, business cards, reference letters, in-house production, ongoing support, and promotional materials.
Profit Potential: Net profit for a 100 ad map is $30,000.
Comments: This can be run part-time or as an absentee ownership. Part of the training course is devoted to hiring, training, and managing sales teams.

FILE-RITE, P.O. Box 17738, San Diego, CA 92177.
Franchise: No.
Description: File-Rite is a much needed loose-leaf filing service for accountants, attorneys, and corporations. You would render this service to them on a monthly basis. The time spent at one office may vary from 15 minutes to 12 hours per month with fees ranging from $45 to $550 per month.
Requirements: The cost is $149.
Provisions: The investment covers a training manual.
Profit Potential: The annual income per location ranges from $30,000 to $50,000 and up working part-time hours.

GENERAL BUSINESS SERVICES, P.O. Box 3146, Waco, TX 76707; (800)583-6181.
Franchise: Yes.
Description: Full service financial planning (including tax planning) and financial management for small businesses.
Requirements: The franchise fee is $25,000 and start-up costs are about $5,000. Royalties are on a sliding scale of none to 10%.
Provisions: The investment covers manuals, ongoing support, field-support training, and initial inventory.
Profit Potential: Not available.
Comments: This is one of the oldest franchises around. It was started in 1962 and now has over 500 franchise operators.

GREETINGS, P.O. Box 25623, Lexington, KY 40524; (606)272-5624.
Franchise: Yes.
Description: Advertising business utilizing hot air balloons.
Requirements: The franchise fee is $15,000. In addition to the franchise fee, you will need approximately $11,950 for supplies, equipment, working capital, etc. All franchisees are required to attend training in Lexington at their own expense. There is a 5% royalty based on gross sales.
Provisions: The fee covers training, operating system, promotional programs, a recordkeeping system, customer references, and ongoing support.

HEALTHTEK, INC., 6416 Moriah Run, Apt. 202, Memphis, TN 38115. (615)352-4200.
Franchise: No.
Description: Operators screen for factors the American Heart Association has recognized as being modifiable in the control of heart disease. The equipment used is completely portable and individual screenings can be performed in about 20 minutes. The data obtained from the screenings, in conjunction with a lifestyle profile, are used to generate a printed risk assessment. The goal is to help corporate clients solve health care cost problems by providing effective employee wellness assessments and wellness programs.
Requirements: Costs start at $12,000.
Provisions: Turn-key system
Profit Potential: Providing assessments for 120 people would take a staff of two, one week to complete and could potentially generate a gross income of about $3,750 to $6,570, based on 20 minutes per person.

HOLLAND-LANTZ AND ASSOCIATES, INC., 407 Wekiva Springs Road, Suite 225, Longwood, FL 32779. (407)884-6000.
Franchise: No.
Description: Holland-Lantz and its employees have been successfully providing executive search, outplacement and temporary employment services to Fortune 500 companies for over a decade.
Requirements: The cost of the program is $4,950. (There is also a correspondence course available for those unable to attend classroom instruction for only $500.)
Provisions: There is classroom and hands-on training which gives new business owners proven, tested and professional techniques on developing their markets and capturing sales. The program provides manuals, forms and contracts (resident in software and hard copies) and professional information necessary for the daily operation of an ex-

ecutive search, outplacement or temporary employment business. There is also a help-line available during the initial start-up period.

I.D. USA, 2810 Scherer Drive, Suite 100, St. Petersburg, FL 33716; (800)890-1000.
Franchise: No.
Description: This is a new offering from the very successful company, IDENT-A-KID (see Photo and Video Services). In this business you establish your own I.D. card production service bureau utilizing the latest in high resolution badge production technology. The need for employee identification affects every small business owner in the country and has even been mandated by some local government agencies.

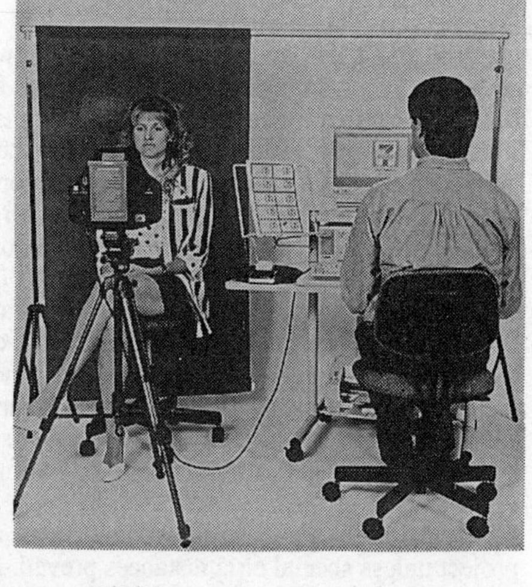

Requirements: The total investment is $7,995 with several different financing options available including leasing. The unique "lease to own" option can provide you with the entire system for as little as $250 per month with a down payment of $500.
Provisions: This is a turn-key system including: Pentium computer with super VGA, high-resolution composite color camera, full-color I.D. card printer and all production equipment, production supplies, integral card production software, and system training videos and manual. There is also technical support as well as business and marketing support. It will take an hour or less to set up the system. You can be making your first badges in a few hours and be making money in a few days.
Profit Potential: It costs less than 75 cents to produce a badge that sells for $10 or more. With over 6 million businesses that need the service and virtually no competition, there is certainly a great opportunity for profit.

IMPACT, 205-8475 Ontario St., Vancouver, B.C. Canada V5X 3E8; (604)324-6600.
Franchise: No.
Description: Impact's basic service is an advertising display called Tel-Ad. It is a case that holds as many as 100 professional advertising photos. The photos are identified with stick-on numbers that coincide with a push button pad located in the counter top for direct access to the advertiser's business premises. The heart of the display is a programmable logic board that is capable of storing up to 100 numbers in its memory. Once a patron has selected a service to contact, they would simply pick up the handset and press the number of the advertiser shown on the photo. The Tel-Ad displays are placed by independent business operators wherever tourists traffic such as hotel lobbies.
Requirements: The purchase price is $5,000.
Provisions: The price covers the price of a complete display plus supplies and four manuals. The manuals include installation instructions, business start-up procedures, complete instructions on how to work with hotels, signs, contracts, ads, phone scripts, and everything needed to make this a viable business.
Profit Potential: One system should generate from $20,000 to $45,000 a year.

Comments: Impact has more than 75 operators.

INDEPENDENT CONSULTANT NETWORK (ICN), 8855 Atlanta Ave., Suite 356, Huntington Beach, CA 92646. (714)753-3312.
Franchise: No.
Description: This is a nationwide network of offices and over 400 affiliates to serve its national client list, and an international network of over 100 affiliates serving other countries for its multinational clients. It was founded in 1974. ICN's network concentrates on top level management consulting assignments in over 150 specialty areas. Their nationwide offices are involved in consulting, staffing, career planning and outplacement. ICN's network concentrates on staffing assignments from middle management to corporate CEO assignments. Both the consulting and staffing division work together to provide a cohesive nationwide consulting network. Both divisions work a wide spectrum of industries and commerce including accounting, banking, data processing, engineering, financial services, insurance, sales and marketing, and many more.
Provisions: ICN provides start-up coaching, on-line training and support services, and client base building. You'll begin with an individually tailored training program that includes real consulting assignments for organizations that may become continuing clients for you. These projects are specifically selected to match your professional interests. Also included are training and operating manuals and personal instruction from experts.
Profit Potential: Fees are quoted in advance and are based on a minimum $10,000 per project unless special circumstances prevail. Executive search consulting assignments pay usually 30% of the successful candidate's finally agreed salary.

INFORM BUSINESS, INC., 1562 1st Ave., #246, New York, NY 10028. (212)831-7337.
Franchise: Yes.
Description: Business forms and printing. Franchisees are connected electronically to Inform's main office and works closely with headquarters.
Provisions: Fee includes training, ongoing support services, and an industry and marketing manual. Also provided are a computer with modem along with Inform software to hook up with headquarters.
Profit Potential: Not available, however, this is a huge industry that is growing at 11% annually.

JUST THE FAX, P.O. Box 96, Trail, OR 97541; (503)878-5352.
Franchise: No.
Description: A unique service that faxes restaurant lunch specials to businesses daily. This business only requires five to ten hours a week once it is set up.
Requirements: $1,200 licensing fee and a computer with fax software. A payment plan is available.
Provisions: The fee buys you the Restaurant Specials Fax Service Manual which gives you everything you need to know to set up this business. Materials you will receive on disk include: Templates for all stationery, business cards, forms, faxes and letters; contracts; invoices and renewal forms; scripts for signing up businesses and restaurants; promotion letters; public relations release and cover letter; and more.
Profit Potential: From $60 to $360 per day.

LOUSIG-NONT & ASSOCIATES, 3740 S. Royal Crest St., Las Vegas, NV 89119. (800)477-3211.

Franchise: No.
Description: Giving sales aptitude tests to prospective employees.
Requirements: The cost of a dealer package is $999.
Provisions: The dealer starter package contains approximately $3,000 retail value in sales tests. It also includes sales material and training tapes.

MEDICAL MANAGEMENT SOFTWARE, 1730 S. Amphlett Blvd. #217, San Mateo, CA 94402; (800)759-8419.
Franchise: Yes.
Description: Medical Management Software is an electronic medical billing system. Medical billing has been rated one of the top ten businesses of the '90s. Electronic billing is particularly appealing to clients since it yields 98% payment in 14 to 18 days response time versus only 70% payment in 30 to 90 days for traditional "paper billing."
Requirements: A limited package costs $3,495 and a full accounting with electronic claims package costs $6,995. You will also need an IBM or compatible with Windows 95 or Version 3.1, Hayes compatible fax/modem, and printer.
Provisions: The limited package includes software, manuals, and two full days of training for two people plus 90 days of toll-free marketing and technical support. The full package also includes additional software, lodging and meals during training, marketing manuals, audio tapes, personalized help in developing your marketing materials, updates, memberships to several online services, unlimited in-house support and training, and 1,000 names and addresses of medical providers NOT processing claims electronically.
Comments: This is a great opportunity for anyone no matter where they live. One of MMS's franchisees lives in the country, 35 miles from the nearest small town. Yet, she was able to land a three-year contract with a medical clinic that has over a million dollars in billing annually.

CLOSEUP: Medical Management Software

It's been less than a year since Nanci Lee Chavez of San Mateo, California, decided it was time to put more balance in her life. Community work had become very important to her and working in the insurance industry left little time for that.

"I went looking for something totally new," she said, "I only knew that it had to be a business that I could do at home." She read about the opportunities in medical billing and researched half a dozen companies including Medical Management Software. "I chose this company because they were very knowledgeable and had actually done the billing themselves, they were not just sales people." Nanci checked all the companies very thoroughly and advises anyone else to do the same. "I checked all the way from the Attorney General to the Better Business Bureau to the banks. Medical Management Software was the only one with a totally clean record."

Shortly after training with MMS, Nanci chose one of the company's sample sales letters and sent it out to 25 of the 1,000 qualified leads MMS provided. She was surprised when she landed an account within two weeks. "It's an easy sell," she explains. "It's less expensive for doctors to out-source their billing. They don't have to worry about overhead in terms of employee cost and insurance and I bring them a completed package. All the doctor has to do is give me the patient accounts and I keep the money coming in to him."

Nanci's knowledge of computers was very limited, but she found MMS's menu-driven software easy to use. "Some things I'm familiar with and a lot I'm not. At each phase the company is supporting me."

It's only been five months since Nanci started her business and she already has the life she was looking for. She works at the business in the early morning and the evening. That leaves plenty of daytime hours free to work as a City Commissioner and be on the board of directors for the Northern California Arthritis Foundation.

"I used to work a lot of hours before, but honestly I've learned you don't have to work so hard. The market is wide open so I could work 10 hours a day if I wanted. But having balance in my life, that's what's important to me."

MONEY BY THE MINUTE, 3419 Via Lido, Ste 621, Newport Beach, CA 92663; (800)675-3534.
Franchise: No.
Description: Providing 800, 900, and 500 numbers to the pay-per-call industry.
Requirements: $500 to $3,000.

MONEY MAILER, 29783 S.W. Town Center Loop, Wilsonville OR 97070. (800)624-5371.
Franchise: Yes.
Description: Cooperative direct mail advertising for small businesses.
Requirements: The franchise fee is $17,000 and up depending on the territory. You will need another $10,000 for living and operating expenses plus the cost of a Macintosh computer and customized software. Royalties are 10%.
Provisions: The investment buys training and start-up materials (first mailing is free). Money Mailer helps find outside financing.
Profit Potential: Not available.

NATIONAL BANK DRAFTING SYSTEMS, 6707 Brentwood Stair Rd., Ste. 640, Fort Worth, TX 76112. (817)457-9545.
Franchise: No.
Description: Training program to provide pre-authorized payment drafts to small business for improved cash flow on receivables - print bank drafts on your home laser printer.
Requirements: Must have a 386 or better computer with laser printer. The software and training package costs $4,990.

Provisions: Draft printing software, complete training package with marketing samples and complete phone support..
Profit Potential: Unlimited... "center owners now making $20,000+ per month!"

NATIONAL DRIVE BY BROADCASTING, INC., 21346 St. Andrews Blvd., Boca Raton, FL 33433; (407)482-8246.
Franchise: No.
Description: NDBB is a consumer oriented electronics manufacturer that has come up with an interesting service opportunity. This "on the spot" advertising service requires a little explanation. Imagine, while driving around looking for a new home, you find a home for sale that appears to fit your needs, and next to the For Sale sign is another sign that says "This House Speaks For Itself," "Tune Your Car Radio to 91.7FM," and upon doing so, you hear a continuously transmitted message being broadcast from inside the house with all the details you need. Other possibilities include restaurants with broadcast menus.
Requirements: As a distributor you purchase transmitters for $262 each and either sell them retail or rent them for up to $125 a month.
Provisions: New distributors receive the proprietary distribution package which includes marketing materials and sales leads from national advertising.

NATIONAL YELLOW PAGES CONSULTING ASSOCIATES, INC., 675 Fairview Dr., Suite 246, Carson City, NV 89701. (916)626-1106.
Franchise: No.
Description: As a Yellow Pages consultant you will be taught how to advise business clients on the best ways to reduce their yellow pages advertising expenses while maintaining or improving exposure.
Requirements: An initial investment of $9,900 for training plus an on-going 7% of gross receipts for continued assistance and membership in the association.
Provisions: The investment covers four days of intensive training in California including manuals, hotel, breakfasts and lunches.
Profit Potential: Depending on trainee's aggressiveness and follow-through (territories must also be considered) some trainees make upwards of $50,000 a year.

NORTHSTAR TELECOMMUNICATIONS, INC., 1821 Hall Ave., Marinette, WI 54143.
Franchise: No.
Description: Agents offer 5% to 20% guaranteed savings every month to local businesses on their phone bill. Also works as an excellent non-profit program.
Requirements: Refundable $25 for information packet and video.
Profit Potential: "Up to $10,000 per month for the committed."

O2 EMERGENCY MEDICAL CARE SERVICE, 5829 W. Maple Rd., Suite 123, West Bloomfield, MI 48322; (800)777-4535.
Franchise: Yes.
Description: In this business you would provide an emergency first aid program (including emergency oxygen unit, first aid kit and first aid training) to businesses.
Requirements: The franchise fee is $12,500 and the estimated total investment is around $50,000. The royalty fee is based on oxygen units only and it is $5.75 per unit. There is also a 3% advertising fee.
Provisions: The investment covers initial training program expenses, three operations manuals, initial inventory, office equipment and supplies, insurance, an exclusive terri-

tory, and toll-free support. The extensive training covers all aspects of business including sales, marketing, office set-up, and business record keeping. A field representative will be assigned to you and will periodically visit your location to help provide any information you require.
Profit Potential: Not available.

THE OFFICE ANSWER, 8445 Keystone Crossing, Suite 165, Indianapolis, IN 46240; (800)678-2336.
Franchise: Yes.
Description: Telephone answering service. During the franchise operator's day, incoming calls are answered with the appropriate company's name and chosen greeting. The message taker sees the vital statistics of the company of a computer display monitor. They can then speak intelligently as company representatives and take accurate messages. Callers may never realize they've reached an answering service.
Requirements: Licence fee with training costs $8,500. The answering system which includes a computer, telephone answering electronics, and work station is leased at a cost of $225 a month.
Provisions: The license fee covers telephone answering computer software with customer billing functions, on-the-job training programs and resource materials, business set-up guidance, operational and accounting systems, professionally prepared advertising material and marketing strategies, all necessary supplies, and ongoing support.
Profit Potential: Not available.

PDP, INC., 400 West Highway 24, Suite 201, Box 5289, Woodland Park, CO 80866; (719)687-6074.
Franchise: Yes.
Description: Business consulting service matching jobs to people and people to jobs using an array of software programs to aid in the analysis.
Requirements: The licensing fee is $14,900.
Provisions: The fee covers five days of formal training at corporate headquarters, a coordinator/technical manual, software user's guide, the software operating system, and ongoing support services.
Profit Potential: Not available.
Comments: PDP is a 13 year old company with 30 franchises as far-flung as Brazil.

PRICECHECK, 2970 Lakeshore Blvd. West, Suite 205, Toronto, Ontario, Canada, M8V 1J6; (416)255-9385.
Franchise: Yes.
Description: Hands-on marketing service for local businesses. Examples of the service include checking prices; gathering market information; distributing coupons, pamphlets, products; making local advertising and promotional copy changes; in store merchandising; shelf-stock counts; arranging local tie-in promotions, etc. The head office does bookkeeping of interoffice payments and all billing and collecting work.
Requirements: The franchise fee is $12,900. About $1,500 working capital plus three months income will also be necessary.
Provisions: The fee covers four days of field training and other business start-up activity in your market, office equipment and furniture, operating manual, artwork for office forms, referrals from the head office, and ongoing support.
Profit Potential: Not available.
Comments: Opportunities exist throughout the U.S. and Canada. No experience is necessary.

PRIORITY MANAGEMENT SYSTEMS, 500 108th Ave., NE, Suite 1740, Bellevue, WA 98004; (800)221-9031.
Franchise: Yes.
Description: Priority Management has designed a program to help corporate employees develop personal effectiveness skills. Specifically, employees are taught to manage time and projects, cope with stress, run meetings, delegate tasks, and communicate effectively. The purpose is to teach busy professionals to be able to control personal business lives while simultaneously reducing stress.
Requirements: Franchisees are required to be educated, experienced, and highly motivated. The total investment required for this opportunity is in the $30,000 to $35,000 range, including the franchise fee. There is financing available.
Provisions: Training starts with an intensive two-week session at company headquarters. Followup support is offered in several different ways.
Comments: This franchise is for experienced professionals who need to polish their skills. This is a lucrative market, but only heavy hitters survive.

PROFESSIONAL DYNAMETRIC PROGRAMS, P.O. Box 5289, Woodland Park CO 80866; (719)687-6074.
Franchise: Yes.
Description: PDP is a management and employee consulting franchise that uses behavioral assessment profiles to match employees to jobs best suited to their skills.
Requirements: The franchise fee is $29,500. You will also need operating expenses. Financing is available. There are no royalties.
Provisions: Training, forms, office supplies, and support.

PROFORMA, INC., 4705 Van Epps Rd., Cleveland, OH 44131; (216)741-0400.
Franchise: Yes.
Description: Sales of business products including forms, commercial printing, and computer and office supplies.
Requirements: The franchise fee is $39,500. You will need $5,000 for living expenses while you get started. The royalty is 8% and the advertising royalty is 1%. Marketing or executive management experience is required.
Provisions: The fee buys marketing systems, license agreement, ongoing support, trademarks, vendor relations, and lines of credit.
Profit Potential: Not available, but this is a huge industry.
Comments: This is a highly rated company with about 100 franchise operators.

RESEARCH MARKETING, 2561-C Nursery Road, Clearwater, FL 34624; (813)530-4330.
Franchise: No.
Description: Dealers sell a point-of-purchase communications device called the "Magic Message" as an interactive marketing tool. It is a device that can allow a department store display, for instance, and when the customer touches it as instructed, it will immediately begin talking, explaining the product or service.
Requirements: Minimum dealership costs $285.
Provisions: Sales tools including a demonstration case, printed materials such as brochures, and pre-recorded audio demonstration tapes.
Profit Potential: Not available.

RESPOND SYSTEMS, P.O. Box 39925, Denver, CO 80239; (303)371-6800.
Franchise: Yes.

Description: Respond First is a van-based route business. It provides quality first aid and emergency medical supplies service and training to employers. Respond targets the majority of employers which are the small businesses that do not have the resources for in-house medical clinics staffed with doctors and nurses.
Requirements: The total initial investment is $35,000. There are no royalties.
Provisions: Complete training is provided in technical, legal, personnel, and financial areas. Followup training and support are available at any time.

SANDLER SYSTEMS, 10411 Stevenson Rd., Stevenson, MD 21153; (800)669-3537.
Franchise: Yes.
Description: Franchisees offer corporate training programs designed to help client companies boost productivity and generate more profits.
Requirements: The franchise fee is $30,000 with limited financing available.
Provisions: Complete training and followup support is provided.

SERVING BY IRVING, Woolworth Building, 233 Broadway, Suite 1036, New York, NY 10279; (212)233-3346.
Franchise: Yes.
Description: Serving by Irving is a franchised, nationwide network of process servers. Law firms use Serving by Irving to serve the papers that notify people when they are required to appear in a court of law, or that a legal action has begun. The company has an extraordinary success rate of 98%.
Requirements: The fee is $85,000. The company's tongue-in-cheek motto is "If they're alive, we'll serve them, if they're dead, we'll tell you where they're buried."
Provisions: This is a turn-key franchise. The fee covers a complete equipment package that includes a fax machine, personal computer, photocopier, typewriter, electronic beeper, paperwork and forms, bookkeeping supplies, and inventory supplies. All of the above will be installed for you and you will be trained how to use them. Your fee also includes an exclusive territory, an operations manual, a proven grand opening advertising program, continual promotion by the company, and training. Training is conducted in the classroom and in the field and covers management, administrative, and marketing techniques as well as successful investigative techniques and the rules and methods for proper and efficient service of process.
Profit Potential: Although a franchise by law cannot make income claims, this is clearly a sophisticated business with high income potential.
Comments: Company started in 1977.

SUPER COUPS COOPERATIVE DIRECT MAIL, The Mail House, 180 Bodwell St., Avon, MA 02322; (800)626-2620.
Franchise: Yes.
Description: Franchisees sell ad space in their mailings to local and national businesses. They also design and write copy for the ads, but with extensive help from Super Coups.
Requirements: The franchise fee is $22,900.
Provisions: Complete training as well as exceptional followup support is provided.

SURVEILLANCE VIDEO SYSTEMS, 258 'A' Street #12, Ashland, OR 97520; (503)482-4500.
Franchise: No.
Description: Selling security cameras, both live and simulated, to business owners with shoplifting, holdup and bad check problems.

Requirements: Under $100 puts one in business with sample products, sales aids, and point of sale material.
Provisions: You get 23 years of proven, profitable and needed products.

TALKING ADS, P.O. Box 14804, Lenexa, KS 66285; (913)492-7283.
Franchise: No.
Description: Talking Ads is a money- and time-saving marketing alternative for businesses.
Requirements: $477 for the license/consulting program.
Provisions: Start-up manual, sample forms, sample marketing plans, and ongoing consultation.

TREASURE PAK, INC., 6303 Pelican Creek Xing Apt. D, St. Petersburg, FL 33707. (800)237-8896.
Franchise: No.
Description: Direct mail coupon business.
Requirements: A distributorship costs $19,600. (The company will waive the start-up cost provided that you have the necessary background.)
Provisions: The fee covers training, sales materials, sales tools, production services, and ongoing support.
Profit Potential: One mailing a month should net $71,352 a year.

TRIMARK, INC., 184 Quigley Blvd., P.O. Box 10530, Wilmington, DE 19850-0530.
Franchise: Yes.
Description: Direct mail coupon advertising for the local small businesses.
Requirements: The franchise fee is $5,000 and up depending on the territory. Start-up costs are about $5,000. There are no royalties. Sales experience is preferred, but not required.
Provisions: The fee buys two weeks of training (one week at corporate headquarters and one week in the field), ongoing support, and the first six months of supplies (presentation packet, stationery, and contracts.)
Profit Potential: Not available.
Comments: TriMark, a company that has been in business since 1969, offers the best deal in the industry to potential franchisees.

USA FOR HEALTHCLAIMS, INC., 100 Springdale Rd., Ste A3 #270, Cherry Hill, NJ 08003; (800)681-9191.
Franchise: No.
Description: Licensing program enables individuals to process medical claims electronically through a central clearinghouse.
Requirements: $4,990 plus IBM compatible computer.
Provisions: Fee buys software, manuals, marketing manuals, brochures, training class, ongoing technical support and all updates.
Profit Potential: Unlimited.

VIDEO/AD, P.O. Box 111, Willows, CA 95988, (916)934-8827.
Franchise: No.
Description: This is an advertising business that places ads inside rental video cassette cases.
Requirements: $769 for the basic system.
Provisions: The fee covers a turn-key system including business manuals, protected

territory, presentation materials and samples, a discount printing source, forms and contracts, promotional materials, and continuing support.
Profit Potential: Video/Ad says that just three video stores can earn you over $7,200 per month.

HOME AND COMMERCIAL PROPERTY IMPROVEMENTS

To most of us, property improvement means remodeling. And there are indeed remodeling opportunities in this chapter. But there is much more to the property improvement industry than paint and carpentry. Included in this chapter's assortment of businesses are services that you may have thought of, such as carpet dyeing and repair, decorating services, floor coverings, handyman services, drapery cleaning, and lawn care. There are also a few that you may not have considered. Water and gas leak detection provides a unique and valuable service. Porcelain refinishing is a popular alternative to bathroom fixture replacement for hotels, schools, interior decorators, and landlords. And businesses such as HOMEWATCH offer the kind of personalized services - everything from plant watering to building maintenance - that have become so popular with today's busy working couples.

Generally, the businesses in this chapter are very straightforward with no fancy image or special skills required. Down-to-earth working people who want the advantages of owning a business, such as greater income potential and freedom, will find some good possibilities here. Most of these businesses can also be run part-time, which is helpful if you are looking for something with flexibility.

ALL AMERICAN BLIND SALES, 23052 Alicia Parkway #H202, Mission Viejo, CA 92692; (714)258-7068.
Franchise: No.
Description: Own your own discount shop-at-home mini-blind sales company. Sell major brands of at discount prices.
Requirements: $1,700.
Provisions: Fee covers training, samples, marketing and advertising, videos, workbook and membership in buyers group for low pricing.
Profit Potential: $4,000 to $7,000 per month net.

ANCHOR CUSTOM PRODUCTS, P.O. Box 3477, Evansville, IN 47733. (812)867-2421.
Franchise: No.
Description: Design, sell, and install custom-made fabric awnings, canopies, and retractable patio awnings.
Requirements: $100 for dealer information.
Provisions: The $100 gets you the necessary sales tools; training is available by request.
Comments: This is a good add-on business for carpenters or remodelers.

ARCHADECK, P.O. Box 5185, Richmond, VA 23220; (800)722-4668.
Franchise: Yes.
Description: Franchisees work with homeowners and builders to design and construct decks and gazebos. This is a very fast-growing company with over 80 franchise units added since 1985.
Requirements: The franchise fee is $32,500. Financing for half the franchise fee is available.

Provisions: Training and support.

BATH GENIE, 1 Brigham St., Marlborough, MA 01752. (800)255-8827.
Franchise: Yes
Description: Porcelain resurfacing service.
Requirements: $24,500.
Provisions: Fee includes protected territory, $1,000 of initial advertising paid by the company, expense-paid training at company headquarters, all necessary porcelain resurfacing equipment, all advertising and marketing materials, office supplies, ongoing support, and enough resurfacing supplies to completely recoup your investment.
Profit Potential: Performing five jobs a week (10 hours time) you would earn $54,875 per year.

BATHCREST, 2425 S. Progress Dr., Salt Lake City, UT 84119; (801)972-1110.
Franchise: Yes.
Description: Bathcrest is in the porcelain refinishing business.
Requirements: The franchise fee is $3,500 plus you will need an additional $21,000 to pay for training, the costs of attending training sessions, a complete equipment package, printed materials and enough product to return $20,000 in gross sales.
Comments: This is a family business that has been around since 1974. They have substantial experience to offer.

CARPET SCULPTURE GALLERY,® 510A W. Central Ave., Brea, CA 92621; (800)348-6934.
Franchise: No.
Description: A unique art form that allows the operator to change the shape and texture of carpets using special patented tools. The finished designs are all one-of-a-kind and can be anything from company logos to portraits to matching the wallpaper. This is not just a product for the rich; even middle class home owners can enjoy the fine art of carpet sculpting making this a wide open market.
Requirements: One time fee of US $19,900 covers 40 hours of training, all the necessary tools and supplies, marketing, proprietary software to estimate jobs, public relations and headquarters support, leads, newsletters, conventions, etc.
Provisions: During the workshop at the company's "Gallery," you will receive one-on-one training in every aspect of the business, from inlay to carving and Bas-Relief techniques to bidding a job through to acquiring materials and delivering the finished product. The marketing package includes proven marketing and promotional materials, area rights, an inlaid and sculpted carpet sample, and an artist's portfolio with 20 stunning photos to show the client what you're capable of doing.
Comments: The results of carpet sculpting are quite spectacular; call for a video that shows beautiful examples of carpet sculptures. This can be run part-time, full-time, or as an add-on to an existing business such as interior design, carpet cleaning or restoration, floor and wall covering, etc.

CLOSEUP: Carpet Sculpture Gallery®

Have you always wanted a creative business but thought you couldn't because you have no artistic talent? Even if you can't draw, Carpet Sculpture Gallery® can teach you the fine art of carpet sculpting.

Carpet Sculpture Gallery® of San Francisco skyline behind Gina Bauerle, Margo Hemmingway, and Volker Bauerle.

This unique process that creates three-dimensional custom inlaid and sculptured carpet is one of the hottest trends in interior design. CSG's proprietary technique and patented tools make it possible to take any design and handcraft stunning custom carpets as beautiful as paintings. The designs can be as simple as a company logo or as detailed as a portrait.

When Werner Lindemaier of Battle Ground, Washington, got tired of the corporate world, he made a list of requirements for himself. "I said if I'm going to make a change, I know I have to be creative with my hands. I want to be independent, work out of my home, and make a six figure income. Carpet Sculpture Gallery® met all 11 requirements." Werner says when he first saw the sculptured carpets in an ad, they looked really nice. But it wasn't until he saw the real thing that he realized how incredibly beautiful they are.

Werner fell in love with the work during training and couldn't wait to get started. The company had promised to show him how to line up more work than he could handle. Within three months of working part-time (he was winding down his existing business) he had recouped most of his initial investment. "I got my first orders from interior decorators and carpet stores. But then I went to a Home and Garden Show to display my work. I got wonderful feedback from so many people who had never seen anything like this. It really gave me a big boost. Now I do two shows a year and it keeps me busy."

Most of Werner's customers are home owners. With carpet designs starting at only $500, anyone can afford the one-of-a-kind personalized artworks. But, of course, some designs are more complex than others. "I recently delivered a $17,000 custom carpet that took me 12 days to finish, and I earned almost $9,000 after expenses. I don't know of any other business that is as satisfying and profitable."

Werner never repeats the same thing twice. "I don't do production work or crank out the same pattern over and over. That would be boring. I love the work. After five years, I still get excited to get up Monday morning."

COLOR/MATCH, 1872 Del Amo Blvd., #C, Torrance, CA 90501; (800)228-3240.
Franchise: No
Description: On-location carpet and upholstery dyeing.
Requirements: Training is at company headquarters in Los Angeles and is $300 for the first person for the first day; it is $250 a day thereafter.
Provisions: The company offers marketing assistance and technical training.
Profit Potential: Not available.

CONCRETE TECHNOLOGY, INC., 1255 Starkey Rd., Largo, FL 34641; (800)447-6573.
Franchise: No.
Description: Company manufactures state-of-the-art concrete resurfacing product sold to a network of dealers and distributors worldwide.
Requirements: Exclusive territories are available through an initial inventory purchase of at least $10,000.
Provisions: 100% product inventory along with marketing materials, etc. to offer a turnkey operation.
Profit Potential: Average crew dealer has the opportunity to make $100,000 annually.

CREATIVE COLORS INTERNATIONAL, INC., P.O. Box 112, Oak Forest Il 60452. (800)933-2656.
Franchise: Yes.
Description: The CCI franchise system specializes in providing services for the repair, coloring, cleaning and restoration of leather, vinyl, cloth, velour, plastics and other upholstery surfaces and related services on a mobile basis primarily to commercial customers.
Requirements: One white mini-van and $11,000+.
Provisions: Two weeks of training at headquarters, one week in franchisee's territory, and ongoing support through newsletters, seminars, and an advisory council.
Profit Potential: This business can be expanded into all markets that have a need for repairing and re-dyeing of leather, vinyl, velour, plastics, etc.

CREATIVE CURB, 23362 Madero Road, Ste E, Mission Viejo, CA 92691; (800)292-3488.
Franchise: No.
Description: Concrete curb and landscape border installation business.
Requirements: Cost of equipment starts at $5,000.
Provisions: Equipment, training manuals, videos, hands-on training when required.
Profit Potential: Average cost per linear foot of concrete curbing is $.40; average retail price of concrete curbing is approximately $3.00 to $5.00 per linear foot.

DECORATING DEN, 7910 Woodmont Ave., #200, Bethesda, MD 20814; (301)652-6393.
Franchise: Yes

Description: Decorating Den is a shop-at-home decorating service. The franchisee goes by appointment to a customer's home in a "ColorVan" containing over 5,000 samples of fabrics, wall coverings, carpets, draperies, furniture, and accessories. There is no charge for the decorating service because the profit comes from the difference between the wholesale and retail prices on the products sold to the customer. There are over 1,100 franchises operating throughout the U.S., Canada, United Kingdom, Japan, Europe and Australia.
Requirements: The franchise fee is $8,900 for an Associate franchise or $23,900 for a Senior franchise. An additional $5,000 to $15,000 working capital is needed. Some business and decorating experience is preferred.
Provisions: The franchise fee covers complete training which takes about six months, national advertising, promotional materials, business and record keeping systems, access to quality products at wholesale discounted prices, a selection of product samples, and all the necessary paperwork down to printed checks and business cards.
Profit Potential: Not available.

DEKRA-LITE, 3041 S. Orange Ave., Santa Ana, CA 92707; (714)436-0705.
Franchise: Yes.
Description: Dekra-Lite offers new and different services that involve designing and installing decorative exterior lighting. Although the original service was basically intended for the Christmas season, Dekra-Lite services now include figurines and other decorative displays for other holidays during the year and special occasions such as weddings and graduations.
Requirements: The franchise fee starts at $7,500. The company estimates about $17,500 is needed for office supplies, various business expenses, inventory, and equipment.
Provisions: The fee buys complete training, professionally prepared advertising materials, and a sales manual.

DR. VINYL & ASSOCIATES, LTD., 9501 E. State, Route 350 Highway, Raytown, MO 64133; (816)356-3312.
Franchise: Yes.
Description: Dr. Vinyl franchisees repair vinyl, cloth, leather, strip molding, windshields, and plastic for car dealerships, restaurants, and doctors' offices.
Requirements: The franchise fee starts at $20,000 and you will need a van.
Provisions: The fee buys $5,000 worth of inventory, training, and ongoing support.

DYNAMARK SECURITY CENTERS, 19833 Leitersburg Pike, Hagerstown, MD 21742; (800)342-4243.
Franchise: Yes.
Description: Franchisees help homeowners secure their homes against burglary and fire by selling, installing, and maintaining alarm systems.
Requirements: The total investment is about $20,000 with financing available.
Provisions: Training and ongoing support.
Comments: This company has been around since 1977.

FLOOR COVERINGS INTERNATIONAL, 5182 Old Dixie Hwy., Forest Park, GA 30050. (800)955-4324.
Franchise: Yes.
Description: Mobile floor covering retailer offering convenient shop-at-home service to today's time-starved consumers.
Requirements: The franchise fee is $14,000 to $29,000; start-up costs range from

$8,320 to $13,780; royalties are 5%; and the ad fund is 2%.
Provisions: Comprehensive training program, regional workshops, monthly newsletter, national accounts, national advertising, toll-free help line, marketing manual and materials, operations manual, annual convention, and buying group discounts.

FOLIAGE DESIGN SYSTEMS, 1553 S.E. Fort King Ave., Ocala, FL 32671; (904)629-7351.
Franchise: Yes
Description: Interior foliage design, sales, and or maintenance.
Requirements: The franchise fee depends on a market analysis performed by the company, but it ranges from $10,000 to $40,000 with additional costs amounting to about $5,000. The royalty is 4% of gross.
Provisions: Each franchise receives a protected territory, two weeks of training in Florida, operating manuals, operation systems, a computerized management information system to minimize administrative chores, leads from national advertising, and toll-free support. Plant materials can be obtained from over 200,000 sq. ft. of company owned greenhouses. Training covers tested and proven methods of record keeping, order writing, marketing, filing, collections, and accounting, as well as the care, design, and use of foliage in commercial and residential spaces.
Profit Potential: Not available.
Comments: This company has been in business since 1971 and has won numerous nationally recognized awards.

FURNITURE MEDIC, 277 Southfield Pkwy, Suite 130, Forest Park, GA 30050. (800)877-9933.
Franchise: Yes.
Description: Mobile, on-site furniture repair and restoration service using the most technologically advanced techniques and products to offer customers quality, convenient furniture repair and restoration.
Requirements: **Franchise** fee is $9,400; start-up costs range from $7,260 to $9,100; royalties are $200 per month; and the ad fund is $30 per month.
Provisions: Three-week training program, top quality proprietary products and supplies, marketing manual and materials, operations manual, monthly newsletter, national advertising, national accounts, toll-free 24-hour Help Line, ongoing training and research and development.

HANDYMAN HOUSE CALLS, 640 Northland Rd., #33, Forest Park, OH 45240; (513)825-3863.
Franchise: Yes.
Description: This opportunity is not about being one "jack-of-all-trades"; rather it is a job brokerage service. The franchisee manages not one, but many, workers who can collectively "do it all." The goal is to provide reasonably priced alternatives to traditional forms of home maintenance and repair.
Requirements: The franchise fee is $6,250. Financing is available.
Provisions: Complete training and ongoing support is given.

KOTT KOATINGS, 23281 Vista Grande Dr., Suite B, Laguna Hills, CA 92653; (714)770-5055.
Franchise: No
Description: Porcelain and fiberglass refinishing.
Provisions: A dealer package includes 5 days of training at company headquarters, a

complete custom "factory on wheels" trailer unit with generator, a complete equipment package of all necessary tools and supplies, a protected territory, and manuals.
Profit Potential: Not available.

LANGENWALTER INDUSTRIES, INC., 1111 S. Richfield Rd., Placentia, CA 92670; (714)528-7610.
Franchise: Yes.
Description: Franchisees do carpet color correction work for apartment, hotels, and commercial properties, saving the owners up to 85% on carpet replacement costs.
Requirements: $17,750 is the franchise fee. This company is on the SBA approved list for financing. You will also need a white van.
Provisions: Fee includes five days of intensive training, operations manual, marketing package, complete equipment package, technical assistance, and ongoing support.

LIQUID WALL CREATIONS, INC., 2304 11th St., Columbus, NE 68601; (402)564-8591.
Franchise: No.
Description: The liquid wallpaper system is a very interesting method of "faux finish decorating" which means painting on what looks like wallpaper.
Requirements: Investment requirements range from $1,450 for a full equipment package to $4,950 for a complete start-up business package.
Provisions: See above.
Profit Potential: "All of our dealers average $35 to $50 per hour installing Liquid Wallpaper at half the cost of wallpaper."

MIRACLE METHOD, 2767 W. Broadway, Los Angeles, CA 90041; (213)550-1561.
Franchise: Yes
Description: Bathroom restoration.
Provisions: Start-up training takes two to three weeks of intense on-the-job work. Training covers the use of the Miracle Method bonding agent and all aspects of restoring tubs, tile, fiberglass, and cultured marble. The fee includes equipment and enough supplies to restore 20 tubs. Marketing assistance is also provided with company representatives actually accompanying you on sales calls to hotels, construction sites, and private homes.
Profit Potential: Not available.
Comments: Opportunities exist throughout the U.S., Europe, and Australia.

NATIONWIDE CARPET BROKERS, P.O. Box 1472, Dalton, GA 30720. (800)322-7299.
Franchise: No.
Description: This is a national floorcovering and decorating business that offers agents major mill purchasing. You could elect to set up your car or van with the Nationwide logo and be ready to call on your in-home or in-office shoppers. Presently about 20% of Nationwide agencies are full-time businesses with the rest on a part-time basis.
Requirements: Minimum investment is $4,900 in areas where there are no other agents.
Provisions: For the minimum investment you would receive a complete collection of samples, training in your area, technical support, an 800 number for free quotes and inventory availability, video tape training, cards, invoices, letterheads, and basic forms to start your business.
Profit Potential: $30,000 and up depending on the person.

PARKER INTERIOR PLANTSCAPE, INC., 1325 Terrill Rd., Scotch Plains, NJ 07076; (800)526-3672.
Franchise: Yes.
Description: Sale and lease of plants, trees, flowers, silks, Christmas decorations, containers, etc. to offices, malls, atriums, etc. The main business is then to go out and care for these items.
Requirements: $35,000.
Provisions: Training from the largest, most successful, privately-owned interior plantscaping company in the U.S. You will be taught all the secrets, operations, sources, etc. "We will start them in a successful enterprise."
Profit Potential: First year - after costs and salaries $20,000, second year $40,000, third year $60,000, etc. "It is almost like a pyramid. Each time you get an account, you should keep the monthly billing coming in. Each new account just adds to the last."

PARKER INTERIOR PLANTSCAPE, 1325 Terrill Rd., Scotch Plains, NJ 07076; (201)322-5552.
Franchise: No
Description: Your business would be delivering plants and jardeniers to offices and maintaining them as long as they're there. There is no inventory for you to keep.
Requirements: The complete cost of the training program, plus one year of advice and sales leads is $35,000.
Provisions: See above.
Profit Potential: Average profit is $2,000 per job.
Comments: This company has been in business for 45 years.

PERMA-GLAZE, INC., 7310 E. 22nd St., Ste 167, Tucson, AZ 85710; (602)885-7397.
Franchise: Yes.
Description: This business is about restoring and refinishing bathroom and kitchen fixtures such as bathtubs, sinks, and ceramic wall tiles.
Requirements: The franchise fee is $19,500.
Provisions: You get an exclusive territory, complete training, a personalized marketing consultation, printed materials, the operations manual, and equipment.

REPAIR-IT INDUSTRIES, INC., P.O. Box 43680, Phoenix, AZ 85080; (602)465-0165.
Franchise: No
Description: Repair and recoloring of vinyl, leather, windshield glass, fabric, velour, formica, and laminate.
Requirements: Between $150 and $300.
Provisions: Financing may be available. You get the complete kit of supplies for specific repairs, along with instructional manual and video. The kit contains enough supplies to practice and begin doing repair for profit before having to reorder.

SCREEN MACHINE, 19636 8th Street East, Sonoma, CA 95476; (707)996-5551.
Franchise: Yes
Description: A mobile service business specializing in the custom fabrication, replacement, and repair of window and door screens as well as other related services.
Requirements: The franchise fee is $13,500. An equipment and supplies package costs at least $11,350 and general business expenses are $5,500 minimum. The total

initial investment ranges from $30,350 to $49,500.
Provisions: Your investment buys training in marketing strategies, advertising techniques, business management, basic accounting methods, operational procedures, and "hands-on" technical instruction on how to custom fabricate screens and perform screen repair and related work. Also provided are advertising materials, audio visual training, ongoing support, and all of the materials, supplies, and equipment necessary for the basic operation of the business. A custom built mobile workshop with a generator and power miter-box saw are all part of the equipment package.
Profit Potential: Not available.

SPRING-GREEN LAWN CARE, 11927 Spaulding School Dr., Plainfield, IL 60544; (815)436-8777.
Franchise: Yes.
Description: Franchisees offer to residential and commercial customers regular lawn fertilization, weed control, lawn aeration, and pruning and feeding of trees and shrubs.
Requirements: The franchise fee is $12,900.
Provisions: You get an exclusive territory and complete training.

STAINED GLASS OVERLAY, INC., 1827 N. Case St., Orange, CA 92665. (800)654-7666.
Franchise: Yes
Description: The Stained Glass Overlay business is a patented process used to manufacture solid, seamless, one-piece stained glass in any design or pattern. It turns everyday glass into designer glass.
Requirements: The minimum investment is about $50,000. The franchise fee is $34,000, the franchise package that provides training, support materials, a business start-up package, and show quality display materials is $8,000, and other materials cost an additional $3,000. Royalties run 5% of gross sales plus another 2% for the advertising fee.
Provisions: Training starts with 40 hours of classroom and hands-on instruction and includes manuals.
Profit Potential: Not available.
Comments: This franchise is available in the U.S., Australia, the United Kingdom, Israel, Japan, Norway, Thailand, and has locations in 13 other foreign countries.

SURFACE DOCTOR, 5182 Old Dixie Hwy., Forest Park, GA 30050. (800)735-5055.
Franchise: No.
Description: Surface restoration and refinishing service for tile, countertops, bathtubs, sinks, metal appliances and more. Surface Doctor's technology allows bathrooms and kitchens to be transformed without the chaos and expense of conventional remodeling methods.
Requirements: **Franchise** fee is $9,800; start-up costs range from $7,800 to $11,780; royalties are $175 per month; and the ad fund is $25 per month.
Provisions: Comprehensive training program, marketing manuals and materials, operations manual, toll-free Help Line, annual convention, newsletter, ongoing training, and research and development.

URO-TILE, INC., 302 S. Federal Hwy., Boca Raton, FL 33432. (407)394-6701.
Franchise: Yes
Description: Uro-Tile is a patented system which enables on-site manufacturing of

tile, stone, and wood. There are no limitations to the designs, colors, textures, or finishes that can be created with the system. It is an interior-exterior system that can be used on floors and walls or on the facings of home or roof-tops.
Requirements: A non-exclusive contractor's license costs $5,000; an exclusive 100,000 population area costs $20,000.
Provisions: Training and supplies.
Profit Potential: Not available.
Comments: There are currently over 20 franchisees in the U.S. and in foreign countries.

VINYLMAN, 13453 Pumice Street, Norwalk, CA 90650. (213)921-9993.
Franchise: No.
Description: Vinylman is unique in the vinyl repair industry, in that they not only manufacture vinyl repair materials and have schools that are taught by IPVRA accredited teachers, but they are also in the business of vinyl repair. They maintain service trucks that work everyday at vinyl repair, recolor and recover of restaurants and other commercial accounts.
Provisions: Classes are not only available with Vinylman but there are also VCR tapes available for use at home with manuals. The tapes are available for rent for $1.00 per day with a $60.00 deposit. This industry is ideal for either full-time or part-time work.

LON WALTENBERGER TRAINING SERVICES, 5410 Mt. Tahoma Dr. S.E., Olympia, WA 98503; (360)456-1949.
Franchise: No.
Description: Repair/refinish porcelain, gelcoat and acrylic bathtubs; sinks; counters (formica-type and cultured marble); ceramic tiles; spas; ranges and hoods; refrigerators; and dishwashers. Use only primer that requires no acid etching or sanding for savings in labor and durability.
Requirements: The training fee is $295 and you will need about $2,000 for equipment and supplies. "You will repay your total investment with your first 10 jobs."
Provisions: The $295 buy a 14 hour video program plus two manuals with advertising examples, forms, prices, inventory of equipment, and all the information you will need to successfully manage your business. The company president insists that you should shop your hometown sources and manufacturers for all supplies. Technical support is available.
Profit Potential: Profit margin for this industry is high.

THE WINDOW MAN, 2123 E. 7th St., Charlotte NC 28204; (704)377-1995.
Franchise: Yes.
Description: The window Man is the country's largest replacement window franchise. Franchisees sell exclusive solid vinyl replacement windows to customers at home. In 1986, over 23,000,000 windows were sold in the U.S., and a projected annual growth of 15% promises to make this a solid market for the next ten years.
Requirements: The franchise fee is $30,000. You must have some sales or business management experience to qualify.
Provisions: You get complete training, ongoing support and training, a marketing and advertising package, and an exclusive territory.

WOOD REVIVERS, P.O. Box 2230, Danville, CA 94526. (800)545-6603.
Franchise: No.
Description: Restoring beauty to old, weathered, exterior wood. This is part of the

$140 home remodeling industry.
Requirements: Start-up costs amount to $7,500.
Provisions: You receive personal training and joint marketing programs.

WORLDWIDE REFINISHING SYSTEMS, 508 Lake Air Dr., Waco, TX 76710; (817)776-4701.
Franchise: Yes.
Description: Worldwide does bathroom and kitchen fixture refinishing and repair on location.
Requirements: The franchise fee is $6,950.
Provisions: You get an exclusive territory, complete training, ongoing support, and a custom-tailored marketing plan based on the franchisee's background, experience, goals, and territory.

RESIDENTIAL & COMMERCIAL CLEANING & MAINTENANCE

Residential and commercial cleaning businesses are the essence of service businesses. No products are exchanged, and no special skills are required. The basic purpose is to save customers time.

Home cleaning services is a $92 million a year industry, and it is growing all the time. "In John Naisbitt's best seller, Megatrends, maid services is listed among the six growth industries for the nineties," says Frank Flack, chief executive officer of Molly Maid, the fastest growing international maid service. "Roughly 52% of American households are two-income families. That figure is expected to grow to 66% in the next few years, and maid services will grow along with it. There are fifty million women in the work force - about 40% of them have some form of domestic help. Juggling a career and family can take some doing. A working woman is likely to exchange money for time - something she has precious little of. She can save five or six hours a week to do things that are more gratifying than cleaning windows or dusting under the bed."

There are dozens of maid services, and more are entering the field every day. Most can be operated from home. Although they are not the least expensive homebased opportunities to get into, the potential return on investment is excellent. A well-run maid service, utilizing the team cleaning method, can expect to gross over $100,000 by the second year.

Also targeting the residential customer are carpet cleaning, chimney sweeps, and window washing services.

Other businesses in this chapter cater to commercial customers. Office cleaning, janitorial services, mobile power washing, and restaurant cleaning are among these opportunities. Commercial cleaning businesses tend to require bigger investments and more commitment in terms of time and effort. On the plus side, commercial customers are often repeat customers and long-term contracts offer extra security.

AIR CARE, 5115 S. Industrial Rd., #506, Las Vegas, NV 89118; (800)322-9919.
Franchise: No.
Description: Indoor air quality specialists clean and decontaminate air conditioning and heating systems in residential and commercial buildings.
Requirements: $20,500 total.
Provisions: Complete equipment package plus one week training in all aspects of the business. This also includes a toll-free help line.
Profit Potential: $50,000 to $200,000 annually.

AMERICAN LEAK DETECTION, P.O. Box 1701, Palm Springs, CA 92263; (800)755-6697.
Franchise: Yes.
Description: Franchisees use electronic instruments and tools to find and repair water, gas, and sewer leaks in both commercial and residential buildings.
Requirements: The franchise fee is $29,500.
Provisions: Complete training, both business and technical, is provided.

AMERICLEAN, 943 Taft Vineland Rd., Orlando, FL 32824; (407)855-2215.
Franchise: Yes.
Description: This is a mobile power wash and restoration service that has been offering franchises since 1985. The seven different hot and cold water systems make it possible to handle just about anything from restoring historical monuments to cleaning airplanes.
Requirements: The franchise fee is $10,000. Another $20,000 is required for the equipment package. Some financing is available.
Provisions: The franchise fee buys training on equipment use and maintenance as well as business management techniques. There is also a complete advertising package.

BASEMENT DE-WATERING SYSTEMS, INC., 162 East Chestnut St., Canton, IL 61520; (800)331-2943.
Franchise: NoRequirements: $15,900 for the business system. An additional $2,000 will be needed for tools (some of which you may already have.)
Provisions: Fee covers enough baseboard material and epoxy to recoup the entire investment. You will also receive an inventory of sales forms, business cards, presentation materials, advertising slicks, prepared radio commercials and television commercials. The three-day training workshop covers the proper method of installing the system through hands-on-training. Ongoing support is provided.
Profit Potential: Most dealers average from $15 to $22 per installed foot of baseboard. The company founders generated over $100,000 in their first year of business working from home.
Comments: The company has over 110 dealers in 35 states with a success rate of 86%.

BLACK MAGIC, 55 Hercules Drive, Colchester, VT 05446; (800)334-1497.
Franchise: No
Description: The Black Magic commercial kitchen vent cleaning system is a specialized cleaning technique that removes cooking grease from exhaust hoods, ducts, and fans. A self-contained pressure washer forms on a special cleaner, then blasts away stubborn grease. Also available from Black Magic is a chimney sweeping service and automotive detailing business.
Requirements: The systems start at $1,850 and go up to $7,485.
Provisions: This is a turn-key system.
Profit Potential: $65 per hour.
Comments: Can be run part time.

CEILING CLEAN, 5115 S. Industrial Rd., #506, Las Vegas, NV 89118. (702)736-4063.
Franchise: No.
Description: Ceiling fan cleaning service. There are over 400 dealers currently.
Requirements: The cost of the package is $4,750.
Provisions: The fee covers a protected area, complete training manual and video, ongoing support, and corporate referral system.
Profit Potential: "We have many dealers who are earning $1,000 to $5,000 per week, many of them working this busies part-time."

CEILTECH, 825 Gatepark Drive, #3, Daytona Beach, FL 32114; (800)662-9299.
Franchise: No
Description: Ceiling cleaning service.

Requirements: The system sells for $3,495 complete with leasing plans available.
Provisions: The system includes all necessary equipment, supplies, and accessories to generate over $4,000 in gross income. Also included are marketing materials and a training manual.
Profit Potential: You can net in excess of $150 per hour.

CHEM-DRY CARPET, DRAPERY AND UPHOLSTERY CLEANING, 1530 North 1000 West, Logan, UT 84321; (800)841-6583.
Franchise: Yes.
Description: Chem-Dry franchises clean carpet, drapery, upholstery and most fabrics with a patented, heated carbonating system. Chem-Dry specializes in the hard-to-remove stains and has four patents with several more pending.
Requirements: $4,950 down payment with a full purchase price of $17,950. Remaining $13,000 is financed over 56 months at 0% interest.
Provisions: Your fee will get you all of the equipment, solutions, paperwork and training needed to start the business. Plus you can expect the constant support of the parent company, a technical department to help with any questions, newsletters, etc.
Provisions: The investment covers everything necessary to start a full-time business.

COVERALL CLEANING CONCEPTS, 3111 Camino Del Rio North, Suite 1200, San Diego, CA 92108; (800)537-3371.
Franchise: Yes
Description: Commercial cleaning service.
Requirements: The initial franchise fee ranges from $4,250 to $33,600 and up with the total investment ranging from $4,450 to $33,360.
Provisions: This is a turnkey commercial cleaning business that includes training, equipment and supplies, customer accounts as well as billing and collection services. In addition, the company also provides insurance, equipment leasing, volume purchasing discounts and ongoing quality assurance checks. Initial training covers cleaning techniques, product usage and business development. Manuals are included. Ongoing training and business related seminars are offered at no extra charge. There are nine different business levels to choose from beginning at $500 per month in cleaning contracts to $25,000 per month and above.

CLOSEUP: Coverall Cleaning Concepts

Most people go into business risking the uncertainty of having enough income to cover expenses while getting the business off the ground. It is not uncommon for a new business to take one to three years just to turn a profit.

Now imagine buying into a business that not only gives you all the training you need to get off to a good start, but hands you as many customers as you want whenever you want them. Sound too good to be true? That's exactly what Coverall, a commercial cleaning franchise, does for its 4,200 franchisees.

When Craig Wolff of Spring Valley, New York, went looking for a new business opportunity he was already a seasoned business owner. But the one thing that most successful business owners have come to expect, financial freedom, had eluded him. "I wasn't satisfied with the amount of money I was

making," he says. He also didn't like to have to travel as much as he did and went looking for a homebased business.

"I looked into quite a few cleaning services, but the Coverall support system definitely looked the best to me. The company has an operations department I can call on if I get stuck. Once I had a really big job and they sent a guy right out to help me." That kind of support can be invaluable when you're new to a business you know little about.

When Craig purchased his business, he says he got more than was actually promised. In addition to supplies and equipment, he received training in business management for himself and training in cleaning procedures for his crews. Now his time, usually in the evenings, is spent managing the crews and accounts.

All of Craig's accounts came from Coverall. Special services such as carpet cleaning and window washing are not part of the regular service and add extra income. "All it takes is a phone call to grow," says Craig. "I choose to grow $1,000 at a time, but the growth potential here is just unlimited. My business could become enormous. It's up to me." Coverall has a full sales and marketing department that responds quickly. "Every time I've asked for more business, I've had it within two weeks. When I do well they do well."

DELCO CLEANING SYSTEMS, 2513 Warfield, FT Worth, TX 76106; (800)433-2113.
Franchise: No
Description: Environmental mobile power wash service, i.e.: truck washing, building washing for store fronts and shopping malls, and restaurant kitchen washing.
Requirements: Equipment, supplies, and training are all sold separately. Minimum required: $2,000.
Provisions: See above.
Profit Potential: $10,000 to $100,000.

DIAL-A-MAID, 823 Oakdale Rd., Johnson City, NY 13790; (607)798-8871.
Franchise: Yes.
Description: Residential and commercial cleaning service.
Requirements: The franchise fee starts at $5,000. Financing is available. An additional $9,000 will be needed for equipment, supplies, and advertising.
Provisions: Complete training, a protected territory, and an operations manual.

FABRIZONE, 315 Bering Ave., Toronto, Ontario, Canada M8Z 3A
Franchise: Yes

Description: Drycleaning and purification process for carpets and upholstery, ceiling cleaning, and insurance damage restoration.
Requirements: Total investment requires $8,000. There is financing available from the company.
Provisions: Training and ongoing technical and promotional support.
Profit Potential: Not available.
Comments: **Franchise** opportunities exist in both the U.S. and Canada.

HEAVEN'S BEST CARPET & UPHOLSTERY CLEANING, P.O. Box 607, Rexburg, ID 83440. (208)359-1106.
Franchise: Yes.
Description: An alternative to the traditional wet saturation carpet cleaning offering the advantages of modern, low moisture cleaning. "Our operators receive professional training. These factors with a low flat rate royalty fee insure success."
Requirements: The franchise fee is $9,500 and the royalty is $80 a month.
Provisions: Complete equipment and training package, exclusive territory, and enough initial supplies to re-coop $10,000.

JANI-KING INTERNATIONAL, INC., 4950 Keller Springs, Ste 190, Dallas, TX 75248; (214)991-0900.
Franchise: Yes.
Description: Jani-King is the world's largest janitorial franchise. Operators perform light office cleaning and janitorial services for commercial and industrial buildings on a long-term contract basis.
Requirements: The franchise fee starts at $6,500. Financing is available.
Provisions: All franchisees receive training, business forms, and ongoing support.

JANTIZE AMERICA, INC., 15449 Middlebelt, Livonia, MI 48154; (800)968-9182.
Franchise: Yes
Description: Commercial cleaning service.
Requirements: The franchise fee ranges starts at $3,200 and the initial start-up package (computer system, equipment, supplies, etc.) is another $4,000. You can lower that cost by using the company's computer service instead which reduces the cost by $2,500. Monthly royalties are 8% of gross sales and the advertising fee is %1 of gross.
Provisions: In addition to the provisions stated above, Janitize provides all business forms, a supply of uniforms, and ongoing support.
Profit Potential: Not available.

LASER CHEM INTERNATIONAL CORP., 7022 South 400 West, Midvale, UT 84047; (800)272-2741.
Franchise: Yes.
Description: The Laser Chem advanced carpet dry cleaning system thoroughly cleans carpet, dries quickly, and does not resoil. "This new system has revolutionized the carpet cleaning industry."
Requirements: The franchise fee is $6,975.
Provisions: Month to month support via newsletter, toll-free technical assistance, and benefits of in-house research and development.

MAID BRIGADE, 850 Indian Trail, Lilburn, GA 30247; (404)564-2400.
Franchise: Yes
Description: Supervised team cleaning services for single family homes.

Requirements: The franchise fee is $16,900. Operating expenses will require an additional $15,000+. The royalty is 7% and the advertising royalty is 2%. A business background is preferred.
Provisions: The fee buys the right to use the name, a one-week training class, operations manual, and a start-up kit that includes janitorial supplies, printed materials, training videos, and marketing materials.
Profit Potential: Not available.

MAID EASY, 43 Orchard Lane, Glastonbury, CT 06033; (800)395-MAID.
Franchise: Yes
Description: Residential maid service.
Requirements: Total investment is about $22,000.
Provisions: Fee includes an advertising program, sales training, operational manual, motivational training, employee training video and manuals, protected territory, and ongoing support. Equipment and supplies are purchased separately.
Profit Potential: Not available.
Comments: Can be operated part-time, without any office employees. The company boasts of having a system that allows you to pay maids almost twice the going rate.

THE MAIDS INTERNATIONAL, 4820 Dodge St., Omaha, NE 68132; (402)558-8797.
Franchise: Yes.
Description: Completely computerized residential cleaning service.
Requirements: The franchise fee is $16,900. Another $25,000 will be needed for operating capital including leases for cars and computers, labor and advertising. The royalty ranges from 5% to 7% and the advertising royalty is 2%.
Provisions: The fee buys the use of the company name, the exclusive system, pre-training, corporate training, post-training, and a complete equipment and advertising package. Financing is available only for expanding territories.
Profit Potential: Not available.

MCMAID, INC., 10 W. Kinzie, Chicago, IL 60610; (312)321-6250.
Franchise: Yes
Description: Residential cleaning service utilizing team cleaning methods.
Requirements: A business background is preferred. The franchise fee ranges from $15,000 to $30,000 based on numbers of households in the population. You will also need $22,400 for cleaning equipment, supplies, office space, insurance, office furniture, advertising, car leasing, and operational expenses. Royalties are 6% and advertising royalties are 2%.
Provisions: The fee includes the use of the name, two weeks of training, ongoing support, and supplies at cost. There is financing available with a $15,000 minimum down payment.
Profit Potential: Not available.
Comments: The costs for this particular maid service franchise are out of line and there are much better deals available.

MOBILE SERVICES, INC., 5020 Ritter Road, Suite 201, Mechanicsburg, PA (800)444-CLEAN.
Franchise: No
Description: Mobile power wash and restoration.
Requirements: The economy starter unit system costs $6,995.

Provisions: The above package includes complete training in every aspect of the business, equipment, and supplies as well as ongoing support.
Profit Potential: Not available.

MOLLY MAID, INC., 540 Avis Dr., #B, Ann Arbor, MI 48108. (800)666-6559.
Franchise: Yes.
Description: Regularly scheduled cleaning services with weekday business hours. This is an affordable investment in an exploding industry. Repeat cash business. "Award winning technology."
Requirements: No experience is necessary, but a business background is considered a plus. The franchise fee of $9,900. Is included in the total investment of $35,000. The additional working capital is needed for leased cars, insurance, and bonding of the employees. The royalty decreases from 6% to 3% as sales increase. The advertising royalty is 2%.
Provisions: The fee buys exclusive rights to the territory, equipment and supplies, training, and start-up business documents.
Profit Potential: Not available, however, franchisees said that they were earning well into the six figures and grew so fast it was hard to keep the business at home.
Comments: This is the largest maid service franchise with over 400 operators and 16 years of experience. The company believes in projecting a quality image and it works.

PRIME SHINE AMERICA, INC., 2525 Hospital Road, Saginaw, MI 48603; (800)456-8588.
Franchise: No
Description: Residential maid service.
Requirements: The complete start-up package costs $1,295.
Provisions: Included in the complete package are supplies and equipment for your first maid team, a maid training video, an operations manual, and two days of training at company headquarters. Any of the above may be purchased separately.
Profit Potential: The company claims that following their procedures, you should be able to gross over $80,000 a year within two years.

PROFESSIONAL CARPET SYSTEMS, 5182 Old Dixie Hwy., Forest Park, GA 30050. (800)925-5055.
Franchise: Yes.
Description: Professional Carpet Systems is a leader in on-site carpet redyeing and a total carpet maintenance service. PCS services include carpet cleaning and repair, water/flood damage restoration, smoke removal, guaranteed odor control and more.
Requirements: Franchise fee is $10,000; start-up costs range from $13,000 to $17,400; and the royalties are 6%.
Provisions: Comprehensive training program, annual convention, newsletter, toll-free Help Line, and ongoing research and development.

PROFESSIONAL CLEANING ASSOCIATES, 1902 Central Dr., Ste C, Bedford, TX 76052; (817)267-7287.
Franchise: No.
Description: Commercial cleaning service.
Requirements: $295.
Provisions: Complete manual on how to start your own cleaning service in your home plus seven tapes on bidding new accounts. Follow-up is provided.
Profit Potential: $50,000 plus.

INTERNATIONAL CLEANING SERVICES, INC., Family Acres Estates, Rt 1 Box 2400, Ranger, GA 30734; (800)289-8642.
Franchise: No
Description: Residential maid service.
Requirements: Fees are $6,990 and $9,900.
Provisions: The lowest priced package includes training manual, master copies of forms needed for all aspects of the business, a marketing format package, two bookkeeping manuals with a "fill in the blanks" accounting system, desk organizer, five training videos, and one full year of consultation and support. The higher priced package also includes hands-on training with hotel and airfare included, computer software tailored to the maid service system, and complete instruction in five additional businesses: floor refinishing, post-partum service, movers helper, window cleaning, and office cleaning.
Profit Potential: The company claims anyone following their system should be able to gross $250,000 annually by the end of the second year. There is also a new system, sold separately, for a mobile mini-blind washing system.
Comments: The company has an exceptional record. Of its 700+ operators, none have failed.

CLOSEUP: International Cleaning Services, Inc.

"You would think," says Joyce Pierson, of Montgomery, Alabama, "that running a maid service would be easy. It isn't. I seriously considered starting one myself, but I'm glad I didn't." Instead Pierson bought an independent maid service system from International Cleaning Services, Inc. There are many franchised maid services in the $9.2 billion industry, but International Cleaning Services offers a complete system with no royalty payments and no territorial restriction.

The system leaves nothing to chance. Included in the base fee ($6,990) are training manuals, master copies of every form needed to run an efficient maid service, a marketing format package, a customized accounting system, a desk organizer, five videos, and one full year of consultation. Customized software and a computer system are separate options. The price is much lower than that of any franchised maid service.

The add-on business plans - an option unique to the industry - are particularly impressive. For $3,000, you can buy five more business plans designed to bring additional profits. Pierson is especially excited about the Post-Partum Services (for new mothers).

The ICS maid service has over 800 clients (operators). None have failed in the company's 16 year history. Only five have not grossed $80,000 in the first year and $250,000 in the second, according to the company. The average net profit is 41% of revenues.

"A tried and true business system is the only way to go," says Pierson, who is likely to gross $250,000 in her second business year. "It took me less than a month to start making money."

RUG DOCTOR PRO, 2788 North Larkin Ave., Fresno, CA 93727; (209)291-5511.
Franchise: Yes.
Description: As its name implies, Rug Doctor Pro is in the business of cleaning carpets, It also cleans upholstery and drapes and does water damage restoration for residential and commercial customers.
Requirements: The franchise fee starts at $5,000.
Provisions: The fee buys an exclusive territory, complete training, and all necessary forms.

SERVICEMASTER, 2300 Warrenville Rd., Downers Grove, IL 60515; (708)964-1300.
Franchise: Yes
Description: Professional residential and commercial cleaning and lawn-care services with more than two million customers worldwide.
Requirements: The franchise fee ranges from $6,000 to $18,000 depending on the type of franchise. You will need up to $10,000 for training, equipment, and supplies. The royalty is 10% and the advertising is 1%.
Provisions: The fee buys one week of training at headquarters and ongoing support. Financing is offered to up to 65% of total investment.
Profit Potential: Not available.
Comments: This is a franchise that everyone knows. It has been around since 1947 and now has over 4,200 franchise operators!

SERVPRO, 575 Airport Blvd., Gallatin, TX 37066; (800)826-9586.
Franchise: Yes.
Description: Full-service residential and commercial cleaning business that also specializes in fire restoration.
Requirements: The franchise fee is $18,000 with an equal amount needed for startup.
Provisions: Complete training and technical support are provided. Financing is available.
Comments: This is one of the oldest services businesses in the industry with over 800 franchisees.

SHINE A BLIND, P.O. Box 7, St. Clair, MI 48079. (800)446-0411.
Franchise: No
Description: Ultrasonic window blind cleaning.
Requirements: The initial investment is between $14,000 and $55,000 (the latter includes a fully equipped truck mounted machine).
Provisions: The basic business start-up package includes marketing materials, business forms, a marketing guide, and supplies.
Profit Potential: One job is work about $325.
Comments: The initial investment can be financed through the company.

SPR INTERNATIONAL, INC., 3398 Sanford Dr., Marietta GA 30066.
Franchise: No
Description: Bathtub restoration.
Requirements: The complete start-up package costs $1,995.
Provisions: Provided are business supplies and printed materials, all equipment and supplies to perform the work, a proven marketing plan, and training.
Profit Potential: $150 an hour minimum.

STEAMATIC, INC., 1320 S. University Dr., Ste 400, Fort Worth, TX 76107; (800)527-1295.
Franchise: Yes.
Description: Steamatic bills itself as a total cleaning service for the general public. Actually, many customers are commercial as well as residential, and most accounts come from working with insurance companies on settling claims stemming from fire and water damage, floods, storms, and accidents. The Steamatic cleaning service started with controlled-heat carpet cleaning and portable in-home drycleaning for upholstery and drapes. Services also include document restoration, odor removal, ceiling and wall cleaning, water removal (usually flood repair), electronics cleaning, wood restoration, and air duct cleaning and corrosion control. The company considers being able to offer a single source for all of these cleaning services its biggest advantage over the competition. There is no other company that offers customers all of the eleven services which are available from Steamatic.
Requirements: The franchise fee ranges from $5,000 to $18,000 depending on population of the exclusive territory. The equipment package costs $17,545 to $27,500. Upon approval there is 100% financing available. Also needed is a white van and working capital.
Provisions: A complete 50 year old system, proprietary equipment, training, ongoing support, and industry name recognition.

SWISHER INTERNATIONAL, 6849 Fairview Rd., Charlotte, NC 28210; (800)444-4138.
Franchise: Yes.
Description: Commercial rest room cleaning and sanitation. Products and services provided to 35,000 customers every week. "We are the top 50 franchise in North America."
Requirements: Franchise fee of $55,000 plus $44,000 for existing business.
Provisions: Full initial and ongoing training, and access to an extremely successful business.

TWO TWINS FROM TEXAS, 23052 Alicia Parkway #H202, Mission Viejo, CA 92692; (714)258-7068.
Franchise: No.
Description: Own your own discount mobile mini-blind cleaning service. With over 500 million blinds that need cleaning, there is a huge market available. You charge $6 to $7 per blind and earn over $250 per day.
Requirements: $2,700 to $4,300.
Provisions: All equipment, marketing and advertising plan, and training video.
Profit Potential: $3,000 to $5,000 per month net.

ULTRASONIC BLIND CLEANING SYSTEMS, 4464 Industrial St., Simi Valley, CA 93063; (800)669-8227.
Franchise: No
Description: Mini-blind cleaning service.
Requirements: The total investment is under $20,000.
Provisions: All necessary equipment and a training video.
Profit Potential: About $100 an hour.

UNICLEAN SYSTEMS, INC., 642 West 29th St., North Vancouver, British Columbia, Canada V7N 2K2; (604)986-4750.

Franchise: Yes
Description: Commercial cleaning service.
Requirements: The franchise fee is $19,500. Royalties start at $50 per $10,000 gross revenue.
Provisions: The franchise package includes training, office materials, equipment and supplies, an initial customer base, and ongoing support.
Profit Potential: Not available.

THE UNWALLPAPER CO., P.O. Box 757, Silver Spring, MD 20901; (301)680-2512.
Franchise: No
Description: Design wallprinting with paint rather than wallpaper.
Provisions: Training and supplies.
Profit Potential: High net profit is $60,000 annually.

WASH ON WHEELS, 5401 South Bryant Ave., Sanford, FL 32773; (800)345-1969.
Franchise: Yes.
Description: The basic service is a mobile power cleaning service for external cleaning, acoustical tile, wall cleaning, and carpet cleaning.
Requirements: The franchise fee is $4,000. An additional $10,000 to $40,000 is needed for operating capital.
Provisions: Training in all aspects of the business.

COMPUTER AND TECHNICAL SERVICES

After a dozen or so years of computers making their way into the workplace, it is difficult to find a business without one. This chapter is comprised mostly of businesses that either service computer equipment or are based specifically on the services a computer can provide.

There are several opportunities in the laser printer recharging industry. Although this is a relatively new industry, it is huge and recharging cartridges rather than buying new ones has become the norm. In addition to being an excellent part-time business, it is also a good way to get started in other technical services.

There are two businesses that offer computer cleaning services and one that has a unique computer portrait service. Computertots has an excellent curriculum for teaching computer skills to small children. And there are two businesses that can show you how to offer dozens of different computer-based services.

ALPHA LASER CARTRIDGE, INC., P.O. Box 1178, Ormond Beach, FL 32175; (800)627-ALPHA.
Franchise: No.
Description: Basic service is laser cartridge recharging. Optional services include repair, cleaning, and maintenance of laser printers and copiers.
Requirements: The basic cost of becoming a "trainee" is $2,295.
Provisions: The fee covers two days of one-on-one instruction at company headquarters in Florida including hotel accommodations, all tools and supplies necessary to start recycling laser and copier cartridges, a business start-up seminar, a technical manual, and toll-free technical support. To help get you started, the company also provides training on how to acquire new accounts, a list of the most recent laser owners in your area, and samples of ads.
Profit Potential: Gross profit from recharging four cartridges per day amount to $1,000 per week.
Comments: Can be part-time.

ALU, INC., 17717 Vail St., #524, Dallas, TX 75252; (800)752-7370.
Franchise: No.
Description: Laser recharging service.
Requirements: The cost of repair class is $1,295 and includes enough inventory and equipment to perform 60 recharges. There are no ongoing royalties, however, there is a $1 per cartridge royalty only for accounts that ALU acquires for you.
Provisions: In addition to technical training, ALU offers a marketing program and addresses of laser printer and copier owners in your zip code areas (free), and co-op advertising. Training is conducted for two days in Dallas and hotel accommodations are included. A training manual and ongoing consulting service are also provided.
Profit Potential: For no more than 15 minutes of work, your profit will be about $32.
Comments: ALU claims to have a unique process that sets them apart from the numerous other recharging systems. Their cartridges print at least 25% longer than a new one because they put in more toner than the original manufacturer.

COMPU-FRESH, 2512 Caledonia Ave., North Vancouver, B.C., Canada V7G 1T9; (604)929-7187.
Franchise: Yes
Description: Business service that cleans the external surfaces of computer equipment and related accessories, like printers, plotters and computer furniture. The cleaning procedures protect equipment from static and the transmission of bacteria and viruses.
Requirements: Area distributorship costs $15,000 plus $2,000 training fee. There are no royalties, however, there is currently an annual registration fee of $4,000. Additional start-up costs average $2,000 minimum.
Provisions: Fee includes a total equipment package with two full field kits and enough cleaning fluids to last for the first year in business. Also included are an area business plan, a marketing plan, five days of classroom and field training in Vancouver, exclusive territory, initial set-up of business procedures, training manual, training video that demonstrates every marketing, operational and administrative step of the business. The annual registration fee covers the use of the company's trademarks, continuing field training and promotional assistance, emergency consultation, and updating seminars.
Profit Potential: Following the system, you should be able to net $17,000 working part-time, two days a week or over $65,000 working full-time.
Comments: This franchise is available in both Canada and the U.S.

COMPUTER BUSINESS SERVICES, CBC Plaza, Sheridan, IN 46069; (800)343-8014, ext. 2273.
Franchise: No
Description: This is a proven business a couple or individual can run full or part-time from their home. It includes state-of-the-art hardware, software, training material (videos and manuals), and extensive support from the company's technical and marketing staffs. The package consists of over 30 profitable computer-based businesses, including: Bi-Weekly Mortgage, Electronic Medical Claims Processing, Information Broker, Voice Mail/Voice Messaging, Personalized Children's Books, Financial Aid For College, Utility Bill Auditing, Computer Appointment Verification, Real Estate Inspection and Community Bulletin Board.
Requirements: $3,500 to $13,500.
Provisions: See above.
Profit Potential: "People can earn up to $4,000 or more per month with this system."

COMPUTERTOTS, P.O. Box 408, Great Falls VA 20066; (703)759-2556.
Franchise: Yes.
Description: Computertots is a computer enrichment program offered through day-care centers and private preschools to children ages three to six years. In addition to a complete computer system and an extensive software library of the latest educational software, Computertots uses alternate keyboards, light pens, graphic tablets, and computer-controlled robots to introduce computers to children in a fun and nonthreatening way.
Requirements: The franchise fee starts at $15,900 with an additional need for at least $13,000 to get started.
Provisions: The fee includes an exclusive territory, a collection of computer software programs, eight monthly curriculum packages, some hardware, master copies of printed materials, and complete training in every aspect of the business.

CYGNUS SYSTEMS, INC., 3416 S. Dixon Rd., Kokomo, IN 46902. (317)453-7077.
Franchise: No

Description: Graphics imaging system.
Requirements: $5,370 for the black/white video system and $24,000 for the color photography system complete with a 386 computer with digitizing hardware.
Provisions: A complete computer portrait system to do computer pictures.

DEMOSOURCE, INC., 8502 E. Via de Ventura, Ste 220, Scottsdale, AZ 85258; (800)283-4759.
Franchise: No.
Description: Company offers a wide variety of moneymaking opportunities using PC-driven, reasonably-priced voicemail. "Our 'cash machines' bring in money with very little effort on your part. Our basic voicemail answers your phones, faxes back marketing literature and can even drum up leads with outbound calling, perfect for homebased businesses."
Requirements: $295 for a one-line system. Multi-lines start at $1,295. A complete system including PC is $5,995, otherwise you need your own PC. Financing is offered at 50% down with monthly payments at no interest.
Provisions: Package includes voicemail software and hardware, a PC (if applicable), easy-to-follow instructions, a marketing package with ideas, suggestions and samples, and technical support.
Profit Potential: Unlimited; "We have made millionaires."

INKY DEW, 7297 University Ave., La Mesa, CA 91941. (619)465-9339.
Franchise: No.
Description: Turn-key package for printer ribbon re-ink and reloads and inkjet refills.
Requirements: The initial license package costs $2,000. You can get an information packet for $2 and a video for $10.
Provisions: Fee covers a turn-key system with equipment and supplies, instructions, videos, toll-free technical and order lines.
Profit Potential: Up to $125,000.

LASERFAX, INC., 17944 N.E. 65th St., Redmond, WA 98052. (206)883-9398.
Franchise: No.
Description: Laser cartridge recycling.
Provisions: Two days of training in office set-up, marketing, remanufacturing toner cartridges for laser printers, and servicing of laser printers.
Profit Potential: Not available.
Comments: This company was started in 1987 in the president's garage, but now is housed in a 2,000 square foot warehouse and office. That is some indication of how this industry is growing.

LASER PRODUCT CONSULTANTS, 1075 Bellevue Way N.E., Suite 501, Bellevue, WA 98004; (800)878-7008.
Franchise: No.
Description: Laser cartridge recharging.
Requirements: Prices start at $495 and go up to $5,995.
Provisions: All packages include home study training materials and supplies. All training packages have a marketing and advertising package, which includes sample advertisements and flyers as well as proven marketing strategies. Technical training includes correct gapping methods, drum care and lubrication, cleaning and inspection, proper toner refilling and sealing procedures, worn parts replacement, troubleshooting, and cartridge testing.

Profit Potential: Not available.
Comments: This company has over 800 dealers in the U.S., Canada, Europe, Asia, Africa, Australia, Central America, and the Middle East. Their training program appeared in a book entitled "100 Best Spare Time Businesses in America" published by John Wiley & Sons.

LCR TECHNOLOGIES, INC., P.O. Box 871237, Dallas, TX 75287-1237; (214)418-6658.
Franchise: No.
Description: Toner remanufacturing and repair/service maintenance business for laser printers and PC copiers. The company offers a variety of different programs, from home study instruction manuals and videos to comprehensive on-site training.
Requirements: A complete turn-key system costs $4,900. The cost for the home training program is $1,695; with technical training is $3,390. Add $1,400 for a laser printer.
Provisions: See above.
Profit Potential: About $60 per hour.
Comments: Can be run part-time.

SCOTT DIRECT, INC., 2501 22nd Ave. North, Ste 1002, St. Petersburg, FL 33713; (813)528-2677.
Franchise: Yes.
Description: Professional computer cleaning at the client's location. The service entails vacuuming all the dust and contaminants from the inside of the computer, plus washing the electrical boards with a liquid cleaner made especially for electrical components. The keyboard, printer and monitor are also cleaned.
Requirements: Must be able to follow instructions. The cost ranges from $39 to $1,495 for computer cleaning, repair and upgrades.
Provisions: You get five videos on cleaning computers and printers, five sales letters and flyers, a manual on how to start the business, and step-by-step instructions on how to perform the service.
Profit Potential: $20,000 to $50,000 per year.

SUNSTATE LASER PRODUCTS, 7011 Warner Ave., #E205, Huntington Beach, CA 92647.
Franchise: No.
Description: Sunstate is a toner cartridge recycler on contract.
Requirements: The Basic program costs $3,995.
Provisions: The cost includes materials, supplies, equipment, and training. Training consists of two and a half days of intensive hands-on training on how to recharge toner cartridges plus two manuals covering both technical and marketing aspects of the business, and video tapes to be used with the technical manual. There are enough initial supplies to recharge 101 toner cartridges.
Profit Potential: Not available.
Comments: The company points out that this industry is expected to exceed $1 billion by 1993.

REAL ESTATE AND FINANCIAL SERVICES

Real estate is a business commonly based in a home office. Although there are no real estate businesses per se listed in this chapter, there are a variety of businesses closely associated with the industry. Home inspection services, for instance, are employed by real estate brokers and home buyers to carefully check out buildings for hidden problems. Lindal Cedar Homes franchisees do more than sell homes, they offer personalized design services and sometimes act as contractors too. Income property owners need to check out new tenants before renting, and the National Tenant Network offers computerized tenant screening services.

Closely related to the real estate industry is financial services. U.S. Mortgage Reduction offers creative ways to reduce a home owner's mortgage costs. Triple Check is an income tax service for individuals. And Creative Asset Management can teach you to become a financial consultant with clients that return year after year.

All of these businesses require a higher level of expertise and business acumen. If you consider buying one of these businesses, you should have a strong interest in the business and be able to deal effectively with people and project yourself professionally.

AMERICAN ACCENT HOMES, 300 North Cannon Blvd., P.O. Box 131, Kannapolis, NC 28082-0131.
Franchise: No.
Description: Sales of contemporary "kit" homes.
Requirements: Representative must have a company-approved model home erected within their sales area. A $4,000 non-refundable deposit, which applies fully toward the purchase of an approved models, is sufficient to secure a representative agreement. No real estate license is required.
Profit Potential: A representative earns 20% of the retail price on the sale of a kit; gross profits of $8 t0 $12 per sq. ft. are generally expected on completed homes; therefore gross profits of $16,000 to $20,000 can be realized on a 2,000 sq. ft. house.

AMERICAN ELITE HOMES, INC., P.O. Box 1160, Kannapolis, NC 28082; (800)792-3443 ext. 567.
Franchise: No.
Description: Market a full line of panelized homes and commercial buildings.
Requirements: There is no charge to become a representative, however, you are required to purchase or sell a house to get started. The initial down payment is $5,000.
Provisions: Model home to sell, live in, or use as office. Also books, manual, literature, blueprints, and complete construction information.
Profit Potential: $5,000 to $50,000 per sale.

AMERISPEC HOME INSPECTION SERVICE, 1855 West Katella Ave., Suite 330, Orange, CA 92667. (800)426-2270.
Franchise: Yes.
Description: Conduct inspections throughout North America. "Our primary business is home inspections, but our network of independently owned and operated franchisees,

conduct a broad range of services including tests for radon, carbon monoxide, water, energy assessment, and Environmental Phase I Inspections. We conduct more inspections than anyone else in North America."
Requirements: Initial franchise fees range from $11,900 to $22,900. Franchisees pay a 7% royalty fee, and a 3% national advertising fee on an ongoing basis.
Provisions: Fully developed business system includes: business management, technical, and marketing programs. Starter materials and proprietary software provided. Complete initial training and comprehensive ongoing support.
Profit Potential: Varies based on size of territory and resources.

THE BUILDING INSPECTOR OF AMERICA, INC., 684 Main St., Wakefield, MA 01880; (617)246-4215.
Franchise: Yes.
Description: Building inspectors are hired by the franchise operators and trained by the franchisee to produce written reports for customers within a few days.
Requirements: The franchise fee starts at $15,000.
Provisions: Franchisees receive training, an operations manual, an inspector training manual, an advertising package, printed materials, and a prepared press release for local grand opening publicity.

CREATIVE ASSET MANAGEMENT, 120 Wood Avenue South, Suite 300, Iselin, NJ 08830. (800)245-0530.
Franchise: Yes.
Description: Franchisees act as financial consultants to individual clients. This is a fee-based investment advisory franchise using MMA's, CD's, no-load mutual funds, fixed and variable annuities primarily. **Franchise** is building a practice with a client base they will service year after year, helping clients put together a diversified investment portfolio.
Requirements: The franchise fee starts at $17,500. Additional start-up is approximately $3,000. The monthly maintenance fee is $150/$300.
Provisions: Franchisees get a proven marketing system (13 marketing techniques), implementation system (set up investment portfolio with client), and a business system. There is also continual ongoing support.

CREDIT AND DEBT CONSULTANTS INSTITUTE, Box 145087, Coral Gables, FL 33114. (305)661-0606.
Franchise: No.
Description: Work as a debt reduction consultant. You will learn to reduce client's debt to a fraction of the original amount due.
Requirements: $99 to $495.
Provisions: Complete at-home training.
Profit Potential: $40 to $60 an hour.

THE HOMETEAM INSPECTION SERVICE, INC., 4010 Executive Park Dr., Suite 420, Cincinnati, OH 45241. (800)598-5297.
Franchise: Yes.
Description: HomeTeam is a home inspection service for resale of homes and new construction that utilizes a unique approach. This is the fastest growing franchise in this booming industry.
Requirements: The franchise fee ranges from $11,950 to $22,900. The total investment ranges from $13,000 to $33,650. There is a ten year contract period with two ten-

year options.
Provisions: Designated franchise area; an extensive 14 days of training which includes: marketing, technical knowledge and business procedures; and continuous ongoing support.
Profit Potential: Average $100,000 annually.

HOUSEMASTER OF AMERICA, INC., 421 W. Union Ave., Bound Brook, NJ 08805; (201)469-6565.
Franchise: Yes.
Description: HouseMaster has developed a complete system for doing business in the home inspection industry. It is not necessary to know anything about housing, engineering, real estate, or law to take advantage of this opportunity.
Requirements: The franchise fee starts at $17,000.
Provisions: The fee buys training, customized data base software, and ongoing support.

LINDAL CEDAR HOMES, INC., P.O. Box 24426, Seattle, WA 98124; (206)725-0900.
Franchise: Yes.
Description: Lindal Cedar Homes is the world's largest manufacturer of cedar homes.
Requirements: The first requirement of a Lindal distributor is to purchase and build a Lindal home, which will be used as a model and an office. There is no franchise fee.
Provisions: Franchisees receive comprehensive training and a comprehensive cooperative advertising program.

NATIONAL PROPERTY INSPECTIONS, 224 S. 108th Ave., #2, Omaha, NE 68154; (402)333-9807.
Franchise: Yes.
Description: Home inspection.
Requirements: The franchise fee is $14,000.
Provisions: The fee includes an exclusive territory, complete training, sales and marketing manuals, complete advertising package, inspection tools, specialized accounting and bookkeeping system, company blazer with logo, stationery and business cards, business forms, marketing materials, and ongoing assistance.

NATIONAL TENANT NETWORK, INC., P.O. Box 1664, Lake Grove, OR 97035; (50)257-7961.
Franchise: Yes.
Description: This is a unique computerized tenant tracking and screening system for residential and commercial tenants.
Requirements: The franchise fee is $4,000. An additional investment of $15,000 is required for a marketing and feasibility study and for equipment.
Provisions: The franchise investment covers the cost of two fully programmed access terminals, modems, and telecommunications software as well as training and marketing assistance.

NEW ENGLAND LOG HOMES, INC., P.O. Box 57, Hamden, CT 06518; (203)562-9981.
Franchise: Yes.
Description: This company manufactures log homes. Franchisees act as dealers who start out as home buyers.

Requirements: The franchise fee varies.

RESIDENTIAL BUILDING INSPECTORS, 701 Fairway Drive, Clayton, NC 07520. (919)486-3429.
Franchise: Yes.
Description: Building inspection service.
Requirements: The franchise fee is $6,875 with start-up costs amounting to an additional $1,600 to $4,000. Royalties are 10% of gross monthly income.
Provisions: The fee covers marketing materials, camera-ready artwork for all kinds of ads, an operations and procedures manual, territorial protection, office supplies and forms, and ongoing support. The company provides a very comprehensive training program that includes a temporary certification process taking about six weeks to complete, on-site training in your area, and an inspection review process that results in final certification upon satisfactory completion.
Profit Potential: Performing only one inspection per week (2.5 hours of work) will result in $7,920 a year.
Comments: The company offers a great deal for anyone who doesn't have a lot of cash to get started. They will waive the franchise fee and instead charge a 20% royalty. All you have to come up with is the start-up capital.

SELL YOUR OWN HOME, P.O. Box 14804, Lenexa, KS 66285; (913)492-7283.
Franchise: No.
Description: Service offers affordable alternatives to traditional high cost of selling homes. Various programs such as "flat fee" pricing give the homeowner choices as to the amount of their involvement in the selling process.
Requirements: $477 for the license/consulting program.
Provisions: Fee includes a manual, sample forms, marketing procedures, and ongoing consultation.

TRIPLE CHECK INCOME TAX SERVICES, 727 S. Main St.,]Burbank, CA 91506; (800)283-1040.
Franchise: Yes.
Description: In addition to tax preparation services, franchisees also provide a full range of financial planning products.
Requirements: The total investment is only $1,500 to $3,000.
Comments: This is a very reliable company that started in 1941 and now has over 350 franchisees. They are known for their quality and integrity.

U.S. MORTGAGE REDUCTION, 7272 E. Broadway Blvd., Suite 260, Tucson, AZ 85710. (800)456-8982.
Franchise: No
Description: Through a national network of sales agents, U.S. Mortgage Reduction offers its Equity Acceleration Program to homeowners. As an agent for the firm, you will be demonstrating to homeowners why paying for their home with a long term mortgage is a waste of many thousands of dollars in mortgage interest.
Requirements: $295.
Provisions: The fee covers a presentation binder/flip kit, training manual, computer software, brochures, contracts, cassette training tapes, and client presentation video.
Profit Potential: Not available.
Comments: There are also opportunities in regional management.

WES-STATE MORTGAGE, INC., 834 Pearl St., Eugene, OR 97401-2727; (503)485-4741.
Franchise: No
Description: Loan broker.
Requirements: $70.
Provisions: The program includes all documents, forms, step-by-step instructions, samples of brochures and advertising, source of lenders, and basically everything needed to run the business.
Profit Potential: Up to $100,000 a year.
Comments: Can be run part-time.

PERSONAL SERVICES

These days, busy working people are demanding all kinds of services. Some services are designed to make more quality time available while others help enhance the quality of life.

Through these businesses, customers can have their meals delivered to their door at dinnertime, have their pets and plants tended to while on vacation, find sitters for their children temporarily or nannies permanently, and find all kinds of help through personal referral services. They can also find potential mates, have someone else shop for them while they work, have their clothing custom-made, or have custom-made gift baskets sent to their kids in college.

There's something here for everyone, customers and entrepreneurs alike.

ALBERT ANDREWS LTD., 10 Newbury St., #4, Boston, MA 02116. (508)879-9510.
Franchise: Yes.
Description: Albert Andrews is in the business of custom menswear. From your home office you would prospect for clients, telephone, send information, and keep records. All measuring and fitting is done at your client's home or office using a special computerized fitting system. The computerized system allows the suit to be custom-made at company headquarters using corresponding computerized machinery. You act strictly as a person clothier offering service and convenience, not as a tailor.
Requirements: The start-up costs amount to about $34,550. There is an ongoing royalty of 10% of gross sales plus a 2% advertising fee. The minimum royalty is $400 per month.
Provisions: The initial investment covers a complete computer fitting system, training, manuals, office improvements, and working capital. Training includes self-study, classroom lessons, and actual field training. How to use the computer fitting system, proven marketing techniques for maximizing sales, customer service methods, hiring guidelines, and day-to-day support, professionally designed ad slicks and radio copy, advice on buying media, and follow-up customer service letters provided by headquarters.
Profit Potential: Actual numbers are not available, however this is a high-class business with very impressive materials.

BRIGHT BEGINNINGS, 1150 Main St., #D, Irvine, CA 92714. (714)752-2772.
Franchise: Yes
Description: Neighborhood welcoming service. Franchisees visit new homeowners and tell them about products and services that are available in their new neighborhood. Local businesses pay franchisees for advertising their products or services.
Requirements: The franchise fee is $11,000. You will also need a computer and laser printer. Royalties are 10% and advertising fees are 2%.
Provisions: The fee covers all the materials needed to start the business, as well as marketing rights, software, ongoing support, an exclusive territory and five days of training.
Profit Potential: Not available.

DO-IT-YOURSELF PARTY YARD SIGNS, 709 W. Mulberry Dr., West Bend, WI 53095; (414)334-2303.
Franchise: No.
Description: The company designs colorful 6-foot special occasion announcement signs that you produce and rent to consumers.

Requirements: $499.
Provisions: You get a comprehensive, professionally illustrated business operations manual, step-by-step sign making instructions, 10 life-size patterns, sample ads, forms, business cards, promotion ideas, and free consultations.

ENTREES ON TRAYS, INC., 3 Lombardy Terrace, Fort Worth, TX 76132; (817)735-8558.
Franchise: No
Description: A dinner delivery service operated without labor or inventory. You would work with 20-50 local restaurants within a six mile radius, acting as a home delivery service, not a caterer. The business is run from home from 5:00 to 9:00 p.m.
Requirements: The one-time license agreement fee is $8,750.
Provisions: You will receive two days of training, working hands-on in Fort Worth. Also included with your fee is all equipment and materials necessary to initiate business (except radios negotiated on a local basis).
Profit Potential: See below.
Comments: This is a great business idea that has been perfected by this company. Entrees on Trays has delivered 100,000 dinners amounting to over $1 million annually in the Fort Worth metroplex while 11 out of 11 competing companies have gone out of business.

EVE'S AGENCY OF AMERICA, INC., 2625 N. Meridian Street, Suite 204, Indianapolis, IN 46208. (317)924-3787.
Franchise: No.
Description: Eve's Agency, in business since 1975, has been described as the only agency actually offering legitimate escort services. It only offers companionship for social events, not erotic entertainment in private settings. Adjuncts to the business include model and entertainer agency and person business services such as tour guide, valet, shopping assistant, driver, etc.

FAMILY FRIEND MANAGEMENT SYSTEMS, INC., 895 Mount Vernon Highway, Northwest, Atlanta, GA 30327; (404)255-2848.
Franchise: Yes.
Description: This unique personal referral service provides child care elder care, tutoring, pet care, home secretaries, errand service, and other types of personnel referrals for employment in the home.
Requirements: The total package fee is $15,000.
Provisions: The fee buys training, software, manuals, forms, and operations support.

FRIEND OF THE FAMILY, 10825 Stroup Rd., Roswell, GA 30075.
Franchise: No.
Description: This is a personal referral service which provides eldercare, childcare, tutoring, petcare, home secretaries, shopping and errand services, and other types of personnel referrals for employment in the home. The in-home service industry is still in its infancy and represents at least a $7 billion potential market according to national studies. Founder Judi Merlin generated over $100,000 in agency fees per year within two years of opening, while working from her home. Today, she and her agency has achieved more than four times that sales level, and she is still operating from her home!
Requirements: The total package fee is $7,500. The minimum telephone market area population of 100,000 is necessary to support an agency (resort areas or large elderly population areas are possible exceptions).

Provisions: The system consulting package consists of the integrated database and accounts receivable computer software system; a business operations manual, computer operations manual; "Interview Skills" video, over 100 forms, manuals, contracts, and documents; and five days of hands-on training. Continuing support is available for a low monthly fee.

GIFT BASKET CONNECTION, 3 Juniper Ct., Schenectady, NY 12309; (800)437-3237.
Franchise: No.
Description: International gift basket wire service similar to FTD.
Requirements: For already existing retailers $200 per year. The manual is $56.

HOME SITTING SENIORS, 5851 Antigua Blvd., San Diego, CA 92124; (619)576-4417.
Franchise: No.
Description: A referral agency for seniors seeking supplemental income providing housesitting, pet care and assisted living for the elderly. Company was established in 1982.
Requirements: $4,000 for distributorship package with no exclusive territory. Priced by population served for exclusive territory and use of company name and logo.
Provisions: You will get three days of one-on-one training at the San Diego office and a complete manual with forms, procedures on accounting and marketing.
Profit Potential: Depends on area and population served as well as aggressiveness of owner.

HOMEWATCH, 2865 South Colorado Blvd., Denver, CO 80222; (303)758-7290.
Franchise: Yes
Description: Full service housesitting by trained, bonded, and insured adults for people who are away from home on business or vacation; companion sitting (nonmedical); and handyman services.
Requirements: The fee is $18,500 for a franchise, but you can get a smaller area for less. Some management background or previous business ownership is preferred.
Provisions: The fee buys a geographic area with a population of 200,000, five days of training including software training, logo, manual, bond/insurance for one year, exclusive area, ongoing support, and advertising materials. You will also get a grand opening at your location. Financing is available, but only when buying multiple territories.
Comments: This is a good part-time business for retired or semi-retired people.

THE HOUSESITTERS, 530 Queen Street East, Toronto, Ontario M5A 1V2 Canada; (416)947-1295.
Franchise: Yes
Description: Services include live-in housesitting, periodic visit housesitting, and live-in family care. Ongoing service include dog walking, hourly family care, and residential cleaning.
Provisions: The franchise fee includes two weeks of training, customized computer software that not only handles all administrative tasks but runs a customized voice information system as well, the operations manual, and marketing support. The Housesitters head office prepares and mails announcements of your new operation to appropriate businesses while you are in training. The advance publicity usually generates enough sales leads to get you off to a running start.
Profit Potential: A population territory of 100,000 should yield a net profit of $29,200.

Naturally, profits go up with the populations density.

MAIN EVENT LAWN SIGN, INC., 911 E. Brookwood Drive, Arlington Hts., IL 60004; (708)670-7777.
Franchise: No.
Description: Special event signs are ordered to announce the many special occasions in a family's life throughout the year.
Requirements: The price of the complete business package is $2,295. You can get a "Do It Yourself Kit" for $299, or ready-made plastic signs for $199. Space requirements are about four feet by six feet against a wall to store the signs waiting to be rented.
Provisions: Included are 6 signs, 12 announcement inserts, two letter kits, an operations manual, camera ready advertising proofs, 20 store window posters, 5 store counter displays, and flyers.
Profit Potential: About $35 an hour.

NANNIES PLUS INC., 615 W. Mt. Pleasant Ave., Livingston, NJ 07039. (800)752-0078.
Franchise: No.
Description: Nanny placement service.
Requirements: One-time licensing fee is $22,500 with operating capital of an additional $5,000. Financing is available.
Provisions: Licensees receive a complete package: five days of training in New Jersey, three days training on-site, promotional materials, ongoing support, a hotline, and office forms.

PARAGRAVE, 1455 West Center, Orem, UT 84057-5104; (800)624-7415.
Franchise: No
Description: Ultra high-speed custom engraving to personalize valuables for decoration and anti-theft purposes.
Requirements: The complete "Parapak" system costs $2,399.
Provisions: The fee covers dealership privileges, an ongoing support program, all equipment necessary to perform the service, training videos, and illustrated manuals.
Profit Potential: Not available.

PET NANNY OF AMERICA, INC., 300 N. Clippert St., Ste 13, Lansing, MI 48912; (517)336-8622.
Franchise: Yes.
Description: A Pet Nanny franchisee visits pets in their own home, maintaining the regular diet, exercise, and play routines while their owners enjoy worry-free travel. The main idea is to eliminate the unnecessary trauma of removing pets from the home environment. Pet Nanny service representatives are bonded, insured, and trained. The comprehensive veterinarian-developed training program covers basic care, illness detection, animal behavior, and the administration of injections and medications. In addition to the pet care provided, clients are offered several extra services at no additional cost: the representative will bring in the mail and newspapers, water plants, turn lights on and off, open and close drapes, and give the home an overall security check.
Requirements: The franchise fee is $8,700; 75% can be financed. The royalty fee is 5% of gross. An investment of approximately $1,500 in equipment is also needed.
Provisions: An exclusive territory, one-on-one training program, start-up business materials, nationally recognized name, and ongoing consultation.

Comments: Pet Nanny offers a nice little business for pet lovers who prefer to spend more time with animals than with people.

PET SITTERS, PLUS!, 20031I Powers Ferry Road, Marietta, GA 30067; (770)933-8679.
Franchise: Yes.
Description: Pet sitting in homes of clients while they are away. Also house sitting, errands, etc.
Provisions: Logo, company name, expertise of owner, two days of hands-on assistance to set up the business.

PET-TENDERS, P.O. Box 23622, San Diego, CA 92193; (619)283-3033.
Franchise: Yes
Description: In-home pet/housesitting service that cares for pets in the comfort of their own home.
Requirements: The total investment is between $10,500 and $13,900. The royalty fee is 5% of gross sales per month and the advertising fee is 2%.
Provisions: The costs include the franchise fee for which you are given an exclusive territory, training, and a complete operation and training manual for your business. The training package includes up to five days of lectures, hands-on training, telephone techniques, voice training, and on-the-job training with a working pet-sitter.
Profit Potential: Not available.

PRE-FIT FRANCHISES, INC., 10340 S. Western Ave., Chicago, IL 60643; (312)233-7771.
Description: A homebased mobile preschool fitness program of sports, exercise, and health classes designed for two to six year olds.
Requirements: The franchise fee is $6,500; additional start-up costs are $250 to $350.
Provisions: Your fee buys uniforms, initial and continuous training program, lesson plans, workout routines, marketing tools, bookkeeping materials, class equipment, exclusive territory, and toll-free support.

SAFE-T-CHILD, INC., 401 Friday Mountain Road, Austin, TX 78737. (512)288-2882.
Franchise: Yes.
Description: Child safety and I.D. products.
Requirements: The complete franchise is $13,500. There are no royalties.
Provisions: The investment includes a protected territory and turnkey business package: equipment, supplies, sales aids, manual, 7 hour audio cassette training course, camera-ready forms, a software program to run your business, and ongoing support.

SINGLE SEARCH NATIONAL, 13176 N. Dale Mabry, Ste. 202, Tampa, FL 33618; (813)264-1705.
Franchise: No.
Description: Computerized, mail order, match-making service designed by a marriage counselor. The system matches for 350 items of compatibility.
Requirements: $1,500 per exclusive territory, plus approximately $1,000 start-up capital. Also need computer and printer.
Provisions: Software, manual on disk, two hours free technical and marketing training, marketing kit, newsletter, Internet referrals, co-op advertising opportunity.
Profit Potential: $70,000 to $100,000 annually depending on territory.

SPECIAL SELECTIONS, P.O. Box 3243, Boise, ID 83703; (208)343-3629.
Franchise: No
Description: Licensees offer personal and business gift shopping services to busy corporate executives, physicians, attorneys, professionals, and wealthy individuals and community leaders.
Requirements: The licensing fee is $495.
Provisions: The complete licensing package includes the right to use an internationally recognized trademark and a training manual. Instruction covers how to write a business plan, how to target and approach clients, a complete marketing plan, how to shop profitably without ever paying full retail, and how to price your services.
Profit Potential: You earn income two ways: first by charging an hourly fee, and second by obtaining commissions on the gifts you purchase. It is possible to earn thousands of dollars for a single situation.

SITTERS UNLIMITED, 23015 Del Lago Dr. #D2152, Laguna Hills, CA 92653. (714)752-2366.
Franchise: Yes
Description: A coast to coast sitting service for children, the elderly, homes, and pets, on both a temporary and permanent basis. In addition to quality in-home care, traveling families can rely on hotel and convention care services.
Requirements: The franchise fee for an exclusive territory is $13,000.
Provisions: The fee includes five days of corporate training, ongoing training and support, and one month's free supply of required materials. Literature, business cards, and all required forms are designed for you. No purchasing of products except an answering machine and forms is necessary.
Profit Potential: Not available.
Comments: The company has been in business since 1979.

TGIF PEOPLEWORKS, P.O. Box 828, Old Lyme, CT 06371; (203)434-1262.
Franchise: No
Description: Domestic and special help search-and -referral service for in-home help such as child care, elder care, and housekeeping.
Requirements: There is an initial cost of $350 to receive the complete and comprehensive Operations Manual which is used in your training. This manual includes camera-ready artwork for printing of materials to be used in the business. Set-up costs to get started should not exceed $800.
Provisions: You will be working as an independent business owner, but instead of paying royalties like a franchisee would, you will be paid a commission from the company.
Profit Potential: Not available.
Comments: This is a great business for women, especially those who are people-oriented.

PHOTO AND VIDEO SERVICES

Of the opportunities described in this chapter, just one actually involves traditional, still-shot photography. Sports Section Photography caters to the parents of budding athletes by photographing sports teams and individual players.

Some other businesses here are in the booming video market. Each services a different and unique function. Video Data Services franchise operators use videotape to record weddings and other special events in a modernized version of standard photography services. Dr. Video owners offer repair and maintenance services for the eighty million videocassette recorders owned by U.S. consumers.

These opportunities offer some interesting possibilities for people interested in photography or video. It is a market that is sure to continue growing and changing.

AERIAL PHOTOGRAPHY, LTD., 1040 Airport Rd., Salem, IL 62881. (618)548-6691.
Franchise: No.
Description: This system provides precision low level aerial photographs superior in quality and less expensive than those taken by planes or helicopters. You can operate in areas inaccessible to them and get exactly the shots your clients need. Hi-Shots currently supports over 100 affiliates worldwide and several international distributors.
Requirements: The complete system costs $19,500 with no ongoing fees. You must have proven business skills, an available slot in your area, and the necessary capital to qualify.
Provisions: The system includes the Nikon 35mm system, complete training, service, and support. There is limited operator placement (1 per 500,000 population. There is ongoing marketing, training, and support.

BIRD'S EYE VIEW PHOTOGRAPHY, INC., P.O. Box 394, Station A, Burlington, Ontario, Canada L7R 9Z9.
Franchise: No
Description: Aerial photography. The "Hi-shots" system consists of a tethered balloon which carries either a 35mm or Medium Format camera that can be rotated through 360 degrees. Both systems have a tilt feature which allows the camera to be adjusted vertically. A video picture is relayed to the operator on the ground. The monitor allows you to choose the perfect shot.
Requirements: The total investment is $22,900 for a 35mm system or $24,900 for the Medium Format system.
Provisions: The investment covers complete training and start-up assistance as well as all equipment.
Profit Potential: The photos sell for $250 and up and cost between $235 and $40 to produce. Each location takes only 20 minutes to photograph.
Comments: This can be a part-time, full-time, or absentee ownership business.

COLORFAST, 9522 Topanga Canyon Blvd,. Chatsworth, CA 91311; (818)407-1881.
Franchise: No
Description: Distributorship to sell photographic business cards and promotional prod-

ucts such as postcards, magnets, rolodex cards, etc..
Requirements: A distributorship costs $100 plus the desire to make money.
Provisions: The fee covers a home training video tape, advertising tools, portfolios, order forms, use of the Colorfast name, a 10% discount on personal cards, and support.
Profit Potential: Unlimited.

DEOS VIDEO, 800 Turnpike St.,. Suite 100, North Andover, MA 01845. (508)682-6400. Contact: Paul C. Quintal.
Franchise: No.
Description: Personalized Children's VideoMaker. Computer animated video storybooks lets the child become the star of their very own video. The star's name appears visually and is spoken by the narrator. You determine the gender, skin tone, hair color and from whom the video is given. Made in minutes on VHS tape.
Requirements: Startup costs to $9,995. Financing is available.
Provisions: Complete turnkey system including multimedia PC, software, videotape supply, sales and marketing materials, comprehensive marketing guide, lifetime warranty and unlimited technical support.
Profit Potential: Videos sell for $9.95 to $14.95; raw materials cost less than $2.50 per tape.

DR. VIDEO, 1131 Bay Ave., Point Pleasant, NJ 08742; (201)892-8877.
Franchise: Yes.
Description: Dr. Video is a VCR repair and maintenance service.
Requirements: The franchise fee is $17,500; the total investment is about $25,000.
Provisions: The investment covers training, an exclusive territory, and an advertising campaign.

IDENT-A-KID Services of America, Inc., 2810 Scherer Dr., Ste 100, St. Petersburg, FL 33716; (800) 890-1000.
Franchise: Yes
Description: Identification cards for children.
Requirements: Franchise Fee is $12,500
Provisions: Fee covers an exclusive territory, complete training, an IBM PC and custom designed software to produce the printed cards and forms, automatic identification camera, video presentation deck, laminator, marketing materials, and other supplies and equipment necessary to perform the service.

CLOSEUP: IDENT-A-KID

IDENT-A-KID, a franchise based in Florida, provides credit-card-sized ID cards for parents to carry; the card contains the photograph, fingerprint, weight, measurements, and other identifying information about their child. The cards sell for one dollar to five dollars depending on quantity. Since the service is primarily offered through schools, those quantities can run into the thousands.

Not only does IDENT-A-KID provide a much needed service, but it offers the kind of flexibility necessary to have a fulfilling family life as well.

Before starting her franchise five years ago, Joyce Johnston, of Greens-

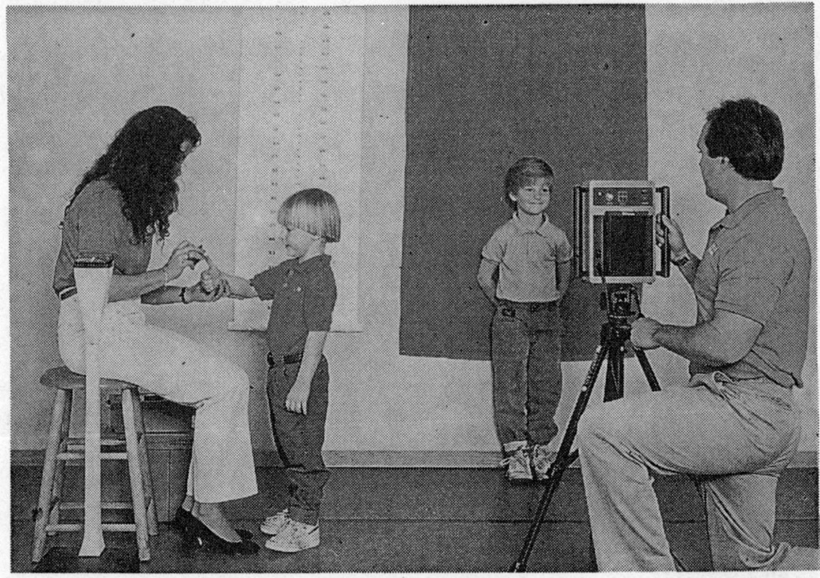

boro, North Carolina, worked as a supervisor for a mortgage corporation. As a single parent, getting home after six each night made her very unhappy. Now her schedule is hers to make as she sees fit.

"I work when I want to," she says. "I don't work on Monday, I reserve Fridays for computer work, and when the kids come home from school I'm done. With children you can't beat that." Joyce's job is to take the photos and gather all the necessary data at the schools, then return home to produce the cards, a process that takes about four days. To further reduce her time away from home, she recently hired somebody to go out and do the photo shoot.

Joyce actually bought her franchise secondhand from an owner who had to move out of the area. She received the original package of computer, software, printer, laminating machine, camera equipment, and presentation video. She also got to take over the training and support from the parent company, something that you don't normally get when buying a non-franchise business.

"The company was great. I could call them and they would give me ideas. They had me up and working within a week."

As a parent, Joyce felt comfortable in the school and daycare environment. Her first order of business was to line up appointments to make her presentations. She has yet to be turned down and her business grew so fast she was working to capacity right away. She now services over 100 schools. "I do the schools during the school year and save the daycares for summer."

You might think that cutting down on hours means cutting down on income. But Joyce says, "You can't even compare incomes. My business went over $100,000 this year. I could never go back to working for someone else."

HIGH READERSHIP FEATURES, P.O. Box 1601, Solana Beach, CA 92075. (800)798-1824.
Franchise: No.
Description: Newspaper column business. It can be run part-time and you can hire salespeople. Since there is no inventory or fixed hours, an office is unnecessary. As a HRF associate, you'll have ready access to an extensive library of columns on a growing list of subjects. Specialized columns focus on a specific type of business, such as real estate, insurance, jewelers, etc. You'll be able to offer interesting and informative column features to your clients, regardless of their type of business. They can then use them to promote their businesses.
Requirements: The one-time investment is $5,900. No prior writing or sales experience is required.
Provisions: Exclusive territories. You will receive training, a large column inventory, an operating manual, visual presentation manual, operating supplies, and ongoing support.

IMAGE MAKERS UNLIMITED, 1018 W. El Norte Parkway, Suite 200, Escondido, CA 92026.
Franchise: No
Description: Photographic business cards.
Requirements: $3,000.
Provisions: The fee includes six video training tapes, toll-free support, a professionally prepared sales presentation video tape that makes sales for you, and a complete set of all business forms needed to run this business.
Profit Potential: Not available.

SKY VIEW AERIAL PHOTO, INC., 2021 Midwest Rd., Oakbrook, IL 60521; (800)9SKYVIEW.
Franchise: No.
Description: Ground-based remote control aerial photography and video using helium blimp and telescopic tripod poles. In business since 1990.
Requirements: From $4,995 to $25,000.
Provisions: Equipment, two days of training, brochures and sample marketing kit, and training video.

THE SPORTS SECTION, INC., 3120A Medlock Br. Rd., Norcross, GA 90071. (404)416-6604.
Franchise: Yes.
Description: Homebased childrens and sports photography franchise offering over 120 keepsakes.
Requirements: Investments at $9,900 and $29,500.
Provisions: On-site training in sales and marketing, photography training, sample materials, and headquarter support.

UNIVERSAL ART, 1525 Hardeman Lane, N.E., Cleveland, TN 37311; (615)479-5481.
Franchise: Yes
Description: Photo processing and graphic communication specializing in photo portraits.
Requirements: The franchise fee is $9,000, photographic equipment is $6,000, and the company recommends you have access to around $10,000 to $12,000 in working

capital. Some financing is available from the company.
Provisions: Comprehensive training and a guarantee of 2,000 to 3,000 customers per year.
Profit Potential: Not available.

VIDEO DATA SERVICES, 30 Grove St., Pittsford, NY 14534. (716)385-4773.
Franchise: Yes
Description: Videotaping service.
Requirements: $15,900 for a turn-key system.
Provisions: The price includes a complete equipment package based on the Amiga computer, training, marketing materials, and ongoing support.
Profit Potential: Over $100,000 annually.

VISUAL IMAGES, 300 Richfield St., Suite 201, Pittsburgh, PA 15234; (800)648-2105.
Franchise: No
Description: Marketing of full color, lithographed photo business cards.
Requirements: Total investment is $199.
Provisions: The initial investment includes samples of all products, templates, layout forms and other production materials, and toll-free support. You will also need a 35mm camera. The $199 is refunded with your 52nd order.
Profit Potential: Not available.

PUBLISHING

There has been an opportunity explosion in the publishing industry that has not been seen since Guttenberg invented the printing press. Technology has made it possible for anyone, anywhere, interested in any subject, to become a publisher with a minimal amount of money and experience. This is the only industry where homebased business operators can buy into a low-cost business opportunity and realistically expect to make it big. There are actual cases of business owners who started at home and built publishing empires worth millions of dollars. Without a doubt, the opportunities in this chapter offer the greatest potential of any of this book. Fees start as low as $495 and top out at only $25,000. Some require experience, but most do not.

The actual involvement in the business of publishing ranges from simply signing up advertisers, to snapping some pictures and writing editorials, to performing every task necessary to publish a complete book.

Probably the best way to choose a publishing business is to decide what subject you are most interested in. If you like children's books, then you might want to take a closer look at Hefty Publishing. If public relations is your chosen profession, FINDERBINDER would be a better choice for you. Other opportunities presented in this chapter cover real estate, television, bingo, entertainment, shopping, travel, and wedding information.

BINGO BUGLE NEWSPAPER, K & O Publishing, Inc., P.O. Box 51189, Seattle, WA 98115; (206)527-4958.
Franchise: Yes.
Description: Monthly publication for bingo players. Franchisee is responsible for sales, publishing, and distribution.
Requirements: $2,500 to $10,000 plus cost of telephone, camera, automobile, typewriter and/or computer if franchisee doesn't' own one.
Provisions: A 2-day training session is provided to franchisees, along with manuals and start-up materials. A monthly package is provided each month that includes camera-ready copy, clip art, industry news, etc. Other support is given as needed.

THE BRIDE'S DAY MAGAZINE, 750 Hamburg Turnpike, Pompton Lakes, NJ 07442; (201)835-6551.
Franchise: Yes.
Description: Franchisees produce a magazine that includes every possible product and service provider needed by brides-to-be. The profit comes from selling the ad space; the publication itself is offered free to brides through retail outlets.
Requirements: The total investment is $14,900.
Provisions: Complete training, exclusive territory and support.

BUYING & DINING GUIDE, Community Publications of America, Inc., 80 Eighth Ave., New York, NY 10011; (212)243-6800.
Franchise: Yes.
Description: This is a free community guide to dining and shopping. It is aimed at prime spenders. The guide is published every two weeks, allowing advertisers to buy twice the advertising time for the cost of just one week in a weekly newspaper.

Requirements: The franchise fee is $29,500.
Provisions: Each franchise includes an exclusive territory, classroom and on-site training, a free printing credit of $1,000, a grand opening promotion program, a free promotional mailing to 100,000 prime prospects, sales kits, advertising art books, display racks, free stationery and forms, operations manual, sales training cassette tapes and films, company-paid contests and sweepstakes for readers, a support hotline, and advanced training sessions.

CATHEDRAL DIRECTORIES FRANCHISES, INC., 1401 W. Girard Ave., Madison Heights, MI 48071; (810)545-1415.
Franchise: Yes.
Description: Company publishes church and organization membership rosters. The publications are free to members of the congregation as they are advertising supported. You would sell ads to the leads supplied by the Pastor such as banks, funeral homes, etc.
Requirements: Costs are $14,500 for the franchise fee plus living expenses while developing the business. There are no royalties. "We look for people with a little marketing background, somewhat computer literate, and comfortable in the church environment."
Provisions: The franchise system, proprietary software, ongoing support, training at headquarters and in franchisee's home territory, and all necessary supplies.
Profit Potential: Franchisee profit margin is approximately 35%.

THE COUPON TABLOID, 5775 Jean Rd., #101, Lake Oswego, OR 97035. (800)888-8575.
Franchise: Yes
Description: The Coupon Tabloid is a direct mail advertising business. All graphics are done through the company's production department.
Requirements: The one-time investment is $3,500. Sales experience is necessary.
Provisions: The fee covers an exclusive territory, one week of intensive training in your area, marketing materials, start-up materials, printed business supplies and other support materials, and ongoing support by team of professionals.
Profit Potential: "Excellent."

D & K ENTERPRISES, 3216 Commander Dr., #101, Carrollton, TX 75006.
Franchise: No
Description: Personalized children's books. With the D & K system, you can produce full color, hard cover, laser printed books in less than four minutes.
Requirements: The dealership fee is $2,495; other supplies bring that cost up to $2,990, and you will need a computer and laser printer.
Provisions: Included in the dealership package is the software to produce the books, a dealer manual with step-by-step instructions, a marketing manual and support, practice books, and location assistance with Sears concessions.
Profit Potential: A part-time dealer operating on week-ends only should profit over $10,000 a year.

FINDERBINDER and SOURCE BOOK DIRECTORIES, 8546 Chevy Chase Dr., La Mesa, Ca 91941; (619)463-5050.
Franchise: Yes
Description: Publishing of news media and association/club directories for metropolitan areas or states. This is designed as an add-on small business for consulting firms and community relations institutions.

Requirements: The franchise fee is only $1,000, but you will need at least $8,000 more for printing costs, supplies, and a research staff. You must have an established compatible business. Royalties run 5% to 15% (decreasing as sales increase).
Provisions: The fee buys a detailed operations manual, camera-ready art for advertising and promotion, software, and ongoing operational support.
Profit Potential: $20,000 a year as an add-on business.
Comments: Entrepreneur Magazine declared this one of the best low-cost franchises several years in a row.

HEFTY PUBLISHING (formerly Create-A-Book), 1232 Paula Circle, Gulf Breeze, FL 32561. (800)732-3009.
Franchise: No
Description: Personalized children's books.
Requirements: The cost of a dealership is $3,995 and the operator needs a computer. The annual software renewal fee of $200 is also required.
Provisions: The price includes the software, a training video that shows how to make the books and a list of available supplies, The company manufactures the books' pages and covers and then supplies the materials to the dealers. Also included in the price is a manual with instructions, tips, and camera ready ads.
Profit Potential: The books sell for about $12.95 and take about 15 minutes to put together. High-end earnings can be as much as $1,000 a day.
Comments: This 11-year old company has over 350 dealers in the U.S., 40 in Canada and three in Australia.

HOMES & LAND PUBLISHING CORP., 1600 Capital Circle S.W., Tallahassee, FL 32310; (904)574-2111.
Franchise: Yes.
Description: Homes & Land is the largest publisher of community real estate magazines in the United States with over 275 communities now being serviced by franchisees. The pictorial magazines are published either in black and white or in color, and each contains property listings of real estate companies. Franchisees sell advertising space to real estate brokers and distribute the magazines throughout the community.
Requirements: There are several different franchise offerings starting at a remarkably low $1,500. Royalties vary. Aside from the franchise fee, about $2,000 will be needed to cover initial printing costs and operating expenses. It is common for franchisees o own more than one franchise, and the company expect that all franchisees will operate on a full-time basis. No experience is required.
Provisions: The fee pays for training, field assistance for obtaining initial sales, sixty distribution racks, business cards, invoices, copy folders, stationery, and rate sheets. Training is a one-week orientation at company headquarters covering production, sales, and financial management. An operations manual and sales aids are provided at this time. Franchisees can start as soon as training is completed.

NETWORK PUBLICATIONS, INC., P.O. Box 100001, 2 Pamplin Dr., Lawrenceville, GA 30245; (404)962-7220.
Franchise: No
Description: Network Publications publishes "The Real Estate Books" which is the nation's largest full color real estate magazine network. Distributors act as "associate publishers" and handle the photography, set up distribution, and make contact with real estate brokers and builders who become advertising customers. The company provides the logo, graphic, and printing.

Requirements: The initial investment is about $15,000.
Provisions: Training starts at company headquarters and is followed by a field visit to your market.
Profit Potential: Not available.
Comments: This is a full-time business only.

PENNYSAVER, Community Publications of America, 80 Eighth Ave., New York, NY 10011; (212)243-6800.
Franchise: Yes.
Description: Pennysavers are weekly advertising newspapers.
Requirements: The franchise fee is $29,500.
Provisions: See Buying & Dining Guide.

PREMIER PERSONALIZED PUBLISHING, INC., 11419 Mathis Ave., Ste 210, Farmers Branch, TX 75234.
Franchise: No
Description: Personalized children's books (formerly known as About Me! Books).
Requirements: The initial licensing fee is $2,995 and is renewable each year for $195. Your initial inventory order should be about $525. You will also need an IBM computable computer and printer.
Provisions: The start-up package will include complete training with a manual and video, software, and sample books.
Profit Potential: Not available.

QUAIL CREEK COMPUTING, 7301 Burnet Rd., Ste. 102-528, Austin, TX 78757; (512)834-8927.
Franchise: No.
Description: Publish job guide publication for job seekers.
Requirements: $249 plus a PC or Macintosh, laser printer and desktop publishing software. This is a part-time business requiring only 20 hours a month.
Provisions: The $249 buys the business manual, production manual, Job guided template, and disks with clip art, business letters, flyers, etc. There is also one free hour of support.

REGAL PUBLISHING CORP., 321 New Albany Rd., Moorestown, NJ 08057; (609)778-8900.
Franchise: No
Description: Distribution of the company's publication, Lottery Player's Magazine. Lottery sales totaled $18.8 billion in 1989. Lottery Player's Magazine is the consumer's window to the industry. The magazine acts as a clearinghouse of information for the recreational gaming public. Independent dealers distribute the magazine to retail outlets and other distributors and wholesalers.
Requirements: A contract must be signed, there is no fee involved.
Provisions: Order forms, samples, and limited instructions.
Profit Potential: Commissions are paid on subscriptions sales equal to 60% of the base rate.

SPECTRUM UNLIMITED, 2261 Market St., Ste 276, San Francisco, CA 94114; (415)647-1070.
Franchise: No.
Description: Computer software for IBM compatible systems that creates beautiful

birthday or anniversary greetings. The cards highlight the events that occurred on any date back to the year 1880.
Requirements: $99.95 for the software plus the access to a personal IBM compatible computer.
Provisions: The fee includes News of the Past software and 200 greeting forms.
Profit Potential: The individual greetings sell for $1 to $3 each; the greeting forms cost only 20 cents each.

TV NEWS, Community Publications of America, 80 Eighth Ave., New York, NY 10011; (212)243-6800.
Franchise: Yes.
Description: This publication works very much the same as Buying & Dining Guide. The home office creates the layout and designs the ads. Franchisees sell ads, help clients in writing copy and deliver the finished product to retailers.
Requirements: The franchise fee is $29,500.
Provisions: See Buying & Dining Guide.

WEDDING INFORMATION NETWORK, 11106 Mockingbird Dr., Omaha, NE 68137. (402)331-7755.
Franchise: Yes
Description: Publishing of "The Wedding Pages", a 250-page wedding planner, workbook, and local advertising directory offered free to newly engaged couples. Advertisers in "The Wedding Pages: are supplied with a market database compiled from reply cards that gives them a competitive edge in this $33 billion industry.
Requirements: Experience is required in marketing, sales, media and advertising. The franchise fee ranges from $7,500 to $40,000 depending on the territory. Additional start-up costs range from $1,000 to $10,000 depending on the size of the territory. The royalty is 10%.
Provisions: The fee buys products and rights to be the local publisher of "The Wedding Pages".
Profit Potential: Not available.

TRAVEL

Computers have made it possible for the first time for travel agencies to be run from home. You will find several companies here that can get you set up in your own agency or work as an associate.

Discount travel has also become big recently. Through Hotel Express you can offer major discounts to traveling consumers.

ATA TRAVEL GROUP, 1810 Merchants Dr., Birmingham, AL 35209; (800)477-ATA1.
Franchise: No.
Description: Home or office based travel business.
Requirements: $8,995.
Provisions: All inclusive training and top of the line support. Discounted travel computer system and complete software is included.

HOTEL EXPRESS, INC., 3052 El Cajon Blvd., San Diego, CA 92104; (800)634-6526.
Franchise: No
Description: Distributors sell hotel discount memberships.
Requirements: $395 billed for ten months with no interest.
Provisions: Distributor discounts and ongoing toll-free support.
Profit Potential: Discount memberships sell for $49.95 and cost the distributor $4.95.
Comments: There are over 1,000 distributors in 9 different countries.

LEISURE GROUP, 58 River St., Milford, CT 06460; (800)999-1152.
Franchise: No
Description: Travel service.
Requirements: There is no investment or maintenance fee. Because Leisure Group members do not do domestic ticketing, costs are extremely low for both the company and the affiliates. The major requirement is a telephone to call suppliers, who all have toll-free numbers. Brochures and other reference data are provided free by the suppliers.
Provisions: The Leisure Group licenses its members to sell travel. Training is minimal. A manual is provided that tells members how to operate and newsletters are issued every two to three weeks that include numbers to call for brochures, new offerings, selling hints, etc. Optional training will cost $1,000.
Profit Potential: Each booking which takes about 1.5 hours should generate about $300 in commissions. The maximum you could earn in a year is $300,000.
Comments: The company has 158 members in 34 states and foreign countries.

TPI TRAVEL SERVICES, 3030 Rocky Pt., Suite 100, Tampa, FL 33607; (813)281-5670.
Franchise: No.
Description: Own your own travel agency at home.
Requirements: Initial investment $5,995 plus monthly computer access fee of $135.
Provisions: Complete start-up manuals and procedures, reservations software, extensive five days of training class including airfare and hotel, document processing, sales and marketing guidelines, supply of brochures, full technical and operational support.

TRAVEL PARTNERS, 1691 Kettering, Irvine, CA 92714. (800)445-7333.
Franchise: No
Description: Travel service.
Provisions: The company provides training in sales and marketing, travel guides, training manuals, a travel video library, 24-hour travel information service, ticket delivery, camera-ready art package, and the 800 reservations number.
Profit Potential: Up to $100,000 per year.

TRAVEL SERVICE NETWORK, INC., 2560 Foxfield Road, Ste 302, St. Charles, IL 60174. (800)557-5462.
Franchise: No.
Description: Travel agency.
Requirements: $4,995.
Provisions: Nine days of training including airfare and accommodations, software, manuals, toll-free support, and ongoing marketing support.

MISCELLANEOUS

Many changes in consumers' needs have taken place in recent years, and homebased businesses have proven flexible enough to meet those needs. New businesses are started all the time to fill market niches that never even existed before. In this chapter you will find an assortment of business opportunities, most of which defy classification. If you are looking for something just a little different, this chapter is for you.

ALOETTE COSMETICS, 345 Lancaster Ave., Malvern, PA 19355; (215)644-8200.
Franchise: Yes.
Description: Aloette is the only cosmetics franchise opportunity that does not require a storefront.
Requirements: The franchise fee is $60,000. Financing is available.
Provisions: Training in sales and management skills is provided along with manuals and videos, an accounting manual and journals.
Comment: The franchise fee is high for a home-based business. However, the profit potential is tremendous for those who follow through with the training.

BALLOON BOUQUET, INC., 69 Kilburn Rd., Belmont, MA 02178; (617)484-5907.
Franchise: Yes.
Description: This is one of the first companies to offer balloon delivery services. Balloons and decorating services are used for parties, weddings, bar mitzvahs, new product introductions, corporate kick-offs and conventions, grand openings, and all kinds of special occasions. The service works much like a florist.
Requirements: The franchise fee starts at $5,000.
Provisions: You get training in all aspects of the business, national advertising, access to wholesale inventory, and ongoing support.

THE BASKET CONNECTION, 17715 S. Fieldstone Lane, Oregon City, OR 97045; (503)631-7288.
Franchise: No.
Description: The business involves running home parties with special and unique baskets from around the world, featuring gift baskets. Women are encouraged to hire others to do the parties and build up substantial businesses.
Requirements: Minimum investment is $2,995. Financing is available.
Provisions: The investment includes $1,500 worth of specially selected baskets, consulting, a manual and four videos. Training covers all aspects of running the business including how to pre-book parties, coach a hostess, hire sales women, conduct sales meetings, how to market gift baskets, paperwork procedures, freight information and other pertinent details.

BETTER BIRTH FOUNDATION, 733 Main St., Stone Mountain, GA 30083.
Franchise: Yes.
Description: This company's concept is to provide prospective parents with comprehensive educational courses on the childbirth process. Medical professionals are trained to teach classes in nutrition, exercise, fathering techniques, and interaction with the health care community.
Requirements: The franchise fee is $18,500; there is virtually no other investment

needed. You must be a registered nurse, certified nurse midwife, or similar health care professional.
Provisions: The fee buys complete training in all aspects of the business.

CAJUN COUNTRY CANDIES, P.O. Box 53549, Lafayette, LA 70505-5534; (318)232-1229.
Franchise: No
Description: Distribute homemade candy via mail order.
Requirements: Cost of total business package is $53.95. There is a 30 day unconditional refund privilege. Must be able to follow directions.
Provisions: You will receive a business operations manual with marketing instructions, drop ship directions (so you don't have to stock candy), a box of candy samples, 100 promotional advertising mailers, sample ads, plus unlimited phone consultation.
Profit Potential: Unlimited.

CHILD SHIELD, U.S.A., 103 West Spring St., Titusville, PA 16354; (800)488-2445.
Franchise: No.
Description: Child safety products and services including videotape registration service.
Requirements: Complete business start-up packages begin at $495.
Provisions: The package basic includes 50 kits for resale, 75 promotional brochures, and receipt forms.

COMMUNIDYNE, INC., 636 Anthony Trail, Northbrook, IL 60062. (708)498-2444.
Franchise: No.
Description: Alcohol breath analyzer. The company has over 600 dealers in North America
Requirements: The sample unit with complete dealer support package costs $1,695. Financing is available.
Provisions: Included in the package are training videos and complete outlined instructions, the sample unit, and business forms.
Profit Potential: The national average in 1987 was $138 per week per machine.

COMPLETE MUSIC, INC., 7877 L St., Omaha, NE 68127; (402)339-3535.
Franchise: Yes.
Description: Music disc jockeys provide the entertainment for parties and celebrations of all kinds. About 70% of the time, they are used for wedding receptions. The disc jockeys bring everything, including stereo sound and light equipment as well as a music tape library. The tape collection is the largest music disc jockey collection in the country, with over 30,000 selections in all categories. The entire system packs easily into a compact car.
Requirements: The entire initial investment is under $20,000.
Provisions: Start-up package, 14 days of training, and ongoing support.
Profit Potential: 33% net.
Comments: This is the nation's largest DJ entertainment service with 129 franchisees now in operation.

DUNKA-DUDE, 8772 Aquarius Ave., Elk Grove, CA 95624. (916)685-5358.
Franchise: No.
Description: Distributors rent and deliver dunking tanks; end users have an easy way

to raise funds at events. This is primarily a part-time business.
Requirements: The minimum investment is $2,700.
Provisions: The investment covers everything necessary for an immediate business start-up including one dunk tank with all necessary accessories, printed promotional materials, written marketing plan, training video, owner's manual, uniforms, magnetic signs, forms, sample ads, etc.

GLOBAL SECURITY PRODUCTS LTD., 2522 Hanover St., Unit #3, Aurora, CO 80010; (800)783-4676.
Franchise: No.
Description: This is a manufacturer of pepper spray personal protection products offering distributorships.
Requirements: No minimum purchase requirement.
Provisions: Purchase products at wholesale, sell at retail.

GLOTZBACH DISTRIBUTORS, 600 Elgin Ave., Forest Park, IL 60130; (708)488-1125.
Franchise: No.
Description: Glotzbach Distributors offers coffee vending dealerships for either part-time or full-time business.
Requirements: $495 minimum.
Provisions: In the minimum start-up package you receive three displays and 600 serving units of top quality, individual packets of gourmet coffee. Discounts are given for larger start-up packages. They may be obtained in increments of 5, 10, 15, 20, 30 and up.

HOPE CAREER CONSULTING CENTER, 2735 S. Newton St., Denver, CO 80236; (303)934-1018.
Franchise: No.
Description: Hope offers a business of helping others by providing education and financial aid information including scholarships, funding assistance, career planning, college planning, corporate reimbursement programs for displaced workers, undergraduates, veterans, college bound students, disadvantaged citizens, and people wanting career change. $659 buys a complete turnkey package.
Provisions: "Over 15 lbs of marketing materials," free phone support, software, audio cassettes, manuals, camera-ready art work, forms and supplies, etc.
Profit Potential: From $200 part-time to well over $125,000 full-time per year.

KINDERDANCE INTERNATIONAL, INC., P.O. Box 510881, Melbourne Beach, FL 32951; (407)723-1595.
Franchise: Yes.
Description: Kinderdance is a program for preschool children that is designed to develop motor and cognitive skills through dance and movement. Ballet, tap, acrobatics, and modern dance are blended with numbers, colors, and shapes in the basic program. This is taught to boys and girls three to five years of age, and it is offered through nursery schools and day-care centers.
Requirements: The franchise fee is $5,000; start-up capital is under $2,000.
Provisions: The fee buys training, an operations manual, printed materials including promotional materials and forms, props, dance wear, cassette and video tapes, and file cabinet.

Comment: This company has an excellent reputation and the opportunity is ideal for someone who loves children, has an educational background, and enjoys dance.

KIDS CAN SEW PROGRAM, P.O. Box 1710, St. George, UT 84771. (800)KIDS-SEW.
Franchise: No.
Description: This program is a unique and highly successful business centered around teaching children ages 6-12 how to sew. There is also a limited curriculum for beginning teens and adults. Qualified individuals are able to purchase the exclusive licensing rights to establish a KCS Sewing School. Classes can be given in your home and you can begin your new business within 30 days.
Requirements: The licensing fee is $295 plus $100 per month (or 10% of gross) to lease a zip code territory.
Provisions: The investment buys the right to use the curriculum, an exclusive territory, training materials explaining how to establish and operate the business, liability insurance, and an annual sales and training convention in Las Vegas. Training can take place in your own home. There is plenty of ongoing support available as well as national advertising and student referrals.
Profit Potential: Most licensees work part-time (10 to 15 hours a week) earning $25 to $60 an hour. Income potential is $30,000 plus.

CLOSEUP: Kids Can Sew, Inc.

What could be better than making money doing something you love? Turning a hobby into a viable business is a dream for many. For Sunshine O'Brien, of Prairie Village, Kansas, it is a reality.

Sunshine always loved two things: sewing and teaching. Five years ago, she discovered a way to combine both. "I found an ad for Kids Can Sew in the back of a sewing journal. I sort of called it on a whim, not knowing what to expect."

What Sunshine found was a unique business opportunity that cost only $295. "I didn't even know where to look for commercial patterns and here was a program in place with simplified patterns and age appropriate instruction books that made it possible for kids to make their own garments in just two to four sessions. It was just what I needed."

Sunshine started her first class with her daughter who was in the second grade and four of her little friends. From there it grew by word of mouth. She has had as many as 200 students but says, "That was a really bad idea, too much stress." Today, about 50 students ranging in age from 6 to 15 make it possible for Sunshine to work part-time and produce a full-time income that supports the family.

The Sunshine's Sewing School takes place in the O'Brien family room. Classes are after school for three hours, three days a week, and then seven and a half hours on Saturday and three on Sunday. Each class is an hour and a half in length. "I limit classes to no more than four. That way I can give a lot of individual attention."

The kids seem to love it as much as Sunshine does. "I've heard moms say, 'I can't get little Jane out of her shorts to wash them!'" But their pleasure may have as much to do with the family atmosphere as the learning experience. "It is a really comfortable feeling here. The kids are always asking about the cats and dogs and they help themselves to drinks or whatever they need."

Sunshine credits the parent company for much of her success. "They go far beyond the call of duty in their support. It is really nice to have a supplier that you know will stand behind you. You don't find that much in companies anymore."

KINDERMUSIK INTERNATIONAL, P.O. Box 26575, Greensboro, NC 27415; (910)273-3363.
Franchise: Yes.
Description: Kindermusik is a unique, highly creative, music and movement learning experience for children 18 months to 7 years of age. Professional curricula workshops are designed to acquaint participants with the principles of the Kindermusik curricula and prepare them to teach the program.
Requirements: $125 to $200.

MARTEK LTD., P.O. Box 15160, Charlotte, NC 28211; (704)364-7213.
Franchise: No.
Description: Make and market a wide variety of customized clocks for a number of different markets. Clock faces are changed to suit the markets.
Requirements: A kitchen table and $3,995.
Provisions: You get everything you need to start the business.

MARTY WOLF GAME COMPANY, 2120 "G" So. Highland Dr., Las Vegas, NV 89101. (702)385-2963.
Franchise: No.
Description: You would own and operate a charity gambling casino for fundraising activities. It can be started in your garage part-time.
Requirements: The total investment for the complete party business package is $6,000.
Provisions: The investment covers all the tables, equipment and supplies required to stage a Las Vegas Style Gambling Party. A complete gambling casino accommodates 100 charity party gamblers. It also includes a five day, casino dealer workshop in Las Vegas where you will learn and qualify to deal Blackjack, Craps, and Roulette; learn and qualify to training your own party dealers. There is ongoing support.

MEISTERGRAM MONOGRAM AND EMBROIDERY SYSTEMS, 3517 W. Wendover Ave., Greensboro, NC 27407; (919)854-6200.
Franchise: Yes.
Description: Meistergram was the first to manufacture monogram embroidery equipment and supplies, and it is still the largest company of its kind. The company places a great deal of emphasis on individuals who buy the equipment to start their own monogram services usually at home.
Requirements: There is no franchise fee, but the cost of a monogram system starts at $5,000. A complete set of supplies and spare parts are included. Meistergram offers a leasing and financing plan for qualified applicants.
Provisions: The franchise includes training and ongoing support.

MRS MARKETING, 6348 66th Ave. N., Pinellas Park, FL 34665; (813)546-6153.
Franchise: No.
Description: Place weight loss displays in retail stores. They may be placed on a purchase basis or consignment.
Requirements: Start-up costs are under $300. Must have the ability to communicate with business people.

PHOTO ADVERTISING INDUSTRIES, INC., 262 S. Coconut Lane, Palm Island, Miami Beach, FL 33139; (305)673-3686.
Franchise: No
Description: Photo-keying concessions and distribution.
Requirements: The complete start-up package is $1,800.
Provisions: The package includes equipment, one-on-one training, all necessary business forms, and ongoing support.
Profit Potential: Not available.

PARTY ANIMALS, INC., 180 Allen Road, Ste 204, Atlanta, GA 30328; (404)303-7789.
Franchise: Yes.
Description: Unique costumed entertainment company provides corporate entertainment for conventions, trade shows, holiday events and theme parties. Also perform for birthdays, family reunions, etc.
Requirements: $12,500. Can start as a part-time company, but must agree to go full-time within a year.
Provisions: Three training manuals, one week of hands-on training, regional meetings, annual convention, ongoing phone and marketing support.

PEE WEE WORKOUT, 34976 Aspenwood Ln., Willoughby, OH 44094; (216)946-7888.
Franchise: Yes.
Description: Aerobic fitness program for children.
Requirements: The franchise fee is $1,500 and start-up costs are another $300.
Provisions: Programs, training, and start-up materials.

PROFUSION SYSTEMS, 2851 S. Parker Rd., Suite 650, Aurora, CO 80014; (303)337-1949.
Franchise: Yes
Description: Repair of vinyl, leather, Naugahyde, and all types of plastics with perfect color matches. About 82% of the clientele served by the company are corporate accounts.
Requirements: The total investment is $20,500.
Provisions: The investment covers training, field supervision, initial equipment, and supplies. Training is held for two weeks in Denver and covers both technical and management topics. After this initial training program, a company trainer will spend three days in your territory to help get your business started. Any client contracts from national advertising negotiated by the company are your without additional charge.
Profit Potential: Not available.

SPECIALTY COATINGS & CHEMICALS, INC., 7360 Varna Ave., North Hollywood, CA 91605; (213)875-0233.
Franchise: No.
Description: Liquid window glass tinting for residential, commercial, and automobile applications.
Requirements: $1,800 to $2,800.
Provisions: Materials, equipment and coatings. Training videos and manuals (hands-on training available for an additional fee).
Profit Potential: $100 to $300 per hour and up.

SPECIALTY COATINGS & CHEMICALS, INC., 7360 Varna Ave., North Hollywood, CA 91605; (213)875-0233.
Description: Bathtub, tile and countertop repair, recoloring and refinishing (porcelain, fiberglass and formica).
Requirements: $2,500 to $35,000.
Provisions: Materials, equipment and coatings plus training manuals and videos.
Profit Potential: $75 to $100 an hour and up.

SPECIALTY COATINGS & CHEMICALS, INC., 7360 Varna Ave., North Hollywood, CA 91605; (213)875-0233.
Franchise: No.
Description: Vinyl and leather repair, recoloring and reconditioning for commercial and automobiles.
Requirements: $1,500.
Provisions: Materials, equipment, and coatings plus training videos and manuals.
Profit Potential: $50 to $100 an hour.

SPORT IT, INC., 4196 Corporate Square, Naples, FL 33942. (800)762-6869.
Franchise: No.
Description: Sport It dealers market competitively priced brand name sporting goods

equipment and apparel from their homes.
Requirements: The dealership fee is $1,500 and the monthly service fee is $25.
Provisions: Access to major brand name sporting goods suppliers, operations manual, free telephone consultation, and monthly newsletters.

STORK NEWS OF AMERICA, INC., 5075 Morganton Rd., Suite 12A, Fayetteville, NC 28314; (919)868-3065.
Franchise: Yes.
Description: Stork News is a newborn announcement service primarily providing outdoor display signs. Other products include announcement cards, newborn clothing for christening, and party supplies.
Requirements: The franchise fee starts at $5,000. Additional tools, advertising expenses, operating capital, equipment, and inventory can cost as much as $3,000.
Provisions: The fee buys a complete start-up package including introductory advertising materials, administrative supplies, and enough equipment and supplies to get started.

TALKING BALLOONS, Atlanta, GA; (800)328-2551.
Franchise: No
Description: A talking balloon has a 2 foot ribbon that is specially made like a record. The ribbon is pre-recorded with little grooves all the way down and when you attach it to anything that is thin or hollow like a balloon you can make it talk just by running your finger down it. It can be used for special occasions and sold through florists and balloon shops, or as an advertising specialty for any business.
Requirements: The starter package costs $346.
Provisions: The starter package includes enough talking balloons to gross you over $1,415. Training, particularly in marketing the product, is also included.
Profit Potential: Not available.

THRIFTY INSTANT SIGNS, 13199 Brookhurst St., Garden Grove, CA 92643. (800)659-SIGN.
Franchise: No.
Description: Producing "instant" signs, banners, magnetic signs, vehicle graphics, lettering, T-shirts, hats, advertising specialties, etc. Easily operated from home, either full or part time.
Requirements: Complete systems start at $9,950. Requires $600 in start-up costs for material.
Provisions: Computer, sign machine, hands-on training, unlimited telephone support, price lists, sources of supply, newsletters, marketing ideas, tie-in sale sources, artwork for direct mailers, etc.
Profit Potential: This business has very high mark-ups. Magnetic signs retail for $52; cost to make is just $6.50.

UNCO INDUSTRIES, INC., 7802 Old Spring Street, Racine, WI 53406. (414)886-2665.
Franchise: No.
Description: The business concerns producing nightcrawlers and organic fertilizer. The company has been in business for 17 years.
Requirements: You will need a small spare room, a portion of your garage, or a corner of your basement. You will need t spend 2 hours every 2 weeks per kit. Each kit costs $249 and includes complete training.
Provisions: Everything is supplied including step-by-step training.

UNITED BRONZE, INC., Dept. SB, 181 Greenwood Ave., Rumford, RI 02916; (401)434-7312.
Franchise: No
Description: Bronzing service. Although bronzing is usually for baby shoes, it can be used for numerous other items that will become keepsakes.
Requirements: The "starter bronzing shop kit" costs $499.95.
Provisions: You will receive detailed instructions, marketing plans, and tested classified ads to run in your local newspaper. You will also get enough materials to bronze 300 to 400 pairs of baby shoes and booties...Nike's too - in 13 metallic and porcelainized finishes.
Profit Potential: Cost of materials to bronze a pair of baby shoes is about $3 and a pair of unmounted shoes sells for $39.95 to $49.95. Most people want a "shoe mount" and there are several styles you can offer which brings in additional profits.
Comments: The company claims to be able to show you how to receive at least five or six appointment cards from potential customers every day. It sounds good, if that's true.

UNLIMITED VOICE MAIL, 7010 Brookfield Plaza, Springfield, VA 22150; (703)644-1088.
Franchise: No.
Description: Business consists of reselling toll-free voice mail products.
Requirements: The only requirement is that you must subscribe to the system so that you are familiar with the product and can demonstrate it.
Provisions: Ongoing residual commissions.

VALET PARK INTERNATIONAL, Ocean Park Plaza, 1602 Lawrence Ave., Ste. 110, Ocean, J 07712; (908)493-9087.
Franchise: Yes.
Description: This company has been in the valet parking industry for over 10 years. Typical customers of this specialized service are hotels, shopping centers, restaurants, caterers, entertainment centers, hospitals, office buildings, and private parties. Customers are attracted by the professionalism of the two fully trained attendants that remain on duty and by the fact that all services are completely insured against property and bodily injuries. As an extra bonus, the service is extended to include rides home for customers who may have had too much to drink.
Requirements: The franchise fee is $14,500.
Provisions: The fee buys an exclusive territory, intensive training, uniforms, signs, and other supplies. The business is computerized, and a complete computer system and software package is included. The software has been customized for the valet parking industry and handles everything from word processing to payroll. Printed materials from stationery to media kits are also provided.

VENDX, 1550 Jones Ave., Suite G, Idaho Falls, ID 83401. (800)527-8363.
Franchise: No.
Description: Bulk candy/nut vending of nationally advertised products such as M&Ms, Skittles, etc.
Provisions: You will be advised of which candies sell best, and where to purchase your products. You will be provided with proven management tools. You will receive a sample route record keeping system, bi-monthly newsletter, product and vending information, operations manual, support materials, and ongoing support. Financial assistance is available.

Profit Potential: On most products, you will receive 64-84% gross profit.

WILLIAM STREVEL, INC., P.O. Box 71891, Las Vegas, NV 89170. (702)593-7476.
Franchise: No.
Description: Long distance telecommunications. No quotas, no physical inventory.
Requirements: No experience is necessary. $195 set-up fee. No exclusive territories.
Provisions: Constant and ongoing training, no layoff guarantee, and a solid future in a field growing at $500,000,000 a month.
Profit Potential: Unlimited.

MARKETS FOR HANDCRAFTS

The listings in this chapter include shops and galleries willing to consider buying your handcrafts. While these shops and galleries are willing to give new artisans a chance, they have no patience for hobbyists. You must deal with them on a professional level, making them believe you mean business.

To approach each shop, follow the instructions exactly. Start with a letter of introduction, preferably typed on letterhead. Always supply a self-addressed envelope. Keep the information brief and concise. Describe what you have to offer, stressing the quality of the work and materials used.

Include a price list. Keep in mind that a shop that buys outright will generally split 50/50, while you can expect another 10% if it is a consignment sale. Don't price yourself out of the market, but make sure you can make a healthy profit. Otherwise, you won't be in the handcrafts business for long. It is an acceptable practice to set minimum orders, but keep them small, say a half dozen for example.

Send the best quality photos or slides of your work that you possibly can. You don't have to hire a professional photographer. Set up one or two items on a plain contrasting background such as a sheet or drapes. Keep the focus close enough to show the detail of your work. Remember, this is the first, and possibly only, impression that a potential buyer will have. Never send samples unless asked. Label the back of every photo with your name and address.

Contact more than one shop at a time. By doing business with several, you can be assured of making it through seasonal fluctuations and other lean times. Give plenty of time for them to respond. Rather than contacting the same shops repeatedly, go on to some others if you need more business.

Finally, make sure that you are capable of handling the volume of business each shop requires. It's very disappointing for everyone when an item is selling well, but the crafter can't - or won't - produce enough.

AMY LAX, 53 Ryefield Road, Lattingtown, NY 11560.
Items Wanted: Wearable art: clothing, sweaters, separates, dresses, jackets, that are woven, printed, or silkscreened. "Anything interesting!"
Payment: "I take things on consignment for a sale I hold biannually lasting 4 weeks."
Instructions: Send photos, slides, sketches, swatches with a return envelope. "I sell interesting and different clothing - no jewelry please."

ARTIQUE, INC., 259 Godwin Avenue, Midland Park, NJ 07432.
Items Wanted: Good quality items based on Early American designs. Also, items that can be customized. Only interested in items that can be reordered. No precious metal items. No extremely fragile items or paper items.
Payment: Purchase with terms; credit references can be furnished.
Instructions: Send photos and price list. Later, samples may be requested. If necessary, would like craftsperson to drop ship via UPS.

ARTISTIC TREASURES, INC., 112-B South Street, S.E., Leesburg, VA 22075.
Items Wanted: Any and all handmade items with uniqueness a plus.
Payment: Consignment only.
Instructions: Send photos, with list of prices you need for items. Consignees pay small rental fee for space, plus 20% commission at end of monthly sales. There is a one time registration fee of $45 to begin.

ARTISTS' PARLOR, 126 Laurens Street, NW, Aiken, SC 29801.
Items Wanted: Pottery, wood, jewelry, whimsical but not country. Animal images are good.
Payment: Purchase outright.
Instructions: Any information is helpful; all will be returned.

ARTS & ARTISANS, LTD., 63 E. Adams, #501, Chicago, IL 60603.
Items Wanted: Blown glass in all forms, jewelry, wood, ceramic, frames, clocks, dolls, boxes - all media.
Payment: Purchase; net 30.
Instructions: Send photos, slides and prices (wholesale). Your background would also be helpful. This is a group of 4 galleries in downtown Chicago.

AYOTTES' DESIGNERY, 43 Maple St., Center Sandwich, NH 03227.
Items Wanted: 36" - 60" wide handwoven cloth made to our design specification or woven to prior approved design.
Payment: Cash upon quality acceptance at our facility.
Instructions: Write and include samples. "We'll sell yarn for our projects at cost and purchase quality cloth. We'll pay inbound freight charges for purchased cloth. Our designs may NOT be sold elsewhere. We'll purchase narrower cloth upon occasion. We also publish and support a home study course in handweaving. Graduates have easiest time selling back to us!"

BARBARA'S LACE & CRAFTS, 13817 E. Sprague #12, Spokane, WA 99216.
Items Wanted: Finely done handcrafted gifts and decorative accessories. No children's items,crochet or plastic canvas.
Payment: Consignment: store keeps 25%, pays by the 5th of the month following sale. Outright wholesale purchase pays net 30 days.

Instructions: Okay to send photos, but samples are better. "We also carry a very few imported handcrafts, most are from the U.S. We are a Dreamside Club Center."

BEARPAW SANDALS & LEATHER, 36 Main Street, Clinton, NJ 08809.
Items Wanted: Leather jackets, hats, belts, briefcases, wallets, handbags, stationery and inexpensive earrings.
Payment: Net 30 preferably.
Instructions: Send photos and catalogs.

BEAUREGARD TOWN GIFT SHOP, 201 St. Charles St., Baton Rouge, LA 70802.
Items Wanted: Handmade gift items and baby items such as clothes, bibs, receiving blankets, bonnets, and booties.
Payments: Pays approximately the "15th to the 20th" of each month for items sold the previous month.
Instructions: Prefers photos or a sample of product. "We are a member of the Federation of Woman's Exchanges, that are consignment shops throughout the U.S."

BOATEAK, Bluff Island, 102 Holly Circle, Fayetteville, NY 13066.
Items Wanted: Varies. Good quality and unusual.
Payment: 50% wholesale; 1/3 commission on consignment with 2/3 to craftsperson.
Instructions: Contact Cookie Tomaiuoli. "The Boateak is a seasonal store open from Memorial Day through the second week in September. My customers are those islanders who move up to the river from all over the country. They in turn bring their company, many of which are from all over the world. The store will be in existence 12 years next summer. To day, we represent over 300 craftsmen from all over the U.S. and Alaska. January and February are the months in which I plan for the season. I would be happy to hear from any craftsmen."

BROADWAY, 819 Gallery, 817 S. Broadway, Baltimore, MD 21231.
Items Wanted: Emerging contemporary art and ceramics.
Payment: Outright.
Instructions: Send photos or slides and resume with self-addressed stamped envelope.

BROOKLYN WOMEN'S EXCHANGE, INC., 55 Pierrepont St., Brooklyn, NY 11201.
Items Wanted: Hand-knitted sweaters, handmade toys, dolls, clothing for children.
Payment: Consignment 70/30 (this is a non-profit group).
Instructions: Send photos and prices to be reviewed by consignor committee. This is a non-profit organization staffed by volunteers continuing operation since 1854.

CABOT'S OLD INDIAN MUSEUM, P.O. Box 1267, 67-616 E. Desert View Ave., Desert Hot Springs, CA 92240.
Description: Leather and beadwork.
Payment: Pays in cash.
Instructions: Send photos and include prices.

CANTRY ARTISANS COLONY MILL MARKETPLACE, Keene, N 03431.
Items Wanted: Jewelry, gargoyle reproductions in plaster or stonelike, quilted or fabric photo albums, woven chenille/velour clothing, cut and pierced lampshades.
Payment: Monthly, in month following sale. Consignment gets 50% of retail price.

Instructions: Send photos or slides to Florence Rosenstock, Inventory Manager. "We are limited to consignment at this time."

CARNEGIE ART CENTER, 109 South Palouse, Walla Walla, WA 99362.
Items Wanted: Handcrafted art items including pottery, jewelry, weavings, glass paperweights, vases, wooden toys, fabric toys, etc.
Payment: Consignment preferred; 60% of retail price goes to the artist.
Instructions: Send photos or slides, artist's catalog, resume, and personal statement if available. "The Center is a non-profit art gallery with a gift shop. Art classes for children and adults are offered."

THE CITY GARDENER, INC., 3510 Wade Ave., Raleigh, NC 27607.
Items Wanted: Items for the home and garden - pottery, sculpture for the garden, fountains.
Payment: Consignment paid by the 15th of each month.
Instructions: Call Al Newsom or Allen Taylor at (919)821-2718. The store has 2,000 sf inside and 6,000 sf outside with patio area and display gardens for sculpture. There are two annual shows: May - Outdoor Sculpture Invitational; October - Clayworks for the Home & Garden.

CJ'S CRAFT COTTAGE, 7 High St., Butler, NJ 07405.
Items Wanted: Quality handcrafts. CJ's is established in an eleven room Victorian home.
Payment: Checks mailed to crafters monthly. Consignment: 3 month and 6 month contracts. 3 months $100/6 months $180 plus 25% of selling price.
Instructions: Send photos.

COLLAGE CRAFT BOUTIQUE, 366 Main St., Stoneham, MA 02180.
Items Wanted: Country crafts; no jewelry, no knits or crocheted items.
Payment: Checks by the 10th of the month following sale.
Instructions: Send photos. "We rent space for $40/month with a t-month contract. No up-front fee is required. This is not 'booth' space! We intermingle crafts for better exposure. Contact: Shirley Estrello."

COLLAGE GALLERY, Attn: Delisa, 1345 18th St., San Francisco, CA 94107.
Items Wanted: Contemporary crafts, bowls, clocks, jewelry, mirrors, picture frames, candleholders, and furniture.
Payment: Consignment; 50/50.
Instructions: Send photos or slides with price list. "Functional crafts sell really well."

CONGREGATION BETH ELOHIM SISTERHOOD GIFT SHOP, 86 Hasell St., Charleston, SC 29401.
Items Wanted: All Judaica only! Candleholders, sabbath, sever, matzo plates, dreidles, menorahs, and jewelry.
Payment: Outright purchase and consignment.
Instructions: Send photos, slides, and/or brochures. "we are open to the public - tourists are welcome."

CORVALLIS ARTS CENTER, LINN-BENTON COUNCIL FOR THE ARTS, 700 SW Madison, Corvallis, OR 97333.

Items Wanted: Jewelry, fine crafts, mostly functional.
Payment: On consignment: 60% to artists by the 20th of the month.
Instructions: Send photos or samples. Items are "juried" by a panel of several people so it often takes at least a full week to make a decision. Contact Alice Hall or Hester Coucke.

COUNTRY COURIERS, P.O. Box 8143, Prairie Village, KS 66208.
Items Wanted: This is a wholesale representative company that will represent unique American handmade items. They are currently expanding and looking for new lines to represent in the wholesale market. There are showrooms in the Kansas City Merchandise Mart and the Atlanta Mart. Items are exhibited at top wholesale trade shows across the country with buyers from around the world. "We are looking for people that are not only creative but serious about their business."
Instructions: Send for details. There is no cost to apply. If you are accepted, there is a one time fee of $50 at start-up time. The company then takes a commission of 20% of all sales.

THE COUNTRY STORE, 201-45 Estes Dr., The University Mall, Chapel Hill, NC 27514.
Items Wanted: Reasonably priced home accessories, novelties, and gifts. Also children's toys and baby gifts. No adult clothing.
Payment: Consignment only.
Instructions: Send photos for approval committee.

CRAFTER'S COTTAGE, 46 Henderson Rd., Sandy Creek, NY 13145.
Items Wanted: Any new country crafts. NO knits, crochet, leather, plastic canvas needlepoint or large ceramics and nothing over $50.
Payment: Consignment 25% paid every month as long as at least $20 is earned.
Instructions: Send photos or slides and prices. Crafter's own tags okay. Enclose SASE for return of pictures. Shop is open May through October in a tourist area at eastern end of Lake Ontario (nowhere near New York City).

CREATIVE TREASURES, 6836 Duckling Way, Sacramento, CA 95842.
Items Wanted: Creative Treasures is a home party business that markets quality handcrafts of all kinds. Crafter can submit any item for approval.
Payment: If an item is approved, it is included in the company's regular line and sold one of three ways. Consignment orders: company receives 40% of retail price. Party orders: items are ordered from a sample that is provided by the crafter. Company receives 45% of retail price. Delivery for these items is 15 days from order date. Wholesale orders: these items will be stocked and paid for by Creative Treasures for wholesaling. Company receives 50% of retail price.
Instructions: Send good photo of item, or a sample, with letter of interest including suggested retail price for consideration. Home party demonstrators and their supervisors also used. Write letter of introduction.

COUNTRYVILLE COTTAGE, 2400 N. Loretta Dr., Tucson, AZ 85716.
Items Wanted: Handcrafted, quality-made items such as painted wood, dolls, and floral.
Payment: Wholesale; consignment 33% mark-up. Paid out once a month.
Instructions: Send photos with SASE. "I look for up-to-date trends in the items I purchase or accept on consignment. Must be top quality. Some with a primitive 'look'."

DAVLINS, 125 S.E. Main St., Minneapolis, MN 55414.
Items Wanted: Quality, unique wood gifts (some furniture), no country.
Payment: Consignment - monthly; net 30.
Instructions: Send photos, slides, or brochures. Contact Dave Loonet.

ESPECIAL DAY, 10-A Trolley Square, Wilmington, DE 19806.
Items Wanted: Creative, useful gifts, jewelry cards made in the USA- "in this economy the more practical items are best".
Payment: Net 30 days.
Instructions: Send all information to the attention of Elizabeth Clayton.

EXTREMES, 759 Somerset St., Watchung, NJ 07060.
Items Wanted: Unique jewelry, glass, wood, frames, and candle holders.
Payment: Consignment: 60% to artist.
Instructions: Contact MaryLou Disano. "Always looking for handcrafted items with pizaaz! Usually under $100 retail."

FISHSCALE & MOUSETOOTH, Attn: Susan Taylor-Schran, 9406 Main St., Manassas, VA 22110.
Items Wanted: Fine crafts: handmade pottery, jewelry, blown glass, turned wood forms, textiles (original - no kits).
Payment: Consignment only - 60% (artist) - 40% split. Artists paid month following month of sale.
Instructions: Photos or slides acceptable, include SASE with adequate postage. "In business 3 years, Fishscale & Mousetooth is housed in a unique brick building, constructed as a bank in 1895. We currently represent over 50 artists and will provide references on request."

FOUR SEASONS SHOPPE, Betty Phillips, FM 488 Rt. 1, Box 831, Fairfield, TX 75840.
Items Wanted: Decorative painted pieces from smallest (signs, etc.) to as large as crafter wishes to ship.
Payment: Buys out right.
Instructions: Provide photos and wholesale prices. "In addition to placing items in my shop, I also place some items in local craft malls for resale acting as an agent or representative. Crafter also needs to inform me if they can handle mass production if larger quantities are needed."

FUSION FINE CRAFTS, 121 E. Tarpon Ave., Tarpon Springs, FL 34689.
Items Wanted: Fine, handcrafted goods - no country crafts.
Payment: Purchase at wholesale and keystone.
Instructions: Send brochure or photos and wholesale price list to above address.

GALERIA ELDORADO, 1054 Ashford Ave., Condado, PR 00907.
Items Wanted: High end sculptures in glass, wood, metal or ceramic.
Payment: Consignment with end of month inventory/payment.
Instructions: Prefer color pictures returnable upon selection. "We are an art and decor gallery, specializing in fine pieces of art, sculpture and porcelain. We are located on main avenue with both tourist and local trade."

GALLERY OF THE SANDIAS, Box 311, Sandia Park, NM 87047.

Items Wanted: Most crafts (interested in proven crafts), also discontinued items and slight irregulars.
Payment: COD or check within 7 days of receipt.
Instructions: Send photos or slides.

GALLERY OF TWO SISTERS, 1298 Prospect St., La Jolla, CA 92037.
Items Wanted: All crafts except fabric crafts (no fiber).
Payment: Consignment only; monthly check.
Instructions: Send photos or slides of work along with description and SASE. Contact Linda Brenner.

GALLERY/SHOP AT WESLEYAN POTTERS, 350 S. Main St., Middletown, CT 06457. Contact: Maureen LoPresti.
Items Wanted: Fine, contemporary American handcrafts in all media except clay. Items are juried first. No country.
Payment: All work, after jurying, is on consignment at 37%; payment made every 60 days.
Instructions: Invitation to submit work for jurying is made after viewing photos and price list. Send SASE for return of photos. "We are primarily a craft education center, non-profit, run as a cooperative. Most of our members are potters so we have more than enough clay work from them to sell."

GARY TREASURES, 629 Plank Road Plaza, Clifton Park, NY 12065.
Items Wanted: Quality handcrafted items retailing from $10 to $150. Decorative home items (kitchen, bath, general), woodcrafts (kitchen, general), pottery, glass, jewelry, wedding, baby, religious, and Victorian country.
Payment: Consignment: 60% to artisan; 40% to shop.
Instructions: Send photos and wholesale price list. Contact Kimberly M.A. Swift.

THE GIFT CUPBOARD, LTD., 104 Lafayette Ave., Suffern, NY 10901.
Items Wanted: Any quality handmade items.
Payment: Mainly consignment 60/40; or purchase 50%.
Instructions: Send photos, prices, and lead time needed. "We do large volume at holiday times - babies and 'country'.

GOLDEN ENTERPRISES, HACAP, Skywalk Level, 308 3rd St., S.E., Cedar Rapids, IA 52401.
Items Wanted: Handcrafting of gifts and keepsake type items: baby things, dolls, wall signs, hangings, quilts, and comforters. Program is designed to provide income for home-based senior citizens by marketing handcrafts through retail and catalog orders. Currently has over 100 active participants, but the organization is expanding rapidly.
Payment: Buys some items outright; others are accepted on consignment.
Instructions: Inquiries are welcome from senior citizens in Cedar Rapids only!

H.O.M.E., INC., Route 1, Orland, ME 04472.
Items Wanted: H.O.M.E. stands for Homeworkers Organized for More Employment. It is a non-profit co-operative founded in 1970 for the purpose of marketing handcrafted products from this economically depressed area. H.O.M.E. operates a country store, many types of craft and trade workshops, a child-care center, the Learning Center for adult education, a sawmill, a shingle mill, a woodlot and two hospitality houses. It also publishes a quarterly newspaper ("This Time") and a crafts catalog, and builds homes

for otherwise homeless neighbors. Currently has 3,500 members. Anyone living in the area is encouraged to participate.

HONEYSUCKLE CRAFTS, Rt 3, Box 114, Cambridge, NE 69022.
Items Wanted: Country wood dolls, signs, bunnies, bears, doll furniture; all items must retail for under $20.
Payment: Cash monthly for what has sold on consignment the previous month.
Instructions: Send photos.

HUSTED GALLERY & ART FRAMES, 9776 Holman Road, NW, #111, Seattle, WA 98117.
Items Wanted: Fine American made crafts: wood, glass, jewelry, pottery, Christmas.
Payment: Consignment 50/50 paid monthly or sooner if large sales accumulate.
Instructions: Send sample or photo with SASE for return. "We attract upper middle class repeat customers in this well established N. Seattle business. We dare in our 16th year doing custom picture framing and showing original artwork as well as gifts, cards and crafts."

THE INDIAN CRAFT SHOP, Georgetown Park, 3222 M Street N.W., Washington, DC 20007.
Items Wanted: Only carry authentic American Indian Arts (authenticity required): jewelry, baskets, beadwork, quillwork, pottery, weavings, some small paintings, cards, books, childrens toys (handcrafted), etc.
Payment: Consignment, 60% to artist; purchase by check, net 30 days if outright 50% or less.
Instructions: Send artist documentation, description of work, prices, photos helpful.

JACKIE CHALKLEY, 5301 Wisconsin Avenue, N.W., Washington, DC 20015.
Items Wanted: Sophisticated, design-oriented clothing, accessories and crafts (clay, wood, glass, fiber, etc.)
Payment: Consignment or Net 30.
Instructions: Send photos or slides, resume, artist's statement, wholesale price sheet and SASE for return.

KENNEDY BROTHERS MARKETPLACE, 11 Main St., Vergennes, VT 05491.
Items Wanted: Leather, stoneware, glass, wood and other crafts.
Payment: Pays for consignments on the 10th of each month.
Instructions: Send photos and/or samples to Edwin Grant.

LOVE OF COUNTRY, 137 Ault Rd., Urbanan, OH 43078.
Items Wanted: Collector bears and dolls only.
Payment: Buys outright usually on net 30 days.
Instructions: Send photos. "I no longer buy and sell crafts - only dolls and sometimes bears."

MACKION'S, 628 Hanes Mall Blvd., Winston-Salem, NC 27103.
Items Wanted: Handmade jewelry, pottery, handblown glass. Will consider other items.
Payment: Net 30 on items purchased or pay monthly on consignment.
Instructions: Call for appointment to come in or send slides or photos. "We do not carry country crafts. Wearables only on consignment. Would like some southwestern items."

MANSFIELD ART CENTER, 700 Marion Ave., Mansfield, OH 44903.
Items Wanted: The Gallery Shop carries work of original design in all of the art mediums ie, jewelry, glass, fiber, ceramics, wood, paintings, metal, etc. "We do not carry work made from kits!"
Payment: Both wholesale and consignment. Net 30 on wholesale; 60/40 on consignment.
Instructions: Photos and slides accepted as well as wholesale catalogs and price sheets. The gallery shop within the art center is open all year. Contact co-buyers Judy Cole and Judy Bemiller.

MIXED MEDIA ARTISANS' GALLERY, Zero Water Street, Newburyport, MA 01950.
Items Wanted: Masculine handcrafted items (oil cloth rugs - handpainted), fused glass, etc.
Payment: 60% to artisan; 40% to shop, net 30 days. Check sent out 1st week of following month.
Instructions: Send photos and background.

MORNING STAR GALLERY, Rt. One, Box 292-10, Banner Elk, NC 28604.
Items Wanted: Excellent quality handcrafts: especially interested in large pieces of turned wood, and all wearables and accessories, i.e., painted silks, woven jackets, quilted vests in contemporary colors and styles.
Payment: Consignment; references available from 8 years of consignees.
Instructions: Send SASE with slides or photos and prices. Note how long item has been in crafter's repetoir. Send any business references and list of awards and shows, if any. Send care and cleaning instructions for wearables. Contact person: Maggie Wilson.

MOSSY CREEK POTTERY, Attn: Jeanne Davis, P.O. Box 368, Gleneden Beach, OR 97388.
Items Wanted: Handmade (thrown, slab or?) pottery. No commercial molds, please! All styles, glazes and price ranges considered.
Payment: Cash upon delivery (50% of retail price) of approved items or 60% of retail paid 1st of every month for consignment items.
Instructions: Send photos or slides; bring samples in person. Phone contact best initially; (503)996-2415. Oregon, Washington potters only. "We require exclusive sales rights within 20 mile radius. Willing to work with young or new potters or potters establishing market for new or different items."

NORTHERN PARADISE GIFT SHOP, Sea-Burns, 44027 Cross Island, Wellesley Island, NY 13645.
Items Wanted: Items that reflect the natural beauty of the flora, fauna and fairies of the 1,000 Islands Region.
Payment: Buys wholesale and/or consign at 30%.
Instructions: Write, send information and photos is available. Send SASE if you want the photos returned.

NORTHFIELD ARTS GUILD, Attn: Ellie Lundblad, Executive Director, 304 Division St., Northfield, MN 55057.
Items Wanted: High quality original handcrafted items - more fine arts - less "crafts".
Payment: Consignment: 60 artist/40 shop. Wholesale: 30 days.
Instructions: Send photos, slides and/or samples. "Our shop is part of a center for the

arts that includes a gallery, recital room, dance school and classrooms. Wed appreciate having information about the artists represented in the shop since many of our customers like this 'personal' touch."

NORTHWOODS TRADING COMPANY, 13451 Essex Ct., Eden Prairie, MN 55347.
Items Wanted: This is a publisher of the Directory of Wholesale Reps for Craft Professionals. In addition to identifying crafts reps, specific information is given on how to choose a suitable rep and how to successfully use one for the first time. Cost of the directory is $17.95.

THE OBVIOUS PLACE, INC., 12 N. Section St., Fairhope, AL 36532.
Items Wanted: Good quality handcrafted items (not "country") priced wholesale from $10 to $100.
Payment: Consignment 60/40 or wholesale purchase.
Instructions: Send photos and prices to Larry or Donna Holt. "We would be interested in pottery, wood, or metal craft."

OCTAGON CENTER FOR THE ARTS, 427 Douglas, Ames, IA 50010.
Items Wanted: Pottery, jewelry, stationery, fiber, children's items, books, wood, metal, sculpture, art.
Payment: Consignment 50/50 paid 15th of the month when items have sold.
Instructions: Contact Alissa Hansen to set up an appointment. Otherwise send letter with photos, slides, etc. "We also buy things outright, but we prefer consignment. We specialize in Iowa handcrafted art and art that coincides with our exhibit in the gallery."

OWINGS CRAFTS AND GIFTS, 51523 Highway 443, Loranger, LA 70446.
Items Wanted: Country items, refrigerator magnets, and folk art.
Payment: "I no longer take consignments, but do still purchase some items at a wholesale price."
Instructions: Send photos and brochure.

PANICH, 26 North Dean St., Englewood, NJ 07631.
Items Wanted: Contemporary jewelry, ceramics, glass. High quality only. Prices must be above $50 retail.
Payment: End of month - 10 days net sale of consignment.
Instructions: Send photos, slides and SASE if things are to be returned. No crafts, please! "We carry high quality, design-oriented jewelry and gifts. No costume jewelry! Sterling silver, vermeil or gold only. Ceramics and glass must have a design element, be contemporary and unique."

PK'S TREASURES LTD, 11 Paterson Ave., Midland Park, NJ 07432.
Items Wanted: Any quality handmade items that will accessorize nicely with antiques.
Payment: Consignment 35/65. Wholesale if minimum order is open.
Instructions: Send photos and retail price list and wholesale price list. "I carry a wide range of handcrafts in addition to antiques. I am always looking for new craftspeople but with times as they are prices are very important. Higher end items are a very hard sell in this area. I am open to anyone with quality work at affordable prices!" Contact Phyllis Kapha.

THE POTTER, ETC., Box 305, Jerome, AZ 86331.
Items Wanted: The shop inventory includes pottery, baskets, jewelry, clothing, candles,

books, cards, handwovens, dried floral arrangements, and wall sprays. "We carry only handcrafted items."
Payment: Prefers wholesale purchase, but consignment considered on very high-end items.
Instructions: Send brochures. "We are interested in high quality crafts. I have no crocheted or knitted items nor am I interested in what I call the work of "loving hands at home!"

PRINTS & PATCHES, Box 1205 Mt. Rd., Stowe, VT 05672.
Items Wanted: Fabric related handmade items that are one of a kind or repeated design of products welcome.
Payment: Consignment: 2/3 goes to artisan.
Instructions: Send samples. "I have an agreement they must sign."

THE QUILT RACQUE, 183 N. Main Street, Shavertown, PA 18708.
Items Wanted: Quilted wallhangings, runners for the table, placemats, coasters, pillows, and baby quilts.
Payment: Prefers consignment with 2/3 to make, 1/3 to shop. Will consider purchase if on approval basis for minimum two months.
Instructions: Photos would be best. "I prefer handquilted items but good machine quilted articles are acceptable, if price can be kept moderate. People want handcrafted look but the price will always get compared to the 'imports'. It's a constant education to the public, i.e. quality, handmade one of a kind, etc. My shop is not a fabric shop with supplies, etc. It is a one of a kind finished product, antique and new quilts, linens and lace and — no imported linens or quilts!"

QUILTS LTD., 625 Canyon road, Sante Fe, NM 87501.
Items Wanted: High quality quilts, pillows, and wearables.
Payment: Consignment; 50/50.
Instructions: Send photos, prices, and SASE to the attention of Trisha.

REFLECTIONS, Attn: Richard, 199 River St., Leland, MI 49654.
Items Wanted: Prints, posters, greeting cards, crafts, pottery, photography, wood, ship and sailboat models.
Payment: Buys outright or 45% consignment.
Instructions: Send photos or slides, brochures, catalog, or samples. "We've been in business since 1970."

SEVENTEENTH COLONY HOUSE, 3991 Main St., Hilliard, OH 43026.
Items Wanted: Hand carved Santas, Noah's Arks, Uncle Sams, decoys, etc. Woven throws, placemats, jewelry, country stoneware.
Payment: COD or AmEx.
Instructions: Send photos and sizes. "We look for any items that are collectible or can be used in the home."

THE SHOP AT GUILFORD HANDCRAFT CENTER, P.O. Box 589, Guilford, CT 06437.
Items Wanted: Original design handcrafted items in all media.
Payment: Consignment 60/40.
Instructions: Committee meets one time per month January through September. They will look at slides or photos. The Center runs a holiday show, too. This is call "Artistry:

A Holiday Festival of Crafts." It runs for two months - November and December in our Mill Gallery. Many more craftspeople can participate in this show than inthe year round Shop. This is a consignment show - also 60/40, checks sent out in January. Applicant should send for an application! This Show is juried by September.

SHOW OF HANDS, 2610 E. Third Ave., Denver, CO 80206.
Items Wanted: Fine American contemporary craft. No country. No wearables except accessories.
Payment: Purchase/ consignment.
Instructions: Send slides and SASE with description, dimensions, and prices. Slides are viewed the second Tuesday of each month except December.

SIGN OF THE COPPER LANTERN, 215 East Central, Mackinaw City, MI 49701.
Items Wanted: Michigan fine art and crafts only. No photography, weavings or basketry.
Payment: On receipt for the first order; 30 days thereafter. No consignment, only outright purchase.
Instructions: Just send a letter and photo of work including description of other marketing.

SIGNATURE GALLERY, 3693 5th Ave., San Diego, CA 92013; second gallery 1110 Camino Del Mar, Del Mar, CA 92014. Contact: John Keaton.
Items Wanted: All good quality, unique crafts. Original artwork: glass, wood, sculpture, painting, soft sculpture, jewelry.
Payment: Consignment only. Pays by check every two months.
Instructions: Send photos and slides. Also resume and description of the piece and technique employed. All items are displayed for approximately four months and are returned if not sold. The retail price is double the artist's price.

SMITHWORKS, 730 Boston Post Road, Sudbury, MA 01776.
Items Wanted: High quality handcrafts: stained glass, clocks, lamps, dolls, wood items, unusual jewelry, slate, small size quilted items (baby's things), doll houses, etc. Object is good quality!
Payment: $50 share per month plus 10% of gross sales for advertising. Will consider 60/40 consignment (60% to artisan).
Instructions: "I have 'art space' where I display art and project slides (via video tape) for $5 per week, plus 30% commission on sale of artwork. The shop is two rooms. One: handcrafts; two: children's retail toy and book shop. I also sell confections and candy. We're on busy Route 20 in an affluent suburb of Boston." Contact Rhoda Smith, proprietor.

THE SOFT TOUCH, 1580 Haight St., San Francisco, CA 94117.
Items Wanted: Unique, quality construction, of wild or quirky items - "curiously artistic". Jewelry, clothing and accessories. Also other unusual items of a smaller scale.
Payment: Consignment: 45% store/ 55% artists.
Instructions: Prefer hand delivery to monthly jury. Will look at photos but generally does not make decisions by them. Prefers local artists.
Comments: "We are a collective just celebrating 20 years in business. We are a small storefront on busy and wild Haight Street. We have many long-term consignees and members as well as new. We pay monthly on the 1st. There is also an upstairs gallery we rent out on a monthly basis."

SPIRIT OF THE WEST, 1095 N. U.S. Highway 1, Ormond Beach, FL 32174.
Items Wanted: Southwest pottery, art, weaving.
Payment: Cash.
Instructions: Send photos or slides. "We are a Southwest store manufacturing our own line of Southwest Santa Fe style furniture. We are always looking for original accessories." Contact Millie Kashuk.

SUITCASE BOUTIQUE, 12228 Spring Place Court, Maryland Heights, MO 63043.
Items Wanted: Suitcase Boutique is a home party business. Company buys many types of handcrafted items included stuffed animals, wood crafts, toys, soft sculpture, framed pictures, and cross-stitch.
Instructions: Crafters should send photo of product and description.

SUSI'S, A Gallery for Children, 348 Huron Ave., Cambridge, MA 02138.
Items Wanted: Whimsical, colorful, jewelry, furniture, clothing, mobiles, and picture frames.
Payment: Consignment 50/50.
Instructions: Send photos or slides. Contact Susi Cooper. "I'm looking for something that appeals to the child in all of us."

TERRY'S COUNTRY SHOPPE, 1049 Queen St., Southington, CT 06489.
Items Wanted: Country items for the home; seasonal, wood, ceramic, etc. No jewelry or contemporary art.
Payment: No consignment, COD, Net 15-30 (preferred).
Instructions: Send written description or photos (no slides) and price list. Include care or safety instructions where required. "We have a 5,000 square foot retail store open year round. We feature many one-of-a-kind items and carry many lines of collectables. We have been in business since 1983."

TESORI GALLERY, 30 East Third Ave., San Mateo, CA 94401.
Items Wanted: Glass ceramics, jewelry, paintings, wood.
Payment: Consignment 50/50. Payments made 1st of month following sale or net 30 with references.
Instructions: Send photos and/or slides.

THREE SISTERS FOLK ART GALLERY, P.O. Box 1121, Sisters, OR 97759. Attn: Gale Hutchinson, Owner.
Items Wanted: Handcrafted art ie; wood, glass, textiles, metal, clay, etc. by artisans in the Pacific Northwest.
Payment: 60/40 consignment contract.
Instructions: Send photos or slides with SASE. Price points (retail) should be in the range of $10 to $200.

TUMBLEWEED, 1919 Rt 6A, West Barnstable, MA 02668.
Items Wanted: Quilting and/or fabric related articles.
Payment: Buys outright; no consignment.
Instructions: Send pictures, price information, etc.

UBG'S IDEA FACTORY, P.O. Box 906, Kalispell, MT 59903.
Items Wanted: This is a store that carries only handmade crafted items, preferably by home-based artisans.

Payment: Buys outright in small quantities.
Instructions: Send samples or photos of products along with pricing information and quantities available.

THE UNIQUE, 11 E. Bijou St., Colorado Springs, CO 80903.
Items Wanted: Handcrafted items in all media; wood, jewelry, glass, etc. Must be of excellent quality and design. Typical "bazaar items" not wanted.
Payment: Pays on the 10th of the month following month of sale.
Instructions: Send photos, slides, or samples. "This is our 30th year in business in the same downtown location."

VILLAGE OF THE SMOKY HILLS, Osage, MN 56570.
Items Wanted: Crafts of all kinds made by local home-based craftspeople are sold at the Village. Currently has over 350 participants.

CLOSEUP: Village of the Smoky Hills

Village of the Smoky Hills is an award-winning cottage industry center in Osage, Minnesota. Fifteen buildings nestled amid 67 acres of pine forest, showcase every imaginable type of handcraft.

Founder Lorelei Kraft came up with the idea in 1984 as a way to employ her neighbors without forfeiting the clear air and natural beauty of the area. At that time, unemployment was over 20%; the area was the poorest in the state. Kraft says she was inspired by Rockefeller's Appalachian quilting project, but rather than send the handcrafted products away to be sold, she gave the plan a whole new twist. She envisioned a village so unique it would not only attract customers, but would charge admissions to cover the cost of personal appearances by the craftspeople.

It took two months to develop the original business plan, during which time Kraft and 11 other social activists formed The Founding Mothers, Inc. From that point, it took only five months to locate the land, apply for a receiving a loan, get a zoning variance, build the entire complex, interview and train employees to run it, and open to the public.

Over 350 local artisans bring their products from home to be displayed and sold. The Village takes care of inventory, staffing clerks, advertising, etc. Everything is of high quality, nothing "plastic" is accepted. Each building houses something different; Woodworking, Stenciling, Pottery, Indian Arts, Mrs. Santa's House, Bake Shoppe, Candle-Dipping, Quilting, Stained Glass, "Country", Old-Tyme Photo, and Ice Cream Parlor.

If this sounds like just another cutesy shopping center, it's far from it. In addition to displaying the crafts, the group demonstrates how they are made. The Pavilion in the center of The Commons features special demonstrations throughout the summer. There's soap-making, birchbark weaving, making tea from common plants, spinning and weaving, chain-saw sculptures, tole painting, basket-making, silver-smithing, and more.

Visitors are invited to get involved, too. Want a souvenir T-shirt? Stencil your own! Or dip your own candles, or grind your own flour at the Bake Shoppe. The biggest project so far has been the erection of an authentic log cabin.

The key to the Village's success is participation. 20,000 visitors were expected the first year, but 100,000 came from all over to get involved in all the fun activities. For that, the Village won the State Travel Marketing of the Year Award, swept the top awards at the 1984 Minnesota Tourism Conference, and the Regional Development Award for outstanding tourism development. The latter was won an unprecedented two years in a row.

What's in the future? Kraft sees a lot of growth. Plans are in the works to build another 30 to 50 buildings (on the 500 acres bought recently) which will expand the number of crafts tremendously. A spin-off will be a direct mail catalog.

Kraft describes her group as the "Superstars of Cottage Industry in Minnesota." Not only has her innovation paid off for 350 home workers, but she breathed economic life into an otherwise impoverished area. She says, "We've proved here that cottage industry is a viable (economic) alternative!"

VILLAGE WEAVERS, 418 Villita, San Antonio, TX 78205.
Items Wanted: Handwoven items.
Payment: Consignment: "after item sells we pay 1st day of following month."
Instructions: Contact Romayne Mertens to discuss. "Village Weavers is located in a tourist area along the San Antonio river. Our customers are from - everywhere."

THE WEED LADY, 122 4th Avenue South, Edmonds, WA 98020.
Items Wanted: Quality handcrafts that are unique; rustic bird houses, jewelry, containers, candles, etc.
Payment: Store keeps 35% of consignment; pays quarterly.
Instructions: "We prefer to view items personally. Our shop is somewhere between country and Victorian. We specialize in dried flower products, and do our own floral design work. We carry antiques and do-it-yourself materials such as ribbon, cards, books, etc."

WENDY GORDON GLASS STUDIO, INC., & CRAFT GALLERY, P.O. Box 878, Stevensville, MD 21666.
Items Wanted: Some whimsical and nautical themes in glass, wood, ceramics, fiber, jewelry. (Not limited to described themes though). No country. Priced at $2 to $2,000.
Payment: Consignment, 70% to artist; purchase 50/50.
Instructions: Send photos and prices. Would like to know delivery time as well. The Craft Gallery is on Kent Island in Chesapeake Bay. It also has a working stained glass studio established in 1980.

THE WOMEN'S EXCHANGE, 88 Racine St., Memphis, TN 38111.
Items Wanted: "We specialize in infant and children's clothing with quality fabric and french seams, handmade linens and toys."

Payment: Consignment.
Instructions: Send actual merchandise if possible.

WOODSTOCK GALLERY OF ART, Route 4 East, Woodstock, VT 05091.
Items Wanted: Only top quality furniture.
Payment: Consignment; pays in 30 days.
Instructions: Send photos or slides first.

TELECOMMUTING AND OTHER EMPLOYEE OPTIONS

If you are like most people, you think that if you want a job working at home, you will have to give up your present job and start from scratch, and look for a new job that could be done at home. The fact is, however, that for 13 million Americans, taking their work home at least one day a week is routine. These home workers are commonly referred to as "telecommuters."

Telecommuting is an often misused term. It means transporting work to the worker rather than the worker to the workplace. This can be accomplished in a number of ways, but most often it involves the use of telephones, computers and modems, and facimile (FAX) machines.

In this book, telecommuting will be defined as an option open to employees who are currently working for a company and have an express need to take their work home. A temporary need might be illness, temporary disability, pregnancy, or the need to take care of family members. Some workers desire to move home in order to work more productively on long projects, cut down on commuting, or spend more time with family.

Some telecommuting is done temporarily, some is part-time, and some is permanent. It is becoming a very common option in the corporate world with as many as 500 corporations reporting some kind of work-at-home option available to employees on an informal basis. A few of those have formal programs with the rules for working at home laid out in very specific detail.

If you are already working and you want to work at home, look in your own back yard first. Many employees have the opportunity to work at home and just don't know it. Before looking elsewhere for a new job that can be done at home, why not start by discussing with your manager the possibility of moving your present job home? You might be surprised by the answer.

The listings in this section should be considered as examples of successful telecommuting programs only. None of them are open to inquiries from anyone who is not currently an employee.

Moving Your Work Home

Moving your present job from its current location to your home is an option that you should explore before looking for a new employer.

Large corporations are most likely to accept the telecommuting arrangement. Of the several hundred major corporations in the U.S. that have home workers on the payroll, very few hire home workers from the outside. As a rule, they want to develop confidence in their employees before allowing them to take their work home. Therefore, the very first thing to do is make sure you are known for being a valuable and trustworthy employee.

Next, develop a plan of action. Define the job tasks which are feasible for home work. Don't ignore problems that could arise later and undermine your position. Consider all of the possible problems and devise a "worst case" scenario and alternative solutions for dealing with each of them. That way, you will be prepared and can confidently assure your company there will be no unpleasant surprises.

You will need to sell your home work idea to your employer, focusing on the ways moving your work home will benefit the company. Remember, your employer is in business to make a profit, and while he/she probably prefers happy employees, the bottom line is ultimately the highest priority. You can take comfort in the fact that the benefits employers gain from work-at-home arrangements are well documented. If you want to refer to some success stories, see the company profiles scattered throughout this book. In addition, the following information is likely to grab your employer's attention.

The number one benefit to employers is increased productivity. The best documented cases are from Blue Cross/Blue Shield of South Carolina, which reported productivity gains of 50%, and from Control Data Corp., which showed gains of 35%. Employees at home tend to work at their individual peak hours, don't get paid for long luch hours and time spent at the water cooler, and often continue to work while feeling slightly under the weather rather than take time off.

The second greatest benefit to employers is the cost savings from not spending money on additional office space, utilities, parking space, etc. This is especially helpful for growing companies and also for home-based businesses that need to expand, but want to limit the costs of doing so. Some companies have even sent employees home and rented out the unoccupied space to compatible firms. As a direct result of its home work program, Pacific Bell closed three offices last year, saving $40,000 in rent alone.

Another advantage to employers is a far lower turnover rate among employees allowed to work at home. In some industries, rapid turnover is a serious problem. The insurance industry, for instance, has a turnover rate between 30% and 45%. As you would expect, recruiting and training costs are very high in such industries.

Even governments have come to view telecommuting as a viable solution to some of society's most pressing problems-air pollution, traffic conjestion, and energy consumption. It has been estimated that a 20% reduction in commuting nationwide could save 110,000 barrels of gasoline a day! For these reasons, several states-including California, Washington, and North Dakota-have formally endorsed telecommuting. California is even considering offering tax incentives to companies that will send some of its employees home to work. And, in a speech on energy conservation, George Bush came out in favor of the idea.

All of this should give you ample ammunition to convince your manager(s) to let you try working at home. It's usually best not to try for an immediate move to full-time home work, though. Start slowly, asking to take your work home a couple of times in the afternoon, and then proposing a two-day project. While you're testing the waters, make sure you check in by phone to see if anything has come up at the office that you need to take care of. After a few months of occasional home work, you'll be ready to go to your manager and point out that you get more accomplished when you're not distracted by office routines and don't have to waste valuable time commuting. Remember, you're not asking for favors. You are simply offering what every employer wants—a motivated, efficient worker interested in increasing productivity.

COMPANIES WITH TELECOMMUTING PROGRAMS

ADC Telecommunications, Inc., Minnesota.

ADC makes telecommuting an option for employees as the need arises. An employee need only get the okay from their supervisor.

AETNA LIFE & CASUALTY, Connecticut.

Aetna has a formal program that includes over 2,000 employees. Among the telecommuters are claims representatives, sales consultants, claims processors, and account consultants.

AIR PRODUCTS & CHEMICALS, INC., Pennsylvania.

This is a very large company with over 10,000 employees. Of those, only 50 are telecommuters which is actually a small percentage. There is no formal arrangement and telecommuting is allowed on an individual basis as needed.

ALLERGAN, INC., California.

Allergan is a well-known manufacturer of eye care products. For the last decade, company programmers have been working at home due to lack of space at company headquarters. The policy has saved the company considerable money (from not having to expand) and given employees freedom and flexibility.

ALLSTATE INSURANCE COMPANY, Illinois.

Allstate's telecommuting program originally started as an option for disabled employees, all of whom were programmers. The first was a systems programmer who was injured in a car accident. Then came some entries placed by Lift, Inc. Now, Allstate is open to the telecommuting option for any current employee with a job suitable to be taken home on an alternating schedule.

AMERICAN EXPRESS TRAVEL RELATED SERVICES COMPANY, INC., New York.

Over 50 travel counselors are offered telecommuting as an incentive program to top performers only.

AMERICAN INSTITUTES FOR RESEARCH, California.

Ten researchers and analysts telecommute; each has made individual arrangements to do so.

AMERITECH CORPORATION, Illinois.

Most of Ameritech's 250 telecommuters are in sales or customer service.

AMF BOWLING PRODUCTS GROUP, INC., New York.

Office-based employees are provided with computer terminals and telecommunications equipment for after-hours telecommuting. Most telecommuting is done by company programmers.

AMTRAK, Washington, DC.

Amtrak's Customer Relations Group has increased its productivity and employee morale by implementing telecommuting on a small scale. Nine writers in the group work at home on a rotating schedule, with one writer working one day at home, then the next taking one day, and so on.

ANASAZI, INC., Arizona.

Programmers, engineers, and other high level technical personnel work at home. Company is very careful who is selected for telecommuting. Only persons who have proven to be self-managing, have some experience working at home, and have proper technical equipment can participate. Employee status remains intact.

ANDREWS GLASS COMPANY, INC., New Jersey.

Glass lampwork and tool work on laboratory glass products is dispensed as an option for extra income for after-hours work for established employees only.

APOLLO GROUP, INC., Arizona.

Apollo Group is the corporation that owns University of Phoenix. About 100 employees in various positions ranging from enrollment representatives to financial aid coordinators work from home.

APPLE COMPUTER, INC., California.

Telecommuting at Apple is a natural. All employees receive an Apple computer for their home use and are part of the company's electronic network automatically. Couple that with the company's liberal attitude toward its employees in general and you have a lot of people working at home whenever it seems appropriate.

ARIZONA, DEPARTMENT OF ADMINISTRATION, Arizona.

The state of Arizona began telecommuting in 1990. Now over 800 employees work at home.

ARTHUR ANDERSEN & COMPANY, Illinois.

Only about 50 of this company's 64,000 employees work at home. They are mostly in management positions.

AT&T, California.

AT&T, like most of the "Baby Bells," is not only a participant in the telecommuting trend, but a leader as well. It's own formal telecommuting program involves almost a hundred employees in various job categories. These people sign contracts that specifically lay out the rules of the arrangement and they then attend orientation training.

But more widespread is the company's informal consent to over 30,000 employees who find it efficient to spend at least part of their work week at home. The policy is so liberal even newly hired employees can arrange to telecommute right from the start if that is the custom of the group they will be working with.

In addition, AT&T helps set up telecommuting programs for other companies in the Southern California area.

BALTIMORE EVENING SUN, Maryland.

The work-at-home option, used by writers of all kinds, is available to any employee with the necessary equipment.

BANKERS TRUST COMPANY, New York.

Bankers Trust recently conducted its initial telecommuting pilot program with the help of Electronic Services Unlimited. 20 employees worked at home for six months on a part-time basis only. The usual time spent at home working was two days a week unless the particular project allowed for longer periods of time. Employees were supplied with IBM PCs tied into the mainframe in Manhattan. The work was done in the local mode using and transferring floppies. The pilot was successful so the program has been expanded to include 10 more people.

BATTERYMARCH FINANCIAL MANAGEMENT COMPANY, Massachusetts.

Batterymarch is an international investment counseling firm with $12 billion worth of funds, mostly corporate pensions, to manage. Operation requires a 24-hour vigilance in order to keep up with world markets. Most employees, 30 out of 35, have terminals at home connected to the company's mainframe. 20 professional brokers are also "on-line" with their own PCs. If a broker has a problem with the system, he/she can call one of the others at home for help. Throughout the night, the company's "Phantom Program" monitors the system automatically and transmits wake-up calls if something goes wrong.

"We've been using this system for over 10 years. Since starting the work-at-home routine, our productivity has increased tremendously. The owner had a vision that at some time everyone would work at home unless they absolutely could not."

BELL ATLANTIC, Pennsylvania.

Bell Atlantic has over 1,500 full-time telecommuters and many other employees who telecommute from time to time. Most are claims representatives and consultants.

BELL COMMUNICATIONS, New Jersey.

Experienced employees in the Research Department can make arrangements with their managers to take their work home on a project-by-project basis. There have been some full-time telecommuters, but the situation is not the rule.

BELL SOUTH, Arizona.

Bell South is conducting an experimental two-year telecommuting program. Telecommuters are all regular employees of Bell South and include both high-tech and low-tech personnel, mostly middle managers and marketers.

BENEFICIAL CORPORATION, New Jersey.

Data processors and the top brass share the telecommuting option at Beneficial.

BEST WESTERN HOTELS INTERNATIONAL, Arizona.

This is an interesting project where the home workers telecommute from their home in prison. About 10 women prisoners in the Arizona State Prison handle telephone reservations for the hotel chain. They are provided with computer terminals, telecommunications hookups, extra phone lines, and complete training.

BLUE CROSS/BLUE SHIELD OF MARYLAND, Maryland.

This particular branch of Blue Cross/Blue Shield is still in the beginning stages of telecommuting. Only a handful of experienced employees are working as cottage keyers. They are part-time employees with part-time benefits.

BLUE CROSS/BLUE SHIELD OF THE NATIONAL CAPITOL AREA, Washington, DC.

This program was fashioned after the similar program at Blue Cross/Blue Shield of South Carolina's data entry program. Basically, cottage keyers key in data from insurance claims. The main difference is that here, all cottage keyers are former employees. Also, instead of keying onto tape, these workers key directly into the company's mainframe.

Each worker has a quota of at least 400 claims per day. IBM terminals with modems are leased to the home workers. Pays so much per claim on a biweekly basis.

BORG-WARNER CHEMICAL COMPANY, West Virginia.

Sales personnel are equipped with PCs at home which are hooked up to company's mainframe. Telecommunications capabilities include E-mail. Sales people can now do analysis and forecasting without going into the office. Other professionals on staff are similarly equipped and can work at home as the need arises.

BRONNER MANUFACTURING AND TOOL COMPANY, New Jersey.

Work to take home is assigned only to regular in-house employees that wish to earn extra money at home. Work involves milling, turning, deburring, drilling, and lathe work. Pays piece rates.

BROWN WILLIAMSON TOBACCO COMPANY, Kentucky.

Systems programmers work on a contract basis and divide their time between home and office. Only programmers that were previously employed in-house are chosen.

CALIFORNIA STATE DEPARTMENT OF GENERAL SERVICES, California.

After two years of planning, The California State Telecommuting Project is finally underway. State workers from 14 different state agencies can volunteer to participate. Anyone who thinks his/her job can be done at home can volunteer. A minimum of 200 will participate with job titles ranging from clerk typists to managers. Locations have been scaled back to include the greater Los Angeles area, San Francisco, and (primarily) Sacramento.

Those chosen will be outfitted with PCs and ergonomically correct furniture. An electronic bulletin board will replace the "water cooler" as the center of internal communications. All workers are required to return to the office of origin at least once a week.

Jack Nilles, sometimes known as the "father of telecommuting" wrote the 150-page "Plan For Success" and has been selected to direct the project. David Fleming, who initiated the idea, hopes the experiment will serve as an example of successful telecommuting and thereby open up telecommuting opportunities elsewhere in government and private industry. To that end, many aspects will be monitored and evaluated to conclude how much fuel was saved, effects on traffic flow, possible effects on air quality, etc.

CHATAS GLASS COMPANY, New Jersey.

Glassblowing and grinding of laboratory glassware can be done as a secondary income opportunity by established employees. Only part-time work is allowed at home. Pick up and delivery of supplies and finished work is provided. This is handwork, so no machinery is needed. Pays piece rates.

CHILTON CREDIT REPORTING, Massachusetts.

In-house employees must be thoroughly experienced before moving work home. About 14 workers have taken advantage of the option. They proof computer sheets and analyze the "decisions" made by the computers. Pays piece rates equaling approximately the same as in-house workers doing similar work.

CIGNA CORPORATION, Pennsylvania.

Several hundred employees telecommute including underwriters, claims representatives, and accountants.

CITIBANK, New York.

Citibank offers telecommuting as an option to regular employees on an informal basis as the need arises. Employees most often work at home during temporarily disability or pregnancy.

COLORADO DEPARTMENT OF PERSONNEL, Colorado.

About 60 employees in a wide variety of positions telecommute in a formal program.

COLORADO NATIONAL BANK, Colorado.

This major Colorado bank is currently conducting a pilot telecommuting program within the MIS department only. The purpose of the project is to determine whether telecommuting can help cut costs as it has in so many other organizations. The telecommuters write systems documentation four days a week. The PCs are provided by the workers. Colorado National expects to expand the program to perhaps two dozen telecommuters at the end of the pilot phase.

THE COMPUCARE COMPANY, Virginia.

Several high level employees have found working at home necessary for various personal reasons.

COMPUTERLAND, California.

Computerland is conducting a two-year telecommuting experiment for current company marketing personnel and their managers. All necessary equipment is provided.

CURTIS 1000, Connecticut.

Company offers home work arrangement as option to in-house employees with proven need. For example, one disabled worker does hand inserting and other mail processing work at home.

DATA GENERAL CORPORATION, Massachusetts.

Data General manufactures, designs, and sells business systems. One product is the "Comprehensive Electronic Office" system which includes E-mail, spreadsheet analysis and more. Working at home is an option to in-house employees on a departmental level. Those taking advantage of the option are most often programmers, engineers, and word processors involved in software development.

Employee's department is responsible for providing necessary equipment, generally a PC and modem which will be logged onto the company mainframe. This is usually older equipment that has already been costed out. "Working at home has proven to be a convenient and useful tool. The key benefits are convenience and being close to family."

DECORATED PRODUCTS COMPANY, Massachusetts.

About 8 employees here make extra money by taking extra work home. They inspect nameplates manufactured at the plant. They are required to pick up and deliver the work themselves. Pays piece rates.

DENVER, CITY AND COUNTY, Colorado.

In an effort to combat air pollution in the Denver area, the city and county offered telecommuting wherever it was feasible. There are now about 150 employees including data entry operators, engineers, and supervisors working at home on a regular basis.

DETROIT FREE PRESS, Michigan.

Reporters, columnists, and editors telecommute. PCs (IBM, AT&T #6300, or Leading Edge) are supplied. Work is transmitted to mainframe via telecommunications network. Examples of telecommuters include one-person bureaus in Los Angeles and Toronto, and a columnist who lives 40 minutes away from the office and has no reason to commute anyway for that type of work. Telecommuting was implemented as a company policy in 1984. Detroit Free Press also has several home-based freelance photographers who work on an assignment basis. Currently has about 20 home workers. All telecommuters are staff members and are paid the same salary and benefits they could receive if they were in-house. Freelancers are paid by the job.

DIGITAL EQUIPMENT CORPORATION, Massachusetts.

Digital, like Apple, has a very progressive attitude about its employees. Most of the technical workers have computers in their home offices and are allowed to work at home at their own discretion. Informally, the number of telecommuters (who work at home only part of the time) may run into the thousands.

EASTMAN KODAK COMPANY, New York.

About 25 sales representatives work from home with full benefits.

EQUITABLE LIFE ASSURANCE, New Jersey.

Several programmers and managers are participating in a pilot telecommuting program. Work involves database development, technical support, troubleshooting, budgeting, project monitoring and progress reporting. All equipment is supplied. Home terminals are connected to the large mainframe IMS. There is also a $400 allowance for furniture. Employees are salaried with employee status intact. After final review of pilot, Equitable will decide whether to expand telecommuting option to other departments. So far, it is reported to be successful.

CLOSE UP: Equitable Life Assurance

Success is a word that is rapidly becoming synonymous with telecommuting pilot programs. Equitable Life Assurance is no exception.

Last year Equitable relocated some of its departments from corporate headquarters in midtown Manhattan to Secaucus, New Jersey. For most employees involved, this was merely a matter of traveling in a different direction; some even lived in New Jersey and it meant less traveling. But, for those who lived on Long Island, travel time would double and it was feared that would be too much for some.

It was clear that something had to be done to avoid the costs of replacing valuable personnel. Telecommuting was offered to key people as an incentive to stay with Equitable. Six people, programmers, analysts, and one administrative assistant, were encouraged to stay home two or three days a week. They were each given all necessary equipment, a $400 furniture allowance, and retained their salary levels and employment status.

Telecommuting project coordinator, Jack Tyniec, credits Electronic Services Unlimited with providing the necessary training and guidance. ESU worked closely with Equitable's legal department, personnel manager, and prospective telecommuting managers to avoid problems in advance.

"We had no idea how many things could just creep out of the woodwork. ESU helped us spell out the issues and deal with them in advance — things like local zoning restrictions, labor laws, insurance liability both for company provided medical coverage and Workmen's Compensation, and even seemingly innocent wordings in our company personnel policy."

Words like"...work to be performed in company office...," found in standard employment contracts, may not have been intended to restrict working at home, but that is the legal effect, Tyniec points out. To rectify that situation, a supplementary contract was drawn up to specifically allow work at home.

The first formal review of the Equitable telecommuting program indicates that all is going well. The telecommuters love it, Tyniec says, and their managers are equally enthusiastic. "Not only have we kept good people, but productivity has increased as well. We've measured productivity in terms of quality, not quantity, from a managerial point of view. The managers are unanimously in favor of continuing the program. The consensus is that these people (telecommuters) were good anyway, but now they're even better."

It is expected that telecommuting will be formally integrated into Equitable's overall personnel policy. In the meantime, though, "It will spread now of its own accord," says Tyniec. "Our personnel manager gave a presentation to other company PMs at their urging. It seems that somebody has to slay the dragons first, but once that's been done and it's been clearly demonstrated that it works, others will follow. At least for corporations, someone has to champion the effort to get telecommuting started."

FEDERAL RESERVE BANK, Georgia.

Federal Reserve Bank offers a work-at-home option to its regular professional staff. First started as an experiment in the early 80's with more than 65 employees in the research department participating, working at home is now an option incorporated into departmental policy for anyone who performs tasks such as writing or editing either full-time or part-time. Computers, when used, are usually PCs owned by the employees. "Reports of our home work program have been greatly exaggerated by the media. When they (employees) can work better at home, they do. It's a simple as that."

FIRST NATIONAL BANK OF CHICAGO, Illinois.

Company has a formal home work program intended especially for data processing and other non-technical personnel. Program guidelines are designed to insure success. "It basically uses a foundation of trust and it's up to the managers to make it work. There is support from top management in the company." There are no number goals or monitoring of employees. Working at home is considered a career option which managers can use as a possible solution to employees' problems as they arise. "We've had some good experiences. In the case of some clerical, there has been a 30% increase in productivity." Any necessary equipment is paid for by the business unit budget. This is a program for experienced current employees only.

FT. COLLINS, Colorado

Working at home is a city-wide option open to all city employees. If work can be done at home, it will be permitted. Several hundred city employees are currently working at home in Ft. Collins. Any necessary equipment, furniture, or supplies will be provided. Employees retain full status, pay and benefits.

GANNETT, Virginia.

Newspaper reporters and editors who are currently employed by Gannett can work at home with manager approval.

GE PLASTICS, West Virginia.

Although the bulk of GE Plastics 100 telecommuters are sales and sales support staff, anyone here may telecommute as long as there is manager approval. Most employees have their own computers at home, but the company will sometimes supply the necessary equipment for telecommuting.

GENERAL TELEPHONE, California.

GTE first experimented with telecommuting during the '84 Summer Olympics as part of a citywide call for people to reduce commuting as much as possible. The pilot program involved technical and programming personnel and systems analysts. All were provided with PCs, modems, printers, and pagers and all were kept on straight salary. The experiment was considered a complete success and now GTE is broadening the scope of telecommuting across departmental lines. Planners of the program feel management skills should improve after telecommuting employees are trained in self-management skills and managers learn to gauge productivity rather than count heads. GTE is also participating in telecommuting as part of the Southern California Association

CLOSE UP: Fort Collins, Colorado

Ft. Collins, Colorado, a city of 85,000 located 60 miles north of Denver, is the first municipality to institute routine telecommuting. The foundation for the project is a large electronic mail network set up by Peter Dallow, Information and Communications Systems Director. The system was originally designed as a good means of communications between city employees and city council members. Each user had to be supplied with a computer, of course, and once several hundred of them were linked together by the system, telecommuting was simply the next logical step.

Asked about surveys or other scientific bases for the project, Dallow shrugs off any such notion. "It was no big deal once the equipment was in place."

As a matter of fact, the program's policies and procedures are found on a one-page sheet outlining blanket acquisition procedures for necessary hardware and software. Any other issues that may arise will be handled on a case-by-case basis. Thus far, no problems have been reported.

"Normally, you don't tell an employee to be sure and take home some supplies—that would be called pilfering. But, now we encourage them to take home the whole office," says Dallow.

It would take a lot of software, disk drives and other equipment and supplies to equal the cost of building more office space. The personal computers had to be purchased regardless of where they would be used, and telecommuting has proven to be an excellent way to deal with Ft. Collins' office space crunch.

Several hundred city workers on many different levels are now participating in the project, which includes council members, accountants, data processors, rate analysts for the utility department and secretaries. Most work at home part of the time with a small percentage doing so full-time. Prime candidates for telecommuting, says Dallow, are top level professionals such as programmers and systems engineer. Just about everybody is eligible for part-time participation except the police and fire fighters.

Dallow cites benefits for both the workers and the city. For the workers, there is flexibility, job enrichment, a way to retain employee status during maternity leave, and new opportunities for Ft. Collins' handicapped citizens. For the city, there is increased productivity, a partial solution to the office space problem, lower costs, greater employee retention and the ability to attract employees in otherwise hard-to-fill jobs.

of Governments' plan to reduce traffic congestion and pollution. "We think telecommuting over a period of time will have a substantial impact on traffic in Southern California. There is a lot of potential here."

GTE, California.

Over 400 employees including administrative staff and marketing representatives telecommute in GTE's formal telecommuting program.

HARRIS TRUST AND SAVINGS BANK, Illinois.

Harris Trust has an informal agreement that allows certain experienced employees to work at home on computer terminals to complete paperwork. There are about 40 telecommuters here.

HARTFORD INSURANCE GROUP, Connecticut.

Data processors and programmer analysts. Hartford has conducted a telecommuting pilot project with guidelines developed by a special committee. Employees, all volunteers, were required to have a good performance record with the company, be highly productive, not be working on "sensitive projects", and have a manager's approval. Each worked four days a week at home and one day a week at the office. Hartford supplied computer equipment hooked up to the company's mainframe plus extra phone lines. Employee status and salary remained unchanged. Although some problems were reported, telecommuting was integrated into Hartford's overall personnel policy, mostly as a reward for highly productive, experienced employees.

HEWLETT PACKARD LABORATORIES, California.

Working at home as an option is offered department-wide. Home workers (over 3,000) are usually programmers, hardware and software engineers, applications engineers, research scientists, speech writers, and managers. Most work at home part of the time during the week; some do so in addition to in-house work. Equipment is provided as necessary. Individuals are responsible for their own phone bills, but can avoid toll charges by calling the company mainframe and requesting a callback - made at company expense.

HIGHLAND SUPPLY CORPORATION, Illinois.

Highland Supply is in the business of converting aluminum foil and films. Employees perform packaging tasks for extra income.

HOLT, RINEHART, & WINSTON, New York.

In-house copy editors and proofreaders can get permission to work at home if they have a need for any personal reason. Employees must have editor's approval.

HOMEQUITY, INC. Connecticut.

Telecommuters do programming, evaluating, systems analysis, and software development. Homequity is a leading relocation service company. Its primary business consists of finding new housing for transferred corporate employees. Phase One of the telecommuting pilot project lasted about four months and gave the company a chance to evaluate cost savings and productivity. The initial findings were excellent and Phase Two, "continuation and expansion," is now in progress. Since most of the participants in Phase One were computer personnel, they were supplied with PCs and modems.

"Telecommuting only makes sense because the future of this business is in computers."

HONEYWELL, INC., Minnesota.

Working at home is an informal option for Honeywell employees on a departmental level. One example of its use involves handicapped phone operators. The operators have dedicated phone lines in their homes which route long distance calls on weekend and nights. Calls are relayed from Honeywell employees on the road who don't have access to touch-tone phones. Home operators patch through the calls, using a network. Pays salary plus benefits.

HOUSEHOLD INTERNATIONAL, Illinois.

This financial services company has several dozen telecommuters, mostly working in customer service.

THE H.W. WILSON COMPANY, New York.

Like Information Access Company (see below), this company is in the abstracting and indexing field. Although the number is smaller than its competitor, H.W. Wilson's indexers also work at home utilizing the company's electronic network and Federal Express.

IBM, New York.

Home work is a company option for IBM employees only. IBM has provided over 8,000 PCs for its employees to use at home, either part-time during regular business hours or after hours. Home work is allowed during regular hours on a project basis as a convenience to employees. Company recently participated in a formal two-year telecommuting experiment conducted by The Center for Futures Research at U.S.C.

INDUSTRIAL INDEMNITY INSURANCE, California.

Approximately 125 insurance auditors in the company have been outfitted with Visual Commuter Portable Computers, Hayes modems, HP printers, and Super Audit software at the expense of the company. The purpose was to reduce commuting time to and from the office and to increase overall productivity. Both goals have been achieved.

INFORMATION ACCESS COMPANY, California.

This company collects information from magazines and trade journals to maintain databases, including Magazine Index, Management Contents, and Trade and Industry Index; all of which are found in most libraries. At one time, Information Access had a fairly large home work operation with over 150 home-based indexers. Upon moving the operation to California, however, the home work program was scaled back severely. Now home-based indexers work only on weekly or monthly publications so deadlines can be met comfortably.

Workers come in once or twice a week to get supplies, materials, and any special instructions and to meet with their supervisor.

Company provides Apple PCs and special software. (Indexes are written on diskettes which are returned to the office.) Workers are full employees with benefits and promotional opportunities equal to those of their in-house counterparts. Home indexers are used because they are more productive and have fewer errors.

JET PROPULSION LABORATORY, California.

Telecommuting is an employee option to be used only for health reasons.

KEATING OF CHICAGO, INC., Illinois.

Keating is in the business of commercial kitchen equipment. Typing for its sales department is performed at home by employees who are either previous in-house employees or referrals.

LAFAYETTE VENETIAN BLIND, Indiana.

About 40 sales representatives work at home on a full-time basis.

LANIER BUSINESS PRODUCTS, INC, Georgia.

Lanier makes "Telestaf," a product used in telecommuting which was used in American Express' initial homebound training program. It includes features such as voice mail and is transcription-facilitated. Within Lanier, home work is allowed as a necessary option. Usually home workers are word processors and secretaries working at home part to the time as the need arises.

LENCO ELECTRONIC, INC., 1Illinois.

Lenco is an electronic manufacturing company. Experienced employees perform a small part of the job at home, connecting and soldering wires onto transformers.

ARTHUR D. LITTLE, INC., Massachusetts.

Telecommuting is an informal option offered to staff members. Most telecommuting is done by information systems consultants. Equipment is provided as necessary.

LOS ANGELES COUNTY, California.

In 1989, Los Angeles County joined a small, but growing, number of government entities who have decided to combat the problems associated with heavy work-related traffic with a telecommuting program. About 150 county employees started working at home as part of the initial pilot program. As many as 2,000 of the county's 17,000 employees could be telecommuting within the next 5 years. All departments have been instructed to identify and select potential telecommuters within their employee pools.

MARINE MIDLAND BANK, New York.

Regular employees of Marine Midland have the option of working at home as the need arises. The option is most often taken by professionals on staff in cases of temporary disability or pregnancy. The company is planning to develop more definitive guidelines for telecommuting in the future after current reorganization is completed.

MCDONALD DOUGLAS, California.

At one time (before company went through reorganization) there were 200 full-time telecommuters, plus another 2,000 employees that worked at home part of the time. These were mostly consultants, project managers, sales and marketing personnel, programmers, and engineers. Home work is not nearly so prevalent now, but it is still possible on an informal basis. Any experienced worker whose job can be done at home can require permission from the manager in charge of their department.

MEGAHERTZ CORPORATION, Utah.

It only makes sense that a company that designs and manufactures communications products for mobile computer operators would have telecommuters. About three dozen sales representatives and their managers work from home.

Linda Anapol, Director of Teleservices Applications for Pacific Bell, at work in her home office. (Photo curtesy of Pacific Bell.)

MELLON BANK, Pennsylvania

Mellon Bank has made personal computers available to its programmers and other personnel for several years. Mostly the PCs are used at home for after-hours work, but some employees, programmers in particular, can work at home full-time on a project-by-project basis. Working at home is also used as a perk to boost the morale of management level employees.

METROPOLITAN LIFE INSURANCE COMPANY, New York.

Metropolitan has several handicapped computer programmers trained by Lift, Inc. (see listing). Agents are also home-based. Necessary equipment and phone lines are provided. All home workers are paid full benefits.

METROPOLITAN WATER DISTRICT OF SOUTHERN CALIFORNIA, California.

This is one of several southern California government agencies that entered into a formal telecommuting program as a way to ease traffic congestion and air pollution. Most of the 50 telecommuters are computer programmers.

MONSANTO AGRICULTURAL GROUP, Missouri.

About 25 employees, mostly involved in computer programming, telecommute under informal arrangements.

MONTGOMERY WARD & COMPANY. INC., Illinois.

Montgomery Ward uses home-based workers to handle mail opening and other jobs involved in the direct mail operation for insurance companies and other financial service clients. Only current employees or people referred by employees are considered. All are local residents.

MULTILINK INCORPORATED, Massachusetts.

MultiLink is in the teleconferencing business, so telecommuting comes naturally. About a dozen employees involved is setting up teleconferences do so from home.

NEW YORK LIFE INSURANCE COMPANY, New York.

About two dozen home workers are insurance claims processors and contract programmers. Equipment is provided as necessary. Employees retain in-house status and benefits.

NORTH CAROLINA NATIONAL BANK, North Carolina.

Telecommuting is being offered on a limited basis, along with other work options, as part of this company's personnel policy. The purpose of offering options is to answer some of the family issues raised in an employee survey. Currently, three women are taking advantage of the telecommuting option by dividing their work equally between home and office.

NORTHWESTERN BELL INFORMATION TECHNOLOGIES, Nebraska.

Northwestern Bell is involved in a two-year telecommuting experiment involving middle managers, marketing personnel, and data processing personnel. The guidelines for the program were developed by the Center for Futures Research at USC. After conclusion of the experiment, telecommuting will be evaluated and considered as a permanent overall company policy.

ORTHO PHARMACEUTICAL CORPORATION, New Jersey.

Although telecommuting started small here with just a handful of computer programmers and data processors, it is an option that is being offered to any employee who deems it appropriate. Supervisors have reported increased productivity, therefore many more employees will likely be working at home in the future with management's blessing.

PACIFIC BELL, California.

Engineers, marketing planners, project managers, forecasters, programmers, analysts, and some technicians and service reps work for Pacific Bell at home. Currently has over 200 telecommuters in both Northern California and Southern California. Though not all positions require computers, PCs are supplied as necessary. Pagers and extra phone lines are also provided as necessary.

CLOSEUP: Pacific Bell

Pacific Bell has a work-at-home program that, after only five months, was hailed as a complete success. While most telecommuting programs to date have been designed specifically for data processing personnel only, from the start Pac Bell wanted to prove that any job could be done at home. And they have done just that.

75 employees went home in the program's first year, and 100 more are

Rick Higgins, Pacific Bell Marketing Manager

expected to make the move shortly. All are volunteers and no restrictions have been placed on job titles. The range of job classifications is broad—everything from marketing personnel to engineers.

Computers are used only by those who needed them before moving their work home. Second phone lines and pagers are the most added equipment. Geographically, the home workers are spread out all over the state of California.

Being closer to clients was the first noticeable benefit. "This made us much more effective in servicing our clients," says Leslie Crawford, Marketing Manager for the Pacific Bell Telecommuting Department. "We soon realized how much 'windshield time' (time wasted behind the wheel commuting) was actually being spent on driving to the office first, then to the client."

The company was naturally pleased to improve service to clients, but there have been other benefits as well. For one thing, moving the work home has resulted in closing three offices with savings on space leases totaling $40,000 annually. There were no deliberate plans to close the first office; all the employees went home and there simply was no one left to mind the store. Two other offices then closed down and several more are expected to close soon.

But the biggest advantage to the program, according to Crawford, is flexibility for everyone concerned—for the company, for the employees, and for the clients. Increased flexibility has meant many jobs have been redefined with a new look at what they are, what they should accomplish, and how.

The program is working so well that Pac Bell's account executives have been looking at telecommuting as a possible solution to clients' problems. Pointing to themselves as a prime example is often the best way to sell the idea. "To some, however, the very word 'telecommuting' sounds foreign. To them, we point out that their own salespeople have been doing it for years. Telecommuting is just a new word to describe it. When they realize that, it doesn't seen like such a weird idea after all."

This may all sound unrealistically positive, but when asked about disadvantages, Crawford said she couldn't think of any. "Maybe it's because everyone in the program volunteered," she said. "They knew their jobs, their managers knew them, and they knew from the advance planning what to expect. No one has voiced a problem and no one has left the program.

If there is a problem, she added, it would be not enough people. "More bodies in more homes around the state would be good for us," she laughs, "We are very, very pleased with the success of our telecommuting program and the enthusiasm with which it has been received. It has already been established that telecommuting works for data processing professionals. Now we have proved it is possible for all fields."

PEAT, MARWICK, MITCHELL & COMPANY, New York.

Throughout its 100 offices nationwide, this major accounting firm has provided its field auditors with MacIntosh computers in order to increase productivity. The auditors are now able to work for several days without actually returning to the office.

Like most major accounting firms, this one also has a "stable" of on-call accountants that handle assignments on a freelance basis during peak periods. These independent accountants are mostly former employees or are highly recommended by current employees.

J.C. PENNEY COMPANY, INC., New York.

Telemarketers take catalog orders in Milwaukee, Columbus, Sacramento, Richmond, Buffalo Grove (Illinois) and Atlanta, where the company catalog distribution centers are located. This program has increased from about 18 home workers in 1981 to 60 in 1987. The number rose again in 1988 to 206, making it one of the largest and technologically advanced telecommuting programs in the country. Computer terminals (hooked up to the company mainframe) are supplied, along with two phone lines - one for data and one for voice contact with the customer. Supervisors visit home workers to make sure the home work space is adequate. They expect a minimum of 35 square feet of work space that is isolated from family activities (noise).

Home workers are paid the same as in-house workers. In order to qualify to participate in the telecommuting program, a worker must have worked in a Penneys phone center for at least a year. The program is expected to grow even more, since it will save the company a lot of money by not having to build new facilities.

PRIME COMPUTER, INC., Massachusetts.

At any given time, about 100 of Prime's 12,000 employees are working at home on company provided computers. Most are in the customer service area, but others are in management and marketing. To take advantage of the telecommuting alternative, employees must first demonstrate the need.

PUBLIC SERVICE COMPANY OF NEW MEXICO, New Mexico .

Working at home is an option offered to permanent employees who need it. PCs are provided as necessary.

REDMOND, Washington.

Redmond's telecommuting program began as an effort to ease traffic congestion. So far there are only a few dozen telecommuters, but any city employee can apply for the option.

SNET, Connecticut.

SNET (Southern New England Telecommunications, Inc.) recently instituted a pilot program that involves about 100 telecommuters in several job categories.

SOUTHERN CALIFORNIA ASSOCIATION OF GOVERNMENTS, California.

SCAG started its telecommuting program two years ago with 20 staff members, including accountants, legal staff members, planners and writers. The purpose of the program is to find a way to reduce work-related driving in Southern California by 12% by the year 2000. This project is one of several being conducted under the umbrella of the Central City Association. During the initial project, the home workers kept a log of transportation charges, telecommunications usage and utilities usage. Each was periodically interviewed to determine the best methods for expanding the program. Workers have their choice of part-time or full-time telecommuting. There is no change in salary, benefits, or employee status for anyone who chooses to work at home.

SOUTHERN NEW ENGLAND TELEPHONE, Connecticut.

Working at home is an option open to all Southern New England Telephone employees. If the option is needed for any reason, working at home will be okayed as long as the job can be done at home.

STATE OF SOUTH DAKOTA, South Dakota.

Working at home is facilitated on a statewide level by several electronic networks and PCs that are provided to all professional personnel in all state agencies. Working at home is considered informal, but is clearly acceptable; especially since it is donated time.

SUN MICROSYSTEMS COMPUTER CORPORATION, California.

About 200 employees telecommute on a regular basis, but up to 4,000 are registered to do so at their discretion.

TANDEM COMPUTERS INCORPORATED, California.

Most of Tandem's 200 telecommuters are software developers and technical writers.

3COM CORPORATION, California.

3Com started experimenting with telecommuting in 1993. Today, there are about 85 employees in a wide variety of jobs who regularly work at home.

TRAVELER'S LIFE INSURANCE, Connecticut.

Resident claims operations adjusters are provided with briefcase computers so they don't have to return to the office from the field to finish work. Data processors are also provided with home terminals, E-Mail, formal training in telecommuting procedures, and a telecommuting handbook. Telecommuting is a formal program for established DP employees only.

TRAVELING SOFTWARE, Washington.

Traveling Software started a telecommuting program as part of an effort to reduce long commuting times and enhance productivity. There are about 60 programmers, sales staff, and public relations staff involved.

UNION MUTUAL LIFE INSURANCE COMPANY, Maine.

Union Mutual's "Flex-Program" is an option offered to employees as needed. Examples of need include, but are not limited to, pregnancy or temporary disability. "Currently, the program is driven solely by managers/employees' interests. After expressing a desire to work at home, employees must demonstrate a legitimate need for an alternative work arrangement to their managers."

UNITED PRESS INTERNATIONAL, Washington, DC.

Most of UPI's news bureaus are small operations scattered around the country and abroad. It only makes sense to allow the news correspondents and sales reps to work from home if they choose. Since home-based correspondents and reps are regular salaried employees of UPI, normal hiring procedures and requirements apply.

UNITED SERVICES AUTOMOBILE ASSOCIATION, Texas.

Programmers for this insurance company are provided with PCs, both for after-hours work and also on a project-by-project basis.

UNIVERSITY OF WISCONSIN HOSPITAL AND CLINIC, Wisconsin .

Medical transcribers handle physicians' notes for 50 clinics. To qualify for working at home, employees must first gain experience by spending six months in the office doing the same work that will be done at home. Work is to completed on 24 to 48 hour turn-around schedule; same as for in-house workers.

Dictaphones and word processors are provided. Home workers are regular employees with salaries and benefits identical to that of in-house workers. Performance is measured by characters typed (home workers are found to be 40-50% more productive than in-house workers). Home workers are represented by Local 2412 of the Wisconsin State Employees' Union. "There is an interest here in expanding the program. We can add one home worker for every one-and-a-half in-house workers."

U.S. GENERAL SERVICES ADMINISTRATION, Washington, DC.

The federal government's telecommuting program is called Flexiplace and is sponsored by the President's Council on Management Improvement. Almost 3,000 employees now participate regularly.

US WEST, Colorado.

Nearly 6,000 engineers, writers, computer programmers, and their supervisors work at home. Telecommuting has become a fully-accepted way of working at US West because it has proven to be very economical for the company. Equipment is supplied as necessary. Home workers are represented on the project planning team by The Communications Workers of America. Employee status remains unchanged.

WENDY'S INTERNATIONAL, INC., Ohio.

A couple dozen employees in a wide variety of administrative positions work at home as needed. Wendy's has supported telecommuting for a number of years and now provides laptop and portable computers to those who need them at home.

WEYERHAUSER COMPANY, Washington.

Marketing personnel can work out of their homes full-time. In-house employees in Washington have the option to work at home part-time on an informal basis. The option is usually used on a project-by-project basis. Weyerhauser has a very flexible time policy in general. The work-at-home option is most common among systems developers, technical professionals and sales personnel in the Research & Development and Data Processing departments.

LEARNING AT HOME TO WORK AT HOME

Although there are plenty of opportunities listed in this book for people with limited skills, you have probably noticed many more that do require education or skills you don't possess. Of course, additional skills generally brings additional pay, so the incentive to learn new things is strong.

The same reasons you have for wanting to stay home to work probably affect your ability to leave home to go to classes. How do you attend classes 35 miles away after working all day? And even if you were able to find childcare during the day, can you also find it in the evening? For these reasons, home study courses have become more popular than ever before.

Home study involves enrolling in an educational institution that offers lessons specially prepared for self-directed study. The lessons are delivered, completed, and returned by mail one at a time. Each lesson is corrected, graded, and returned to the student by a qualified instructor who provides a personalized student-teacher relationship.

Generally, home study courses include only what you need to know and can be completed in much shorter time than traditional classroom instruction. With home study, you don't have to stick to somebody else's schedule. You don't have to give up your job, your time, leave home, or lose income. As in a home-based job, you work at your own pace with the school coming to you instead of you going to the school.

Listed in this section are dozens of home study schools. All of them are fully accredited by the National Home Study Council. Although there are hundreds more such institutions, the ones presented here have been selected because they offer instruction that could help you take advantage of opportunities listed in this book.

ACCOUNTING

Citizens's High School, 188 College Drive, Orange Park, FL 32067.

Educational Institute of the American Hotel & Motel Assoc., Stephen S. Nisbet Bldg., 1407 So. Harrison Rd., East Lansing, MI 44826.

Hemphill Schools, 510 S. Alvarado St., Los Angeles, CA 90057-2998.

ICS Center for Degree Studies, 925 Oak St., Scranton, PA 18515.

North American Correspondence Schools, 925 Oak St., Scranton, PA 18515.

ADVERTISING

Columbia School of Broadcasting, 5858 Hollywood BLvd., 4th FLoor, PO Box 1970, Hollywood, CA 90028.

ICS Center for Degree Studies, 925 Oak St., Scranton, PA 18515.

ADVERTISING ART

Art Instruction Schools, 500 South Fourth St., Minneapolis, MN 55415.

ARTICLE AND FEATURE WRITING

Art Instruction Schools, 500 South Fourth St., Minneapolis, MN 55415.

ARTS, FINE AND COMMERCIAL

Art Instruction Schools, 500 South Fourth St., Minneapolis, MN 55415.

BOOKKEEPING

American School, 850 East 58th St., Chicago, IL 60637.

Educational Institute of the American Hotel & Motel Assoc., P.O. Box 1240, East Lansing, MI 48826.

Hemphill Schools, 510 S. Alvarado St., Los Angeles, CA 90057-2998.

Home Study International, 12501 Old Columbia Pike, Silver Spring, MD 20914.

McGraw-Hill Continuing Education Center, 4401 Connecticut Avenue, N.W., Washington D.C. 20008.

North American Correspondence Schools, 925 Oak St., Scranton, PA 18515.

BUSINESS WRITING

American School, 850 East 58th St., Chicago, IL 60637.

The Hadley School for the Blind, 700 Elm St., Winnetka, IL 60093.

CARTOONING

Art Instruction Schools, 500 South Fourth St., Minneapolis, MN 55415.

CLERICAL

American School, 850 East 58th St., Chicago, IL 60637.

Citizen's High School, 188 College Drive, Orange Park, FL 32067.

COMPUTER PROGRAMMING

Grantham College of Engineering, 34641 Grantham College Road, Slidell, LA 70469.

Heathkit/Zenith Educational Systems, Hilltop Road, St. Joseph, Michigan 49085.

Hemphill Schools, 510 S. Alvarado ST., Los Angeles, CA 90057-2998.

ICS-International Correspondence Schools, 925 Oak St., Scranton, PA 18515.

ICS Center for Degree Studies, Scranton, 925 Oak St., PA 18515.

McGraw-Hill Continuing Education Center, 4401 Connecticut Ave., N.W., Washington, D.C. 20008.

Microcomputer Technology Center, 8303 Arlington Blvd., Suite 210, Fairfax, VA 22031.

People's College of Independent Studies, 233 Academy Drive, Kissimmee, FL 34742.

COURT REPORTING

Stenotype Institute of Jacksonville, Inc., 500 9th Avenue North, P.O. Box 50009.

DRAWING

Hemphill Schools, 510 S Alvarado St., Los Angeles, CA 90057-2998.

ICS-International Correspondence Schools, 925 Oak St., Scranton, PA 18515.

DRESSMAKING

Hemphill Schools, 510 S. Alvarado. Los Angeles, CA 90057-2998.

ICS-International Correspondence Schools, 925 Oak St., Scranton, PA 18515.

Lifetime Career Schools, 101 Harrison St., Archibald, PA 18403.

ELECTRONICS

Citizens' High School, 188 College Drive, Orange Park, FL 32067.

Cleveland Institute of Electronics, Inc., 1776 East 17th St., Cleveland, OH 44114.

Grantham College of Engineering, 34641 Grantham College Road, Slidell, LA 70469.

Heathkit/Zenith Educational Systems, Hilltop Road, St. Joseph, Michigan 49085.

Hemphill Schools, 510 S. Alvarado St., Los Angeles, CA 90057-2998.

ICS-International Correspondence Schools, 925 Oak St., Scranton, PA 18515.

ICS Center for Degree Studies, 925 Oak St., Scranton, PA 18515.

McGraw-Hill Continuing Education Center, 4401 Connecticut Avenue, N.W., Washington, D.C. 20008.

NRI Schools, 4401 Connecticut Ave. N.W., Washington D.C. 20008.

Peoples College of Independent Studies, 233 Academy Dr., Drawer 1768, Kissimmee, FL 32742.

INCOME TAX

National Tax Training School, 4 Melnick Drive, P.O. Box 382, Monsey, NY 10952.

JEWELRY DESIGN & MARKETING

Gemological Institute of America, 1660 Stewart St., Santa Monica, CA 90404.

JOURNALISM

ICS-International Correspondence Schools, 925 Oak St., Scranton, PA 18515.

LANGUAGES, FOREIGN

American School, 850 East 58th St., Chicago, IL 60637.

Citizens' High School, 188 College Drive, Orange Park, FL 32067.

The Hadley School for the Blind, 700 Elm St., Winnetka, IL 60093.

Home Study International, P.O. Box 4437, Silver Spring, IL 20914.

Laural School, 2538 North 8th St., Phoenix, AZ 85006.

LEGAL SECRETARY

Laural School, 2538 North 8th St., Phoenix, AZ 85006.

North American Correspondence Schools, 925 Oak St., Scranton, PA 18515.

MARKETING

ICS Center for Degree Studies, 925 Oak St., Scranton, PA 18515.

MEDICAL TRANSCRIPTION

American Health Information Management Association, 919 North Michigan Avenue, Suite 1400, Chicago, IL 60611.

At Home Professions, 2001 Lowe St., Fort Collins, CO 80525.

The Hadley School for the Blind, 700 Elm St., Winnetka, IL 60093.

Laural School, 2538 North 8th Street, Phoenix, AZ 85010.

NOTEREADING

At-Home Professions, 2001 Lowe St., Fort Collins, CO 80525.

Stenotype Institute of Jacksonville, Inc., 500 9th Ave., N., P.O. Box 50009,
Jacksonville Beach, FL 32250.

PHOTOGRAPHY

Hemphill Schools, 510 S Alvarado St., Los Angeles, CA 90057.

ICS-International Correspondence Schools, 925 Oak St., Scranton, PA 18515.

McGraw-Hill Continuing Education Center, 4401 Connecticut Avenue, N.W., Washington, D.C. 20008.

NRI Schools, 4401 Connecticut Avenue, N.W. Washington, D.C. 20008.

Southern Career Institute, 164 W Royal Palm Rd., P.O. Drawer 2158, Boca Raton, FL 33427.

SALESMANSHIP

ICS International Correspondence Schools, 925 Oak St., Scranton, PA 18515.

SECRETARIAL

American School, 850 E. 58th St., Chicago, IL 60637.

Laural School, 2538 N. 8th St., Phoenix, AZ 85006.

North American Correspondence Schools, 925 Oak St., Scranton, PA 18515.

SEWING

Hemphill Schools, 510 S. Alvarado St., Los Angeles, CA 90057.

ICS-International Correspondence Schools, 925 Oak St., Scranton, PA 18515.

Lifetime Career Schools, 101 Harrison Ave., Los Angeles, CA 90064.

TYPING

American School, 850 E. 58th St., Chicago, IL 60637.

Citizens' High School, 188 College Drive, Orange Park, FL 32067.

The Hadley School for the Blind, 700 Elm St., Winnetka, IL 60093.

Home Study International, 12501 Old Columbia Pike, Silver Spring, MD 20914.

WRITING

Art Instruction Schools, 500 So. Fourth St., Minneapolis, MN 55415.

Columbia School of Broadcasting, 5858 Hollywood Blvd., 4th Floor, P.O. Box 1970, Hollywood, CA 90028.

Hollywood Scriptwriting Institute, 1605 N. Cahuenga Blvd., Suite 211, Hollywood, CA 90028.

McGraw-Hill Continuing Education Center, 4401 Connecticut Ave., N.W., Washington, D.C. 20008.

NRI, 4401 Connecticut Ave., N.W., Washington, D.C. 20008.

THE WORK-AT-HOME JOB BANK

Getting a Home-Based Job, Step-by-Step

The first step in getting the home-based job of your choice is to define exactly what it is you want. You should ask yourself what kind of a commitment you are willing to make. Are you looking for a long-term career or just a short-term job? Do you need to support yourself or do you just need some extra income? Do you want to work in the same industry where you've always worked or try something new?

A wide range of occupations are covered in this book. Do you see something you like? If not, back up and give some thought to the type of jobs that can be done at home. While opportunities for home work span a wide spectrum of employment possibilities, not all work can effectively be moved home.

First of all, home work is work which can be easily measured. Why? Because you and your employer need to know what to expect, such as when the work will begin and when it will be completed. If you are paid a piece rate, which is very common, this factor is crucial. Besides that, your employer wants to know that he's getting his money's worth. Along these same lines, the work should require minimal supervision after initial training.

It is also important to know whether there are physical barriers to doing a particular type of work at home. Work which requires minimal space and no large and/or expensive equipment is ideal. In some cases, the type of equipment and the amount of space used for home work is restricted by local zoning ordinances.

Where The Work Is

In general, home work tends to be available at very large corporations and at very small companies. Mid-sized firms often lack the management expertise available at large companies and may be less willing to take risks than small companies. There are many exceptions to this, however, especially among companies originally started using home workers.

Information-intensive industries such as the banking industry, the insurance industry and the computer software industry are prime candidates for home work because so much of their work is done via computer and telephone.

All types of sales organizations have traditionally been open to working at home. Real estate, publishing, insurance, pharmaceuticals, apparel, cosmetics, and printing are just a few of the businesses that typically use home-based representatives.

Home businesses are often forced by zoning ordinances to use home workers or else move out of their original home base. Such businesses may need secretaries, sales reps, bookkeepers, assemblers, shipping clerks, artists, copy writers, public relations consultants, programmers, lawyers, and accountants.

Any rapidly growing company may also be a good bet. Whenever a company suddenly outgrows its available space, the option of having additional workers provide their own space can be very appealing. Besides, if the growth is temporary, the money spent on additional facilities would be wasted. It is normally far cheaper for a company to pay for extra phone lines, computer terminals, or other equipment for employee's homes than to build new office space.

Moving Your Work Home

Now that you have zeroed in on the job you would like to have at home, you have two options. You can either start from scratch and find a new job starting at home or you can move your present (or future) job from its current location to your home.

Large corporations are most likely to accept the latter option. There are presently several hundred major corporations in the U.S. that have home workers on the payroll. Very few, however, hire home workers from the outside. As a rule, they want to develop confidence in their employees before allowing them to take their work home. Therefore, the very first thing to do is make sure you are known for being a valuable and trustworthy employee.

Next, develop a plan of action. Define the job tasks which are feasible for home work. Don't ignore problems that could arise later and undermine your position. Consider all of the possible problems and devise a "worst case" scenario and alternative solutions for dealing with each of them. That way, you will be prepared and can confidently assure your company there will be no unpleasant surprises.

You will need to sell your home work idea to your employer, focusing on the ways moving your work home will benefit the company. Remember, your employer is in business to make a profit, and while he/she probably prefers happy employees, the bottom line is ultimately the highest priority. You can take comfort in the fact that the benefits employers gain from work-at-home arrangements are well documented. If you want to refer to some success stories, see the company profiles scattered throughout this book. In addition, the following information is likely to grab your employer's attention.

The number one benefit to employers is increased productivity. The best documented cases are from Blue Cross/Blue Shield of South Carolina, which reported productivity gains of 50%, and from Control Data Corp., which showed gains of 35%. Employees at home tend to work at their individual peak hours, don't get paid for long lunch hours and time spent at the water cooler, and often continue to work while feeling slightly under the weather rather than take time off.

The second greatest benefit to employers is the cost savings from not spending money on additional office space, utilities, parking space, etc. This is especially helpful for growing companies and also for home-based businesses that need to expand, but want to limit the costs of doing so. Some companies have even sent employees home and rented out the unoccupied space to compatible firms. As a direct result of its home work program, Pacific Bell recently closed three offices, saving $40,000 in rent alone.

Another advantage to employers is a far lower turnover rate among employees allowed to work at home. In some industries, rapid turnover is a serious problem. The insurance industry, for instance, has a turnover rate between 30% and 45%. As you would expect, recruiting and training costs are very high in such industries.

All of this should give you ample ammunition to convince your manager(s) to let you try working at home. It's usually best not to try for an immediate move to full-time home work, though. Start slowly, asking to take your work home a couple of times in the afternoon, and then proposing a two-day project. While you're testing the waters, make sure you check in by phone to see if anything has come up at the office that you need to take care of. After a few months of occasional home work, you'll be ready to go to your manager and point out that you get more accomplished when you're not distracted by office routines and don't have to waste valuable time commuting.

Remember, you're not asking for favors. You are simply offering what every employer wants—a motivated, efficient worker interested in increasing productivity.

Starting From Scratch

If you're presently not working and need to find a job you can do at home right from the start, there is a good chance the type of work you're looking for is secondary to your need to be at home. (This has proven to be true about 75% of the time.)

The first thing you should do is examine your skills and match them up with possible job types. If you don't see anything here that you're already trained in, consider what you would like to learn. Many jobs offer training at a central location or right in your home.

Preparing a Resume

It's time to prepare a resume that stresses skills needed to work at home. In other words, you should emphasize anything that demonstrates your ability to work well without supervision. Because your employer won't see you very often (or ever, in some cases), your reliability is extremely important. For every job you apply for, you should write a cover letter openly stressing your desire and ability to work efficiently and effectively at home.

There are basically two kinds of resumes—chronological and functional. Both include identifying information, work history, and educational background. Neither is necessarily better than the other, but generally speaking, employers prefer the chronological style because its format is quick and easy to read.

The chronological resume simply lists your work history according to dates, starting with the most recent and working backwards. Educational background is handled in the same way.

The functional resume presents essentially the same information, but in a different order. The purpose of this type of resume is to emphasize your skills. Instead of starting with dates, you head each descriptive paragraph with a job title.

Regardless of the style of resume you choose, the following rules apply:

- Include only information that is directly relevant to the job for which you are applying. While it is great to have many skills and accomplishments, employers are only interested in what you can offer them in particular.

- Limit your resume to two pages. A ten page resume may look impressive, but what employer has time to read it? It will be easier to keep your resume brief if you carefully follow the rule above.

- Present a professional image. Your resume should be typed or typeset in a neat and orderly fashion. Leave sufficient margins and double space between paragraphs. Proofread carefully. Grammatical errors and typos could cost you a highly desirable job.

The Cover Letter

A cover letter is a personalized letter stating your interest in a job in clear, concise terms. You should indicate which job you are applying for and point out a few good reasons why you should be considered. There is no need to repeat any of the information included in the resume.

Letter of Interest

In some cases an employer is more interested in your aptitude and enthusiasm than in your background. This is often the situation when a training course will be provided, or for "people jobs" such as sales, customer service, and market research positions. The basic requirement here is an ability to relate to people and communicate effectively. How do you prove that ability with a resume? You can't, really, so you use a letter of interest.

A letter of interest is similar to a cover letter except that you (briefly) describe any background or personality traits that are applicable to the position and then request an application or an interview, or both.

Phone Interviews

Prospective home workers are often interviewed over the phone; many are hired without ever meeting their new employers.

After sending in an application, you can normally expect to be called within a week or two if you are going to be considered for an opening in the near future. Of course, you won't know exactly when to expect the call, but you should be prepared right from the start.

- Find out as much as you can about the company ahead of time. Then, make a list of questions you want to ask about the job. Keep the list and a copy of your application near the phone. Don't forget to keep a pen or pencil and paper handy, too.

- Try to use a phone in a quiet part of the house where you will not be interrupted.

- Listen carefully, take your time and answer all questions in a clear, steady voice. Don't mumble. Speak with confidence and honesty.

- Be polite and friendly, but not "chummy."

- Be enthusiastic even if you're not sure you want the job. You can always change your mind later.

- Be prepared to give references if asked.

Most important, you want to present yourself as the right candidate for the job. Ask yourself one question: "Why should this company hire me?" This is, after all, what they are calling to find out.

Don't Expect Too Much

Looking for a job that you can do from home is essentially no different, and definitely no easier, than looking for a job in a "traditional" work place. You cannot assume that because an employer uses home workers, that somehow means the employer is desperate for help and getting the job is going to be easy. On the contrary, employers often offer the work-at-home option as an incentive in order to have a larger pool of applicants to choose from. A single small ad in a local newspaper mentioning a job that can be done at home typically elicits hundreds of responses. That means competition, and lots of it, for you.

It's up to you, and you alone, to convince any prospective employer that you're a cut above the rest and that you will handle the job professionally with a minimal amount of supervision.

Most home worker employers never advertise at all (like most of the ones in this book). They don't need to because the jobs are so sought after, word-of-mouth alone often creates a waiting list of eager applicants. If you should apply to any of these firms and don't receive a reply, understand that they don't have the manpower or the time to do so and your name has been placed on file for possible future openings. Rather than sit around waiting for a response that may not come for quite a while, your time would be better spent seeking out new opportunities in your field that nobody else knows about yet. Moving Your Work Home

IN ANSWER TO YOUR QUESTIONS....

1. How are the listings in the book obtained?

Compiling a list of opportunities as diverse as those in this book requires constant searching. The listings actually come from many different sources including government agencies, industry associations, trade directories, advertisements, and telephone surveys of certain types of businesses. Of course, some companies write in asking to be listed, but most of the time it's not that easy.

2. How do I know these listings are legitimate opportunities?

There are thousands more real work-at-home opportunities than are listed in this book, and yet *The Work-at-Home Sourcebook* is still the most extensive listing of real work-at-home jobs and business opportunities available. To the best of our knowledge, there have been no reports of deceptive practices among the employers listed—and this is after nine years of publication. Each listing has been verified, and those firms which write in asking to be listed are screened with special care. If there is any question as to the legitimacy of the offer, an interview with at least one worker is required before listing the company.

3. What if I don't find what I'm looking for in my area?

There are over 350 listings in the job bank that can be done either in a large region or anywhere in the country. And, most of the business opportunities can likewise be operated from where ever you are. But if you still want to pursue a particular job type in a town where there is none listed in this book, you need only follow the instructions found at the beginning of The Work-at-Home Job Bank. Do not contact an employer that can only hire local residents if you don't live in the same area. You will only be wasting your time and theirs.

4. Is it okay to call a prospective employer?

Unless there is a telephone number published with the listing, the answer is definitely no. Most employers simply don't have the manpower available to talk to anyone who might have questions or be somewhat interested in their company. If you call before you are invited to, you will only alienate a potential employer.

5. Is it better to send a letter of interest or a resume?

That depends. If an employer has a preference, it will be stated in the listing. Most of the time, a letter of interest is more welcome. A resume is best in the case of professions requiring a high level of education and experience.

6. What should I do when I don't get a reply to my letter of interest or resume?

If you don't get a response within a few weeks, you have to assume that there is no interest or no openings. In either case, you shouldn't sit around waiting for that to change. Look for opportunities elsewhere. Finding the work-at-home job you want takes time and diligence.

7. Will I have to pay money to work for any of these companies?

Just as a general rule, you should always be wary of any employer that requires money to work for them. (This does not pertain to business opportunities, which almost always involve an investment.) There are exceptions, however. Positions in sales often require a deposit for a sales kit to get started. And there are a handful of crafts and assembly jobs listed in this book that likewise require a fee for a start-up kit. All of the listings in this book that require money upfront will refund your money if you change your mind and return the kit in reusable condition. Never pay money to a company if you don't know exactly what the job is and what you are getting for your money.

8. How do you handle complaints about listings?

Fortunately, this is a rare problem. Readers' complaints are usually about a company that has moved, changed its policy towards working-at-home, or simply hasn't responded. Sometimes, an employer will become swamped with applications and ask to be removed from the listings. These requests are always complied with at the first available opportunity.

9. Can I work for more than one company?

Since most work-at-home job opportunities are for independent contractors, it is your right (and obligation according to the I.R.S.) to seek out multiple sources of income. Most employers know that you will need to do this and understand if there is an occasional conflict. If the position or business will require full time participation, the company will tell you before you begin.

10. Are there any shortcuts to find the listings I want in the book?

Much thought has gone into the organization of this book. It is not always easy to categorize an opportunity. The lines between job opportunities and business opportunities, for instance, are not always clear. Likewise, it is not always easy to decide in what grouping a particular type of opportunity should be placed. For these reasons, and so that you will not miss out on anything, you should take the time to browse through the entire book. You would do yourself a disservice to go to the location index and, seeing that there are not many listings in your particular area, give up before you even get started. If you know exactly what you're looking for, though, you can save a lot of time by looking first at the Table of Contents. There you will see the layout of the book and find the general categories broken down into major sections. There are also several indexes in the back of the book to help you zero in on specific companies and their locations.

OPPORTUNITIES IN ARTS

Artists of all kinds have been working at home since the beginning of time. An artist is a special breed of worker, with a need for freedom that may be stronger than the need for security. To be able to work when the flash of inspiration strikes is important to the artist; not being forced to work when there is no inspiration is equally important.

Included in the following pages are freelance opportunities for graphic artists, illustrators, designers, calligraphers, photographers, writers, and editors. To get work in any artistic field, the primary requirement is proof of talent, skill, and dependability. Some prospective employers may require evidence of previous publication; others are on the lookout for new talent and will take a look at samples.

Graphic art is a growing field that has traditionally accepted the work-at-home option. Currently, about 75% of all graphic artists work in their own studios as independent contractors. They design, by hand or computer, the visuals for commercials, brochures, corporate reports, books, record covers, posters, logos, packaging, and more. Their major clients are ad agencies, publishers, broadcast companies, textile manufacturers, and printers.

Illustrators and calligraphers may find that work is more sporadic. Illustrators often work for publishers, but both illustrators and calligraphers will find the most opportunities among ad agencies and greeting card publishers. Both of these are huge industries. The greeting card industry has grown rapidly over the past five years, and it is now worth $3.8 billion a year. Photographers, writers, and poets will also find this to be fertile ground for home work.

The biggest field for photographers is still advertising. Agencies large and small are in constant need of professional photographers who can deliver high quality work according to the concept developed by the agency. Rarely will an agency use an inexperienced photographer; the business is too fast-paced to risk losing time on a photographer who may not work out. A freelance photographer looking for any kind of work should be prepared with a professional portfolio of his/her best work, tearsheets of previously published photos if possible, a resume, business cards, and samples that can be left on file.

ABBEY PRESS, Hill Dr., St. Meinrad, IN 47577.
Positions: Freelance artists, poets, and photographers. Abbey Press produces greeting cards, gift wrap, and statuary. Greeting cards are all occasions; gift wrap is for Christmas only. This company is owned and operated by the Benedictine Monks of St. Meinrad Archabbey. All products stress religious and inspirational themes.
Requirements: Prefers long poetic verses; poets send samples. Artists should submit several sketches. Photographers submit tear sheets. Be sure to include SASE when inquiring.
Provisions: Average assignment pays $200 - $400. Up to 500 designs are assigned each year.

ADELE'S II, INC., 2832 Angelo Dr., Los Angeles, CA 90077.
Positions: This producer of high quality personalized giftware uses freelance artists for product design.
Requirements: Submit resume along with photographs of work samples.

ALBION CARDS, Box 102, Albion, MI 49224.
Positions: Artists are used in the production of greeting cards and related products. Albion uses a very special style of high contrast line art accented with calligraphy. Interested artists should send for guidelines first; include SASE with request. If you send no SASE, your request will be ignored.
Requirements: Only serious artists that can produce very high quality work should inquire. After studying the guidelines, send a letter of interest with samples.
Provisions: Pays a royalty.

AMBERLY GREETING CARD COMPANY, 11510 Goldcoast Dr., Cincinnati, OH 45249.
Positions: Freelance writers and illustrators for studio style cards.
Requirements: Writers can live anywhere, but artists work on assignment and must be local. Both writers and artists can send for market guidelines before submitting work samples.

AMCAL, 1050 Shary Court, Concord, CA 94578.
Positions: Artists and writers for greeting cards and fine art calendars. Themes include country, nostalgia, Christmas, and many others that fall within the fine art categories.
Requirements: Artists send samples in 5" x 7" size along with SASE. Writers send samples of verses. No humor or long poetry. Most commonly purchased are friendship and birthday messages. It's best to check out company's style first before submitting.
Provisions: Pays royalties.

AMERICAN CRAFTS, 13010 Woodland, Cleveland, OH 44120.
Positions: Contemporary fiber arts are accepted on consignment.
Requirements: Submit slides (only) and prices you want. Include SASE.
Provisions: Pays 50/50 split.

AMERICAN GREETING CORPORATION, 10500 American Rd., Cleveland, OH 44102.
Positions: Artists, writers, and photographers. Company makes cards, wrapping paper, posters, calendars, stationary, and post cards. Work is on a freelance basis; some is assigned, some is bought.

Requirements: Must send for submission forms first, then send samples of work with letter of interest. If appropriate, ask to arranged for a personal interview to show portfolio.

ARGONAUT PRESS, 1706 Vilas Ave., Madison, WI 53711.
Positions: Photographers. Company produces postcards with contemporary themes.
Requirements: Submit transparencies along with resume. A guideline sheet is available upon request.
Provisions: Pays for photos outright or in royalties.

ARGUS COMMUNICATIONS, One DLM Park, Allen, TX 75002.
Positions: Argus publishes humorous, quality greeting cards, posters, post cards, and calendars. Freelance assignments are available for artists, photographers, and writers.
Requirements: To be considered, you must first contact company and ask for guidelines. Then send six samples of your work in any form (originals, copies, slides, etc.) along with SASE for their safe return. Resume is also required; include a list of credits and a business card to be kept on file.
Provisions: Writers are paid from $50 to $125 depending on the assignment. Some royalty arrangements are made.

AVANTI PRESS, 84 Wooster, #505, New York, NY 10012.
Positions: Freelance photographers for this publisher of quality greeting cards, invitations, calendars, etc. Humorous animal, children, and other people themes.
Requirements: Send letter of interest first. Ask for specific submission guidelines.
Provisions: Pays flat fees only for about 150 photos a year.

CAROLYN BEAN PUBLISHING, 1129 N. McDowell Blvd., Petaluma, CA 94954.
Positions: Writers, artists, and photographers for contemporary greeting card company.
Requirements: To be considered, writers should send SASE with 25c postage for guidelines. Artists send samples of work (any medium okay) along with SASE. Do not send originals. Photographers should arrange personal interview to show portfolio. Bring slides only, tear sheets and business card; the two latter items will be kept on file. "About 90% of our work is done by freelancers."

BEAUTYWAY, Box 340, Flagstaff, AZ 86002.
Positions: Photographers. Company produces postcards, calendars, and posters. Interested mostly in scenics and animals.
Requirements: Submit any size transparencies. Guidelines are available; include SASE with request. Prefers to work with previously published photographers.
Provisions: Pays one-time fee for each photo used.

BENTLEY HOUSE, P.O. Box 5551, Art Sources Department, Walnut Creek, CA 94596.
Positions: Bentley House has been a major national publisher of art for over eight years. They sell to major accounts, print shops, and distributors at the rate of 100,000 per month. For the first time, new artists are being sought. Preferred subject matter includes anything of interest to "Middle America"; nostalgia, country, scapes, local folk arts, people, animals, etc. Can be any medium; oils, water color, acrylics... Original art will be reproduced for mass sale.
Requirements: No prior publishing is required. Bentley House is most interested in long term working relationships. To be considered, send slides (only) of your work

plus a cover letter to introduce yourself. Be sure to number your slides and keep a file of them at home for later reference. Bentley House requires no investment of any kind and suggests strongly that any artist who is approached by a buyer of any kind asking for money up front Beware.
Provisions: Reproduced prints sell in the $15 to $60 range. Different arrangements are worked out with different artists; buys outright, on commission, and other. A new line is introduced every four to five months.

BLAH BLAH BLAH CARDS, 1208 Baylor, Austin, TX 78703.
Positions: This small company produces postcards only, using art and written verses. Alternative themes only.
Requirements: Send resume and copies of work samples along with SASE.
Provisions: Pays about $50 for artwork assignment.

B.M. Enterprises, Box 421, Farrell, PA 16121.
Positions: Freelance artists. Company is a clip art service bureau. Assigns line drawings and cartoons to previously published artists only.
Requirements: Write first for market guide. Then submit letter of interest with tear sheets.
Provisions: Payment is a 50/50 split.

BRADFORD EXCHANGE, 9333 Milwaukee, Chicago, IL 60648.
Positions: Bradford is a manufacturer of collectible plates. Freelance professional artists are used to design landscapes and portraits that will be reproduced on the plates.
Requirements: Submit resume, samples that can be kept on file, and references or tear sheets.

BRETT-FORER GREETINGS, INC., 790 Madison Ave., Suite 201, New York, NY 10021.
Positions: Freelance artists and writers. Brett-Forer cards are whimsical; mostly Christmas and everyday with a few other occasions. Writers can submit verse for consideration. Artists are usually assigned.
Requirements: Writers should send batches of 10 verses. Artists submit samples and business card.
Provisions: Pays flat fee.

BUCKBOARD ANTIQUES, 1411 N. May, Oklahoma City, OK 73107.
Positions: Folk art and other traditional country crafts like rag dolls and quilted items will be considered.
Requirements: Send photos and prices you want along with an SASE.

BURGOYNE, INC., 2030 E. Byberry Rd., Philadelphia, PA 19116.
Positions: Company produces greeting cards and calendars with Christmas theme only. Uses freelance artists for design, illustration, and calligraphy.
Requirements: Experienced artists only. Submit letter of interest with work samples and business card.
Provisions: Pays about $225 for design work on first assignment. Buys about 150 designs a year.

CANTERBURY DESIGNS, INC., Box 4060, Martinez, GA 30907.
Positions: Freelance artists are used to produce new designs for needlework design

books.
Requirements: Send photographs of your work samples. Include letters of interest that indicates professional background.
Provisions: Pay methods vary.

CAPE SHORE PAPER PRODUCTS, INC., 42A N. Elm Street, Box 537, Yarmouth, ME 04096.
Positions: Freelance artists for design and illustrations of gifts and stationery products. Company uses primarily nautical theme with some Americana, Christmas, and other traditional themes such as floral, birds, and animals.
Requirements: Send for guidelines first. Then submit letter of interest with samples.
Provisions: Pays flat fee.

CARLTON CARDS, 10500 American Rd., Cleveland, OH 44144.
Positions: Artists, writers, and photographers design cards and calendars.
Requirements: Artists should submit sketches; photographers submit color transparencies. Send sample portfolio with return postage included. Writers should submit ideas on 3x5 index cards. Be sure name and address is on the back of each card submitted.
Provisions: Payment depends on individual situation. Sometimes ideas are purchased outright, sometimes work is assigned and paid for by the project. New talent is actively solicited.

CHESAPEAKE BAY MAGAZINE, 1819 Bay Ridge Ave., Suite 200, Annapolis, MD 21403.
Positions: Freelance writers and photographers.
Requirements: Any material about the Chesapeake region will be considered. Photographers submit color photos only. Writers can submit either proposal or complete manuscript.
Provisions: Pays on acceptance.

CMP PUBLICATIONS, 600 Community Dr., Manhasset, NY 11030.
Positions: Editors, associate editors, reporters, and writers are all outfitted with computers and modems in order to transmit material from the field. Freelance stringers are hired to cover business news from all over the country.
Requirements: Hard news reporting experience a must. Must feel comfortable going

to top industrial companies looking for stories and information. Apply with resume and previously published clips.
Provisions: Payment varies. Some reporters are salaried, some are paid by individual contract. Phone charges are reimbursed.

COMMUNICATIONS DYNAMICS CORPORATION, Box 3060, Glen Ellyn, IL 60137.
Positions: Freelance copy writers and technical writers.
Requirements: Must be reliable and experienced. Send resume and work sample. Must be local resident.
Provisions: Pays by the job.

COMMUNICATIONS ELECTRONICS, Box 1045, Ann Arbor, MI 48106.
Positions: Freelance artists for advertising work.
Requirements: Send resume and samples or tear sheets to be kept on file. Request an appointment to show portfolio. Only local artists will be considered.
Provisions: Pays by the project.

COMSTOCK CARDS, INC., 600 S. Rock Blvd., Suite 15, Reno, NV 89502.
Positions: Photographers, artists, and writers are used to design outrageously funny stationery and novelty items.
Requirements: Submit color transparencies, cartoon drawings, or brief verses with strong, but short lead.
Provisions: Pays $50 for each assignment. Will consider royalty arrangement.

COURAGE CARDS, 3915 Golden Valley Road, Golden Valley, MN 55422.
Positions: This is a non-profit rehabilitation and independent living center for children and adults with various disabilities. They produce mostly Christmas and other holiday cards using fine art theme only.
Requirements: Unsolicited samples are not accepted. Send letter of interest first.

CRAIG COMMUNICATIONS, 3095 Lawson Blvd., Oceanside, NY 11572.
Positions: Graphic art.
Requirements: Experience required in marketing graphics, advertising and printing. Also, strong desktop publishing skills required. Local residents only send resume.

CREATIVE CARD COMPANY/CENTURY ENGRAVING, 1500 W. Monroe, Chicago, IL 60607.
Positions: This publisher of personalized Christmas and holiday cards uses artists.
Requirements: Submit samples on slides; conventional themes are best.
Provisions: Average payment for a card is $250 - $400.

CUSTOM STUDIOS, 1337 W. Devon Ave., Chicago, IL 60660.
Positions: Freelance photographers on assignment basis only for Christmas card department. Offer over 100 assignments annually.
Requirements: To be considered, send letter of interest with SASE requesting "Photo Guidelines". Include business card.
Provisions: Pays by the job, $50 minimum.

DAVID M & COMPANY, 7723 Densmore Avenue, Van Nuys, CA 91406.
Positions: Company produces watercolor and calligraphy cards and paper goods. Both

artists and writers are used.
Requirements: Artists submit samples of work in the form of slides, originals, or color photocopies. Writers send samples along with SASE.
Provisions: Artwork pays about $250; verse $50 - $100.

DEADY ADVERTISING, 17 E. Cary St., Richmond, VA 23236.
Positions: Freelance illustrators.
Requirements: Must be very experienced in the advertising field. Local artists only. Submit resume and work samples.
Provisions: Pay methods vary from project to project.

DIGITAL NEWS, P.O. Box 9192, Framingham, MA 01701.
Positions: This is an in-house publication that covers equipment made by Digital. Writers and reporters routinely work at home.
Requirements: Resumes are accepted from experienced computer industry writers.
Provisions: Some home workers receive benefits; others do not.

DISPLAYCO, 2055 McCarter Highway, Newark, NJ 07104.
Positions: Freelance artists. Company manufacturers advertising display fixtures.
Requirements: Must have experience working in the advertising field and, in particular, with display fixtures. Submit work samples or photos of work and resumes. Prefers local artists.
Provisions: Pays by the project.

ENESCO IMPORTS CORPORATION, Attn: Ms. Karen George, Art Department, 1 Enesco Plaza, Elk Grove Village, IL 60007.
Positions: Enesco provides freelance opportunities in their art department for artists, designers, and sample makers for their giftware line.
Requirements: Artists and designers must have exceptional creativity and the work samples to prove it. Sample makers must have all necessary tools to produce samples from artists' renderings. Must be local resident. To inquire, write to the address above. Absolutely no phone calls will be accepted!
Provisions: Artwork is often bought outright. Others are paid by the project or by the hour.

ENVIRONMENTAL DESIGN & RESEARCH CENTER, 26799 Elena Rd., Los Altos Hills, CA 94022.
Positions: Free-hand artists to do presentation graphics representing technical concepts by cartoon figures and objects.
Requirements: Send resume and work samples.
Provisions: Pays on a per-piece basis.

EVERETT STUDIOS, INC., 22 Barker Ave., White Plains, NY 10601.
Positions: Graphic artists and freelance photographers.
Requirements: Need experienced people who have worked in production, lab, or studio end of the business. Local residents only. Send resume.

THE EVERGREEN PRESS, INC., 3380 Vincent Rd., Pleasant Hill, CA 94523.
Positions: Artists for design and illustrations of cards, gift wrap, children's picture books, and bookmarks. Cards are generally produced in a series with a common theme. Especially in need of Christmas card designs. Gift wrap is also for Christmas; prefers

country or folk art theme.
Requirements: Send for guidelines first. To be considered for assignment, send a group of samples and resume.
Provisions: Generally pays royalty.

FELLERS LACY GADDIS, 5th Floor, 5918 W. Courtyard Dr., Austin, TX 78730.
Positions: Freelance photographers are used by this advertising agency. Photos are used in consumer publications.
Requirements: Prefers to work only with local photographers. Must be experienced and have professional portfolio. Write letter of interest requesting appointment to show portfolio.
Provisions: Pays photographers regular rates.

FINELINE ILLUSTRATIONS, 2840 Jerusalem Ave., Wantagh, NY 11793.
Positions: Artist.
Requirements: Need Macintosh with Adobe Illustrator to do textbook illustration from technical charts and graphs to full color artwork. Local residents only send resume.

FREEDOM GREETING CARD COMPANY, P.O. Box 715, Bristol, PA 19007.
Positions: Writers and artists. Writers sell verses outright. Artists work on assignment only.
Requirements: Samples of work, letter of interest, and SASE required for either type of work.

G.A.I., INC., Box 30309, Indianapolis, IN 46203.
Positions: G.A.I. is a licensing agent in the collectibles industry. Freelance artists that seek representation are encouraged to submit samples of people-type art in any medium. There is no fee; G.A.I. takes a commission for successfully completed projects.
Requirements: Send resume and color photographs of work samples. Include SASE for reply.
Provisions: Artists are generally paid a royalty.

GERBIG, SNELL, WEISHEIMER & ASSOCIATES, Suite 600, 425 Metro Pl. North, Dublin, OH 43017
Positions: Freelance illustrators and photographers used for the production of advertising materials.
Requirements: Works only with local experienced people. Submit resume, tear sheets, and business card.

C.R. GIBSON, COMPANY, 32 Knight Street, Norwalk, CT 06856.
Positions: Freelance artists. Company produces stationery products and buys new designs.
Requirements: Only previously established artists are considered. Submit samples and resume.
Provisions: Pays flat rate for each design accepted.

GIBSON GREETINGS, INC., 2100 Section Road, Cincinnati, OH 45237.
Positions: Gibson buys about 2,000 designs from freelance artists and 500 verses from writers each year. Company publishes cards and other paper products with a wide range of themes and styles.
Requirements: Send resume and request guidelines first.

GLENCOE PUBLISHING COMPANY, 15319 Chatsworth St., Mission Hills, CA 91345.
Positions: Freelance artists illustrate textbooks.
Requirements: Work must be top notch. Submit resume and tear sheets. Will consider only previously published illustrators.
Provisions: Pays by the project.

HARCOURT BRACE JOVANOVICH PUBLICATIONS, 1250 6th Ave., San Diego, CA 92101.
Positions: Freelance writing assignments are available from this major business publisher. Artists also work on assignment.
Requirements: Only very experienced writers will be considered. Apply with resume and writing samples along with letter of interest. Artists should send samples of work along with letter of interest and bio describing in detail background experience.

HERFF JONES, Box 6500, Providence RI, 02940.
Positions: Freelance illustrators and designers. Company makes medals, trophies, and class rings.
Requirements: Several years of experience is required. Submit resume and samples.
Provisions: Pays by the project.

Want additional information on any aspect of working from home? See the *Resource Guide* at the end of this book.

IN TOUCH, The International Tours Travel Magazine, 192 Newbury St., Boston, MA 02116. .
Positions: Freelance writers and photographers. All material is travel related.
Requirements: Both writers and photographers should send for guidelines first; include SASE.

THE INQUISITIVE TRAVELER, 6 Lakeshore Lane, Asheville, NC 28804.
Positions: Freelance writers and photographers for quarterly travel magazine.
Requirements: Writers should send for guidelines first; include SASE with request. Photographers send samples of travel photos.

INTERCONTINENTAL GREETINGS, LTD., 176 Madison Ave., New York, NY 10016.
Positions: Freelance artists for greeting cards, gift wrap, calendars, posters, and stationery. Prefers very graphic designs with some cartoon style illustrations.
Requirements: Works only with professionals. Send resume, work samples, and include SASE.
Provisions: Generally pays royalties.

KERSTEN BROTHERS, P.O. Box 1765, Scottsdale, AZ 85252.

Positions: Writers and artists for greeting cards. All cards are humorous and seasonal; Christmas, Thanksgiving, Halloween, Mother's Day, Father's Day, Graduation, Easter, Valentine's Day, and St. Patrick's Day.
Requirements: Writers submit batches of short verses for consideration. Artists send sketches or photocopies of finished originals.

KLITZNER INDUSTRIES, 44 Warren St., Providence, RI 02901.
Positions: Freelance designers and illustrators for advertising specialty products.
Requirements: Must have experience in the advertising field and the proven ability to follow through on assignments. Submit resume and tear sheets. Prefers local artists.
Provisions: Pays by the project.

LASER CRAFT, 3300 Coffey Lane, Santa Rosa, CA 95401.
Positions: Established greeting card company always on the lookout for artists with new ideas for greeting card designs. Company prefers humorous themes, but anything innovative (and good) will be considered.
Requirements: Submit ideas/designs in card format and send with SASE.
Provisions: Pays for each design.

LILLIAN VERNON CORPORATION, 543 Main Street, New Rochelle, NY 10801.
Positions: Freelance artists. Lillian Vernon is one of those rare "kitchen table" success stories. The company is one of the most successful of all direct mail catalog marketers. Products include all kinds of paper products, textiles, housewares, Christmas decor, etc. Freelance artists design and illustrate on assignment only.
Requirements: Only New York metropolitan area artists are used. Only uses artists with previous experience. Send letter of interest with tear sheets or samples that can be kept on file.
Provisions: Pays flat fee.

LOS ANGELES REVIEW OF BOOKS, 7536 Circuit Dr., Citrus Heights, CA 95610.
Positions: Stringers and staff writers for reviews, features, and interviews with writers and others in the publishing industry.
Requirements: At least one sample of previous (published) work. Knowledge of the publishing industry is preferred.
Provisions: Staff members are salaried employees. Stringers are paid per assignment.

MANGAN, RAINS, GINNAVEN, HOLCOMB, 911 Savers Federal Building, Little Rock, AR 72201.
Positions: Freelance artists work on a variety of advertising materials.
Requirements: Prefers experienced local artists. Submit letter of interest and business card. Request appointment to show portfolio.
Provisions: Pays hourly rates.

THE MARCEL SCHURMAN COMPANY, INC., 2500 North Watney Way, Fairfield, CA 94533.
Positions: Company produces high quality greeting cards, stationery, and social occasion books. Only museum quality art is used. Illustrations include trendy graphics and traditional florals. Uses professional artists experienced in sophisticated juvenile, humorous, and general styles. Calligraphers, fine art painters, fabric designers and graphic designers are also used. Experienced writes are used to produce verse.
Requirements: Artists submit slides or prints (no originals please) and send to the attention of the Art Director. Writers submit ideas on 3" x 5" typed index cards. Label each card with your name and address. Send to the attention of the Editor. Include SASE with any samples.

MASTERPIECE STUDIOS, 5400 West 35th St., Chicago, IL 60650.
Positions: Freelance artists for seasonal greeting cards. Especially needs highly stylized designs for Christmas cards.
Requirements: Send for guidelines first. Submit full color sketches or finished art. Samples will not be returned.
Provisions: Pays flat fee for each design. Pays higher fees for assigned illustration.

MECKLER PUBLISHING CORPORATION, 11 Ferry Lane West, Westport, CT 06880
Positions: Meckler publishes books and journals about computer databases and other electronic information storage products. There are about 40 home-based writers, editors, and even some local keyboarders.
Requirements: Resumes are accepted from qualified writers and editors with experience in this field.

MEDIA REVIEW, Box 146717, San Francisco, CA 94114.
Positions: Freelance writers and editors. Media Review is a humorous new magazine that parodies mainstream media.
Requirements: Submit resume with copies of articles, sample ideas, and include SASE.

MEDIA TRENDS, P.O. Box 134, Metuchen, NJ 08810.
Positions: Photographers for weddings in photojournalistic style.
Requirements: Must own necessary equipment and be very skilled and experienced. Local residents only. Send resume and samples of work.

MERION PUBLICATIONS, INC., 636 School Line Dr., King of Prussia, PA 19406.
Positions: Freelance staff writers for newspaper read by health professionals.
Requirements: Must live in the area. Need experience and resume with samples.
Provisions: Story leads are provided for features.

METRO CREATIVE GRAPHICS, 33 West 34th St., 4th Floor, New York, NY 10005.

Positions: Freelance illustrators. Metro is a clip art dealer that works with dozens of artists.
Requirements: Must apply with resume and request personal interview to show portfolio of professional work samples. Prefers New York artists, but will consider anyone with real talent.
Provisions: Pay worked out on an individual basis.

MIDWEST LIVING, 1912 Grand Avenue, Des Moines, IA 50336.
Positions: Freelance writers work on assignment for this monthly travel and leisure magazine.
Requirements: Send proposal along with clips of previously published material.
Provisions: Pays excellent rates upon acceptance.

NATIONAL HARDWOOD MAGAZINE, P.O. Box 34808, Memphis, TN 38184.
Positions: Freelance writers work on assignment basis in various metropolitan areas around the country. Publication is a wood industry trade journal.
Requirements: Send resume and writing samples.

THOMAS NELSON PUBLISHERS, Box 141000, Elm Hill Pike, Nashville, TN 37284.
Positions: Freelance artists illustrate religious publications and design advertising materials.
Requirements: Only local experienced artists are considered. Submit letter of interest and tear sheets.

NEW DOMINION, P.O. Box 19714, Alexandria, VA 22320.
Positions: Freelance writers write most of this quarterly magazine for northern Virginia.
Requirements: Must be regional writer. Send for guidelines and sample issue first.
Provisions: Pays by the word.

NEWSBYTES NEWS SERVICE, 406 Olive St. W., Stillwater, MN 55082.
Positions: Newsbytes is similar to AP and UPI in that it is a news service. The difference is that it specializes in news about the computer industry. The entire staff is comprised of a dozen writers scattered throughout the world, each running his or her own bureau from home. Each is a permanent, though part-time employee of the company.
Requirements: Resumes are accepted from experienced computer industry reporters.

NOBLEWORKS, 113 Clinton Street, Hoboken, NJ 07030.
Positions: This company has been called the "Marx Brothers" of the greeting card industry. They purchase photos and some illustration. It is important that you study this company's line first before submitting anything.
Requirements: Send letter of interest first.
Provisions: Pays royalties.

NU-ART, INC., Box 2002, Bedford, IL 60499.
Positions: Writers and artists for greeting cards, wedding invitations and accessories, and boxed stationery. Cards are for Christmas only.
Requirements: Writers submit verse along with design ideas for total concept. Artists submit color roughs or finished art.

OATMEAL STUDIOS, Box 138, Rochester, VT 05767.

Positions: Writers and illustrators for greeting card design.
Requirements: The first step for both positions is to send for Oatmeal's guidelines and current market list. Include SASE with your request. Then send several samples with a letter of interest.
Provisions: Writers are paid for each idea that is accepted. Pay for artists depends on the situation. 90% of Oatmeal's work is done by freelancers.

OUTREACH PUBLICATIONS, P.O. Box 1010, Siloam Springs, AR 72761.
Positions: This conservative Christian greeting card publisher uses freelance writers and artists.
Requirements: Artists should send samples or photos of their work. Writers submit verse ideas on index cards. Send for guidelines first.
Provisions: Pays artists $200 - $300 per design. Buys up to 400 designs per year. Buys up to 800 verses per year.

PALM PRESS, INC., 1442A Walnut Street, Berkeley, CA 94709.
Positions: Freelance photographers are used by this greeting card publisher.
Requirements: Submit transparencies or prints.

PAMCO SECURITIES AND INSURANCE SERVICES, 16030 Ventura Blvd. #500, Encino, CA 91436.
Positions: Freelance writer for composing banking training manuals.
Requirements: Must be local resident. Minimum five years experience in this type of writing is required. Must have thorough knowledge of banking industry. Must own IBM compatible word processor. Submit resume and references.

PAPEL, Box 9879, North Hollywood, CA 91609.
Positions: Freelance illustrators, designers, and calligraphers work on greeting cards and ceramic souvenir items.
Requirements: Several years experience is required. Submit resume and tear sheets.
Provisions: Pays by the project.

PARAISO PUBLISHERS, INC., 160 W. Slauson Ave., #3, Los Angeles, CA 90003.
Positions: Artists and writers used by this manufacturer of Spanish greeting cards.
Requirements: Send letter of interest requesting permission to submit samples or ideas.
Provisions: Artists are paid at least $50 per design. Pays $4 for a verse.

PARAMOUNT CARDS INC., 400 Pine Street, Providence, RI 02863.
Positions: Writers, artists, and photographers for greeting card production and promotional work. Cards are seasonal and everyday with a humorous theme (studio style).
Requirements: First send for instruction sheet, including SASE with request. Then send samples with letter of interest. Be sure to include SASE with any samples.
Provisions: Specific art assignments and purchase agreements are given to freelance artists/designers. Pay methods vary.

PC WEEK, 800 Boylston Street, Boston, MA 02199.
Positions: Technical analysts review computer software and hardware.
Requirements: Only the best technical reviewers will be considered. Send resume.

PENDLETON HAND WEAVERS, P.O. Box 233, Sedona, AZ 86336.

Positions: Will consider hand woven and other fabric art pieces for inclusion in regular retail line.
Requirements: Send either slides or photos along with written description and prices of your offerings. Include SASE.

PHILLIPS PUBLISHING, INC., 7811 Montrose Road, Potomac, MD 20854.
Positions: This newsletter publisher uses up to ten freelance writers.
Requirements: Must have the necessary expertise to write on high technology topics. Prefers local residents.
Provisions: Equipment such as personal computers and fax machines are provided as needed.

PICTURA, INC., 4 Andrews Drive, West Paterson, NJ 07424.
Positions: Freelance artists are used for Victorian, floral, children and "cute" illustrations for greeting cards.
Requirements: Send a letter of introduction along with one sample.

PLUM GRAPHICS, INC., P.O. Box 136, Prince Station, New York, NY 10012.
Positions: Realistic art in oil paint, acrylic or water color is used for greeting cards.
Requirements: Artists send samples of style including SASE. Writers submit ideas on index cards along with SASE. Be sure to study company's line first.

PORTAL PUBLICATIONS, 21 Tamal Vista Blvd., Corte Madera, CA 94925,
Positions: Freelance writers. Company produces greeting cards especially for young adult working women.
Requirements: Study the line first and send for market guidelines. Then submit verses on index cards in small batches with SASE.

PROFESSIONAL MARINER, 55 John Street, New York, NY 10038.
Positions: Freelance writers/stringers produce most of the articles on marine subjects for this magazine.
Requirements: Send sample ideas along with clips of previously published work. Must have some particular knowledge of marine subjects.

RAINBOW WORLD CARDS, 6247 W. 74th St. #2002, Bedford Park, IL 60499.
Positions: Freelance designers and illustrators for contemporary greeting cards.
Requirements: Send for market guidelines first. Then send samples along with resume.

RECYCLED PAPER PRODUCTS, INC., 3636 N. Broadway, Chicago, IL 60613.
Positions: Freelance artists and calligraphers. Company produces greeting cards and other stationery items.
Requirements: Submit samples and letter of interest. Guidelines are available for SASE.

RED FARM STUDIO, P.O. Box 347, 334 Pleasant St., Pawtucket, RI 02862.
Positions: Writers and artists. Company produces greeting cards, gift wrap, and note papers. Artwork used is mostly watercolor.
Requirements: Send for a current market list; include a business size SASE. Then send letter of interest with work samples.
Provisions: Writers are paid by the line. Artists' pay varies depending on the situation.

REED STARLINE CARD COMPANY, P.O. Box 2368, Lake Arrowhead, CA 92352.
Positions: Artists and writers for work involved in the production and promotion of greeting cards. 100% of all work is done by freelancers on assignment basis only.
Requirements: To be considered for any of the hundreds of project assignments each year, start by sending for company guidelines and market list; include SASE with request. Then send samples of your style with SASE. Include business card which will be kept on file for future assignments.

REGIONAL GRAPHICS, P.O. Box 47033, St. Petersburg, FL 33743.
Positions: Freelance artists are used to design Christmas cards.
Requirements: Send photos or slides only along with resume.

REMIGRAPHICS, P.O. Box 171, Oak Park, IL 60303.
Positions: This company makes custom designed cards and paper products. Freelance artists are used for design and illustration.
Requirements: Experience is a must. To be considered, send samples and resume. They will be kept on file.

RENAISSANCE GREETING CARDS, P.O. Box 845, Springvale, ME 04083.
Positions: Writers and artists for all occasion and Christmas cards.
Requirements: Writers send verse ideas; especially likes humorous verse. Include ideas for design. Artists send samples of full color work in batches of a dozen; include resume. Prefers bright cartoons. Guidelines are available. Be sure to include SASE with your request.

ROUSANA CARDS, 25 Madison Ave., Clifton,, NJ 07011.
Positions: Writers and artists for everyday and seasonal cards.
Requirements: Works only with established greeting card designers. Submit work samples with resume and/or tear sheets.

SAN FRANCISCO BAY GUARDIAN, 2700 19th St., San Francisco, CA 94110.
Positions: Freelance writers produce over half of the contents of this alternative news weekly.
Requirements: Only previously published Bay Area writers will be considered. Especially interested in investigative reporters. Send query with clips of previously published work.

SANGAMON COMPANY, Route 48 West, Taylorville, IL 62558.
Positions: Writers and artists for greeting card and gift wrap design.
Requirements: Writers should submit verses with SASE included. Artists submit finished art or color sketches.

SAWYER CAMERA & INSTRUMENT COMPANY, 1208 Isabel St., Burbank, CA 91506.
Positions: Freelance photographers work on assignment for this multimedia ad agency.
Requirements: Local photographers only. Must have experience in multimedia production. Submit resume, business card, and tear sheets.
Provisions: Pays by the project..

SECRETARY SUPREME, 3008 Spaulding Ave., Baltimore, MD 21215.
Positions: Graphic artists.

Requirements: Must be qualified with verifiable experience and skill. Local residents only mail resumes.

SEYBOLD CONSULTING GROUP, INC., 148 State Street, Suite 612, Boston, MA 02109.
Positions: Independent writers are contracted by the year to write stories from evaluation reports of automated office systems and software. Company publishes 35 to 40 reports each month on UNIX and Office systems.
Requirements: Experience and references are required. Send letter of interest with work samples. Prefers to work with writers in Boston.
Provisions: Pay is worked out on an individual contract basis.

SHULSINGER SALES, INC., 50 Washington St., Brooklyn, NY 11201.
Positions: Freelance artists design greeting cards and gift wrap with Jewish themes.
Requirements: Submit work samples and resume.

ST. MARTIN'S PRESS, 175 Fifth Ave., New York, NY 10010
Positions: Freelance copy editors.
Requirements: Must be computer literate and experienced. New York residents only.
Provisions: Apply by sending resume to the managing editor, trade division.

SUNRISE PUBLICATIONS, INC., P.O. Box 4699, Bloomington, IN 47402.
Positions: Writers and artists for production of greeting cards.
Requirements: First, send for Sunrise's Creative Guidelines and current market list. Then send letter of interest with work samples. Include SASE.
Provisions: Payment varies..

SUPPORT OUR SYSTEMS (SOS), 1 W. Front St., 3rd Fl., Red Bank, NJ 07701.
Positions: SOS has a pool of over 60 home-based technical writers that produce user guides for computer systems at large companies.
Requirements: Experience and top skills are a must. You will be tested before starting work for your writing ability and study habits. You must own a computer and a modem and have the ability to communicate electronically by several means. Although your schedule is your own, you will be required to check in with the company several times a day.

SYNDICATION ASSOCIATES, INC., P.O. Box 400, Jenks, OK 74037.
Positions: This company sells patterns and plans for fabric, craft, and woodworking projects through newspaper syndication which amounts to a potential readership base of a whopping 34 million. Submissions of new, original, and unpublished designs are accepted.
Requirements: Send for submission instructions.
Provisions: Payment for accepted material is worked out on an individual basis for either lump sum payment in advance and/or royalties.

TAVERNON PHOTO ENGRAVING COMPANY, 27 First Ave., Paterson, NJ 07514.
Positions: Company makes silk screens for wallpaper and fabric. Hand work consists of color separation of textile designs. Freelance artists do all the design work.
Requirements: Must live in Paterson in order to pick up and deliver supplies and finished work. Experience is required.
Provisions: Pay depends on the colors and intricacy of the design.

TAYLOR CORPORATION, P.O. Box 3728, North Mankato, MN 56002.
Positions: Freelance artists are used to design wedding invitations.
Requirements: Send samples of work to be kept on file.

TLC GREETINGS, 615 McCall Road, Manhattan, KS 66502.
Positions: Freelance writers are used by this manufacturer of humorous greeting cards.
Requirements: Study the line first, then submit sample verses.

TURNROTH SIGN COMPANY, 1207 East Rock Falls Road, Rock Falls, IL 61071.
Positions: Freelance artists design billboards and other kinds of signs on assignment.
Requirements: Submit letter of interest with sketches or finished work samples. Include SASE with all correspondence.
Provisions: Pays flat rates for each project.

"Talented new writers are especially sought."
—Warner Press, Inc.

UNIVERSITY OF NEW HAVEN, 300 Orange Ave., Public Relations Department, West Haven, CT 06516.
Positions: Freelance photographers take shots of campus life, working on assignment basis only. Work is used in all sorts of PR presentations.
Requirements: Send letter of interest along with resume and at least one sample shot to be kept on file. Include SASE and business card. You will be contacted for an interview. Be ready with a portfolio. Local photographers only.
Provisions: Pays by the hour at a minimum of $20.

UNIX, MULTIUSER, MULTITASKING SYSTEM, Tech Valley Publishing, 444 Castro St., Mountain View, CA 94041.
Positions: Freelance writers work on assignment for this monthly magazine.
Requirements: Must have thorough knowledge of this end of the computer industry. Send query along with clips of previously published work.
Provisions: Pays for articles on acceptance. Sometimes pays expenses.

U.S. ALLEGIANCE, INC., P.O. Box 12000, Eugene, OR 97401.
Positions: This company makes greeting cards and post cards for the military market only. Both freelance artists and writers are used.
Requirements: Artists send photocopies of work to establish style.

WARNER PRESS, INC., Box 2499, Anderson, IN 46018.
Positions: Writers and artists for work on greeting cards, calendars, posters, postcards, and plaques. Artists work on assignment. Writers are freelance.
Requirements: Before applying, write for current market list and guidelines. Include SASE. Be sure to study company's style before sending samples. Talented new artists are especially sought.
Provisions: Pay varies.

WILDER LIMITED, P.O. Box 8367, Universal City, CA 91608.
Positions: Silkscreen artists, calligraphers, and translators. Company produces children's wallhangings.
Requirements: Experience is required. Send letter of interest; state fee desired.
Provisions: Pays by the job.

OPPORTUNITIES IN CRAFTS

A craft is any occupation that requires manual dexterity or artistic skill. In this section, you'll find quite a few crafts represented--jewelry making, macrame, knitting, embroidery and merrowing, sewing, and silkscreen among others.

Knitting is one of the original seven industries that was banned from using home workers in 1938 under the Fair Labor Standards Act. The ban was lifted on knitting alone in December of 1985, after many years of struggling in the courts. Now there are dozens of companies that are certified by the U.S. Dept. of Labor to hire home workers. Most of these companies are based in New England, where home knitting has been a traditional occupation for generations.

Most knitting is still done by hand, but knitting machines are being used in increasing numbers. As you can imagine, using a knitting machine speeds up the process and allows the knitter to make more clothing and therefore more money.

Sewing is among the remaining six industries that are still banned from using home workers. Actually, only certain types of sewing are banned and most have to do with women's and children's apparel. That doesn't mean there isn't any home sewing going on. There are tens of thousands of home sewers across the country, but most are working "underground." The companies listed here are all located in states with labor laws that allow home sewing under specific certification procedures. (State labor laws supercede federal laws.) Unfortunately, in March of 1991, New Jersey reversed its longstanding tolerance of home work in ladies apparel. Now any home work involved in the manufacture of ladies apparel is outlawed. That meant dropping over 40 employers from this edition!

Sewing is a skill that most women learn to some extent, but that doesn't mean that every woman is qualified to be a professional home sewer. Most home sewing is specialized so that each sewer works on a particular type of garment or, in many cases, a particular piece of garment. Employers have indicated that it isn't easy finding workers who are capable of doing quality work.

No matter what kind of craft you want to do, in order to get a job you will have to show samples of your work in order to prove that you have the necessary skills. There are a few situations mentioned in the following pages that offer training to inexperienced people, but these are the exceptions to the rule.

ADLER & YORK, 7831 West 1st Avenue, Lakewood, CO 80226.
Positions: Embroidery. There are virtually no opportunities here; the program has dwindled to one home worker.
Requirements: Must be local resident and be skilled.

C. M. ALMY & SONS, INC., Ruth Road, Pittsfield, ME 04967.
Positions: Embroidery. There are virtually no opportunities here; the program has dwindled to one home worker.
Requirements: Must be local resident and be skilled.

AMERICAN GLOVE CO. INC., P.O. Box 51, Lyerly, GA 30730
Positions: Home manufacture of work gloves. There are currently 34 home workers.
Requirements: Must be local resident and be skilled.

AMSTER NOVELTY COMPANY, INC., 75-13 - 71ST Ave., Middle Village, NY 11375.
Positions: Sewing, trimming, stringing, and other hand work involved in the manufacture of soft tote bags, pouches for cosmetics , and decorations (bows and appliques) for little girls' dresses. Currently has about 100 home workers.
Requirements: No experience is necessary. Must be local resident.
Provisions: Pays piece rates.

ANDREA STRONGWATER DESIGNS, 465 West End Ave., Manhattan, NY 10024.
Positions: Home-based knitting of outerwear.
Requirements: Must be local resident and be skilled.

ATLAS MFG. CO., INC., 5511 Resthome Rd., Claremont, NC 28610.
Positions: Home-based stitchers produce gloves. There are currently 8 home workers.
Requirements: Must be local resident.

BARRY MANUFACTURING COMPANY, INC., Bubier St., Lynn, MA 01901.
Positions: Stitching and hand assembly of infant and children's shoe parts.
Requirements: Experience is required.. Must be local resident.
Provisions: Some of the work requires machinery, which is supplied by the employer. Pays piece rates equal to minimum wage, which is the same in-house workers are paid for the same work.

BERLIN GLOVES CO., 150 W. Franklin, PO Box 230, Berlin, WI 54923-0230.
Positions: Home stitchers manufacture gloves. Currently there are 18 home workers.
Requirements: Must be local resident and be skilled.

BLUEBERRY WOOLENS, P.O. Box 318 Randall St., Anson, ME 04911.
Positions: Machine knitting of whole sweaters for wholesaler. This is an established and growing company with close to $1 million in annual sales. Currently has a pool of 60 knitters.
Requirements: Enrollment in company's training classes and submission of acceptable samples is required. Must own a knitting machine or purchase one from the company. Must be local in order to pick up and deliver supplies and finished sweaters.
Provisions: Pays per finished sweater. Hours can be full time or part time. Workers are independent contractors. Inquiries are welcome as company continues to grow.

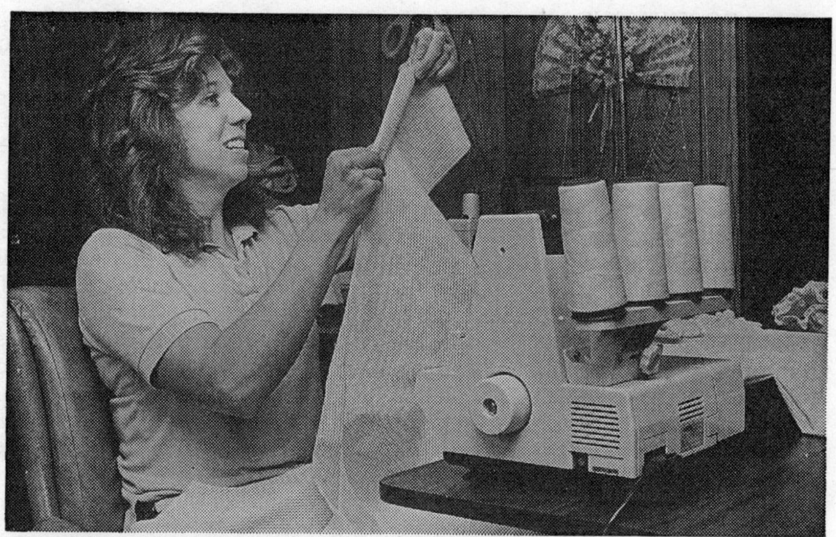

Janet Nagel sews at her home for Boston-based Rocking Horse clothing store for children. Photo courtesy of The Salt Lake Tribune.

BORDEAUX, INC., 102 East Washington Street, Clarinda, IA 51632

Bordeaux has over 150 home workers sewing appliques onto ladies' sportswear, mostly sweatsuits. The company was started by Bertha Turner and her two partners six years ago. Since then, the company has grown to a $3.5 million a year business. Clarinda is in an economically depressed farm community. All of the home workers are farm wives (or ex-farm wives). Each day, a van delivers work to farmhouses up to 50 miles away from headquarters. Each seamstress is considered by Bordeaux to be an independent contractor and is paid piece rates. Unfortunately, this independent contractor status is being challenged in court by the U.S. Department of Labor at the insistence of the Ladies' Garment Workers Union. Unfortunate, because if Bordeaux loses, all work will have to be conducted in a factory. Not only is the idea of working in a factory dismal, but most of the workers will not be able to commute and will simply lose their jobs. Bertha Turner says all applications for home work are on hold until the matter is resolved.

BRC INTERNATIONAL, INC., 7760 W. 20th Ave., Bay #5, Miami, FL 33016.
Positions: Embroidery. Currently there are 15 home workers.
Requirements: Must be local resident and be skilled.

BRYSTIE, INC., P.O. Box 1106, Mountain Rd., Stowe, VT 05672.
Positions: Home-based knitters produce outerwear. Currently there are 115 home workers.
Requirements: Must be local resident.

CARBAREE, 4904 Briar Grove, Dallas, TX 75287.
Positions: This company uses home-based knitters to produce outerwear. This is a small operation with only 4 home workers at present.
Requirements: Must be local resident.

CHICAGO KNITTING MILLS, 3344 West Montrose Ave., Chicago, IL 60618.
Positions: Home-based sewing of emblems onto outerwear. Currently there are no openings available.
Requirements: Must be local resident and be skilled. Must obtain a home workers certificate from Illinois Department of Labor.

CHIPITA ACCESSORIES, P.O. Box 1250, Walsenburg, CO 81089.
Positions: Between 75 and 250 home workers handcraft jewelry using beads, stones, semi-precious stones, silver, crystal, and gold. The number of home workers fluctuates with the time of year, number of orders, and number of available workers in this rural area in southern Colorado. Walsenburg is, like most rural areas, economically depressed, but has a history of handcrafts of all kinds created by local artisans. Chipita started by producing and selling one kind of beaded earrings and grew from there. Home workers here are completely independent, having total control over their hours, how often and when they work, etc. The company will sell kits to workers, will show and attempt to sell from new sample designs for workers, or will buy outright as much jewelry as a worker can produce as long as it meets quality standards. A worker can work part -time or full-time, with the opportunity to earn a "regular income".
Requirements: Must be a local resident. Contact the company with letter of interest.

COUNTRY CRAFTS, P.O. Box 150, Nashville, IN 48448.
Positions: Jewelry making. Currently there are 12 home workers.
Requirements: Must be local resident.

COUNTRY CURTAINS, INC., Main St., Stockbridge, MA 01262.
Positions: Sewing trim on basic curtains. Currently has about 31 home workers.
Requirements: Need sewing machine. Must be local resident.
Provisions: Pick up and delivery provided. Pays piece rates equal to minimum wage.

COUNTRY SETTLE, THE, 810 Gail Drive, Weatherford, TX 76086.
Positions: Embroidery. Currently the company has 8 home workers.
Requirements: Must be a local resident with experience.

DABEC, INC., 19230-144 Ave., N.E., Suite D, Woodinville, WA 98072.
Positions: Knitting of outerwear. Currently there are 8 home workers here.
Requirements: Must be a local resident and be experienced.

DAINTY MAID MANUFACTURING COMPANY, 12 North St., Fitchburg,MA 10420.
Positions: Sewing aprons.
Requirements: Must be local resident and own sewing machine. Experience is required.
Provisions: Material is supplied. Pays piece rates equal to approximately $4 an hour. Company only has 2 home-based employees; opportunities are extremely limited.

DEER HILL KNITTERS, P.O. Box 25, Weeks Mills, ME 04361.
Positions: Knitting of outerwear. There are 5 home workers at present.
Requirements: Must be local resident with experience.

DEVA CLOTHING COMPANY, a Cottage Industry, Box C, 303 East Main Street, Burkittsville, MD 21718.

Dana Cassell, President
Writer Data Bank

"To make it as a writer, you've got to be competitive. Start by making your manuscript look better. The look of it has a lot to do with whether you get the assignment. It's just like you look and talk, it's the image that sticks.

"If you have no specific field, try a little bit of everything until you find your niche. Look for the field where you are getting the highest ratio of return from query letters, then sales, and so on...One writer I know makes $50,000 a year in the medical field."

Positions: DEVA has been using the cottage industry method for producing unisex, natural fiber apparel for 10 years. About two dozen local stitchers work as true independent contractors; they work on their own equipment, set their own prices, set their own production schedules, etc. Since the company's philosophy is based upon quality, only quality workers remain. "More of our stitchers wash out for not being businesslike. It is hard for them to get organized working at home. They need discipline and they have to find it for themselves without the structure of the factory."

LEE ENGLAND, 27 Alta St., San Francisco, CA 94133.
Positions: Sewing, bead stringers and hand knitters for jewelry designer. All positions are on an independent contractor basis. Number of worker depends upon orders, season, etc. Averages more than 10. Company was much larger in the past, but it has been reduced to "a more manageable size with creativity the primary emphasis."
Requirements: Sewing requires experience with fine and antique fabrics and trims for high-fashion evening jackets. Sewing machine required. Stringers need no experience. Knitters do need experience. Must be local resident.
Provisions: Limited training available. Pick up and delivery provided only if necessary. Pay rates per production based upon difficulty of project.

EWE FIRST, 2081 Meeting Street, Hennepin, MN 55391.
Positions: Home knitters produce outerwear. There are no openings at the present time.
Requirements: Must be local resident and be skilled.

FIT-RITE HEADWEAR, INC., 92 South Empire Street, Wilkes-Barre, PA 18702
Positions: About a dozen home workers sew industrial headwear.
Requirements: Must be local resident. Must qualify as Pennsylvania industrial home worker (be either disabled or need to care for invalid family member).
Provisions: Pays piece rates.

FRENCH CREEK SHEEP AND WOOL COMPANY, INC., Route 345, R.D. #1, Elverson, PA 19520.

Positions: Knitting sweaters on hand operated machines. Currently has about 40 workers.
Requirements: Must be local resident in order to pick up and deliver supplies and finished sweaters.
Provisions: Some training, specific to the work here, is provided. Pays production rate, which is "well above minimum wage."

GATER SPORTS, 3565 SW Temple, Suite 5, Salt Lake City, UT 84115
Positions: Sewing cold weather sports accessories, socks, face protectors, eyeglass cases, etc. Currently uses 25 to 50 home workers.
Requirements: Need some sewing experience and own sewing machine. Must be local resident in order to pick up and deliver supplies and finished work.
Provisions: Will train for specifics of the job. Pays piece rates. Workers are independent contractors. At this time, most of the available work fluctuates seasonally, but the company is growing and hopes to be able to offer full-time, year-round work in the near future.

ESTELLE GRACER, INC., 950 West Hatcher Rd., Phoenix, AZ 85021.
Positions: Knitting and crocheting jackets and sweaters. Work has previously been done by hand only, but company is now going into machine knitting. Currently has over 50 home workers; that number fluctuates up to 200. "Inquiries are always welcome."
Requirements: Must be experienced. Phoenix residents only.
Provisions: Specific training is provided. Home workers are full employees. Pays for production.

HEADLINER HAIRPIECES, INC., 1532 N. Highland Ave., Los Angeles, CA 90028.
Positions: Hand sewing and assembly of hairpieces.
Requirements: Must live nearby and have specific experience with this kind of work.
Provisions: Pays piece rates equal to about $5 an hour.

HOMESTEAD HANDCRAFTS, North 1301 Pines Rd., Spokane, WA 92206.
Positions: Company markets quality handcrafts with a country theme such as tole painting. Different situations are worked out on an individual basis.
Requirements: Must live in Spokane.

INDIAN JEWELERS SUPPLY, 220 Altez SE, Bernalille, NM 87123.
Positions: Jewelry making. There are currently 7 home workers.
Requirements: Must be local resident.

K-C PRODUCTS, 1600 East 6th Street, Los Angeles, CA 90023.
Positions: Sewing vinyl travel bags, garment bags, mattress covers, and appliance covers. Up to 16 home workers are employed.
Requirements: Need ordinary sewing machine. Must live nearby.
Provisions: Pays piece rates.

K. COMPANY, 2155 Verdugo Blvd., #601, Montrose, CA 91020.
Positions: K. Company is a costume jewelry "manufacturer" that retails both from a storefront and through craft shows in Los Angeles. Uses bead workers.
Requirements: Prefers someone who is dependable and willing to make a minimum commitment of six months. About $50 worth of small tools will be required. Prefers someone with some kind of handcraft experience. Must live in the West Valley in order

to pick up and deliver inventory and supplies.
Provisions: Training will be provided and owner Kim Bovino says the training is very valuable and can be transferred to other companies upon leaving K. Company. The work is part-time, on-call as orders come in. Pays piece rates.

KIRSTEN SCARCELLI, 9 Union St., Hallowell, ME 04347.
Positions: Knitting of outerwear. Currently there are 11 home workers.
Requirements: Must be local resident. Must be skilled.

KNIT PICKEN, RFD #1, Box 1517, Rt. 11, Casco, ME 04015.
Positions: Hand knitting outerwear. There are only 3 home workers a present.
Requirements: Must be local resident.

LEHUA HAWAII, INC., 1001 Dillingham, Suite 319, Honolulu, HI 96817.
Positions: Productions sewing of mu-mus, dresses, bras, and shirts.
Requirements: Must be experienced and own sewing interlocking sewing machine. Must be an in-house employee prior to moving work home. Local residents only.
Provisions: Pays hourly wages.

LEISURE ARTS, INC., P.O. Box 5595, Little Rock, AR 72212.
Positions: Knitting of outerwear. Currently there are 177 home workers.
Requirements: Must be local resident with experience.

LIVING EARTH CRAFTS, 600 E. Todd Rd., Santa Rosa, CA 95407.
Positions: Production of several types of crafts. Most work consists of sewing bags, vinyl pieces, sheets, blankets and pad covers.
Requirements: Must own sewing machine. Must live in Santa Rosa. Experience is required.
Provisions: Materials are supplied. Workers are considered regular employees with medical and dental insurance, paid holidays and sick leave. Pays piece rates equal to an average of $8 an hour. Applications are kept on file indefinitely.

LUCINDA, INC., 80 Second Street, Portland, ME 04106.
Positions: Knitting of outerwear. There are 20 home workers at present.
Requirements: Must be local resident.

MAINE BRAND MFG., INC., P.O. Box 860, Houton, ME 04730
Positions: Stitching of gloves. There are currently 6 home workers.
Requirements: Must be local resident and be skilled.

MAINE MAD HATTER, RFD # 1, Box 790, Augusta, ME 04330.
Positions: Knitting of ski hats. There are currently 24 home workers.
Requirements: Must be local resident and be skilled.

MANDALA DESIGNS, RFD #1, Box 480, Starks, ME 04911.

Positions: Machine knitting of woolen outerwear including sweaters, jackets, socks, scarves, and hats.
Requirements: Prefers local knitters. Must be experienced and own knitting machine.
Provisions: Provides supplies and patterns. Pays piece rates.

MC DESIGNS, 115 Altura Way, Greenbrae, CA 94904.
Positions: Hand knitters are used by sweater designer.
Requirements: Must be local resident. Professional level experience required. Apply with resume only.
Provisions: Pays piece rates.

MORIARTIE'S HATS AND SWEATERS, P.O. Box 1117, Stowe, VT 05676.
Positions: Mrs. Moriartie started this company in the late '50's when she handknitted a hat for her son and almost single-handedly launched the New England home knitting industry as it is today. Moriartie's has a reputation for being the best hat and sweater store in the world. Home knitters make hats, Christmas stockings, ornaments, and sweaters. Work is done on hand-operated machines. Company sells products wholesale as well as retail. Currently has 17 permanent home workers.
Requirements: Must be local resident in order to come in once a week to get supplies. Must own machine.
Provisions: Knitters can select designs, patterns and yarns from stock and make as many or as few items as they like. Can accept custom orders, too. "Each knitter has something they like to do especially and they usually stick to it. Some prefer to knit hats that only take 25 minutes to complete. Others prefer sweaters that take much longer. It's up to them." Pays piece rates.

MOUNTAINSIDE INDUSTRIES, INC., 838 Cliff St., P.O. Box 181, Shamokin, PA 17872.
Positions: Sewing of double drawstring pouches.
Requirements: Must be local resident. Must qualify as Pennsylvania industrial home worker (be either disabled or need to care for invalid family member).
Provisions: Pays piece rates.

MOUNTAIN LADIES & EWE, INC., Box 391 Route 7, Manchester Village, VT 05254.
Positions: Knitters make ski hats and sweaters. Products are sold both retail and wholesale. Currently has 25 permanent home workers.
Requirements: Prefers workers that live within a 60-mile radius of Manchester Village. Must own knitting machine. Pick up and delivery of supplies and finished work is required of each knitter.
Provisions: Specific training is provided. All supplies are provided.
Pays production rates, but workers are considered regular employees and receive basic benefits provided by law. Inquiries are welcome from qualified applicants.

NEUMA AGINS DESIGN, INC., Main St., Southfield, MA 01105.
Positions: Embroidery of sweaters according to custom orders. Decorations may also be applied. Currently has over 200 home workers.
Requirements: Must have experience and do quality work. Local residents only.
Provisions: Pays about $3.65 an hour.

NORTH OF BOSTON, P.O. Box 879, Stowe, VT 06672.

Positions: Knitting sweaters for wholesale orders. Currently has 32 home workers.
Requirements: Must own knitting machine and live in the area. Workers are required to pick up and deliver supplies and finished work or use the mail for that purpose.
Provisions: Some training is provided. Pays piece rates.

PATTY ANNE, 1212 Crespi Dr., Pacifica, CA 94044.
Positions: This well-established retailer/wholesaler of children's apparel and gifts uses home-bases seamstresses. There are different jobs for different types of machines; appliques, blind hems, etc.
Requirements: Industrial overlock machine is necessary. Experience is required. Must live within reasonable proximity to Pacifica.
Provisions: Pick up and delivery provided. Pays piece rates equal to about $7.50 an hour for an average part-time income of $75 to $100 a week. Work tends to be seasonal.

PENELOPE'S WEB, P.O. Box 308, Anson, ME 04911.
Positions: Knitting of outerwear. There are 12 home workers at present.
Requirements: Must be local resident with good skills.

RUTH HORNBEIN SWEATERS, 377 Flatbush Ave., Brooklyn, NY 11238.
Positions: Knitting of outerwear. Currently there are only 5 home workers.
Requirements: Must be local resident.

SOUTHERN GLOVE MFG. CO., INC., Highway 321 South, Conover, NC 28613.
Positions: Stitching of gloves.
Requirements: Must be local resident.

STREAMLINE INDUSTRIES, 234 W. 39th St., New York, NY 10018.
Positions: Hand sewing cloth onto buttons and buckles. Company employs up to 6 homeworkers.
Requirements: Must live nearby.
Provisions: Pays piece rates.

TOMORROW TODAY CORPORATION, P.O. Box 6125, Westfield, MA 01085.
Positions: Hand work consists of tying bows and working with flowers to make decorations. Currently has 23 home workers.
Requirements: Must live in Westfield.
Provisions: Pays minimum wage.

TOP NOTCH KNITS, 14929 N.E. 40th St., Redmond, WA 98052.
Positions: Knitting and sewing of complete garments. Currently has 18 home workers.
Requirements: Must own knitting machine (any type is okay). Will only accept applications from experienced local residents.
Provisions: Pick up and delivery of supplies and finished work is provided. Pays production rates.

UNIQUE 1, P.O. Box 744, 2 Bayview Street, Camden, ME 04843.
Positions: Knitting of sweaters using both wool and cotton yarn for retail shop. Currently has 9 home workers.
Requirements: Must be experienced and be a local resident.
Provisions: Training is provided. If home worker doesn't own a knitting machine, Unique 1 will lease one. Pays piece rates. "Camden is tourist town, so the summer is

the best time for us, especially for custom orders."

VERMONT ORIGINALS, INC., RR2, Box 3554, Hyde Park, VT 05655.
Positions: Knitting of outerwear. Currently there are 9 home workers.
Requirements: Must be local resident with skills and experience.

WAGON WHEEL WESTERN WEAR, 2765 W. Jefferson, Springfield, IL.
Positions: This is a custom shop that has home workers sew together pre-cut pieces.
Requirements: Machinery and experience required. Must be local resident. Must obtain home worker certificate from Illinois Department of Labor.
Provisions: Pays piece rates.

WAIN MANUFACTURING CORPORATION, 589 Essex St., Lynn, MA 01901.
Positions: Stitching and thread trimming of eye glass cases.
Requirements: Must be local resident with experience.
Provisions: Training and machinery are provided. Pays $4 an hour.

WASHINGTON GARTER CORP., 195 Front St., Brooklyn, NY 11201.
Positions: Sewing and hand assembly of ladies garters and men's suspenders. Up to 35 home workers are employed.
Requirements: Must live nearby and be experienced.
Provisions: Pays piece rates.

WEST HILL WEAVERS, Box 108, Stowe, VT 05672.
Positions: Knitting and sewing of outerwear. Also some handwoven clothing and crafts. Currently has about 30 home workers located all over the state.
Requirements: Must own and have full knowledge of proper machinery. Pick up and delivery of supplies and finished work is the responsibility of the home worker; therefore must be local.
Provisions: Training for particular designs is provided. Pays piece rates. Inquiries are welcome.
"When we're hiring, we're hiring. Otherwise we will keep your name on file for future work."

WIRTH MANUFACTURING CO., INC., 335 Hamilton St., Allentown, PA 18101.
Positions: Sewing of children's tops.
Requirements: Must be local resident. Must qualify as Pennsylvania industrial home worker (be either disabled or need to care for invalid family member.)
Provisions: Sewing machines are provided. Pays piece rates.

WOOLENS 'N' THINGS, 175 Vine Street, Barre, VT 05672.
Positions: Knitting of outerwear. Currently has 7 home workers.
Requirements: Must be local resident.

ZAUDER BROTHERS, INC., 10 Henry St., Freeport, NY 11520.
Positions: Hand work involved in the manufacture of wigs, toupes, and theatrical makeup. Up to eight home workers are employed here.
Requirements: Must have specific experience with this kind of work. Must be local resident.

COMPUTER-RELATED OPPORTUNITIES

This section includes any situation that requires a computer to get the job done. This doesn't necessarily mean that you must own your own equipment. In the case of typesetting input, for example, many companies provide computer terminals to their home keyers. On the other hand, a contract programmer not only needs to own a computer, but often several different computers.

By its nature, computerized work generally pays more than office work that is done on conventional typewriters. Therefore, if you are a very good typist, you may find it to your advantage to transfer your typing skills to the computer keyboard. Word processors are in great demand to handle assignments from small businesses and huge corporations alike. It'll take a few months to get the hang of it all; the computer itself, the software, and the printer. There are classes available at most community colleges and vocational schools. If you're sharp, you can get paid while you learn by signing on with a temporary help agency. Kelly Services and Manpower, to name just two, have excellent training programs-including cross-training on different systems-available to anyone who is on the roster and available for work.

Experienced typists with exceptional accuracy can make money by becoming a typesetting input operator. Typesetting is a job that was done on very expensive equipment in composition shops before the personal computer came along. Now it is common for home-based operators to do the job at home by typing material into the computer and embedding code into the text that will instruct the shop's specialized printer to use certain fonts, type size or style, and special characters. Most shops have their own special code and train typists in how to use it. It is most common for typesetters that handle books (rather than advertising or brochures) to use home keyers. Typesetting input operators are paid for each character typed and average earnings run from $10 to $25 an hour.

Contract programmers will find the field a little crowded these days. There is still a lot of work in converting programs to run on different computers than they were written for, but that work will soon disappear. Computers are being programmed to do the conversions automatically. Writing programs to specifications pays better, but only very experienced programmers get this work. The key to getting work as a programmer is to continue learning about languages, compilers, and systems design. Employers like programmers who are enthusiastic about what the company is doing, pay attention to deadlines, document their work properly, and submit bug-free programs.

A TO Z SERVICES, INC., 939 East Schuylkill Rd., Pottstown, PA 19464.
Positions: Data entry and computer run-offs.
Requirements: Equipment and experience required. Local residents only send resume.

AASCO BUSINESS SERVICES, INC., 1313 Old Timber Lane, Hoffman Estates, IL 60195.
Positions: Desktop publishing.
Requirements: Must be very familiar with basic skills and know how to use Ventura 2.0 on an intermediate level. Only reasonably local people considered. Send resume.
Provisions: Will not be top dollar due to client payments.

ABILITY GROUP, 1730 Rhode Island Ave., NW, Ste. 704, Washington, DC 20036.
Positions: Word processing specializing in transcription of medical, legal and verbatim tapes. Occasional assignments are mostly overflow.
Requirements: Must be local resident. Word processing equipment is required. Any major word processing software is okay as long as it is IBM compatible so that it can be converted. Experienced professionals only.

ACADEMY SOFTWARE, Box 6277, San Rafael, CA 94903.
Positions: Contract programmers and technical writers. Contract programmers are used for conversions. Also buys unique educational software from freelancers. Some original programming to company specifications available. Technical writers work on user manuals.
Requirements: Must be local resident. Extensive experience required.
Provisions: Payment for both positions can be by the job, by the hour, or on a royalty basis. Credit is given to both in most cases.

ADDISON-WESLEY PUBLISHING CO., Jacob Way, Reading, MA 01867.
Positions: Contract programmers. Company publishes over 100 programs for IBM and Macintosh. Freelance programmers can submit educational programs for consideration or seek assignments in conversions or original programming to company guidelines.
Requirements: Send resume indicating particular expertise and equipment availability and knowledge.
Provisions: Assignments pay by the project.

ADVANCED AUTOMATION ASSOC., 26 Alpha Rd., Chelmsford, MA 01824.
Positions: About 9 home-based keyboarders input data for this data management service.

ALPHA MICROSYSTEMS, 3501 Sunflower, Box 25059, Santa Ana, CA 92799.
Positions: Contract programmers for Alpha Micro computers only. Contracts include vertical applications in specific business areas.
Requirements: Resume and references required.

ALPHA PRESENTATIONS, 5405 Ahon Parkway 5A433, Irvine, CA 92714.
Positions: Typesetting.
Requirements: Must have Mac computer with Quark Express and Pagemaker for advanced graphic layouts, design and typesetting. Prepare for quick turnover. Local residents mail resume.

ALTERNATE SOURCE, 704 North Pennsylvania, Lansing, MI 48906.

Positions: Contract programmers. Company seeks submissions of vertical applications software for any DOS computer. Submissions must include complete documentation and be bug-free.
Requirements: Send letter of interest that describes finished software. Guidelines are available for SASE.
Provisions: Pays 20% royalties.

AMERICAN EXPRESS BANK, LTD., American Express Plaza, New York, NY 10004.
Positions: Word processors.
Requirements: Must be local, physically handicapped and disabled. Job requires transcription skills.
Provisions: Complete training is provided. Equipment provided includes Wang word processing terminals, Lanier central dictation system, and Exxon telecopier. Telephone lines link the home work station to company headquarters on Wall Street. A company supervisor can dictate into the system from anywhere; likewise a home worker is able to access the system any time 24 hours a day to transcribe the dictation. The finished product in hard copy form is then sent back to headquarters via the telecopier. All activity is identified and monitored through the Control Center. "Project Homebound" currently has 10 full-time regular employees of American Express.

AMERICAN STRATFORD, Putney, Box 810, Brattleboro, VT 05301.
Positions: Typesetting input operators. Currently has 14 home keyers.
Requirements: Must be local resident. Must own computer and be competent word processor.

APPALACHIAN COMPUTER SERVICES, Highway 25 South, P.O. Box 140, London, KY 40741.
Positions: Appalachian Computer Services is among a growing number of service bureaus that has solved the problem of stabilizing workflow with a home work program. The initial pool of cottage keyers was formed out of former in-house employees. Most of them had left their jobs because they needed to be at home with their families. The program accomplished what it was supposed to. The workflow went smoothly, the keyers were happy with the arrangement (no one dropped out), and the company overhead fell. Now that Appalachian Computer Services is sure the home work program is the solution they've been looking for, plans are underway to expand the program to an ultimate goal of 200 home keyers. These additional workers will be hired from outside the company.
Requirements: Since there are no telecommunications available, all recruiting will have to be done within the township of London. The only requirement will be a typing speed of 45 wpm. Experienced applicants will spend two days in-house learning to use the Multitech PC. Those with no experience in data entry will spend an additional 3 days in the company's standard training program. There is no pay for time spent in training. Each worker goes into the office to pick up the work and receive instructions. When the job is finished, he or she returns the work on disks (which are provided).
Provisions: The cottage keyers are all treated as part-time employees, not independent contractors. Each works a minimum of 20 hours a week. No one works over 30 hours a week at any time so the part-time status remains intact. There are no benefits due to this part-time status, however, the company is looking into ways of providing some benefits as the program progresses. In the meantime, there are production bonuses offered in addition to the guaranteed hourly wage. The equipment, Multitech PCs, are

provided at no charge.

AQUARIUS PEOPLE MATERIALS, INC., Box 128, Indian Rocks Beach, FL 34635.
Positions: Contract programmers. Company publishes educational software for all grade levels. Original programs will be considered for publication. Contracts are available for conversions.
Requirements: Must be very experienced with IBM equipment.

ARTSCI, INC., P.O. Box 1848, Burbank, CA 91505.
Positions: Contract programmers to translate programs between IBM and Macintosh systems. Programmer's guidelines are available only to those who send acceptable resumes.
Requirements: Resume and references required.
Provisions: Pays by the project.

ARTWORX SOFTWARE COMPANY, 1844 Penfield Rd., Penfield, New York 14526.
Positions: Programmers are contracted to do conversions from other computers to major brand computers.
Requirements: Resume, work samples, and references required.
Provision: Pays by the job.

ATC SOFTWARE, 804 Jordon Lane, Huntsville, AL 35816.
Positions: Contract programmers. Original programs are considered for publication; any type of business application software IBM computers. Also assigns contracts for programming. There are programmers guides for coding available for each language for $20 each.
Requirements: Extensive knowledge and experience required. Resume and references required.
Provisions: Pay methods vary.

AWARD SOFTWARE, 777 E. Middlefield Rd., Mountain View, CA 94043.
Positions: Contract programmers write data management programs to company specifications.
Requirements: Prefers local programmers. Must have extensive knowledge. Submit resume and references.
Provisions: Pay methods vary according to project.

BI-TECH ENTERPRISES, INC., 10 Carlough Road, Bohemia, NY 11716.
Positions: Contract programmers write communications and database software according to company specifications for IBM computers.
Requirements: Must be local resident. Extensive experience required. Submit resume and references.
Provisions: Pays by the project.

BLACK DOT, INC., 6115 Official Road, Crystal Lake IL 60014.
Positions: Typesetting input operators. Company has a very long waiting list.
Requirements: All operators are independent contractors and own their own equipment. Previous typesetting experience is required. Local residents only.

BLUE CROSS/BLUE SHIELD OF MARYLAND, 1946 Greenspring Drive, Timonium, MD 21093.
Positions: Cottage keyers (data entry operators) for coding health forms.
Requirements: Local residents only. Considerable experience is required.
Provisions: Part-time work only; partial benefits.

BLUE CROSS/BLUE SHIELD OF SOUTH CAROLINA, Columbia, SC 29219.
Positions: Local cottage keyers (data entry operators) for coding health claims. Full-time, 8-hour days. Openings are offered first to in-house employees, who are preferred for their company experience, but will also hire from outside applicants. Prefers to train in-house for 6 to 12 months if possible. Currently has over 100 workers.
Requirements: Must live in the area.
Provisions: Pays by the line on computer. Training and equipment (including computer and modem) is provided. Home workers are considered part-timers and receive virtually no benefits; employer/employee relations are excellent, however, and the program is considered by all parties concerned to be very successful. Inquires are welcome, but you should expect to be put on a waiting list.

BOYD PRINTING COMPANY, INC., 49 Sheridan Avenue, Albany, NY 12210.
Positions: Typesetting input operators.
Requirements: Must be local resident. Experienced operators with own equipment only.
Provisions: Pays by the word.

BRAUN-BRUMFIELD, INC., 100 North Staebler Rd., Ann Arbor, MI 48106.
Positions: Typesetting input operators for book typography.
Requirements: Local residents only. Experience and equipment required.
Provisions: Pays by the keystroke.

BREAKTHROUGH TECHNOLOGY, 88 Sunnyside Blvd., Plainview, NY 11803.
Positions: Software design.
Requirements: Must be qualified with solid background. Send resume.

B/T COMPUTING CORPORATION, Box 1465, Euless, TX 76039.
Positions: Contract programmers. Company publishes business software for Macintosh.
Requirements: Thorough knowledge of Macintosh and Assembly language programming. Submit resume, work samples, and references.
Provisions: Pays royalties.

BUREAU OF OFFICE SERVICES, INC., 361 S. Frontage Road, Ste 125, Bfurr Ridge, IL 60521.
Positions: About 55 home-based workers do transcription and word processing for both general and medical work.
Requirements: Must have PC and be experienced. Local residents only.
Provisions: Company furnishes all supplies, transcribers, and computer equipment may be rented. Telecommunications has replaced almost all need for pickups and deliveries, but when necessary it is done by company messengers. All homeworkers are employees (not independent contractors) who are paid by production but who also receive benefits.

BUSINESS GRAPHICS, 3314 Baser N.E., Albuquerque, NM 87107.
Positions: Typesetting input operators.
Requirements: Must be local resident. Experience and computer required.

CARLISLE COMMUNICATIONS, 2530 Kerper Blvd., Dubuque, IA 52001.
Positions: Typesetting input operators. Currently has 17 home keyers.
Requirements: Must live in Dubuque in order to pick up and deliver manuscripts and disks. Must be excellent typist with high rate of accuracy.
Provisions: Training and equipment provided. Pays by the character.

CATERED GRAPHICS, 9823 Mason Avenue, Chatsworth, CA 91311.
Positions: Typesetting input operators for book typography.
Requirements: Local residents only. Must be experienced in this business. Must own IBM equipment. Apply with resume.

CENTRAL ILLINOIS LIGHT CO., 300 Liberty St., Peoria, IL 61602.
Positions: Computer programming.
Requirements: Must be local resident with experience and equipment. Apply with resume.

CHECKMATE TECHNOLOGY, INC., P.O. Box 250, Tempe, AZ 85281.
Positions: Contract programmers and technical writers. Company manufactures peripherals such as RAM disks and memory cards for the Apple IIE series, Macintosh, and IBM. Software is needed by company to enhance marketability of programs written to company specifications and also for conversion from Apple programs to others. Technical writers may be needed for documentation.

CIRCLE GRAPHICS, INC., 7484-K Candlewood Rd., Harmans, MD 21077.
Positions: Typesetting input operators. Company has 12 operators on call.
Requirements: Must be local resident in order to pick up and deliver work. Computer required; any brand okay.
Provisions: Pays by the character. Will train for company code.

COGHILL COMPOSITION COMPANY, 1627 Elmdale Avenue, Richmond, VA 23224.
Positions: Typesetting input operators. Company handles all types of commercial typesetting jobs.
Requirements: Must own IBM compatible and have telecommunications capabilities. Local residents only.
Provisions: Pays by the character.

COMMUNIGRAPHICS, 623 Stewart Ave., Garden City, NY 11530.
Positions: Desktop publishing.
Requirements: Experience working a Mac using Quark Express, Adobe Illustrator, and Photo Shop. Must be local and report in daily. Send resume.

"It's really nice to be able to kick back when I want to. I can go out and mingle with my goats and geese and not worry about work for awhile. It'll get done."
—Paul Farr, Remote Control

COMPANION HEALTHCARE, 300 Arbor Lake Drive, Suite 800, Columbia, MD 29223.
Positions: Medical reviewers.
Requirements: Must be registered nurse and own a personal computer and a modem.
Provisions: Workers are independent contractors but retirement program is available.

COMPUTER CENTRAL CORPORATION, 1 Westbury Square, St. Charles, MO 63301.
Positions: Computer Central has been using home-based data entry operators since 1969. While 20 people do work in the office, about 50 work at home.
Requirements: Must be local resident. Must pick up and deliver own work daily. Must be able to type 60 wpm accurately. Must be able to work five hours a day.
Provisions: A two-day training session is provided to learn the equipment and work procedures. PCs are provided. Social Security and unemployment insurance coverage is provided. Pays piece rates which equals about $4 an hour. There is an opportunity to earn more with production bonuses for fast and accurate keyboarders.

DATA COMMAND, Box 548, Kankakee, IL 60901.
Positions: Contract programming. Company publishes high quality educational programming for the top five computers.
Requirements: Innovative thinking is most important here. New ideas in educational programming are highly sought after. You can merely submit a great idea for a new program or submit a resume and references for possible contract assignments to company specs.

DIRECT DATA, 1215 Francis Dr., Arlington Heights, IL 60005.
Positions: Direct Data utilizes the services of about two dozen independent contractors that they call "professional personal computer operators." The actual work performed

Carolyn Hyde
Blue Cross/Blue Shield of SC

"The best thing about working at home is being able to work my own hours, not being confined to a 9 to 5 job. The pay is better, too. Since I get paid by the line, all I have to do is work more to get paid more. It's nice to get paid for what I do."

includes mostly word processing and desktop publishing.
Requirements: Must be a local resident. Equipment and experience are a must.

DISCWASHER, 4623 Crane St., Long Island City, NY 11101.
Positions: Contract programmers and technical writers. Programming is usually conversion work, but company also assigns programs written to client's specifications. Technical writers are occasionally used for documentation.
Requirements: Must own and have thorough knowledge of IBM and Macintosh. Resume should indicate knowledge and experience with languages and operating systems. Include previous work experience and references.
Provisions: Pays by the job or by the hour.

EDWARDS BROTHERS, INC., 2500 State Street, Ann Arbor, MI 48106.
Positions: Typesetting input operators, proofreaders, and layout for book typography business.
Requirements: Local residents only. Must have necessary skills.
Provisions: Equipment and specific training provided. Home workers are considered company employees.

ELECTRONIC ARTS, 1450 Fashion Island Blvd., San Mateo, CA 94404.
Positions: Contract programmers for conversion work. Also regularly backs talented software developers on original programs. Company mainly produces entertainment software for the home market. Some technical writing is assigned for documentation.
Requirements: Must have experience on equipment owned. Must have fervent interest in company's products. "We look for someone specifically suited to the project."

ELITE SOFTWARE DEVELOPMENT, INC., Drawer 1194, Bryan, TX 77806.
Positions: Contract programmers for program components such as algorythms. Currently has pool of six.

Requirements: Must own and have experience with IBM or clone. Prefers programmers who properly test their work and are capable of writing their own documentation.
Provisions: Generally pays by the hour, total sum not to exceed predetermined amount.

EN FLEUR CORPORATION, 2494 Sun Valley Circle, Silver Spring, MD 20906.
Positions: Contract programmers for program sub-routines.
Requirements: Should own and be extremely familiar with MacIntosh, HP, or IBM. Assembly is the language most often used. Send work samples with resume. All work must be well documented.
Provisions: Pays by the job.

EXSPEEDITE PRINTING SERVICE, 12201 Old Columbia Pike, Silver Spring, MD 20914.
Positions: Typesetting input operators for book typography.
Requirements: Must be local resident in order to pick up and deliver work. Experience and computer equipment required.
Provisions: Work is part-time from overflow. Pays by the character.

FEDERATION OF THE HANDICAPPED, Automated Office Services, 211 West 14th St., 2nd Floor, New York, NY 10011.
Positions: Automated Office Systems is the newest of the Federation's programs for homebound disabled workers. It is similar to the typing/transcription department, except that all workers use computers and telecommunications equipment to perform the work.
Requirements: All positions require evaluation through lengthy interviews and personal counseling. All workers must live in New York City.
Provisions: Automated Office Services provides training in word processing procedures. Computers, telecommunication equipment and a phone-in dictation system are provided. All positions pay piece rates.
Disability insurance counseling is provided.

FIELD COMPANIES INC., 385 Pleasant St., Watertown, MA 02173.
Positions: Data entry operators. Work consists of computer data entry (mostly names and addresses for mail order fulfillment). There are currently 5 home workers.
Requirements: Experience is required. Must be local resident.
Provisions: Equipment and pick up and delivery are provided. Pays piece rates.

FOLLETT LIBRARY BOOK CO., 4506 Northwest Hwy., Crystal Lake, IL 60014.
Positions: Data entry for book wholesaler.
Requirements: Must be local resident with experience. Must obtain home worker certificate from Illinois Department of Labor.

GATEWAY TECHNICAL SERVICES, 11403 Cronridge Dr., Suite 200, Owings Mills, MD 21117.
Positions: Software development.
Requirements: Need solid experience in software development for PC applications written in Fox Pro, CC Plus, Visual Basic, Clipper, and Paradox. Send resume.

GRAPHIC TYPESETTING, 5650 Jillson St., Los Angeles, CA 90040.
Positions: Typesetting input operators for work in textbook typography. Currently has 25 operators working all over the U.S.
Requirements: Must be former employee or come with recommendation from another

book typography firm.

GUILD PRINTING COMPANY, INC., 380 West 38th St., Los Angeles, CA 90037.
Positions: Typesetting input operators for book typography.
Requirements: Must be former in-house employee.

HARD SYSTEMS, 200 Stonehenge Lane, Carle Place, NY 11514.
Positions: This data processing service specializes in keeping inventories for major department stores. More than 600 home-based data processing employees and their managers work throughout Nassau and Suffolk counties.
Requirements: Must live in one of the two counties mentioned. Must own a personal computer. There is a 24-hour turn-around requirement and workers must pick up and return their work to the company if they live in Nassau County or to a manager's home if they live in Suffolk County.
Provisions: Pays piece rates (by the line). Pay ranges from $4.50 to $10 an hour depending on the speed of the individual worker. Managers receive a base salary plus a 10 percent override on workers. This can amount to $10,000 to $15,000 for a 94-day cycle. This work is very seasonal and is therefore not available all the time. The best times to apply are July and August and again in January and February.

THE HOME OFFICE NETWORK, 203 Commack Road, Suite 114, Commack, NY 11725.
The Home Office Network is an organization that provides support, networking, and referrals to home-based business owners and freelance professionals. It offers businesses a free referral hotline to call whenever they are in need of office support, creative or technical services.

The service involves a database of Long Island and New York City companies who have expressed interest in using the services of the professional freelancers and home-based business owners who have registered with the network. At present, over 1,500 members work in over 40 occupational categories, including: word processing, typing, data processing, bookkeeping, accounting, computer consulting and programming, electronics, illustration, writing, and more.

The Home Office Network does not act as an employment agency. When a company needs to hire outside help, they call The Home Office Network for free referrals to members listed in the database.

HRM SOFTWARE, 175 Tompkins Ave., Pleasantville, NY 10570.
Positions: Computer programmers for freelance submissions, computer to computer conversions, and company-directed programming. HRM publishes only interactive home education programs
Requirements: Experience programming on Macintosh or IBM. Freelancers can submit finished programs for consideration. All others submit resume, samples, and references.

IMPRESSIONS, INC., P.O. Box 3304, Madison, WI 53704.
Positions: Typesetting input operators for book typography.
Requirements: Local residents only. Excellent keyboarding skills are required. Must own computer equipment.
Provisions: Hours are flexible. Pays by the character.

INSTITUTE FOR GLOBAL COMMUNICATIONS, 1010 Doyle St., #9, Menlo Park, CA 94025.

Positions: On-line computer service for non-profit organizations interested in peace, social justice, environmental issues (Amnesty International, Greenpeace, Sierra Club, etc).
Requirements: Need experience on Internet and Unix and Windows programming. Looking for women technical staff since half the users are women. With modem, can work from anywhere in the country.

INTELLIGENT MACHINES, 1440 West Broadway, Missoula, MT 59802.
Positions: Contract programmers and technical writers. Programmers write software according to company specifications. The company primarily produces business software for most major computers. Technical writers write manuals.
Requirements: Resume and references required for both positions.
Provisions: Pays by the hour and by the job.

INTELLIGENT MICRO SYSTEMS, INC., 1249 Greentree Lane, Narberth, PA 19072.
Positions: Contract programming of utility programs for AT&T, IBM and Macintosh.
Requirements: Extensive knowledge and experience with operating systems and languages. Must live on East Coast.

ISLAND GRAPHICS, 1 Harbor Drive, Sausalito, CA 94965.
Positions: Computer programmers used to develop computer graphics.
Requirements: Must be local resident. Experience is required.
Provisions: All equipment is supplied by the company. Employees are salaried. 10% of company employees work at home. 'We are an opportunity based company."

J & L GRAPHICS, INC., 418 Root Street, Park Ridge, IL 60068.
Positions: Typesetting input operators for book typography.
Requirements: Local residents only. Must be experienced, skilled operator with own computer equipment.
Provisions: Courier service provided. Pays $0.55/1,000 characters.

JOURNAL GRAPHICS, 267 Broadway, New York, NY 10007.
Positions: Journal Graphics transcribes about 40 news and talk show from TV. Home workers are assigned certain shows to tape, then transcribe onto personal computers, and transmit the transcripts via modem to company headquarters where they are printed out. Workers here are independent contractors with their own computer hardware.
Requirements: Tests are given to judge spelling, vocabulary, typing speed and accuracy, and general intelligence. Must own personal computer. Only local residents should apply. Send letter of interest.
Provisions: Word processing and communications software is provided. Pays flat fee per show transcribed.

KJ SOFTWARE, INC., 12629 N. Tatum Blvd., Suite 208, Phoenix, AZ 85032.
Positions: Freelance programmers and technical writers on contract. Company produces only management training programs with workbooks for IBM computers.
Requirements: Programmers can submit finished programs for consideration. Technical writers submit resume, samples, and references.
Provisions: Programmers are paid royalties. Writers are paid by the project.

LABFORCE, INC., 600 Bayview Ave., Inwood, NY 11696.

Positions: Software designers.
Requirements: Need people for software design (customization) on PC with Lotus Suite, Windows. Mail resume.

LAKE AVENUE SOFTWARE, 650 Sierra Madre Villa, Suite 204, Pasadena, CA 91107.
Positions: Contract programmers and technical writers. Company develops accounting software for any size business using dBase on IBM compatibles. Contract programmers are usually called upon to modify existing programs. Technical writers are used on occasion to write manuals. Most workers are local, but some are out of state. Work is handled through the transfer of disks; no telecommunications available at this time.
Provisions: Both positions pay by the job.

LASSEN SOFTWARE, INC., 1835 S. Centre City Pky, #512, Escondido, CA 92025.
Positions: Contract programmers and technical writers. Company produces business utility software, some of which is specifically useful for the home-based business person. Contract programmers are used mostly for conversions. Technical writers are used for documentation and copy writing.
Requirements: Programmers should first send for programming guidelines. Both positions require resumes and samples of previous work.
Provisions: Pays by the job.

THE LEARNING COMPANY, 6493 Kaiser Dr., Fremont, CA 94555.
Positions: Contract programmers and technical writers. Company produces educational software with an emphasis on graphics and sound. Contract programmers are used for conversions from computer to computer. Technical writers produce manuals.
Requirements: Exceptional ability in working with graphics and sound effects is especially sought in programmers. Must be very familiar with IBM and Macintosh computers. Must be local resident. Ability to meet deadlines is important Writers should be experienced and their experience should be documented in their resumes.
Provisions: Pays by the job.

LETTER PERFECT WORD PROCESSING CENTER, 4205 Menlo Drive, Baltimore, MD 21215.
Positions: Company operates a mailing center and publishes three newsletters for businesses in mail order. About a dozen home-based word processors and typists work mostly on mailing lists and the company's two monthly newsletters.
Requirements: Must be Baltimore resident. Must own PC and have experience using it. Word Perfect software is preferred. Typing speed of 100 to 110 wpm is average among workers here.
Provisions: Will train on Nutshell software. Pays piece rates which run from $10 to $20 an hour, much higher than in-house rates.

LIFT, INC., P.O. Box 1072, Mountainside, NJ 07092.
Positions: Lift, Inc., is a nonprofit organization that trains and places physically disabled people as home-based computer programmers for corporate employers. In the past 10 years, program participants have been placed with 52 major corporations.
Requirements: Applicants must have a severe but stable disability, such as MS or impaired limbs. Pilot programs for blind and deaf workers are underway, too. Standard aptitude tests are applied to find traits as motivation, drive, self-control, and an aptitude for computer programming. Occasionally the candidate already has some training, but

prior training is not necessary for entry into the program. Each candidate is trained to specifically meet the needs of the corporate client using whatever language and equipment the employer chooses. Most candidates are trained in systems programming and business applications.
Provisions: Upon completion of training, the programmer will work under contract with Lift for one year. The salary is comparable to that of any other entry level programmer, with medical and life insurance provided. After the year is up, the corporate employer then has the option of employing the programmer directly. The placement record has been exceptional. Lift operates in 15 states now, but expansion is underway, with plans to include all 50. Qualified persons are encouraged to apply from any urban location. (All workers are required to go into the employer's office at least once a week and most corporations are located in densely populated areas.)

E.T. LOWE PUBLISHING COMPANY, 2920 Sidco Drive, Nashville, TN 37204.
Positions: Typesetting input operators for book typography.
Requirements: Local residents only. Experience and equipment required.
Provisions: Pays by the character.

MARILYNN'S SECRETARIAL SERVICE, 207 E. Redwood St., Baltimore, MD 21202.
Positions: Occasional overflow work is available for word processors to type manuscripts, legal briefs, resumes, and general business documents.
Requirements: Baltimore residents only. Must have PC with Word Perfect 4.2. Several years of experience is required. Send resume.

MAVERICK PUBLICATIONS, P.O. Box 5007, Bend, OR 97701.
Positions: Keyboarding and proofreading. This is a small book producing company, established in 1968, that uses cottage labor where economics make it advantageous. An optical character reader is used to transfer manuscripts to magnetic disks. Computerized photo-typesetting allows corrections to be made on a video screen.
Requirements: Must be local resident.

MCFARLAND GRAPHICS & DESIGN, INC., P.O. Box 129, Dillsburg, PA 17019.
Positions: Typesetting input operators for mass market book typography. Currently has 8 operators working full-time and another 4 part-timers handle overflow.
Requirements: Uses former typesetters only. All are independent contractors. Local residents only. Must be disciplined. New applicants are tested.
Provisions: "We are different in that we pay an hourly rate. If an operator is getting paid by the character, there is too much stress built into the situation. They're likely to skip over problems rather than stop and call for help. In order to make a program like this work, there has to be a trust factor and a lot of give and take."

MICROPROSE SOFTWARE, INC., 180 Lake Front Dr., Hunt Valley, MD 21030.
Positions: Company uses contract programmers for conversion work and is always open to freelance submissions of original software, particularly productivity tools.
Requirements: Must be nearby resident. Freelancers should send letter describing finished program on disk along with documentation. Contract programmers, send resume. Both should be thoroughly experienced and work with their own Macintosh or IBM.
Provisions: All programmers are paid on a royalty basis.

MOD-KOMP CORP., 749 Truman Ave., East Meadow, NY 11554.
Positions: Mod-Komp is a typesetting company that uses home-based keyboarders and proofreaders to type manuscripts, books, magazines, and directories from typewritten copy into the computer. Although the keyboarders are actually typesetting input operators, the company insists that any good typist is qualified to do the work and "can be taught in an hour and a half how to use the computer".
Requirements: Applicants must be local residents. Computers are available to those who do not own their own. For those that do, MS/DOS is preferred. Disc swapping is preferred, but company does have modem capabilities and will use modem transmission of work for rush orders.
Provisions: Pays 40 cents per 1000 characters if computer is supplied by company; pays 46 cents per 1000 characters if worker owns computer. There is currently a backlog of applicants, but the company is expanding rapidly and is interested in hearing from more qualified applicants.

MOLECULAR, INC., 251 River Oaks Parkway, San Jose, CA 95134.
Positions: Contract programmers and technical writers. Company produces multi-user software packages. Programmers write according to company specifications. Technical writers handle documentation and copy writing.
Requirements: Send resume and references. Must be local resident.
Provisions: Pays by the job.

MONARCH/AVALON HILL GAME COMPANY, 4517 Hartford Road, Baltimore, MD 21214.
Positions: Monarch/Avalon has been making adult board games for 30 years. Company now produces adult computer strategy games. Contract programmers are used for conversions from one computer to another and also for original program writing to company specifications.
Requirements: Must own and have experience with IBM or Macintosh. Some game experience is preferred, particularly with "our type of games." Send resume and include references. Programmers are encouraged to send for free "Programmer's Guidelines."
Provisions: Pays by the job or royalties or a combination of both. Can live anywhere. "We have programmers as far away as Hungary." Currently has up to 25 contract programmers working at a time.

MONOTYPE COMPOSITION COMPANY, 2050 Rockrose Avenue, Baltimore, MD 21211.
Positions: Typesetting input operators for book typography. This is a union shop, so in-house workers are guaranteed work first. Any overflow goes to independent contractors. There are about 6 full-time and another 12 on-call home keyed on the roster.
Requirements: Local residents only. Must own computer equipment and have experience.
Provisions: Pays by the character.

MOUNTAIN VIEW PRESS, Box X, Mountain View, CA 94040.
Positions: Freelance programmers. Publishes hundreds of programs of all types for all types of computers. All programs are FORTH language programs.
Requirements: High level experience writing in FORTH with resume, samples and references to prove it. Send along with proposal.

NATIONAL READING STYLES INSTITUTE, P.O. Box 737, Syossett, NY 11791.
Positions: Desktop publishing and typesetting.
Requirements: Educational publisher has overflow work only for professionals experienced with Ventura. Local residents only send resume.

Wanda Welliver
Typesetting Input Operator
Network Typesetting
Omaha, NE

"I worked at home for eight years as a typist and never even saw a computer. When I met my boss, he explained typography to me and said if I could type 100 words a minute, the job was mine. A couple of months later, I was completely comfortable working with Wordstar on my new IBM PC. Now I make a lot more money than I would just typing. But, even more important than that is the freedom. I really don't want to go back out there."

NETWORK TYPESETTING, 220 Bank of Nebraska Mall,Center Mall, 42nd Center, Omaha, NE 68105.
Positions: Input operators that key in formats for typesetting. Workers are independent contractors. Currently has six input stations. "We would welcome inquires from high quality input people."
Requirements: Although actual experience is not required, quality of work is important. Need IBM PC with Wordstar and a 50,000 word (minimum) spelling checker; sometimes a modem and/or printer is also necessary. "You should understand the business and the importance of doing quality work." Must live in Omaha.
Provisions: Equipment is supplied if necessary. Pays by the job. No benefits. "Our input people are highly paid, more than in-house workers."

NORTH SHORE MEDICAL TRANSCRIBING, 18 Federal Lane, Coram, NY 11727.
Positions: Medical transcription of discharge summaries and operating reports.
Requirements: Must own PC and have experience. Local residents only.
Provisions: Work is part-time, flexible hours. Pays piece rates up to $400 a week. (Has about 10 home workers; turnover is low. There is a waiting list).

NORTHWESTERN UNIVERSITY, 720 University Place, Evanston, IL 60208.
Positions: Maintaining database.
Requirements: Must be local resident with experience and equipment. Must obtain home worker certificate from Illinois Department of Labor.

NPD, 900 West Shore Road, Port Washington, NY 11050.
Positions: NPD is one of the largest market research firms in the country. They have

begun to employ home-based data entry operators to process batches of source documents. The operators are divided into groups of 20 each, with a supervisor for each group. Supervisors are also home-based and are treated the same as in-house data entry supervisors with salaries, benefits, etc. They are provided with PCs for their homes, but do not do data entry work.
Requirements: Good typing skills are necessary. Must be local resident. Must attend quarterly meetings. Must pick up and deliver work about every three days.
Provisions: PCs and all necessary supplies are provided. Training is provided in NPD office for one to two weeks. Work is part-time, therefore, only sick leave and vacation benefits (prorated) are provided; no insurance benefits. Pays piece rates equal to that of in-house workers. Applications are accepted, but there is a waiting list.

ORANGE CHERRY MEDIA, P.O. Box 390, Pound Ridge, NY 10576.
Positions: Freelance and contract programmers. Company publishes highly graphic educational programs for IBM and Macintosh computers.
Requirements: Freelancers can submit either finished program with documentation or proposal with samples and resume. Contract programmers are sometimes assigned to write to spec; submit resume, samples, and references.

OREGON SOFTWARE, INC., 6915 S.W. Macadam Avenue, Portland, OR 97219.
Positions: Technical writers for user manuals.
Requirements: Must be local writer with minimum five years experience in computer documentation. Submit resume, work samples, and references.
Provisions: Pays hourly rate.

PARKS STORIE, INC., 2880 Holcomb Bridge Road, Building b9, Suite 539, Alpharetta, GA 30202.
Positions: This company contracts computer programmers and support people such as technical writers (for software documentation) to work out of their homes for other companies. Disabled employees are placed whenever possible.
Requirements: Applications from experienced workers, particularly disabled ones, are welcome.

PARKWOOD COMPOSITION SERVICE, 1345 South Knowles Avenue, New Richmond, WI 54017.
Positions: Typesetting input operators, proofreaders, and layout for book typography.
Requirements: Local residents only. Experience and equipment required.
Provisions: All workers are independent contractors with no guarantees of continuous work. Work flow is very seasonal.

PEMBLE ASSOCIATES, 1059 Mackey Pike, Nicholasville, KY 40356.
Positions: Pemble Associates is looking for computer consultants and others knowledgeable in computers to act as distributors for a time and billing software package for the legal industry. "Innertrack" is a PC compatible (only) package designed for both single use and multiuser systems. The product sells for $695 (single user) up to $2795 (multiuser) and the dealer receives a discount (profit) up to 40%.
Requirements: Dealers must purchase a dealer demo package with which they receive free technical support via phone and/or modem (user gets free technical support for the life of the product).

PORT CITY PRESS, INC., P.O. Box 5754, Baltimore, MD 21208.

Positions: Typesetting input operators for book typography.
Requirements: Local residents only. Experience and equipment required.
Provisions: Pays by the character.

PUBLISHERS CLEARING HOUSE, 382 Channel Dr., Pt. Washington, NY 11050.
Positions: Data entry operators work on PCs at home entering names and addresses and other data for mailing lists.
Requirements: Local residents only. Experience, speed, and accuracy are required.
Provisions: Pays piece rates. There is currently a waiting list of 6-9 months because the turnover is so low among the home-based workers.

QUEUE, INC., 338 Commerce Dr., Fairfield, CT 06430.
Positions: Contract programmers for writing educational software for Macintosh and/or IBM computers. Freelance programmers also do conversions and programming to company specifications.
Requirements: Local people are definitely preferred. Apply with resume and references or work samples. Quality of work is very important.
Provisions: Pays by the job or royalty. Inquiries are welcome.

REPRODUCTION TYPOGRAPHERS, 244 West First Avenue, Roselle, NJ 07203.
Positions: Typesetting input operators for book typography. All operators are independent contractors and can work for other companies simultaneously.
Requirements: Must be experienced operators with own equipment. Local residents only. Must pick up and deliver own work.
Provisions: All work is overflow from the plant. Pays by the keystroke.

RESEARCH INFORMATION SYSTEMS, 1991 Village Park Way, Suite 205, Encinitas, CA 92024.
Positions: This company is about two years old now and provides a unique and valuable service to professionals in the medical and bio-medical fields. It is a software company that produces a weekly subscription service whereby about 800 medical journals are indexed into an overall table of contents. Home-based workers input critical information such as title, author, and reprint address, from journals or photocopies of title pages, onto disks. The disks are then returned to the company where they are checked for errors by the company's computer. The work is transported via Federal Express and there is a one week turn-around. All of the 10 home-based indexers are women, mostly with children. They are independent contractors, working their own schedules. Some have their own independent word processing businesses and have other clients.
Requirements: Must own PC (MS/DOS only). Must be local resident and have experience and references.
Provisions: Training is provided. Software is also provided. Pays piece rates. The company is growing steadily, but there is very little turnover so opportunities are limited.

RESOURCE SOFTWARE INTERNATIONAL, 330 New Brunswick Avenue, Ford, NJ 08863.
Positions: Contract programmers work on various assignments writing new programs to company specs or modifying existing ones.
Requirements: Must have experience programming in Assembly language on IBM or Macintosh. Submit resume, samples, and references. Prefers programmers on East Coast.
Provisions: Pays by the project.

Phil Neal
Contract Programmer, Maine

"I live in such a remote area I do as much as possible over the phone. I start each job by traveling to the worksite to do a requirement analysis and determine what needs to be done. I then report on what the client will need, how long it will take, and when they can expect parts of the system to be tested. From there, all the work is done strictly from my house. Living in such a remote area, it would be difficult to envision working in any other way."

RIGHT BROTHERS SOFTWARE, 1173 Niagra St., Denver, CO 80220.
Positions: Right Brothers is a new software publishing company looking for good educational programs. Especially wants thought provoking, problem solving, courseware for higher education levels. Programs are highly interactive and are games only if there is also a strong educational value.
Requirements: Thorough knowledge of languages. Submit disk, printed listing, and any other support materials available.
Provisions: Programs will be analyzed for commercial value and if accepted will offer standard royalty of 12-15%.

RIGHT ON PROGRAMS, 755 New York Ave., Huntington, NY 11743.
Positions: Contract programmers for computer to computer conversions. Company produces educational programs for IBM and Macintosh. Also accepts freelance submissions.
Requirements: Must be highly qualified. Submit resume and references.

ROXBURY PUBLISHING COMPANY, P.O. Box 491044, Los Angeles, CA 90049.
Positions: Freelance home-based typesetters are used by this textbook publisher.
Requirements: Must have typesetting equipment (not PC; this is not embedding, this is actual typesetting). Los Angeles residents only. Minimum of five years experience. Send resume and indicate equipment type.
Provisions: Pay method varies. Inquiries welcome from qualified people, but there is a waiting list.

THE SAYBROOK PRESS, INC., P.O. Box 629, Old Saybrook, CT 06475.
Positions: Typesetting input operators for book typography. Currently has 8 home keyers.
Requirements: Local residents only. Must be accurate typist. Must pick up and deliver own work.

Provisions: Training and equipment provided. Pays by the character.

THE TIM SCOTT CORPORATION, 96 St. James Ave., Springfield, MA 01109.
Positions: The Tim Scott Corporation is in the business of exporting/importing goods and services. Goods include a variety of products from rare books to office supplies. Services include computer programming for small businesses and information services for foreign businesses wanting to do business in the U.S. The company has a specific work-at-home program designed for women, handicapped, or welfare persons with no transportation, and women with small children. Men may also take advantage of the option. No training is needed and the company will provide all the required equipment. Benefits are the same as with other employees with very few exceptions. Jobs vary so always request a current job opening listing. Employees currently hired may also apply, but first choice will always be given to unemployed persons or an employed woman with the company who is expected to have a child within 12 months.
Requirements: Must be local resident.

SELEX, 10 Carlisle Drive, Livingston, NJ 07039.
Positions: Software developers. Company develops highly interactive text on any subject. Some technical writers.
Requirements: Must own and have thorough knowledge of major brand PC and printer. Send list of equipment availability with letter of interest.
Provisions: Pays royalty plus other benefits.

SOUTHWEST TRANSCRIPTION CENTER, 9842 Hybert #161, San Diego, CA 92131.
Positions: Both in-house and at-home medical transcribers are used by Southwest. All work is done on computers (IBM compatible) using WordPerfect and Writing Assistant.
Requirements: Only experienced medical transcribers with strong medical terminology and the proper equipment will be considered. Must live in San Diego. Work can be transmitted via modem or hand delivered, but there is a 24-hour turn-around requirement.

SPAR BURGOYNE MARKETING & INFORMATION SERVICES, 10925 Valley View Rd., Suite 102, Eden Prairie, MN 55344.
Positions: Spar is a service bureau that collects data about retailers in the field and then has home-based data processors enter the information from handwritten form onto disks. The home keyers send the disks to company headquarters to be printed out in report form for clients. About a dozen home keyers work as independent contractors, averaging 20 hours a week. This could mean some weeks there is no work and others there is up to 55 hours of work.
Requirements: Must be Minneapolis resident and able to type accurately.. The company is particularly interested in young mothers who might otherwise be without work options.
Provisions: Training in software and procedures is provided in the company offices. Pays $5.50 an hour.

SPSS, INC., 444 North Michigan Avenue, Suite 3000, Chicago, IL 60611.
Positions: Contract programmers and technical writers. Programmers do conversions of business graphics software. Technical writers are used for documentation and promotional materials.
Requirements: Programmers must have experience with mainframe or super-minis. Applicants for both positions must send resume and previous work samples.

STANDARD DATA PREP, 8400 New Horizon Blvd., Amityville, NY 11701.
Positions: Data entry and keypunch operations with 029 keyboard.
Requirements: Good skills, experience required. Local residents only. Send resume.
Provisions: Home workers are full-time employees with 37 1/2 hour work week, benefits, vacations, holiday pays, and 401K.

STRATEGIC SIMULATIONS, INC., 675 Almanor Ave., Sunnyvale, CA 94086.
Positions: Contact programmers for computer to computer conversions. Company publishes over 100 games for Macintosh computers.
Requirements: There is a lot of conversion work available. However, only programmers with a high level of proficiency and ownership of both computers will be considered. Submit resume and references. Include request for current conversion needs.

STSC, INC., 2115 E. Jefferson St., Rockville, MD 20852.
Positions: Contract programmers do conversion work and write original programs to company specifications. Company works with IBM compatible or UNIX operating systems and produces vertical market applications software for specific business, professional, and educational markets.
Requirements: Area residents only. Programmers must have at least three years of experience in APL programming plus experience in systems analysis, documentation, or project management.
Provisions: Pays hourly rates.

TELE VEND, INC., 111 Croydon Rd., Baltimore, MD 21212.
Positions: Freelance and contract programmers. Company publishes business and financial programs for IBM computers.
Requirements: Prefers local programmers. Freelancers should submit finished program with complete documentation. All others submit resume.
Provisions: Pays royalty.

TOWSON WORD PROCESSING, 31 Allegheny Ave., #100, Baltimore, MD 21204.
Positions: Word Processors handle legal and medical transcription.
Requirements: Local residents only. Must own PC with word Perfect 4.2 and a transcriber (standard or micro). Three to five years experience is required. Good work is very important. Send resume noting available hours and equipment.

THE ULTIMATE SECRETARY, 18231 Los Alimos St., Northridge, CA 91326.
Positions: Medical and x-ray transcribers.
Requirements: Must live in the Valley and be experienced. Must own word processor (and have experience using it) and transcribing machine with either standard or micro cassettes.
Provisions: Training provided. For now workers will have to pick up and deliver their own work, especially during the training period, but a courier service is planned for the near future. Turnaround time on x-ray material is 24 hours and 48 hours on all others. Work can be part-time or full-time. Pays by the line.

UNIBASE DATA ENTRY, 510 Park Land Dr., Sandy, UT 84070.
Positions: This is a data entry service bureau that employs several hundred home-based keyboarders.
Requirements: Must be a Salt Lake City resident, have basic knowledge of keyboarding skills, and perform at the level of 10,000 keystrokes per hour including both letters and

numbers (that's about 55 wpm typing with no errors).
Provisions: Training is provided over a six week period in the head office. Training continues with the "clients" until the worker reaches 99.9% accuracy, then the work can be taken home from that point on. Work is picked up and delivered daily and this is done on a rotational basis by members of a car pooling group of home workers living within close proximity to each other. Home workers are included in company social functions. Home workers are paid per item keyed in which amounts to between $6 and $8 an hour for good workers.

UNIVERSITY GRAPHICS, INC., 11 West Lincoln Avenue, Atlantic Highlands, NJ 07716.
Positions: University Graphics provides services to the book publishing industry and has three pools of home workers: keyboarders for typesetting with embedded code, proofreaders, and page makeup people who key in data to the mainframe. Currently has over 70 home workers.
Requirements: Keyboarders must type 50 to 60 wpm with a low error rate. Proofreaders must have good English skills, "maybe an English major". Only local residents.
Provisions: Training is provided. Keyboarders are provided with IBM PCs; others receive terminals which are hooked up to company's mainframe. Pays piece rates. "We were one of the first in the composition industry to use cottage labor. Now it's becoming the norm because it helps stabilize costing in an industry which is cyclical in nature. By using home workers, we can keep tight controls on our costs and overhead. Inquiries are always welcome."

VICKERS STOCK RESEARCH CORP., 226 New York Ave., Huntington, NY 11743.
Positions: Data entry.
Requirements: Must be local resident. All home-based workers are independent contractors and must own PCs. Experience and references are required.

Looking for companies that don't require their homeworkers to be local? Over 350 companies are listed in the Job Bank Location Index under "National or Multi-Regional Companies." See page 298.

OPPORTUNITIES IN OFFICE SUPPORT POSITIONS

"Desk jobs" are among the fastest-growing categories of home work opportunities. Just about any kind of job that is performed in an office setting can just as easily be done at home. The availability of inexpensive office equipment combined with new telephone service options makes it easier now than ever before.

Some companies hire home office workers directly. More often than not, however, they are hired through service bureaus. For instance, insurance policies have been typed by home workers for many years. But the insurance companies have nothing to do with the hiring of home typists. Instead, the insurance companies contract with policy typing service bureaus. The service bureaus are responsible for all phasaes of the policy-typing process and do all the hiring and training of the home typists.

Service bureaus are popping up everywhere in the medical transcribing field. Medical transcribing is the top of the line for home typists. Not only is it the most financially rewarding of all home typing jobs--it is also an industry that is growing at a breakneck speed and there are more openings for jobs than most employers can fill.

The job involves typing doctors' reports and correspondence from cassette tapes. Employers often require several years of experience and test applicants to ensure they have a thorough knowledge of medical terminology. To get the necessary background, there are "Medical Secretary" courses available through community colleges and private vocational schools. A complete course takes from three to six months. But even then, you will need some practice in order to keep up with the 24-hour turnaround time required by most companies. One good way to gain some experience is to sign up with one or more temporary employment agencies. Explain what you're trying to do and ask to be assigned to any medical office jobs that come up.

Foreign language translation is included in this section because so much of the work requires office skills such as typing, proofreading, typesetting, and transcribing. Again, this is a field handled almost entirely by service bureaus. Most translators work at home and many work for service bureaus located in another state or even another country.

Translation is not a job for amateurs. It requires a high level of proficiency in a foreign language and some bureaus will only hire native language translators. It is also necessary to have special expertise in a given field in order to be able to work with the terminology peculiar to that field. For instance, if you are a translator specializing in the legal field, you would need an understanding of legal terminology not only in English, but in the foreign language as well.

Other requirements for this job might include a typewriter, computer, modem, facimile machine, or transcribing machine.

A TO Z WORD-O-MATICS, 9100 S. Dadeland Blvd., Suite 210, Miami, FL 33156.
Positions: Russian, Spanish, French, German translation.
Requirements: Must have IBM compatible and word processing software and equipment. Must be highly qualified and reliable, in which case you can work from anywhere in the country by modem. Send resume.

A WORD ABOVE, INC., 7062 Lakeview Haven Dr., Suite 105, Houston, TX 77095.
Positions: Medical transcriber.
Requirements: Three years experience transcribing consultations, discharges, and physicals from digital equipment. Need dictaphone to hook into Konex (DX 3000, DX 7000). Local residents send resume.

AA INTERNATIONAL TRANSLATIONS & LINGUISTICS, 2312 Artesia, Redondo Beach , CA 90278.
Positions: Foreign language translators; all languages and all subjects.
Requirements: Experienced native translators only. Send resume.

AAA OFFICE SERVICE, INC., 645 N. Michigan Ave., Chicago, IL 60611.
Positions: Medical transcribers.
Requirements: Minimum three years medical transcription experience required, particularly in radiology and radiation oncology. Need computer and dictaphone equipment. Local residents send resume.

ACADEMIE LANGUAGE CENTER, 8032 West Third, Los Angeles, CA 90048.
Positions: Foreign language translations of documents.
Requirements: Certification required. Local residents only. Apply with resume.

ACCURAPID TRANSLATION SERVICES, INC., 806 Main St., Poughkeepsie, NY12603.
Positions: Technical translators in all languages. Company specializes in business, engineering and scientific documents.
Requirements: Thorough knowledge of foreign language and English is required. Must also have experience in one of the three specialties. For translators outside the area, a computer and modem is preferred. Submit resume noting areas of technical expertise and type of computer and telecommunications equipment.
Provisions: Pays by the word on most contracts.

ACCURATE BUSINESS SERVICES, 801 Arch St., Suite 603, Philadelphia, PA 19107.
Positions: Medical transcribing.
Requirements: Need two years experience in hospital record rooms in multiple areas, x-ray, etc. Prefer candidates with IBM computer with Word Perfect 5.1 Also general word processing and legal typist with exceptional skills. Local residents only send resume.

ACCURATE SECRETARIAL SERVICE, 98 Idlewood Dr., Stanford, CT 06905.
Positions: Word processing and transcribing.
Requirements: This is not an opportunity for a second income, but only "the main job". Looking for accuracy and perfection in work and must be able to provide a disk that is IBM compatible for on-the-spot customer correction purposes. Local residents send resume.

ACCURATE WORD PROCESSING, 3 Harvey Ave., Yardley, PA 19067.
Positions: Word processors.
Requirements: Yardley area people (Levittown, Lower Bucks County) only. Must own and have experience on IBM with Word Perfect, Power Point, Word Excell and Windows. Send resume.

ACCUTECH PROFESSIONAL TYPING, 141 Bunche Blvd., Wilmington, DE 19801.
Positions: Medical transcribing.
Requirements: Need own micro cassette transcribing machine, IBM compatible system, and Word Perfect 5.1 and 6. Need experience in all types of medicine and be able to work with 24 - 48 hours turnover. Local residents only send resume.

ACCUWRITE WORD PROCESSING SERVICE, 63-124 Alderton Rd., Rego Park, NY 11374.
Positions: Medical transcription, legal transcription, and word processing.
Requirements: Medical transcription requires accuracy and experience as well as the ability to understand different accents. Requires an IBM compatible with Word Perfect 5.1 and micro/standard transcribing machine. Legal transcription requires experience with depositions and hearings. Word processing is for manuscripts such as books and technical articles, mailing lists and personalized letters. Must have strong Word Perfect 5.1 experience and skill in addition to own equipment. Must be from surrounding area to get to the office for pick-up and drop-off. Send resume.

ACTION TRANSLATION & INTERPRETATION BUREAU, 7825 W. 101st, Palos Hills, IL 60465.
Positions: Foreign language translators work in all languages and subjects.
Requirements: Thorough knowledge of both foreign language and English is required. Some particular of expertise is also necessary. Residents in Northern Illinois only. Submit resume and references.

ACTIVE TRANSLATION BUREAU, 155 W. 68th St., Apt. 919, New York, NY 10023.
Positions: This is a very old translation bureau that handles all languages and all subjects. Native language translators handle literary, chemical, electronics, commercial, medical, legal, technical and industrial documents.
Requirements: Must be native language translator. Minimum five years professional translating experience required. Submit resume with references.
Provisions: Pay rates vary with different projects.

ADEPT WORD MANAGEMENT, P.O. Box 710438, Houston, TX 77271.
Positions: Legal and medical transcription.
Requirements: Requires remote dictaphone and transcribing unit analog tapes (micro, mini, and standard cassettes). Must have experience. Local residents only send resume.

AD-EX TRANSLATIONS INTERNATIONAL/USA, P. O. 2008, Menlo Park, CA 94026.
Positions: Translators and some technical writers for translation of technical, sales, and legal documents, as well as literature, into any major language, or from other language into English. Word processors and typesetters also used, but only those with foreign language expertise. Work is sent via the U.S. mail, Federal Express, or telecopiers.

Requirements: Only experienced, skilled professionals will be considered. Must be versed in one or more industrial, scientific, technical, military, or bio-med fields. Knowledge of foreign language is secondary, but must be thorough. Need typewriter or word processor. Send resume and work sample. Word processing capability and access to fax machine favored.
Provisions: Payment methods varies. 90% of staff works at home. Average 10 to 40 workers a day.

ADVANCE LANGUAGE SERVICE, 333 North Michigan Ave., Suite 3200, Chicago, IL 60601.
Positions: Translators and typesetters with foreign language expertise work in all languages and subjects.
Requirements: Experienced local translators only. Submit resume and references.

AF TRANSLATIONS, 324 N. Francisca, Redondo Beach, CA 90278.
Positions: Foreign language translation of general and technical documents. All major languages.
Requirements: Prefers to work with Southern California translators. Experience required. Apply with resume and references.

A I C I, P.O. Box 91301/Worldway Postal Ct., Los Angeles, CA 90009.
Positions: Freelance technical translators work at home for this translation service bureau.
Requirements: Must be able to work from and into English with French, German, Italian, Spanish, or Japanese. Will consider experienced translators only. Prefers computer users; any type. Apply with resume and references. Can live anywhere.
Provisions: Pays by the word.

ALL PURPOSE TYPING SERVICE, 1550 McDonald Ave., Brooklyn, NY 11230.
Positions: Word processing on Word Perfect module (not character set) in Russian, Hebrew, and Arabic. Work is on reports, theses, etc.
Requirements: Must know database Paradox. Experience and skill required. Send resume.
Provisions: Offers sizable contracts (over 100 pages).

ALL TYPE TRANSCRIPTION AND WORD PROCESSING SERVICES, P.O. Box 6183, East Brunswick, NJ 08816.
Positions: Medical transcribers.
Requirements: Must be certified medical transcriptionist. Need WordPerfect 1.5, modern telecommunications equipment with extra phone line for data and voice files. Can be anywhere in the metropolitan area. Send resume.

ALLIED INTERPRETING & TRANSLATING SERVICE, 7471 Melrose Ave., Los Angeles, CA 90046.
Positions: Foreign language translation of legal and medical documents. All languages
Requirements: Certification required. Los Angeles residents only. Apply with resume.

ALL-LANGUAGE SERVICES, INC., 545 Fifth Ave., New York, NY 10017.
Positions: Translators handle legal, technical, financial, medical and engineering documents.
Requirements: Prefers native language translators. Prefers New York residents because

some projects require coming into headquarters. Resume and references required.
Provisions: Pay methods vary according to assignment.

ALTRUSA LANGUAGE BANK OF CHICAGO, 332 S. Michigan Ave., Suite 1123, Chicago, IL 60604.
Positions: Foreign language translators. All languages; all subjects.
Requirements: Prefers native language translators; will accept certification instead. Submit resume and references.

ASAP WORD PROCESSING SECRETARIAL SERVICE, 75 E. Wacker Dr., Chicago, IL 60601.
Positions: General transcribing of meetings and interviews on tape, both micro and standard size.
Requirements: Local people only available for quick turnover. Some work is during the week, some is only for weekends. Must be flexible as well as skilled. Send resume.

ASSOCIATED SECRETARIAL SERVICE, 4701 Calhoun, Suite A, Houston, TX 77004.
Positions: Word processors for programs, flyers, resumes, board graphics, and legal work.
Requirements: Must own IBM compatible; sometimes has need for Mac. Work is mostly overflow and is almost always needed ASAP. Local residents send resume.

ATI-AMERICAN TRANSLATORS INTERNATIONAL, INC., 145 Addison Ave., Palo Alto, CA 94301.
Positions: ATI is a leading international translation and interpretation service. Foreign language opportunities involve legal and technical fields. English word processing, transcription, and telemarketing opportunities also exist.
Requirements: Word processing and transcribing positions require ownership of an IBM-compatible computer, WordPerfect, fax machine, and modem. Telemarketers must have at least one year of full-time experience. Translators and interpreters must have at least five years of professional, full-time experience, and must focus on a specific industry.
Provisions: Word processors, transcriptionists, and interpreters are paid on an hourly basis. Telemarketers are paid by commission. Translators are paid on a cents-per-word basis.

BARRINGTON WORD PROCESSING, P.O. Box 1442, Barrington, IL 60011.
Positions: Word processors.
Requirements: Must own a Mac and related software to do resumes, research papers, and transcripts. Local residents send resume.

BAY STATE SERVICE AND SYSTEMS, 160 Baldwin St., W. Springfield, MA 01089.
Positions: Medical transcribers.
Requirements: Need experience in all types of medicine and have good grammar. Requires IBM compatible and dictaphone equipment. Local residents send resume.

BBT&T, 8920 Wilshire Blvd., Suite 404, Los Angeles, CA 90211.
Positions: Medical transcribers.
Requirements: Acute care experience necessary.
Provisions: Pick up and delivery available over large area of Los Angeles. Pays piece rates equal to about $12 an hour

BERLITZ TRANSLATION SERVICE, 660 Market Street, San Francisco, CA 94104.
Positions: Berlitz is a huge translation bureau with offices all over the country and in 23 foreign countries as well. Freelance translators in all languages work in all subject areas.
Requirements: Thorough knowledge of foreign language and English required. Only experienced translators are considered. Can live anywhere, but for those not near a Berlitz office, a computer and modem is preferred. Make note of equipment type on resume.
Provisions: Pays by the word.

BERTRAND LANGUAGES, INC., 370 Lexington Ave., New York, NY 10017.
Positions: Freelance translators handle engineering, scientific, medical, legal, commercial, financial, and some advertising documents.
Requirements: Prefers native language translators. Must have expertise in one of the areas mentioned above. Translators outside the New York area should have telecommunications capabilities. Submit resume and references.

BLESSING HOSPITAL, 1005 Broadway, Quincy, IL 62301.
Positions: Medical transcribers.
Requirements: Minimum three years experience required. Must have own equipment. Local residents only may apply.

BLS SECRETARIAL SERVICES, 4108 Walter Ave., Baltimore, MD 21256.
Positions: General and medical transcription.
Requirements: Must own IBM compatible with Word Perfect, Q & A, and Microsoft Word plus transcribing equipment for all size cassettes. Skills and experience required. Local residents only mail resumes.

BLUE RIDGE TEA AND HERB CO., 26 Woodhull St., Brooklyn, NY 11231.
Positions: Stuffing envelopes.
Requirements: Need intelligent (common-sense) people to stuff envelopes of different classifications for shows and conventions. Approximately daily report in. Vehicle necessary for loading of boxes. Requirements changes (envelopes, data entry, packing teas and herbs) with different stages of business. Local residents send resume.

BUDGET COPY TYPING SERVICES, 1136 7th Ave., San Diego, CA 92101.
Positions: Word processing including data entry of names, addresses and direct mail work in a database format.
Requirements: Must have and be familiar with Word Perfect 5.0, Windows, and use Microsoft Access. Local residents send resume.

CALIFORNIA REPORTING, 1049 Dolores St. #3, San Francisco, CA 94110.
Positions: Transcribers for court reporting firm. Work is part-time only.
Requirements: Experience is required. Must live in San Francisco. Word processor is required. Apply with resume.

CALIFORNIA TYPING EXCHANGE, 4363 Hazel Ave., Ste. 1284, Fair Oaks, CA 94026.
Positions: Typists and transcribers for major metropolitan areas of California.
Requirements: Good typing/transcribing skills needed. Must own good typewriter.

Provisions: Pick up and delivery available within certain boundaries. Pays production rates.

CCA, INC., International Marketing Communications, 7120 Havenhurst Ave., #205/208, Van Nuys, CA 91406.
Positions: Technical translators and multilingual editors for computer manuals and data sheets.
Requirements: Must be highly experienced. Must own computer and modem. IBM compatible preferred; Macintosh okay. In general, Americans are used only for proofing and quality control work. Translators are usually native. Must be professionals, usually degreed. Being able to speak/write in foreign language not enough; technical expertise in a particular industry an absolute must. Time deadlines are critical.
Provisions: Work is transferred nationwide via telecommunications or, in some cases, using Federal Express. Freelance and retainer positions are available. Freelancers are paid on a per-word basis. "A good freelancer can make $50,000 a year.." Translators in all languages are invited to send resume with references.

CERTIFIED TRANSLATION BUREAU, INC., 2788 E. Gage Ave., Huntington Park, CA 90255.
Positions: Foreign language translators for all subjects.
Requirements: Experienced translators only; any language. Apply with resume and references.

CLERICAL PLUS, 273 Derby Ave., Derby, CT.
Positions: Data entry, word processing, and transcription.
Requirements: Must own IBM compatible and have and be adept at WordPerfect, Word, MultiMate, and Microsoft Word. Transcription work is usually medical. For that, you will need a micro tape transcriber and experience. Must be local resident. Submit resume.

COMPUTER SECRETARY, 300 W. Peachtree NW, Suite 11H, Atlanta, GA 30308.
Positions: Word processing, legal and medical transcription.
Requirements: Must own IBM or Mac with Word Perfect 5.1 and 6.0 and Lotus 1,2,3. Experience and good skills required. Local residents send resume.

CONTINENTAL TRANSLATION SERVICE, INC., 6 E. 43rd St., Suite 2100, New York, NY 10017.
Positions: Freelance translators handle technical manuals, legal documentation, marketing projects, and medical transcription in most foreign languages.
Requirements: Thorough knowledge of foreign language and English required. Must have expertise in one of the areas mentioned above. Submit resume. Prefers New York residents.
Provisions: Pay methods vary.

CONTRACT TALENTS, INC., 1550 Mockingbird, Dallas, TX 75235.
Positions: Taylor Publishing is in the business of producing school year books. About 500 independent contractors work full-time and part-time in the Dallas area. Some are home-based, some are not. The home-based work involves typing, proofing, stripping, and other jobs associated with publishing.
Requirements: Must be local resident. Applications are accepted only during June, July, and August.

Provisions: Pays piece rates for completed work associates.

DAVID C. COOK PUBLISHING COMPANY, 850 North Grove Avenue, Elgin, IL 60601.
Positions: Manuscript typing and related clerical work.
Requirements: Must own good typewriter and have good skills. Must be local resident. Must obtain home worker certificate from State Department of Labor.

COSMOPOLITAN TRANSLATION BUREAU, INC., 53 W. Jackson Blvd., Suite 1123, Chicago, IL 60604.
Positions: Cosmopolitan is a very old translation bureau that handles all languages and subjects.
Requirements: Native translators are preferred, but will consider translators with absolute knowledge of a foreign language and good English skills. Must have a particular area of expertise for the terminology of that field (such as legal or medical). Chicago translators only. Submit resume and references.

CPS MED TEXT, 58 Sprucewood Dr., Levittown, NY 11756.
Positions: Medical transcribers.
Requirements: Must be a well seasoned pro with own equipment. Local residents only mail resume.

DALE TYPING SERVICE, 8700 Old Harford Rd., Baltimore, MD 21236.
Positions: Medical transcribers.
Requirements: Local residents only. Minimum three years experience and equipment required.

DATA COMPUTER CORPORATION, 229 Baldwin Rd., Hempstead, NY 11550.
Positions: Data entry.
Requirements: Need IBM compatible and good skills. Local residents send resume.

DATA PROCESSING & ACCOUNTING SERVICES, 1407 Market St., San Francisco, CA 94026.
Positions: Data entry.
Requirements: Must own IBM compatible. Company's software will be taught. Once learning curve is over, you will be on call on an as-needed basis as an independent contractor. Local residents only mail resume.

DJ BUSINESS SERVICE, 842 State Rd., Princeton, NJ 08540.
Positions: General transcription.
Requirements: Need to own IBM compatible with Word Perfect 5.1 and transcribing machine for standard tapes. Local residents send resume.

DWH OFFICE SERVICES, 101 Brightside Ave., Pikesville, MD 21208.
Positions: Word processors and transcribers.
Requirements: Must own IBM compatible with Word Perfect 5.0 plus standard and micro transcribing equipment. Skills and experienced required. Local residents only mail resume.

EASTERN MAIL DATA, 3523 Route 112, Medford, NY 11746.
Positions: Data entry.

Requirements: Must have production quality work. No modem necessary. Need IBM compatible with at least 20 meg minimum hard drive and floppydisc for data entry. Must be highly qualified and test for 10,000 keystrokes with alpha and numeric experience. Local residents only send resume.
Provisions: Company provides software and training for three days only. Turnaround time will be between 24 and 72 hours.

ELEANOR MORRISON SECRETARIAL, 82009 Olive Vine Ave., Citrus Heights, CA 94026.
Positions: Word processing, legal and medical transcription.
Requirements: Need IBM with Word Perfect 5.1 and 6.0. Medical transcription requires micro equipment and OB/GYN experience. Will accept resumes by mail from Citrus Heights, Rosedale, Orangevale, Folsom and Sacramento.

ELITE TYPING CONNECTION, 3108 Beaves Ave., Kettering, OH 45429.
Positions: Legal transcribers.
Requirements: Need 4-track transcribers for court trial transcripts (no court reporters, so all is on tapes only). Average transcription is 160- 200 pages. Must own 4-track transcriber, follow Supreme Court guidelines, and understand citations. Qualified local applicants send resume.

EURAMERICA TRANSLATIONS, INC., 257 Park Avenue, South, New York, NY 10023.
Positions: Freelance translators work in all languages on straight documentation, typesetting and audio-visual services. Especially needs translators with knowledge of automotive, high-tech, medical, financial, legal, or promotional material. Assignments are given on-line only.
Requirements: Thorough knowledge of foreign language "equal to a native" is required. A computer, modem and FAX is required for transmitting work. Submit resume and references. Note any special areas of expertise.
Provisions: Pays by the word.

EXCELLENCE TRANSLATION SERVICE, P.O. Box 5863, Presidio of Monterey, Monterey,. CA 93940.
Positions: Foreign language translators for general and technical documentation. All languages.
Requirements: Thorough knowledge of foreign language and English required. Can live anywhere in California. Submit resume and references.

EXECUTIVE OFFICE SERVICES, 120 Bannon Ave., Buchanan, NY 10511.
Positions: Word processors, data entry, and medical transcribers.
Requirements: Need IBM compatible with Word Perfect 6.0 for word processing, plus D Base 3 for data entry and for medical transcription, amicro/standard transcribing machine. Skills and experience is required for any position. Must be local resident. Send resume.

FEDERATION OF THE HANDICAPPED, 211 West 14th Street, 2nd Floor, New York, NY 10011.
Positions: The Federation operates the Home Employment Program (HEP) for homebound disabled workers only. Within HEP there is a typing/transcription department.

Requirements: All positions here require evaluation through lengthy interviews and personal counseling. All workers must live in New York City.
Provisions: The workshop provides training plus any extra help necessary to overcome any unusual problems an individual might have. Pick up and delivery of supplies and finished work is provided regularly. Necessary equipment is provided. Pays piece rates. Disability insurance counseling is provided.

FRANKLIN RESOURCE CENTER, 1205 Franklin Ave., Garden City, NY 11530.
Positions: Medical and legal transcribing.
Requirements: Must know Word Perfect, type 75 wpm, and dictaphone usage. Local residents send resume.
Provisions: Pay $12 to $13 per hour.

G & L DATA SERVICE, INC., 230 Adams Ave., Hauppauge, NY 11788.
Positions: Data entry of names and addresses.
Requirements: Must own computer and be able to report in weekly. Send resume.

GLOBAL LANGUAGE SERVICES, 2027 Las Lunas, Pasadena, Ca 91108.
Positions: Foreign language translators of general and technical documents. All languages.
Requirements: Prefers native language translators, but will consider certified translators. Some special area of expertise is required. Submit resume.

GLOBALINK, 9990 Lee Highway, Fairfax, VA 22030.
Positions: Foreign language translators for general and technical documents. All languages.
Requirements: Thorough knowledge of foreign language and good English skills are required. Computer and modem is also required. All work is transferred via electronic mail and FAX. Submit resume along with equipment details. Can live anywhere.

GREEN'S MACHINE, 2031 North HiMount, Milwaukee, WI 53208.
Positions: Medical transcription, word processing, legal transcription, database development, and other typing. "We put forward a professional image on behalf of the independent contractors who would otherwise not be able to attract the top corporate clients we have." Currently has 30 home workers.
Requirements: Must live in Milwaukee. Typing skills are needed; accuracy is most important. Workers must own good typewriters. Workers must pick up and deliver their own work.
Provisions: Pays production rate equal to a minimum of $10 an hour.

HART SYSTEMS, INC., 200 Stonehenge Lane, Carle Place, NY 11514.
Positions: Data entry.
Requirements: Must be local for daily drop-off. Call for interview.
Provisions: Training program provided.

HELEN'S MAILING SERVICE, P.O. Box 3116 Bridgeview, IL 60455.
Positions: Typing envelopes and labels.
Requirements: Must be local resident with experience and equipment. Must obtain home worker certificate from Illinois Department of Labor.

HELPING HAND SECRETARIAL SERVICES, 6060 Pickeral Dr., Rockford, MI

49341.
Positions: Medical transcribers.
Requirements: Must own IBM (preferred) or Macintosh with either WordPerfect or Microsoft Word and have thorough knowledge of how to use them. Uses standard micro tapes. Must have accurate vocabulary, spelling, and secretarial skills. Must be thoroughly familiar with medical terminology and keep work confidential. Must live within 45 minutes drive of company. Send resume.

HIGHLAND PARK HOSPITAL, 718 Glenview Ave., Highland, IL 60035.
Positions: Medical transcribers. This is a new and small operation and opportunities are limited.
Requirements: Minimum three years experience required. Must have proper equipment. Local resident only.

HOGARD BUSINESS SERVICES, INC., 462 S. Schuyler Ave., Bradley, IL 60915.
Positions: Typing and stuffing envelopes for this typing and mailing service.
Requirements: Must be local resident. Must obtain a home worker certificate from the Illinois. Department of Labor.

HOME PROFESSIONALS, 1384 William Floyd Parkway, Shirley, NY 11967.
Positions: Data entry to input names and addresses.
Requirements: Must have a computer and be knowledgeable in copying out information onto a disc. Local residents only send resume.

HOOPER-HOLMES BUREAU.
Positions: Commercial reporters. Work consists of gathering information over the phone from businesses, usually for insurance company clients, then writing up the information in a narrative-style report. Company has 100 offices nationwide. Some use homeworkers, some do not. Look in your local phone book to see if there is an office near you. "In rural areas, it's common to have public servants like firemen and policemen do this to supplement their incomes. In this case, there may not even be an office."
Requirements: Excellent verbal and written communication skills required. Typewriter is needed.
Provisions: Training is provided. Workers are independent contractors and are paid per report.

HUNTER PUBLISHING, 25 N.W. Point Blvd., Suite 800, Elk Grove, IL 60007.
Positions: Miscellaneous clerical work in the circulation department. Opportunities are limited.
Requirements: Must be local resident. Must obtain home worker certificate from the Illinois Department of Labor.

ILLINOIS HOSPITAL JOINT VENTURES, 1151 Warrenville, Naperville, IL 60601.
Positions: Medical transcribers.
Requirements: Must be local resident. Extensive experience is required. Must own necessary equipment.
Provisions: Pays piece rates.

INLINGUA TRANSLATION SERVICE, 690 Market St., Suite 700, San Francisco, CA 94104.

A CLOSER LOOK: GREEN'S MACHINE

Word processing businesses are popping up everywhere, but the field has a long way to go before reaching the saturation point. So says Steven Green, who operates Green's Machine with his wife, Joy, from their Milwaukee home.

Steven and Joy have taken their word processing business to an exceptionally high level. Their clients are major corporations which they cultivated over a long period of time. They now have so much business, the work is farmed out to 30 independent contractors in the Milwaukee area.

Steven thinks working at home is great, especially if you need a flexible schedule. But he warns about expecting to make a good living if you have inferior skills. "If you're not good enough, you'll fail. In the 'real world' of jobs, you can hide in the bureaucracy. As an independent contractor, you can't hide. You may think because on a typing test you type 90 words a minute, that means you're good. It doesn't. Typing different material from day to day is not the same as practicing a few paragraphs over and over. To make it as an independent word processor, you have to be better than good."

On the other hand, Steven says that at home, without the office rituals and distractions, you'll find you can accomplish in three hours the same work that used to take you eight hours. The other three hours (not to mention commuting time) can be spent any way you wish.

Positions: Inlingua is a major translation bureau with more than 200 offices all over the world. Freelance translators handle legal, business, and medical documentation in all languages.
Requirements: A thorough knowledge of foreign language and English is required. Submit resume and note special areas of expertise.
Provisions: Pays by the word.

INTER TRANSLATION & INTERPRETING, 1840 North Winona, Los Angeles, CA 94026.
Positions: Foreign language translators for legal and insurance documents. Arabic, Armenian, Italian, Japanese, Russian, and Persian and Turkish languages.
Requirements: Native or certified translators only. Must be Los Angeles resident. Experience in legal and/or insurance field required. Submit resume and references.

INTERNATIONAL DOCUMENTATION, P.O. Box 67628, Los Angeles, CA 90067.
Positions: Freelance translators are used by this service bureau.
Requirements: Thorough knowledge of any language for all types of translating; technical writing, medical transcribing, booklets, brochures, etc. Experience is necessary.
Provision: Pays by the word. Work is transferred via modem or conventional methods.

INTERNATIONAL LANGUAGE & COMMUNICATIONS CENTERS, INC., 79 W. Monroe, Suite 1310, Chicago, Il 60603.
Positions: Freelance translators handle business documents.
Requirements: Must be expert in a foreign language and English. Experience working with business documents is required. Prefers translators with own computers. Must live in the Chicago area. Submit resume and references.

INTERNATIONAL TRANSLATION BUREAU, 123 West Fourth, Room 240, Los Angeles, CA 90013.
Positions: Foreign language translators for general documentation. All major languages.
Requirements: Experienced translators only. Prefers to work with Los Angeles area residents. Submit resume and references.

ISTRA BUSINESS SERVICES, P.O. Box 599, Oakdale, NY 11769.
Positions: Translators of all kinds, especially Lithuanian.
Requirements: Need totally bilingual translators; must be well versed in language and culture and be able to professionally and accurately interpret business contracts. Must have Word Processor with decent printout.

JAPAN WORD TRANSLATION SERVICES, 241 Calado Ave., Campbell, CA 95008.
Positions: Translators and interpreters for Japanese to English and English to Japanese.
Requirements: Must be able to do word processing on either IBM or Mac in Japanese/English. If you have a modem you can work from anywhere in the country. Must sign a confidentiality disclosure.

LEO KANNER ASSOCIATES, P.O. Box 5187, Redwood City, CA 94063.
Positions: Freelance translators in all languages work in all subject areas.
Requirements: Must be a West Coast resident. Only professional-level translators will be considered. Apply with resume and references.
Provisions: Pays by the word.

KEATING OF CHICAGO, INC., 715 S. 25th Ave., Bellwood, IL 60104.
Positions: Keating is in the business of selling commercial kitchen equipment. Home-based clerical workers handle the typing of orders. The home-based work force has not grown here for several years, so there is not much opportunity.
Requirements: Must be local resident.

KING ENTERPRISE OFFICE SERVICES, 1632 Meader Ave., Merrick, NY 11566.
Positions: Data entry, desktop publishing, word processing, and legal transcription.
Requirements: Must be skilled; data entry requires 60 - 100 wpm. Must live on Long Island. Send resume.

KLINE'S DEPARTMENT STORE, INC., 514 W. 14th St., Chicago Heights, IL 60601.
Positions: This retail department store has home-based clerical workers handle miscellaneous paper work. There is a waiting list.
Requirements: Must be local resident. Must obtain a home worker certificate from the Illinois Department of Labor.

MORTAN KRITZER, M.D., INC., 6221 Wilshire Blvd., Los Angeles, CA 90048.

Positions: Medical transcribers.
Requirements: Must be very experienced in internal medicine terminology. Must be local. Good typewriter and transcribing machine is necessary.
Provisions: Pick up and delivery of supplies and finished work is provided daily since a 24-hour turn-around is required. Hours are part-time.

LAMONT TRANSCRIBING, 2701 LeJeune Rd., Suite 301, Coral Gables, FL 33134.
Positions: Word processing and court reporting transcription.
Requirements: Must own IBM compatible using DOS and Wordstar 6. Transcription work requires strong background in court reporting and a standard tape transcribing machine. Local residents only. Send resume.

THE LANGUAGE LAB, 211 E. 43rd St., New York, NY 10017.
Positions: Freelance translators work in all languages for clients in industry, law firms and government agencies.
Requirements: Only highly experienced professionals are considered. Submit resume and references.

LANGUAGE SERVICE BUREAU, 1601 Connecticut Ave., Suite 490, Washington, DC 20009.
Positions: Freelance foreign language translators.
Requirements: Experienced professionals only. Must be nearby resident. Submit resume and references.

LANGUAGES UNLIMITED, 4900 Leesburg Pike, Suite 402, Alexandria, VA 22302.
Positions: Freelance translators work in all languages on documentation for international businesses.
Requirements: Must be very experienced in foreign language translation and in working with business documents such as patents, taxes, or finance.
Submit resume and references.

LEADER TYPING SERVICE, 18 Caroline Ct., North Babylon, NY 11703.
Positions: Leader uses home-based typists to compile lists.
Requirements: Must live within the five surrounding areas of North Babylon, New York. Beyond knowing the keyboard, there are no typing speed requirements because piece rates are paid (per 1,000 characters typed). Typists must pick up and deliver their own work twice a week.
Provisions: Typewriters are provided. Pays $17 to $35 per 1,000 characters. "We always need typists. Home-based typists are hard for us to find."

LEE ENTERPRISES, 17111 S. Wallace, South Hollad, IL 60473.
Positions: Clerical duties for mail advertising business.
Requirements: Must be local resident. Must obtain home worker certificate from Illinois Department of Labor.

LIBRARY OF CONGRESS, National Library Service for the Blind and Physically Handicapped, Washington, D.C. 20542.
Positions: Homebound disabled proofreaders in the Braille Development Section.
Provisions: A training program is available to teach blind people to proofread Braille materials. A certificate is awarded upon completion of the program. Work is farmed out to homebound workers from the Library's production department on a piece rate

basis. Number of participants varies.

E.F. LINDBLOOM, 3636 W. Peterson Ave., Chicago, IL 60659.
Positions: Clerical duties for mail order.
Requirements: Must be local resident with experience and equipment. Must obtain home worker certificate from Illinois Department of Labor.

LINDNER TRANSLATIONS, INC., 29 Broadway, Suite 1707, New York, NY 10006.
Positions: Lindner is a 30-year-old translation bureau with freelance translators working in all languages. Areas include legal, medical, technical, chemical, financial, commercial and advertising.
Requirements: Must be proven professional with references. Prefers New York residents.
Provisions: Pays by the word on most assignments.

LINGUAMUNDI INTERNATIONAL, INC. P.O. Box 2206, Arlington, VA 22202.
Positions: Freelance translators; all languages. Company specializes in foreign language typesetting.
Requirements: Must be experienced professional translator with some area of technical expertise. Especially prefers translators with own computer equipment. Submit resume and references.

LINGUAASSIST, 4 DeHart Street, Morristown, NJ 07960.
Positions: LinguaAssist is a translation bureau that offers translation in 60 different languages. Freelancer translators handle technical and legal documentation, typesetting and printing services, and word processing services.
Requirements: Thorough knowledge of foreign language and English is required. Prefers local residents, but does have FAX capabilities for qualified translators outside the area. Submit resume.
Provisions: Pay varies according to project.

L.O.A.M., INC., 17549 Duvan Dr., Tinley Park, IL 60477.
Positions: About a hundred home-based clerical workers insert mailing pieces for this mailing service. There is a waiting list.
Requirements: Must be local resident. Must obtain home worker certificate from the Illinois Department of Labor.

MAIL BOXES, ETC., 172 N. Plank Rd., Newburg, NY 12550.
Positions: Bulk mailing occasionally with sorting, labeling, stuffing, and stamping. Word processing on contract basis.
Requirements: Must own a word processing system and be skilled and experienced. Local residents only. Send resume.

THE MAILBOX, INC., 521 Bedford Ave., Bellmore, NY 11710.
Positions: Data entry, wafer sealers, inserters.
Requirements: Need local people from East Meadow, Bellmore, Merrick, Levittown, and Wantagh for data entry, sealing stickers on the backs of envelopes, and envelope inserting. The work is available only during overflow time which are unpredictable. Qualified people should send resume.

MARKET FACTS, INC., 676 North St. Clair Street, Chicago, IL 60611.

Positions: Coding, keypunch, clerical, and statistical tabulation relating to market research work. Currently has 94 home workers.
Requirements: Must be local resident. Must obtain home worker certificate from State Department of Labor.
Provisions: Pay varies according to job functions.

MCGINLEY PROCESS SERVICE, 5922 S.W. 29th St., Miami, FL 33155.
Positions: Certified process servers. Company is setting up a nationwide network of process servers and related services.
Requirements: Certification is necessary where required by law. PC and modem are necessary. Send letter of interest.
Provisions: Can be located anywhere in U.S.

MDL SERVICES, 8351 Sperry Ct., Laurel, MD 20723.
Positions: Medical transcription.
Requirements: Two years of hospital experience required. Must own IBM compatible with laser printer plus transcribing equipment for cassettes of all sizes. Local residents only mail resume.

MECHANICAL SECRETARY, 108-16 72nd Ave., Forest Hills, NY 11375.
Positions: Word processors and transcribers. Work covers several areas: medical, legal, insurance, advertising and general business. Currently has 15 home workers and there is a very long waiting list.
Requirements: Must have good skills and own approved equipment; IBM compatible with Word Perfect 5.1 for word processing plus a dictaphone for transcribing. Experience is required. Send resume. Must be resident of Manhattan, Brooklyn, or Queens.
Provisions: Pick up and delivery of supplies and finished work is provided. Pays production rates. Full-time work only.

MID ISLAND TRANSCRIPTION, 100 Washington Ave., Patchogue, NY 11772.
Positions: Medical transcribers.
Requirements: Need strong skills with five years plus background in medical hospital transcription. Must own IBM compatible. Local residents mail resume.

MOBILE STENO, 12439 S. Maple, 1st Rear, Blue Island, Il 60406.
Positions: General typing.
Requirements: Must be local resident. Experience and equipment required.

MODERN SECRETARIAL SERVICE, 2813 South La Cienega Avenue, Los Angeles, CA 90034.
Positions: Typists and word processors. Company specializes in insurance policy typing, but does all types of legal and general work. "We're always looking for good people."
Requirements: Must have good equipment and skills. Test will be given. Los Angeles residents only.

MY OTHER SECRETARY, 1133 15th St., Washington, DC 20005.
Positions: Transcription of big tape jobs of panel sessions, seminars, and discussions. These are big tape jobs, some with eight people speaking.
Requirements: Speed, accuracy, and confidentiality essential. Local residents send resume.

NATIONWIDE SECRETARIAL SERVICE, 305 Broadway, Suite 408, New York, NY 10007.
Positions: Legal transcribers.
Requirements: Need strong legal transcription background and have all necessary equipment. Need to live in New York City, Brooklyn, or Long Island for drop off and pick up. Mail resume.

NEWSBANK, INC., 58 Pine Street, New Canaan, CT 06840.
Positions: About 20 indexers and proofreaders produce current affairs references from their home offices. The work is part-time; each works from 20 to 25 hours per week.
Requirements: Must be local in order to pick up and drop off work twice a week and attend meetings.
Provisions:; There is a three-month training period in-house for learning the company's indexing methods and how to use a personal computer. All equipment is provided.

NODEL/LEE ENTERPRISES, 17111 S. Wallace, South Holland, IL 60473.
Positions: Home-based workers insert coupons into envelopes for this direct mail advertising service.
Requirements: Must be local resident. Apply in person. Workers are called when work builds up.
Provisions: Pays piece rates.

NORTH AMERICAN CO. FOR LIFE & HEALTH INSURANCE, 222 S. Riverside Plaza, Chicago, IL 60606.
Positions: General office work.
Requirements: Must be local resident with office experience. Must obtain home worker certificate from Illinois Department of Labor.

NORTHERN ILLINOIS MEDICAL CENTER, 4201 Medical Center Drive, McHenry, IL 60601.
Positions: Medical transcription.
Requirements: Must be local resident with experience and equipment. Must obtain home worker certificate from Illinois Department of Labor.

NORTHWEST MAILING SERVICE, 5401 W. Grand, Chicago, Il 60639.

Positions: Miscellaneous clerical work involved in mailing services.
Requirements: Must be local resident. Must obtain home worker certificate from Illinois Department of Labor.
Provisions: Pays piece rates.

OMNILINGUA, INC., 2857 Mt. Vernon Rd., S.E., Cedar Rapids, IA 52403.
Positions: Native-speaking translators for work in many different fields. All languages are eligible.
Requirements: Expertise in any area of business is necessary.
Provisions: Can live anywhere. Pay methods vary. Inquiries are welcome from qualified translators.

PACIFIC WORD PUBLISHING, 4250 Terman Dr., #104, Palo Alto, CA 94306.
Positions: Transcription of business meetings.
Requirements: Must have computer, standard and micro cassette equipment, and experience with Page Maker. Local residents send resume.
Provisions: Pay is based on speed with turnaround.

THE PAPER WORKS, 166 W. Washington, Suite 540, Chicago, IL 60602.
Positions: Transcription and word processing.
Requirements: Need computer and Word Perfect 5.1 with experience in transcription of all types. Local resident only send resume.

PARADISE MAILING, INC., 607 Harbor View Boulevard, Somerset, MA 02725.
Positions: Typing addresses on envelopes and flyers for direct mail processing.
Requirements: Good typing skills and typewriter are required. Must be local resident.
Provisions: Pays minimum wage.

PEGASUS TRANSCRIPTION PLUS, INC., 428 S. Cedar St., Palatine, IL 60067.
Positions: Medical transcription.
Requirements: Must be very experienced medical transcriptionist with medical terminology and a background in hospitals or doctor's office. Requires IBM (fax and modem capabilities would be great) with WordPerfect 5.0 and 5.1. Also need dictaphone equipment for micro and standard cassettes. Local residents send resume.

PETERS SHORTHAND REPORTING CORPORATION, 3433 American River Drive, Suite A, Sacramento, CA 95825.
Positions: Court reporting and transcribing.
Requirements: Must be local resident. Some travel is required. Experience is necessary.
Provisions: Pays hourly, plus piece rates, plus expenses.

PHYSICIANS MEDICAL TRANSCRIBING, Chatsworth, CA (818) 938-1553.
Positions: Medical transcribers.
Requirements: Must live in or near the San Fernando Valley. Experience is required in acute care.
Provisions: Part-time hours only. Pays piece rates.

PREFERRED BUSINESS CENTERS, 875 N. Michigan, Suite 3614, Chicago, IL 60601.
Positions: General transcription.
Requirements: Must be experienced and have necessary equipment. Local residents

only.

PRINTED WORD, 6551 Beth Ann Ct., Middletown, OH 45044.
Positions: Word processors.
Requirements: Must own and have experience working on IBM with WordPerfect 5.1, Windows, Lotus, and Pagemaker. Occasionally has need for medical transcriber which requires all types of medical text knowledge and both standard and micro transcribing equipment. Local residents send resume.

REBECCA EMERSON SECRETARIAL, P.O. Box 1964, Belaire, TX 77402.
Positions: Legal and medical transcription.
Requirements: Must own IBM with Word Perfect and Microsoft Word. Experience required. Local residents send resume.

RICHMOND REPORTING, 6800 Jericho Turnpike, Suite 111E, Syosset, NY.
Positions: Legal transcribers.
Requirements: Need people with law industry background and knowledge of legal depositions. Must be able to do 70 wpm with accuracy and be able to report to the office 2 to 3 times a week to drop off work. Must own or have access to a 5.1 computer with laser printer and a Stenorette (a dictaphone machine with a reel-to-reel spool tape, NOT a cassette pop-in). Stenorette must have a foot pedal. Work is based on individual contracts. Send resume.

RMS COMPUTER SERVICES, 11 Kilkea Ct., Perry Hall, MD 21236.
Positions: Word processors and proof readers.
Requirements: Must own IBM compatible with Word Perfect 6.0. Skills and experienced required. Must live close by. Send resume.

MARION J. ROSLEY SECRETARIAL SERVICES, 41 Topland Rd., Hartsdale, NY 10530.
Positions: Word processors, all types of transcription, and graphic art.
Requirements: Need all levels of people for word processing using Macintosh, Word Perfect and Windows. Local residents mail resumes.

RSI, P.O. Box 5510, San Mateo, CA 94402.
Positions: Insurance inspectors/investigators. Independent contractors only.
Requirements: Extensive experience is required. Send resume. Must live in one of the Bay area counties.

SACRAMENTO PROFESSIONAL TYPISTS NETWORK, 9113 Sherrilee Way, Orangevale, CA 95662.
The Network got its start as the original chapter of Peggy Glenn's national home typing group. After the national group disbanded, the Sacramento Network continued as a support group, then eventually formed an organization with bylaws and regular meetings which are held on the second Thursday of each month. Members are professional home-based typists and word processors. Members refer clients and work to other members when there is overflow, rush jobs, jobs that are too big to handle, and in cases of illness or vacations. Often, one member will bid on a large job and then enlist the help of other members to do the job. "This is our lifestyle; it's called freedom," says chairwoman Janice Katz. Currently has 50 members. Inquires and new members are welcome.
Requirements: Only residents of Sacramento can participate. Annual dues are $25.

SCANDIA AMERICA GROUP, 1 Liberty Plaza 34th Fl., New York, NY 10006.
Positions: Word processors and data entry.
Requirements: Experienced required in lower level accounting with insurance industry background. Must own equipment and be local resident. Send resume.

SCRIBE LINK, 124 N. Main St., Forked River, NJ 08731.
Positions: Medical transcribing.
Requirements: Senior level medical transcriptionist with solid medical terminology in all types and fields of medicine. Must be able to discern accents. Local residents send resume.

SCRIPTURE PRESS PUBLICATIONS, 1825 College Ave., Wheaton, IL 60187.
Positions: This religious publisher uses home-based clerical workers to proofread and assemble packets of printed materials.
Requirements: Must be local resident.

SECREPHONE, 2 Kilmer Rd., Edison, NJ 08817.
Positions: Secrephone subcontracts medical transcribing work to home-based medical transcribers.
Requirements: Local residents only. Must own equipment and have minimum three years hospital experience. Minimum 75 - 80 wpm. Send resume.

SECRETARIAL OFFICE SERVICES, 99 W. Apple Ave., Muskegon, MI 49440.
Positions: Legal transcribers.
Requirements: Must be local resident. Requires strong experience in court transcription and knowledge of court proceedings. Must own IBM compatible with Word Perfect. Transcribe from video using VCR with headphones and foot pedal or sometimes standard cassettes. Send resume.

SECRETARIAL SERVICES, 283 Buttermilk Pike, Ft. Mitchell, KY 41047.
Positions: Word processing and desktop publishing.
Requirements: Must own and be skilled with IBM compatible and WordPerfect 6.0, Windows, and Lotus for word processing. For desktop publishing, Corell and Page Maker are required. Local residents send resume.

SENECA INSURANCE CO., INC., 11 John St. 3rd Fl., New York, NY 10018.
Positions: Policy typists.
Requirements: Must be accurate and detail oriented. Experience typing policy insurance forms required. Local residents only. Send resume.

SH3, INC., 5338 E. 115th St. Kansas City, MO 64137.
Positions: Freelance translators for this service bureau.
Requirements: Thorough knowledge of French, German, Italian,, or Spanish. You must be experienced and able to provide telecommunications, IBM PC (or compatible) disks, or COM disks. Send resume.

SHERMAN HOSPITAL, 934 Center St., Elgin, IL.
Positions: Medical transcribing.
Requirements: Must be local resident. Equipment, good skills and a minimum five years experience are required.

SIMULTRANS, 2606 Bayshore Parkway, Mountainview, CA 94043.
Positions: Translators and desktop publishers.
Requirements: Need translating professionals from anywhere in the country with minimum of five years experience. Must own fax and IBM compatible computer. Also need freelance desktop publishers also with translating skills. Must live in the San Francisco Bay Area. Send resume.

SKRUDLAND PHOTO SERVICE, INC., 1720 Rand Rd., Palatine, IL 60074.
Positions: Typing, stuffing envelopes, and other clerical operations.
Requirements: Must be local resident. Must obtain home worker certificate from the State Department of Labor.

SUOBODA PUBLICATIONS, 30 Montgomery, Jersey City, NJ 07302.
Positions: Bilingual English/Ukrainian writers and typists.
Requirements: Must be totally fluent. Send resume.

TAILORED SERVICES, INC., P.O. Box 4767, Silver Spring, MD 20914.
Positions: Word processors.
Requirements: Looking for speed, accuracy, and the ability to work independently. Need IBM compatible with Word Perfect 5.0 and fax machine. Local residents only. Send resume.

TIM SWEENEY & ASSOCIATES, 101 California St., Suite 300, San Francisco, CA 94111.
Positions: Tim Sweeney is a stock broker who conducts financial seminars around the Bay area. He uses home workers for bulk mail processing projects.
Requirements: Must live in San Francisco. Must be dependable for steady, part-time work. Work involves picking up supplies such as mailing labels, brochures, and envelopes, taking them home and stuffing them, then returning them for postage metering (they will be mailed from the office).
Provisions: Pays cash daily, \$.03 or \$.05 per envelope depending on the particular job.

TECHNICAL WRITING AND TRANSLATING ASSOCIATES, 5356 N. Bernard, Chicago, IL 60625.
Positions: Foreign language translators work as technical writers and editors in all languages.
Requirements: Thorough knowledge of foreign language and excellent English skills are essential. Technical writing experience is required. Prefers to work with Northern Illinois residents. Submit resume and references.

TELECOMMUNICATIONS PROFESSIONAL DESIGN, P.O. Box 215684, Sacramento, CA 94026.
Positions: Home-based telemarketers are being sought in the Sacramento area for business-to-business calls. Workers take orders, set appointments, do surveys and market research. No sales calls.
Provisions: Training is provided in workshop area.

THUDIUM MAIL ADVERTISING COMPANY, 3553 North Milwaukee, Chicago, IL 60601.
Positions: Typing, labeling, inserting and other clerical operations involved in letter shop work. Currently has 38 home workers.

A CLOSER LOOK: TRANSCRIPTIONS LIMITED

With over 1,000 home-based medical transcribers associated with 27 offices around the country, Transcriptions Limited may be the largest home work organization in the U.S.

Founder and president Mark Forstein started the company in 1970, he says, "By happy accident." It is by no accident, however, that Transcriptions Limited reached its present level of success.

Forstein says home workers are a tremendous resource in the work force. Aside from the cost savings to employers like himself, he claims home workers are fiercely loyal and supportive of the work-at-home movement and each other.

Some transcribers have been with the company for many years. "These are mostly women who start out with us when they have young children. After the family is older, some of them want to get out of the house and back into the office routine for social contact. These women have been loyal to us and we return the trust by offering them the opportunity to come to work in our offices."

The offices, which are actually a separate business entity, handle any overload that comes up. Since the transcribers are independent contractors, they can refuse work at any time, for any reason. This gives them some latitude (and greatly reduced stress) within the structure which requires a 24-hour turnaround time as a rule.

The company operates on a seven-day week, 24 hours a day. It is managed by key people on a management pyramid.

Inquiries from experienced transcribers are always welcome, but you should be prepared to prove your worth. Experience in acute care would be best and you will be given an extensive test in medical terminology.

The training session lasts only for a few hours—just long enough to get an overview of how things work and what is expected. "We do not offer the luxury of on-the-job training."

If you know your stuff, though, you can make good money. Pay is based on production and varies depending upon the part of the country you are in. In California, average pay is more than $13 an hour and in Chicago, one woman made $60,000 last year.

You will need a typewriter and transcriber, but if you don't own one, Transcriptions Limited will rent it to you at a nominal fee. The same principle applies to pick-up and delivery; it is an option that is available for a small price if you choose. You can also choose the option of working part-time or full-time hours.

These options are the result of Forstein's efforts over the years to comply with any and all aspects of using independent contractors. "Nothing," he says, "has been left to chance."

Requirements: Must be local resident. Must obtain home worker certificate from State Department of Labor.

TOTAL TYPING SERVICES, 311 N.W. St., Jacksonville, IL 62650.
Positions: Word processors.
Requirements: Must own IBM with Lotus, DBase, laser printer, WordPerfect 5.1, 6.0 or AmiPro. Excellent grasp of English language required. Residents of Morgan County only send resume.

TOY TOWN TYPING, 29 Linden St., Winchester, MA 01475.
Positions: Medical transcription.
Requirements: Requires experience and knowledge of all types of medications and terminology. Need IBM or Mac; currently using Microsoft Windows and Multimate. Should also own medical texts for knowledge of medication terms. Will only accept professional work. Local residents only send resume.

TRANSCRIPTIONS LIMITED.
Positions: Medical transcribers for hospital overflow work; discharge summaries and operative reports. Currently has over 1,000 home workers and 30 offices nationwide, including Los Angeles, San Francisco, Sacramento, Denver, and Chicago. If there is an office near enough for you to work for, you will find it listed in your local phone book.
Requirements: Acute care experience is required. A test in medical terminology is given to all applicants.
Provisions: Choice of part-time or full-time hours is available. Equipment is provided on a rental basis if necessary. Daily pick up and delivery of supplies and finished work is provided. Pays production rates that vary depending on the part of the country where you're located. Average hourly pay is about $13 an hour. Inquiries are always welcome from qualified transcribers.

TRANSLATING ASSOCIATES, 104 East 40th , New York, NY 10016.
Positions: Freelance translators work on assignments in all subject areas.
Requirements: Must be New York resident. Only highly professional translators with verifiable references will be considered. Prefers translators with writing and editing experience.
Provisions: Pays by the word.

TRANSLATION COMPANY OF AMERICA, INC., 10 West 37th, New York, NY 10018.
Positions: Translators, interpreters, and typesetters.
Requirements: Prefers native language translators. Must own typewriter or word processor. Expertise in a particular area of business is required. Send resume and references.
Provisions: Pays by the word.

TRANS-LINGUAL COMMUNICATIONS, INC., Quaker Tower, 321 N. Clark St., Suite 3140, Chicago, IL 60610.
Positions: Foreign language translators work in all subject areas. Company specialized in software and technical manual translation.
Requirements: Minimum five years verifiable experience as a professional translator is required. Must have own technical background. Prefers translators with own computer

equipment. Can live anywhere.
Provisions: Pays by the word.

TRANS-LINK, 1850 Gaugh, Suite 701, San Francisco, CA 94109.
Positions: Translators in 55 different foreign languages handle freelance assignments in technical translation, international advertising and audio-visual dubbing.
Requirements: Absolute knowledge of foreign language and English is required. Must be West Coast resident, preferably California. Resume and references required. Note area of technical expertise.
Provisions: Pay methods very according to type of work.

TRI-CITY SECRETARIAL, 640 Northland Blvd., Suite 21, Cincinnati, OH 45240.
Positions: Word processors and desktop publishers.
Requirements: Need IBM and Word Perfect 6.0 and Lotus. Desktop publishers need Express Publisher and Page Maker. Experience required. Local residents send resume.

TUREK - VENTURE 2, P.O. Box 187, Catasauqua, PA 18032.
Positions: Medical transcribers.
Requirements: Experience required in all types of medicine and practices. Need own equipment including micro and standard tape transcribing machines. Local residents send resume.

24 HOUR SECRETARY, 6800 Liberty Rd., Baltimore, MD 21207.
Positions: Medical and legal transcription.
Requirements: At least three years experience with certificate preferred. Must own IBM compatible with Word Perfect 6.0 and the ability to take all types of tapes. Must be from surrounding area and come to the office to pick up documents. Will work with modem, but still needs to be local. Send resume.

TYPE, 7108 Silver Circle, Middletown, MD 21769.
Positions: Word processing and legal transcription.
Requirements: Need IBM with Word Perfect 3.2. Must be able to do professional work on government contracts in a timely way. 4-tracktranscriber is provided, but in-depth legal knowledge is necessary for legal transcribers. Both jobs require good grammar and good ear for dialects and weekly turnaround. Local people send resume.
Provisions: Will pick-up and deliver.

TYPE-A-LINE, INC., 311 Woods Avenue, Oceanside, NY 11572.
Positions: Typing of labels, cards, envelopes, and some inserting for direct mail fulfillment company. Some OCR typing on computers also. Currently has 17 home workers and no applications are being taken as there is a very long waiting list.
Requirements: Typewriter and good typing skills are required. Must be local to either Oceanside or Brentwood in order to pick up and deliver supplies and finished work.
Provisions: Training is provided. If necessary and nearby, company will provide pick up and delivery services. Pays piece rates equal to about $5 an hour. "New York State is tough on home workers. The State demands 'good' reasons for being allowed to work at home. I'd like to hire more home workers, but unless you meet the requirements, I can't."

THE TYPING COMPANY, P.O. Box 955, Davis, CA 95617.
Positions: Typists and transcribers. Most work is academic; term papers, theses,

dissertations, application forms, tables, and grants. Now expanding into medical transcribing.
Requirements: Must have good typewriter and excellent skills. Davis residents only. Home workers pick up and deliver own supplies and finished work whenever they want to during the day.
Provisions: Some training is provided. Pays 60% of the fee paid to the company. The best typist earns up to $12 an hour.

TYPING PRODUCTIONS, 8 Viola St., Milton, MA 02186.
Positions: Medical transcription.
Requirements: Must be computer literate and have good word processing skills. Medical background in internal medicine, urology, orthopedics, cardiology and good grammatical skills required. Be able to take microcassettes and do work on quick turnaround. People from Southshore, Milton, and Quincy send resume.

UMI/DATA COURIER, 620 S. Third St., Louisville, KY 40202.
Positions: About 30 abstracters work at home as independent contractors. Home workers have been used here since 1976.
Requirements: Must live nearby in order to pick up the publications that you will be abstracting once a week. Reasonable good communication skills are needed. Send resume.
Provisions: Computers are necessary for the job and the company does provide them.

BETTY VAN KEULEN, 18215 Jayhawk Dr., Penn Valley, CA 95946.
Positions: Medical transcribers.
Requirements: Hospital transcribing experience is required. Must be local resident in order to pick up and deliver supplies and finished work. A good typewriter is necessary.
Provisions: If a transcriber isn't available, company will lease a transcriber at half price. Pays by the line.

VERNA MEDICAL TRANSCRIPTIONS, 156 Smithwood Avenue, Milpitas, CA 95035.
Positions: Medical transcribers for all types of medical records.
Requirements: Experience is necessary. Must own good typewriter and transcribing machine with either standard or microcassettes. Must be local resident in order to pick up and deliver supplies and finished work.
Provisions: Pays piece rates. Part-time or full-time work is available.

VINCENT LAW OFFICE, P.O. Box 450, Crowley, LA 70526.
Positions: Legal transcription.
Requirements: Experience with sales, mortgages, wills, petitions, and personal injury. Need computer and mini cassette equipment. Local residents send resume.

WCC, 40 Skokie Boulevard, Northbrook, IL 60062.
Positions: Translators for computer-aided technical translation into all major languages.
Requirements: Thorough knowledge of both English and foreign language. Some word processing experience. Apply with resume and references. Prefers local people.

WOMEN'S CLUBS PUBLISHING CO., 323 S. Franklin St., Chicago, IL 60606.
Positions: Miscellaneous typing and clerical work.
Requirements: Must be local resident. Must obtain home worker certificate from the

Illinois Department of Labor.
Provisions: Pays piece rates.

WORD EXPRESS, 250 W. 54th St., Room 606, New York, NY 10019.
Positions: Word processing of long manuscripts, screenplays, and address list.
Requirements: Must have DOS, Word Perfect, and Mac file transfer software. Requires good skills. Local residents only mail resume.
Provisions: Pays per page or per address.

WORD PROCESSING UNLIMITED, 6404 Crestwood Rd., Baltimore, MD 21239.
Positions: Transcribing, data entry, and desktop publishing.
Requirements: Looking for people with higher skill levels and equipment. Strong Word Perfect, tape transcription, and knowledge of database packages required. For desktop publishing, a familiarity with Mac and a strong background required. Local residents only should send resumes including cover letter and statement of monies required.

WORD TECH, 456 Cherokee Ave., S.E., Atlanta, GA 30312.
Positions: Medical and legal transcription.
Requirements: Experience in all types of medicine tapes; you will be tested. Need IBM with modem, Word Perfect 5.1 or 6.0. Local residents send resume.

WORDMASTERS, 1222 O'Berry Hoover Rd., Orlando, FL 32825.
Positions: Straight text typing and chiropractic transcription. Also writing and typing resumes.
Requirements: Must own and have experience on Word Perfect 5.1, Windows, and Lotus. Work on 24 hour turnover. Local residents mail resume.

WORDNET, P.O. Box 164, Acton, MA 01720.
Positions: Professional freelancers translate technical manuals and documentation in and out of all major languages.
Requirements: Must be experienced and skilled both in languages, technical verbiage, and computers. Because translation projects are transmitted electronically all over the world, a computer and modem is required. Send resume.

WORDRHYTHM WORD PROCESSING, 426 B Pennsylvania Ave., Santa Cruz, CA 94026.
Positions: Word processing and transcribing.
Requirements: Need Mac with Microsoft Windows and Pagemaker. Transcribers need standard and micro tape equipment. Experienced local people send resume.

WORDS AND PICTURES, INC., 18220 Harwood, Homewood, IL 60430.
Positions: Word processors. Also graphic designers.
Requirements: Need IBM Word Perfect 5.1 and 6.0 and Windows. Experience required. Local residents send resume.

WORDS PLUS, 18 Park Lane West, New Milford, CT 06776.
Positions: Word processing and data entry. Database work will include 25- 150 page survey sheets, mail merges, mail lists, newsletters, brochures, etc.
Requirements: Need intelligent people with skills and experience. Mustown IBM compatible with Word Perfect 5.1, 6.1, Windows, Corell, and Microsoft Alpha 4 database.

Closeup: At-Home Professions

As you look through this chapter, it's obvious there is a great need for medical transcribers. You'll also notice this job requires knowledge and skill.

So how do you take advantage of such a large, growing opportunity? One option is by learning at home with At-Home Professions. The home study course was designed by people experienced in the field and can be completed in about four months. At-Home Professions boasts a successful at-home job placement service, but graduates say the service is unnecessary because once your skills are in place getting the work is easy.

Three years ago, Rochelle Wexler decided she wanted to have more flexibility in her schedule. Working in Manhattan for a publisher fromnine to five had lost its appeal. She went looking for something that would have a demand in the future, something interesting. "I don't want to be bored to death," she says. "I have a problem with that. And what I didn't have was a burning desire to go back to school."

After seeing an ad for At-Home Professions in a magazine, Rochelle investigated the field of medical transcribing and found it met all her criteria.

The company checked out clean with the Better Business Bureau, still,it took a big leap of faith to go from a secure job to something totally new. "I depended on At-Home Professions to keep feeding me information and telling me 'you can do this.' I kept working in my job, studying the course in the evenings and on weekends."

Within a month of graduation, Rochelle had her first two clients (doctors). "When I started out I didn't want to say I had experience when I didn't so when I got uncomfortable I offered to do something for no charge." That technique worked well, and today Rochelle is working at home full-time. She does all of her own pick-up and delivery, but says she never has to leave the neighborhood. ("Doctors are everywhere!") The doctors give her the tapes that document their every action and Rochelle returns the transcribed copies within a few days.

Rochelle feels anyone could do this. "I was never a typist and had no interest in being a secretary. But now I have a 486 computer and transcription machine and I make my living doing this. The work is piecework so the faster I learn to type the more I make."

To receive information from At-Home Professions call 800-475-0100.

Transcription work requires audio tape equipment. Must be true independent contractors, legitimately set up for taxes, etc. due to strict local codes. Local residents only mail resumes.

WORDSELLER BUSINESS COMMUNICATIONS, 1726 Kirkwood, Houston, TX 77077.
Positions: Translation.
Requirements: Proficient translator with Macintosh for preparing reports. Local resident only send resume.

WORDSEN WORD PROCESSING, 38-30 209th St., Bayside, NY 11361.
Positions: Word processing.
Requirements: Must be able to type a minimum 60 wpm accurately and have excellent grasp of English language. Own computer and Word Perfect 5.1. Must be local resident and pick-up and drop off work on 24-hour turn around. Send resume.

WORDSMART, 250 5th Ave., Suite 202, New York, NY 10001.
Positions: Transcribers.
Requirements: Need only top transcriptionists (70 - 75 wpm) with WordPerfect 5.1 and standard cassette equipment. Much of the work is from phone conversation tapes; familiarity with banking terminology required.
Provisions: Pays $5 per single space page.

WORDTRONICS DIRECT MAIL SERVICE BUREAU, 190 East Post Rd., White Plains, NY 10601.
Positions: Data entry and letter shop services.
Requirements: For data entry, must own IBM PC using ASCII file, D-Base for creating mailing lists. Must be quick and efficient. Also experienced people stuffing, sealing, bulk-rate letter shop services. Local residents only mail resumes.
Provisions: Earn $8 to $12 per hour on a per-piece payment.

WORLD WIDE, P.O. Box 2266, Culver City, CA 90231.
Positions: Medical transcribers for home work out of three Los Angeles offices. Currently has over 100 home workers.
Requirements: Must have experience and knowledge of medical terminology. Work will be for hospitals, clinics, doctors, and government. Must have good typewriter and transcribing machine. Los Angeles residents only.
Provisions: Specific training is provided. Pick up and delivery of supplies and finished work will be provided if necessary. Pays piece rates equal to about $12 an hour. Part-time or full-time hours available. Inquiries are welcome.

WORLDWIDE TRANSLATION AGENCY, 1680 North Vine, Suite 610, Hollywood, CA 90028.
Positions: Foreign language translators work on a wide variety of documents.
Requirements: Los Angeles residents only. Must be experienced professional translator with resume and references.
Provisions: Pays by the word.

WRITERS CRAMP, 6 Norton Rd., Monmouth Junction, NJ 08852.
Positions: Legal transcribers.
Requirements: Candidates need a good solid academic background (college/secretarial);

training in legal end available. Must know WordPerfect and have an IBM compatible computer. Need transcribing machine for tapes. Local residents only mail resume.

YOUR SECRETARIAL ALTERNATIVE, 1516 Marimack Dr., Gulf Breeze, FL 32561.
Positions: Word processing, legal and medical transcription.
Requirements: Experienced word processors to do term papers, leaflets, brochures letters, and home owners association notices. Legal transcribers need standard casset e equipment and experience. Medical transcribers should have experience with fam ly practice and plastic surgery as well as transcribing machine for micro cassette ta es. Local residents send resume.

OPPORTUNITIES WORKING WITH PEOPLE

In this section you will find jobs that have but one basic requirement--the ability to work well with people. Both at-home and from-home jobs are included. At-home jobs include telephone surveying, customer service, fund raising, recruiting, and staffing coordination.

Telephone surveying involves calling consumers to ask specific questions about their buying habits, or more weighty questions of social significance. The names and numbers are supplied and the surveyor is paid for each call. The average pay works out to about $6 an hour. The work is not usually steady; it tends to come and go. This can be good for someone who cannot make a permanent commitment. If you want steady surveying work you should sign up with several companies in order to insure back-to-back assignments.

Customer service is a profession that is just beginning to come into its own. American companies are starting to realize the importance of listening to their customers and trying to satisfy their needs. A customer service representative is basically a problem-solver. The job requires an ability to listen and record customers' comments accurately.

Fund raising can also be an easy job. It doesn't pay as well as surveying, usually only minimum wage plus a small bonus for bringing in so-much in donations. It is, however, very easy work to get and it can be good experience leading to more sophisticated and higher-paying phone work.

Like customer service, staffing coordination is a fairly new opportunity for home workers. This work is found most often in the burgeoning health-care field. Agencies are used to fill the staffing needs of hospitals, nursing homes, and outpatients. Calls come in day and night, but most agencies don't keep their doors open 24 hours a day. After 5:00 on weekdays and on weekends, calls are forwarded to a staffing coordinator's home. It is the coordinator's job to dispatch nurses and home health care workers as they are needed during those hours. Most coordinators have electronic pagers, so they need not be completely homebound.

Field surveying is a job that is custom-made for someone with an outgoing personality. The word "field" indicates that most of the work is done outside— which may mean in a mall, at a movie theatre, or door-to-door. The surveyor collects answers to survey questions in the field and then returns home to fill out the paperwork. It is perfect for the person that needs the flexibility that working from home offers, but who doesn't want to be stuck inside all the time.

Field surveyors work for market research firms and opinion pollers. They generally work as independent contractors, often working for more than one company at a time because each survey may last from only two days to two weeks on average and being on the roster at a number of companies makes steady work more likely.

ADULT INDEPENDENT DEVELOPMENT CENTER OF SANTA CLARA COUNTY, INC. 1190 Benton, Santa Clara, CA 95050.
Positions: Fund raisers request donations over the phone.
Requirements: Must be reliable and self-managing. Must live within Santa Clara County.
Provisions: Training is provided. Pays salary plus bonuses and fringe benefits.

AIS MARKET RESEARCH, 4974 N. Fresno, Bldg. 567, Fresno, CA 93726.
Positions: Field surveyors in the San Joaquin Valley.
Requirements: Must be resident of either Fresno or Modesto. Market research or similar experience required. Send for application.
Provisions: Work is part-time and sporadic. Pays by the survey.

ALL CITY LOCKSMITHS, 160 Del Vale, San Francisco, CA 94127.
Positions: Customer service/dispatchers for locksmiths. Job consists of answering incoming calls at home and determining whether dispatch is necessary.
Requirements: Need to be friendly, alert, and articulate. Locksmith knowledge is preferred. Company works on a 24-hour a day, seven day a week schedule, with home workers working on shift rotations. Calls are forwarded to workers' homes for duration of each shift period only. Must live in San Francisco.
Provisions: Complete training is provided. Commission paid on successfully concluded calls. Company is expanding.

AMERICAN RED CROSS, 2700 Wilshire Blvd., Los Angeles, CA 90057.
Positions: Telephone recruiters locate potential blood donors.
Requirements: Two years telemarketing experience required. Must be available Sunday through Thursday. Excellent communications skills necessary. Los Angeles residents only. Send resume.
Provisions: Pays $4.63 an hour.

AMERICAN TELEMARKETING, INC., 3349 Cahuenga Blvd. West, Suite 5A, Los Angeles, CA 90068.
Positions: Market research is conducted solely over the phone. Part-time hours only. Work is available in most major metropolitan areas.
Requirements: Market research experience is preferred, but not required.
Provisions: Pays about $8 an hour.

AMVETS, 1111 Prospect, Indianapolis, IN 46203.
Positions: Fund raisers call for donations of clothing and household articles.
Requirements: Must live in Indianapolis.
Provisions: Pays hourly wage plus bonus plan.

A-ONE RESEARCH, INC., 2800 Coyle St., Brooklyn, NY 11235.
Positions: Field surveyors for market research studies.
Requirements: Must be resident of New York City or one of the immediate suburbs. Good communication skills and interviewing experience required.
Provisions: Work is part-time only. Pays by the survey.

ARTHRITIS FOUNDATION, 203 Willow St., Suite 201, San Francisco, CA 94109.
Positions: Telephone recruiters find volunteers to go door-to-door for donations. This program repeats every fall and spring for about two months each time.

Requirements: Must live in the Bay area. Experience is not required, but the director says this work is very difficult and may not be suitable for newcomers. Must be available to work (call) during the evening hours of 6 to 9:30 pm.
Provisions: Pays $1.50 per recruitment.

ATLANTA MARKETING RESEARCH CENTER, 10 Lenox Pointe N.E., Atlanta, GA 30324.
Positions: Field surveyors and occasionally, telephone interviewers.
Requirements: Atlanta residents only. Experience preferred.
Provisions: Pays by the survey.

FRANCES BAUMAN ASSOCIATES,, 23 Girard St., Marlboro, NJ 07746.
Positions: Field surveyors and telephone interviewers for market research assignments.
Requirements: Must live in tri-state area of New York, New Jersey, or Pennsylvania. Experience required.
Provisions: Work is part-time on-call only. Pays by the survey.

BLIND & HANDICAPPED, 931 Manor Blvd., San Leandro, CA 94579.
Positions: Telemarketing of household products for fund raising.
Requirements: Must live in Northern California.
Provisions: Training is provided. Pays salary or commission.

CALIFORNIA AMVETS, 747 Twelfth Ave., San Diego, CA 92101.
Positions: Fund raisers telephone for donations of household discards to be sold through thrift shops. Also has locations in El Cajon, Fresno, and Oceanside.
Requirements: Must be dependable and have good speaking skills. Must live in local area.
Provisions: Choice of part-time or full-time; hours flexible. Pays guarantee of minimum wage plus bonus plan. Training provided.

CALIFORNIA COUNCIL FOR THE BLIND, 8700 Reseda Blvd. #208, Northridge, CA 91325.
Positions: Fund raisers telephone for donations of household discards.
Requirements: Must be resident of greater Los Angeles area. Good phone manner necessary.
Provisions: Pays $6 an hour plus bonus plan.

CAMERON MILLS RESEARCH SERVICE, 2414 Cameron Mills Rd., Alexandria, VA 22302.
Positions: Field surveyors and telephone interviewers for market research projects.
Requirements: Must live in Washington, D.C., Northern Virginia, or nearby Maryland. Some experience working with the public necessary.
Provisions: Pays by the survey.

CANCER FEDERATION, San Jose, CA. (209) 287-3088.
Positions: Telemarketers call for household discards in fundraising effort. Work 5 hours each evening, 5 days a week.
Requirements: Some telemarketing experience is required. Must live in Northern California.
Provisions: Training is provided. Pays guaranteed salary plus bonuses.

CAR-LENE RESEARCH, Deerbrook Mall, Deerfield, IL 60015.
Positions: Field surveyors and telephone interviewers for market research assignments.
Requirements: Must live in Deerfield, IL; Pomona, CA; Santa Fe Springs, CA; Northbrook, IL; Hanover, MA; Dallas, TX; or Richardson, TX. Market research experience is required.
Provisions: Pays by the survey.

CERTIFIED MARKETING SERVICES, INC., Route 9, P.O. Box 447, Kinderhook, NY 12106.
Positions: Market Research surveys are conducted nationwide by independent, part-time field workers.
Requirements: Must be over 18 years of age. No experience is required, but good organization and communication skills are helpful. Write for information.
Provisions: Hourly wage, travel expenses and reimbursables.

CHAMBERLAIN MARKET RESEARCH, 1036 Oakhaven Rd., Memphis, TN 38119.
Positions: Field surveyors.
Requirements: Memphis residents only. Experience required.
Provisions: Pays by the survey.

CHECK II MARKET RESEARCH, 900 Osceola Dr., Suite 207, West Palm Beach, FL 33409.
Positions: Field surveyors.
Requirements: Local residents only. Experience is preferred.
Provisions: Work is part-time only. Pays by the survey.

CONSUMER OPINION SEARCH, INC., 10403 Clayton Rd., St. Louis, MO 63131.
Positions: Field surveyors.
Requirements: St. Louis residents only. Good communication skills required.
Provisions: Pays by the survey.

DAKOTA INTERVIEWING SERVICE AND MARKET RESEARCH, 16 Vista Dr., Minot, ND 58701.
Positions: Opinion polls are conducted in the field and on the telephone.
Requirements: Local residents only. Good communication skills required. Must be able to follow directions exactly.
Provisions: Work is part-time, on-call only.

DALE SYSTEM, INC.,1101 Stewart Ave., Garden City, NY 11530.
Positions: Market research surveys are conducted in the field by means of purchases and observations in movie theaters, bowling alleys, restaurants, retail stores, and many other business establishments. Positions are part-time only..
Requirements: Experience in market research is preferred, but other experience dealing with the public could suffice. Need to live in one of the company's sampling areas. Send letter of interest requesting name and address of field supervisor nearest you.
Provisions: Pays per survey, plus reimbursements for related expenses.

DAVIS AND DAVIS RESEARCH, INC., 214 Van Gogh, Brandon, FL 33511.
Positions: Market research surveys are conducted in the field.
Requirements: Must be local resident. Experience required.

Provisions: Must be available for assignments as they come in. Pays by the project.

DAVIS MARKET RESEARCH SERVICES, INC., 23801 Calabasas Rd., Calabasas, CA 91302.
Positions: Field surveyors.
Requirements: Local residents only. Experience working with the public required.

D.C. MARKET RESEARCH, 936 North Second St., Springfield, IL 62702.
Positions: Field surveyors.
Requirements: Experienced interviewers only. Must be local resident.
Provisions: Pays by the project.

DELAWARE INTERVIEWING SERVICE, 811 Sunset Terrace, Dover, DE 19901.
Positions: Field interviewers for market research surveys. Surveys are conducted in Delaware and nearby parts of Maryland only.
Requirements: Interviewing experience required. Must live in one of the sampling points.

DENNIS RESEARCH SERVICE, INC., 3502 Stellhorn Rd., Fort Wayne, IN 46815.
Positions: Market research surveys are conducted in Northern Indiana by independent part-time field surveyors.
Requirements: Must be resident of Fort Wayne or South Bend. No experience is required, but good communication skills are a must.
Provisions: Pays by the survey.

DEPTH RESEARCH LABORATORIES, INC., 1103 Albemarle Rd., Brooklyn, NY 11218.
Positions: Field interviewers for various market research and opinion poll surveys. All are conducted in the greater New York City area.
Requirements: Interviewing experience is required. Send for application.
Provisions: Pays by the survey.

DISABLED AMERICAN VETERANS, 273 E. 800 South, Salt Lake City, UT 84111.
Positions: Telemarketers use the phone to ask for donations of household articles.
Requirements: No experience required. Must live in Salt Lake City.

Provisions: Pays minimum hourly wage plus bonus plan.

DISABLED AMERICAN VETERANS OF COLORADO, 8799 North Washington, Denver, CO 80229.
Positions: Fund raisers call for donations of household discards to be sold through thrift stores.
Requirements: Denver residents only. Must have good phone voice and good self-discipline.
Provisions: Training provided. Pays small hourly wage plus bonus plan.

EVELYN DREXLER INTERVIEWING SERVICE, 8807 Bridlewood Dr., Huntsville, AL 35802.
Positions: Market research surveys are conducted by field surveyors and telephone interviewers in Northern Alabama and Southern Tennessee.
Requirements: Must live in one of the sampling areas. Previous experience is preferred, but not absolutely required.

EL CAMINO MEMORIAL PARK, 5600 Carol Canyon Rd., San Diego, CA 92121.
Positions: Telemarketers conduct surveys over the phone.
Requirements: Experience dealing with the public. Must live in San Diego.
Provisions: Training is provided. Pays salary plus bonus.

E-Z INTERVIEWING, P.O. Box 951, Farmington, CT 06032.
Positions: Field surveyors.
Requirements: Local residents only. Must have interviewing experience.

FACTS 'N FIGURES, Panorama Mall, Suite 78B, Panorama City, CA 91402.
Positions: Market research and public opinion surveys are conducted by field surveyors and telephone interviewers.
Requirements: Must be resident of greater Los Angeles. Interviewing experience is required.
Provisions: Pays by the survey.

FOGARTY MARKET RESEARCH, 5090 Shoreham Pl., #206, San Diego, CA 92122.
Positions: Market research by phone only. Work consists of phone interviewing part-time; some is temporary, some is ongoing.
Requirements: Must live in San Diego.
Provisions: Training is provided. Pays by the survey.

GALLUP POLL, 47 Hulfish Street, 100 Palmer Square, Suite 200, P.O. Box 310, Princeton, NJ 08542. Attn: Field Dept.
Positions: Market researchers for field research. Across the country, there are 360 sampling areas. Market researchers conduct surveys in the field (usually door-to-door), returning home only to do the "paperwork." There are almost 2,000 of these home-based researchers around the U.S. This work is permanent part-time. It is conducted during weekends, approximately 1 - 2 weekends per month.
Requirements: No experience required and no age restriction for persons over 18.

You need only to be able to read well, talk with people and have a dependable car. Send work experience, address and phone number with letter of interest.
Provisions: An applicant must complete sample work which is tested and graded before job begins. After a person is accepted as an interviewer, Gallup's techniques are self-taught using an Interviewer's Manual and by communicating with the Field Administrator in the Princeton Office. All workers are independent contractors and are expected to meet minimum quotas. Pays an hourly wage plus expenses. "We're always looking for responsible people, especially permanent part-timers."

> "We're always looking for responsible people, especially permanent part-timers."—Gallup Poll

L. TUCKER GIBSON AND ASSOCIATES, INC., 3802 Deerfield Dr., San Antonio, TX 78218.
Positions: Field surveyors and telephone interviewers for market research studies.
Requirements: Must be experienced local resident. Bilingual applicants only.

LUANNE GLAZER ASSOCIATES, INC., 98 Ocean Dr. East, Stamford, CT 06902.
Positions: Field surveyors and telephone interviewers for market research.
Requirements: Must be local resident. Excellent communication skills and ability to follow directions explicitly required.
Provisions: Training is provided. Pays by the survey.

RUTH GOLDER INTERVIEWING SERVICE, 1804 Jaybee Rd., Wilmington, DE 19803.
Positions: Field interviewers for market research.
Requirements: Interviewing experience required. Must live in Chester or Delaware County, Pennsylvania, or Salem County, New Jersey.

AURELIA K. GOLDSMITH MARKETING RESEARCH SERVICES, INC., 1279 Guelbreath Lane, #204, St. Louis, MO 63146.
Positions: Field surveyors and telephone interviewers.
Requirements: Local residents only. Interviewing experience preferred.

GOOD SHEPHERD HOME FOR MENTALLY RETARDED, Denver, CO (303)232-7697.
Positions: Telephone fund raisers call for donations of household good and donations.
Requirements: Denver residents only. Must be dependable and sincere. To apply, you must call, do not write. Must be available to work early mornings and evenings.
Provisions: Training is provided in a 2 hour interview/orientation. Names to call are provided. Pays commission per pick up scheduled, averages $3.50 to $6.50 an hour.

LOUIS HARRIS AND ASSOCIATES, 630 Fifth Ave., New York, NY 10020.
Positions: Market researchers and opinion surveyors are needed in the field.
Requirements: No experience is necessary. Louis Harris has "several hundred" sampling areas and it is necessary to live in one of them. Write and ask for an application

which will be kept on file. When something comes up, you will be called. If you are ready for work, you will receive your instructions over the phone. How you go about completing the assignment from there is up to you.
Provisions: Pays by the survey, about $10 to $44 per survey.

HARVEY RESEARCH ORGANIZATION, INC., 600 Perinton Hills Office Park, Fairport, NY 14450.
Positions: Interviewers to work as independent contractors on continuing assignments. Work is available in all major cities. There are 50 to 100 interviewers in each sampling area. Most interviews are conducted in the field.
Requirements: Experience is necessary. Write a letter of interest. You will be sent an application, then a sample survey to complete before being hired permanently .
Provisions: Pays by the survey.

HAYES MARKETING RESEARCH, 7840 El Cajon Blvd., Suite 400, La Mesa, CA 92041.
Positions: Field surveyors and telephone interviewers for market research.
Requirements: Local area residents only. Experience required.
Provisions: Pays by the survey.

HEAKIN RESEARCH, INC., P.O. Box 146, Olympia Field, IL 60461.
Positions: Field surveyors conduct market research survey in 15 areas.
Requirements: Experience is preferred. Must be resident of Los Angeles, Sacramento, San Francisco area, Chicago, Kansas City, Baltimore, Independence, Pittsburgh, Memphis, or Houston.

HOSPICE OF SAN FRANCISCO, 225 - 30th, San Francisco, CA 94121.
Positions: Staffing coordinator for non-office hours.
Requirements: Experience in medical staffing required. Must live in San Francisco. Good phone manner important. Knowledge of medical terminology preferred.
Provisions: Pays hourly rates.

IDEAS IN MARKETING, 14100 N. 46th St., #207K, Tampa, FL 33613.
Positions: Market research surveys are conducted in the field and over the phone.
Requirements: Market research experience is required. Must be resident of Tampa, St. Petersburg, Sarasota, Orlando, or Lakeland.

ILLINOIS AMVETS, 4711 W. 137th St., Crestwood, IL 60445.
Positions: Fund raisers phone for donations of household articles.
Requirements: There are 10 locations in Illinois; you must reside in one of them. No experience necessary outside of good speaking ability.
Provisions: Part-time hours are flexible. Pays commission for every pick-up; averages about $4.50 and hour.

J & R FIELD SERVICES, INC., 747 Caldwell Ave., North Woodmere, NY 11581.
Positions: Field surveyors.
Requirements: Market research experience is required. Must be local resident.

JACKSON ASSOCIATES, 1140 Hammond Dr., N.E. #H, Atlanta, GA 30328.
Positions: Field and telephone interviewers for market research surveys.
Requirements: Experience required. Must be local resident.

Provisions: Pays by the survey.

JAPAN EXCHANGE SERVICES, 3660 Shelby Lane, Marietta, GA 30062.
Positions: Home-based coordinators are needed by this nonprofit educational organization. Responsibilities include finding host families for Japanese students, coordinating activities and tours. Work is part-time starting in March and ending in August each year. A second opportunity exists for area representatives that recruit host families for the academic year. The bulk of recruiting occurs from January through June. Throughout the rest of the year, it is the rep's responsibility to monitor the exchange student's progress by keeping in contact with the school and the student.
Requirements: Must be responsible, have time and energy, and current community involvement is preferred.
Provisions: Area coordinators are paid $100 per student placement plus bonuses for initial paperwork. Also pays for parties, etc. Area reps are paid $380 per student. This is broken down to a split between placement and supervision. Japan Exchange Services is open to inquiries from any area in the country, but some will be screened out on a variety of criteria.

KELLY SERVICES, INC.
Positions: Staffing coordinators. Kelly relies on home-based staffing coordinators to take calls and dispatch temporary personnel during the night as a service to clients who operate on 24-hour shift rotations.
Requirements: Some experience in personnel placement is required. Write to locate the office nearest or find it in the phone book, then apply directly to that office.
Provisions: Positions are considered part-time only. Pays flat salary.

THE KIDNEY FOUNDATION.
Positions: Fund raising on a local level. Work involves calling for donations of household items.
Provisions: Training provided. Pays hourly wage plus bonuses. The Kidney Foundation has branch offices in every city. Call the one nearest you for more information.

LOS ANGELES MARKETING RESEARCH ASSOCIATES, 5712 Lankershim Blvd., North Hollywood, CA 91601.
Positions: Field interviewers.
Requirements: Interviewing experience required.
Provisions: Pays by the survey.

MARKET INTELLIGENCE RESEARCH CORPORATION, 2525 Charleston Road, Mountain View, CA 94043.
Positions: Freelancers write market research reports for various industries including telecommunications and medicine.
Requirements: Experience is required. Apply with resume and clips.
Provisions: Pays by the contract.

MARKET RESEARCH SERVICES OF DALLAS, 2944 Motley Dr. #207, Mesquite, TX 75150.
Positions: Local field surveyors and telephone interviewers are contracted by out-of-town market research firms to conduct surveys in the Dallas area.
Requirements: Good communication skills are necessary. Prefers some kind of experience dealing with the public.

Provisions: Work is part-time on-call only. Pays by the job.

MARKETING INVESTIGATIONS, INC., Osborne Plaza, 1106 Ohio River Blvd., Box 343, Sewickley, PA 15143.
Positions: Field surveyors for market research studies.
Requirements: Interviewing experience required. Must live in Pittsburgh area.

MARSHALS SERVICE BUREAU, P.O. Box 8099, Garden City, NY 11530.
Positions: Skip tracers.
Requirements: Need individuals with law enforcement background to do skip tracing, asset relocation, check personnel records, and employment records by phone. Send resume.

J.B. MARTIN INTERVIEWING SERVICES, INC., 101 Merritt 7, Norwalk, CT 06851.
Positions: Field surveyors.
Requirements: Market research experience required. Local surveyors only.

MARY LUCAS MARKET RESEARCH, Marietta Plaza, 13250 New Halls Ferry Road, Florissant, MO 63033.
Positions: Field surveyors and telephone interviewers.
Requirements: Market research experience is required. Must be resident of greater St. Louis area.

B.J. MAYERSON INTERVIEWING SERVICE, 928 East Hampton Rd., Milwaukee, WI 53217.
Positions: Field surveyors and telephone interviewers.
Requirements: Market research experience required. Must be local resident.
Provisions: Pays by the survey.

MAZUR/ZACHOW INTERVIEWING, 4319 North 76 Street, Milwaukee, WI.
Positions: FIeld surveyors and telephone interviewers.
Requirements: Market research experience required. Must be Milwaukee resident.

T. MCCARTHY ASSOCIATES, INC., 6075 E. Molloy Rd., Ste. 1, Syracuse, NY 13211.
Positions: Market research surveys are conducted in the field and over the phone.
Requirements: Must be local resident. Interviewing experience is required.
Provisions: Pays by the survey.

MEDICAL PERSONNEL POOL, 2050 Spectrum Blvd., Ft. Lauderdale, FL 33309.
Positions: This franchised agency is a nursing staff placement agency with office coast to coast. In some areas where "satellite offices" operate in outlying area, home-based staffing coordinators are used to take incoming calls and dispatch nurses to work assignments. In some offices, this is done only at night and on weekends.
Requirements: Some phone experience is preferred. Staffing experience is also preferred, but not necessary. Must be self-directed. Write to find the office nearest to you or look it up in your local phone book.

MENTOR, 4 Ethel Rd., Bldg. 402A, Edison, NJ 08817.
Positions: Home care for young people, ages 3 - 18, with psychiatric and substance

abuse problems.
Requirements: To be a "mentor" does not necessarily require formal education, but experience, an understanding of people and most of all, compassion. If you qualify, you will be assigned to one patient at a time to live in your home. You'll become a Mental Health Technician, and an integral part of an expert mental health team.
Provisions: Excellent compensation. Openings exist in seven states including Pennsylvania, Texas, New Jersey, Massachusetts, South Carolina, Illinois, and Maryland.

METROPOLITAN FINANCE CORPORATION, 1127-1131 W. 41st St., Kansas City, MO 64111.
Positions: Credit collections brokers for business-to-business accounts only.
Requirements: Some experience in the collections field is necessary.
Provisions: Good company support and training is provided. Pays commission. Can be located anywhere. All brokers are independent contractors.

MISSIONS SURVEYS, 3771 Mt. Arcane Drive, San Diego, CA 92111.
Positions: Opinion surveys are conducted in the field and on the phone.
Requirements: Must be resident of Southern California and have good communication skills.

NATIONAL ANALYSTS, 1700 Market St., Philadelphia, PA 19103.
Positions: Opinion surveys are conducted in the field.
Requirements: Must live in one of the sampling areas. Experience is preferred.
Provisions: Training is provided. Pays by the survey.

NATIONAL OPINION RESEARCH CENTER, Social Science Research Center of the University of Chicago, 6030 South Ellis Avenue, Chicago, IL 60637.
Positions: Interviewers for long-term social science research projects. This nonprofit organization is the oldest research center in the country, founded in 1941. Research contracts come from government agencies and other institutional clients generally to study behavioral changes in specified areas of the population. There are 100 "area probability centers," plus studies are conducted in other locations specifically requested by the clients. All workers are considered part-time, temporary independent contractors though projects often last up to 14 months. Most work is done face-to-face, some is done over the phone. Currently has over 700 interviewers and is actively seeking more, particularly in metropolitan areas.
Requirements: Must be available a minimum of 20 hours a week; some work 40 hours a week. Need to be people-oriented, independent, outgoing, somewhat aggressive, able to follow instructions precisely and pay attention to details. Send letter of interest.
Provisions: Training is provided; general training takes about a day and a half in the office. Project briefings are a combination of written materials and oral instructions over the phone. Pays starting salary of $4.75 plus expenses. Pay goes up with experience or with particular qualifications that may be hard to find. Annual increases are based on performance.

NORTHWEST CENTER FOR THE RETARDED, 1600 West Armory Way, Seattle, WA 98119.
Positions: Telemarketers to call for donations of household goods.
Requirements: Must be local resident.
Provisions: Training is provided. Pays hourly wage of $3.55 plus bonus plan.

CLOSE UP: NORC

Founded in 1941, NORC is the oldest survey research organization established for non-commercial purposes. NORC is a not-for-profit organization affiliated with the University of Chicago.

Survey research is the collection of accurate, unbiased information from a carefully chosen sample of individuals.

Some organizations do opinion polls, asking people to rate the performance of public officials, for example. Others do market research, asking about such things as the products people use. NORC does social science research, asking about people's attitudes and behavior in areas of social concern, such as education, housing, employment (and unemployment), and health care.

NORC's clients include the American Cancer Society, Harvard University, the Rockefeller Foundation, the U.S. Dept. of Labor, and the Social Security Administration to name just a few. Nowhere will you find higher standards of quality in research of this kind.

To date, NORC has conducted more than 1,000 surveys. This may not sound like a lot considering the thousands that are conducted for companies like Gallup. Unlike Gallup, though, NORC's surveys are "longitudinal," meaning the same people are surveyed over long periods of time. Over 900 part-time NORC interviewers are located in cities, towns, and rural areas throughout the United States. Many, but not all, are home-based. Each assignment is on a temporary, per-project basis. The average project lasts about 6 months. All interviewers must be available to work at least 20 hours a week. 40 hour weeks are common.

About half of the people working for NORC have been with the company at least 5 years. That's an outstanding record in an industry where rapid employee turnover is the norm. Nevertheless, NORC is constantly seeking more qualified interviewers--especially in hard-to-staff metropolitan areas such as New York, Chicago, Los Angeles and Miami.

Field Director Miriam Clarke says "We look for someone who is people-oriented, outgoing, and somewhat aggressive. Someone who does not like to be tied to a desk is a good candidate actually. Being able to follow instructions precisely is important, too."

An hour and a half of general training is provided at a central location. After that, project briefings are handled by mail and phone.

The pay range depends upon where you live, but the entry level base rate is $4.50 an hour and up, depending upon experience. Any particular qualifications, such as foreign languages, pay extra. Pay raises come once a year and are based on performance.

OLSTEN HEALTH CARE SERVICES.
Positions: Staffing coordinators. Olsten now has over 300 offices nationwide in its health care services division. Each office has a minimum of two home-based staffing coordinators job sharing on a seven-days-on, seven-days-off routine. The job consists of taking calls during the day, at night, and on weekends to dispatch appropriate personnel for hospital and home health care positions.
Requirements: Some staffing experience or medical background is required. Write to locate the office nearest you, then apply directly to that office.
Provisions: Pays weekly salary plus placement bonuses.

OPINION RESEARCH CORPORATION, Opinion Park, Princeton, NJ 08540.
Positions: Opinion surveyors conduct interviews in the field in New Jersey only.
Requirements: Ability to communicate effectively with people is a must. Send letter of interest.
Provisions: Pays by the survey.

PROFESSIONAL RESEARCH ORGANIZATION, INC., 10 Corporate Hill Drive, Suite 100, Little Rock, AR 72205.
Positions: Market research surveys are conducted in the field and over the phone.
Requirements: Must be experienced. Local residents only.

PROFILE MARKETING RESEARCH, INC., 4020 S. 57th Ave., Lakeworth, FL 33463.
Positions: Field surveyors.
Requirements: Experience required. Southern Florida residents only.

PUBLIC REACTION RESEARCH, One Dillion Rd., Kendall Park, NJ 08824.
Positions: Public opinion surveys are conducted in the field and over the phone.
Requirements: Some kind of interviewing experience is required. Must be resident of greater Princeton area.
Provisions: Pays by the job.

PURPLE HEART SERVICE FOUNDATION.
Positions: Part-time telemarketers solicit for donations.
Requirements: Must work well with the public. Personal interview will be required. Look for the office nearest you in your local phone book and contact that office directly.
Provisions: Hours are flexible. Pays commission of between $5 and $10 an hour.

Q & A RESEARCH, INC., 1701 Sunrise Hwy, Bay Shore, NY 11706.
Positions: Field surveyors.
Requirements: Market research experience required. Must be local resident.
Provisions: Pays by the survey.

RESEARCH TRIANGLE INSTITUTE, Hanes Building, Research Triangle Park, Raleigh, NC 27601.
Positions: Interviewers for opinion research surveys conducted primarily in the field. Research Triangle is a nonprofit social research organization operating nationwide.
Requirements: Good communication skills needed. Send letter of interest.
Provisions: Pays hourly rate in some areas, pays by the survey in others. Training is provided.

THE ROPER ORGANIZATION, 566 Boston Post Road., Mamaroneck, NY 10543.
Positions: Opinion surveyors conduct research within sampling areas around the country. All research is conducted in the field.
Requirements: No opinion surveying experience is necessary, but experience involving some kind of public contact is preferred. Write and ask for name and address of nearest field supervisor.

SALEM SERVICES, 138 Palm coast Pky, NE, #144, Palm Coast, FL 32137.
Positions: Field surveyors and telephone interviewers.
Requirements: Experienced surveyors only. Must be resident of Westchester or Rockland County.
Provisions: Pays by the job.

SALT LAKE ANIMAL SOCIETY, 1151 South Redwood Road, Suite 108, Salt Lake City, UT 84104.
Positions: Telemarketers call for donations.
Requirements: Must live in Salt Lake City.
Provisions: Training is provided. Pays commission and bonus plan.

SOUND IDEA PRODUCTIONS/HPRP, Attn: Personnel Dept. 1-PR, 6547 N. Academy Blvd., Suite 548, Colorado Springs, CO 80918.
Positions: The title of the homebased position with this company is "Human Resource Assistance Representative."
Requirements: Experience in human resource management, public relations or sales and management helpful, but not required. Must enjoy working with and helping others.
Provisions: If selected, you will be trained and certified by the company to work in your area. You can work with complete flexibility and independence. Earnings can go as high as $900 part-time, even higher full-time.

TAYLOR INTERVIEWING SERVICE, 1026 Horseshoe Rd., Augusta, GA 30906.
Positions: Field surveyors and telephone interviewers.
Requirements: Market research experience preferred. Must be Augusta resident.

TAYLOR MANAGEMENT SYSTEMS, 9242 Markville, Dallas, TX 75243.
Positions: Telephone recruiters locate fund raiser volunteers.
Requirements: Telemarketing experience required. Must be Dallas resident.
Provisions: Pays piece rates based on number of volunteers recruited.

TEMPOSITIONS, Home Health Care Division, 150 Post St., San Francisco, CA 94104.
Positions: Staffing coordinator for evenings and weekends.
Requirements: Experience in medical staffing required. Must live in San Francisco.
Provisions: This is part-time work only.

TEXAS GULF MINERALS AND METALS, INC., 1610 Frank Akers Road, Anniston, AL 36201.
Positions: Buyers. Company recycles catalytic converters. Homebased buyers locate and purchase used catalytic converters which will in turn be sold to the company.
Requirements: Write for complete details.
Provisions: Pick up is provided weekly. Pays weekly. Training is provided. Can be anywhere in U.S.

TRI-COUNTY RESEARCH, 3 Rexal Court, New City, NY 10956.
Positions: Field surveyors and telephone interviewers.
Requirements: Market research experience required. Must live in Westchester, Rockland, Bergen, Passaic, or Upstate New York.

CPA, 11401 Rainier Avenue South, Seattle, WA 98178.
Positions: Fund raising involves calling for donations of reusable household items.
Requirements: Must live in greater Seattle area.
Provisions: Pays base salary plus bonus plan. Benefits include paid vacation. Hours can be part-time or full-time. Training is provided.

UNITED CEREBRAL PALSY, 1217 Alhambra Blvd., Sacramento, CA 95816.
Positions: Fund raising by phone. Job consists of calling for donations of household discards for about four hours a day.
Requirements: Must live in Sacaramento.
Provisions: Pays hourly wage plus bonus plan.

VALLEY RESEARCH & SURVEY, 2241 S. 250th E., Bountiful, UT 84010.
Positions: Field surveyors and telephone interviewers.
Requirements: Market research experience required. Salt Lake City residents only.

VALUE VILLAGE PROJECT OF THE NATIONAL CHILDREN'S CENTER, INC., 525 Rhode Island Ave. N.E., Washington, D.C. 20002.
Positions: Telephone fund raising.
Requirements: Must be local resident. Must be articulate and able to work well with the public.

VETERANS' REHABILITATION CENTER, 9201 Pacific Avenue, Tacoma, WA 98444.
Positions: Fund raisers phone for donations of household items, clothing, etc.
Requirements: Must come to Tacoma for short training session. (Can live in Seattle.)
Provisions: Paid training is provided. Pays guaranteed hourly wage. Inquiries are welcome.

VIETNAM VETERANS OF AMERICA FOUNDATION, Ventura, CA (800) 827-2013.
Positions: Fund raisers phone for donations of household items to be sold in thrift stores.
Requirements: No experience required. Must have good speaking voice. Local residents only. Apply by calling.
Provisions: Pays guaranteed minimum wage plus bonus plan. Training is provided.

VISION SERVICES, 9709 3rd Ave. N.E., Ste. 100, Seattle, WA 98115.
Positions: Phone work for nonprofit agency that offers programs to the blind and visually impaired. No sales is involved.
Requirements: Must live in Seattle. Touchtone phone required.
Provisions: One week of training is provided at headquarters. Pays $3.75 per hour. After four months a bonus plan is added.

WEST STAT, 1650 Research Boulevard, Rockville, MD 20850.
Positions: Interviewers conduct social research surveys in the field.

Requirements: Must be able to attend training session.
Provisions: Training is provided. Write for the location of the nearest office.

WHITE VACUUM COMPANY, 215 Brownsville Rd., Pittsburgh, PA 15210.
Positions: Telemarketers do customer service work.
Requirements: Must apply in person (must live in Pittsburgh); after initial application all contact is done via the mail.
Provisions: Training is provided. Customer list is supplied. Work is part-time; three hours a day, five days a week. Pays salary plus commission.

WORLD EXCHANGE, White Birch Road, Putnam Valley, NY 10579.
Positions: World Exchange needs Program Directors for its exchange student program. This year 1,000 students will be arriving from France, Japan, Spain, and Holland and U.S. students will be sent to England, France, Spain and Holland for one month cultural exchange. Program Directors find and interview host families on a part-time, seasonal basis.
Requirements: Experience helps, but is not necessary. World Exchange is looking for people who are "internationally minded"; ability to work well with people and various civic organizations is important. Can live within 300 miles of Los Angeles or San Francisco on the West Coast; and anywhere from Southern Florida to the Canadian Border on the East Coast.
Provisions: Compensates for each placement.

Can't find a job you want in your immediate area? Over 350 companies are listed in the Job Bank Location Index under "National/Multi-Regional Companies." See page 298.

INDUSTRIAL HOME WORK

Industrial home work is the kind of work that most people think of when you mention home work. It is work that is usually performed in a factory setting or sometimes in an office. It generally requires no special skills and therefore it doesn't generally pay very well.

It is simply a myth that this is the most common type of home work. Actually, it is the least common type of home work, because industrial home work is illegal in many states and some types of industrial home work are prohibited by federal labor laws as well. The states that do allow it have very strict standards and certification procedures. In Illinois, for example, any employer who wishes to hire home workers must obtain certification not only for the company, but for each and every employee as well.

All industrial home work is done locally. It is impossible for this type of work to be transported from one location to another, partly because of the labor laws. Also, it is not economically feasible to pay to transport materials to and from a worker's home, pay the worker, and expect to make a profit. Most of the time, an industrial home worker must pick up and deliver the materials and finished work himself. In rare instances, a courier service is set up within a short radius of the employer's factory or office.

As the manufacturing sector of our economic base continues to shrink, so will industrial home work. There is not very much of it available now, and there will be even less available in the future.

AL-LEE JEWELRY, INC., 298 Charles St., Fall River, MA.
Positions: Carding and wrapping. Company currently has 8 home-based employees.
Requirements: Must be local resident.

ALLISON ASSEMBLY, INC., 406 West Fairway, P.O. Box 2650, Big Bear City, CA 92314.
Positions: Electronic assemblers. Loading only, no soldering, of PC boards and ICs. There are currently 28 home workers at Allison.
Requirements: Experience preferred, but not required. Must be local resident.
Provisions: Pays piece rates based on production. Will accept applications, but has a waiting list.

AMERICAN GREENWOOD, INC., 9834 South Kedzie Avenue, Evergreen Park, Chicago, IL 60642.
Positions: Company manufactures novelty and custom design buttons. Hand assemblers insert pins into the backs of the buttons. Currently has19 home workers.
Requirements: Must be local resident. Must obtain home worker certificate from Illinois State Department of Labor.
Provisions: Pays piece rates.

ANGLER'S CHOICE FISHING PRODUCTS, INC., 5140 Primrose Lane, New Holland, PA 17557.
Positions: Hand assembly of various fishing tackle components.
Requirements: Must be local resident. Must qualify as Pennsylvania industrial home worker (be either disabled or need to care for invalid family member).
Provisions: Pays piece rates.

AT&T BELL LABORATORIES, 200 Park Plaza, Naperville, IL.
Positions: Hand assembly.
Requirements: Must be local resident. Must obtain a home worker certificate from the Illinois Department of Labor.

AURA BADGE COMPANY, Clayton Ave., Clayton, NJ 08312
Positions: Hand assembly includes inserting pins into cello buttons and acetate badgeholders.
Requirements: Must be local resident in order to pick up and deliver supplies and finished work. No experience or equipment is required.
Provisions: Pays salary and basic benefits provided by law. Currently has 15 home workers.

BIJAN'S PROTECTIVE EQUIPMENT, INC., 3255 Santa Rosa Avenue, Santa Rosa, CA 95407.
Positions: Hand assembly of industrial kneepads, wristguards, weight lifting belts, and horsebouts.

Requirements: Must be local resident. Currently there are 30 home workers.

BIRCH CUTTING CORPORATION, Crown Avenue & Birch Streets, Scranton, PA 18505.
Positions: Hand assembly.
Requirements: Must be local resident. Must qualify as Pennsylvania industrial home worker (be either disabled or need to care for invalid family member).
Provisions: Pays piece rates.

BROOKLYN BUREAU OF COMMUNITY SERVICE, Program for the Handicapped, 285 Schemerhorn Street, Brooklyn, NY 11217.
Positions: This is a non-profit organization offering many services to the elderly and handicapped citizens of Brooklyn. Home work involves manual assembly of products such as novelties and pharmaceuticals. Products are chosen for suitability - i.e., must be small enough to store in an apartment for a week at a time, light enough to carry up stairs, and suitable for quality control by the individual worker.
Requirements: Must be an elderly or handicapped resident of Brooklyn.
Provisions: Training and supplies are provided. Pick up and delivery of supplies and finished work are provided on a weekly basis. Pays piece rates. Has advocate on staff to insure SSI and disability insurance benefits are protected.

BUTACO CORPORATION, 6051 South Knox, Chicago, IL 60629.
Positions: Butaco is a producer of advertising specialties. Home workers assemble metal pins into lithographic buttons. Currently has 27 home workers.
Requirements: Must be local resident. Must obtain home worker certificate from Illinois State Department of Labor.
Provisions: Pays piece rates.

ANTHONY D. CAPONIGRO CO., 124 Eisenhauer Blvd., Roseto, PA 18013.
Positions: Hand assembly.
Requirements: Must be local resident. Must qualify as Pennsylvania industrial home worker (be either disabled or need to care for invalid family member).
Provisions: Pays piece rates.

CARTRIDGE ACTUATED DEVICES, INC., 123 Clinton Road, Fairfield, NJ 07006.
Positions: Soldering and some bridgewiring of explosive devices.
Requirements: Must be local resident in order to pick up and deliver supplies and finished work. Must own a microscope as prescribed by the company.
Provisions: Training is provided. Pays piece rates, but workers are full employees with basic benefits provided by law. Inquiries welcome.

CENTRAL ASSEMBLY COMPANY, INC., PO Box 398, Addison, IL 60101.
Positions: Light assembly and packaging of small products.
Requirements: Must be local resident. Must obtain home worker certificate from Illinois State Department of Labor.
Provisions: Pays piece rates. Work availability fluctuates according to availability of contracts.

CENTRAL-SHIPPEE, INC., 46 Star Lake Avenue, Bloomington, NJ 07403.
Positions: Manual assembly of color cards, swatching, inserting and mailing;. Central-Shippee is a swatch manufacturer. Home workers put together the swatch cards from

provided samples.
Requirements: Must be local resident.
Provisions: Training, pick up and delivery are provided. Pays piece rates.

COMPONENT PLASTICS, 700 W. Tollgate Road, Elgin, Il. 60120
Positions: Hand assembly and light inspection. This company has only four home workers and the opportunities are nil.
Requirements: Must be local resident. Must obtain a home worker certificate from the Illinois Department of Labor.

CONDON INDUSTRIES, INC., 175 Paterson Ave., Midland Park, NJ 07432.
Positions: Inspection and cutting of woven labels.
Requirements: Must be local resident.

CORD CRAFTS, INC., 530 Mt. Pleasant Ave., Dover, NJ 07801.
Positions: Hand assembly of plant hangers. Currently has over 70 home workers.
Requirements: Must be local resident in order to pick up and deliver supplies and finished products.
Provisions: Training is provided. Pays piece rates.

CYMATICS, INC., 31 W. 280 Diehl Rd., Naperville, IL 60540.
Positions: Circuit board assembly for electronics manufacturer.
Requirements: Must be local resident. Experience is required. Must obtain home worker certificate from Illinois Department of Labor.
Provisions: Pays piece rates.

DAVCO, INC., 42 Walnut Street, Haverhill, MA 01830.
Positions: Hand assembly of shoe findings. There are currently 23 home workers.
Requirements: Must be local resident.
Provisions: Pick up and delivery provided. Pays piece rates equal to minimum wage.

DECORATED PRODUCTS CO., 1 Arch Road, Westfield, MA. 01085
Positions: Handling nameplates and decals. Company currently has 7 home-based employees.
Requirements: Must be local resident.

DONNA JESSICA, INC., 200 Homer Avenue, Ashland, MA 01721.
Positions: Assembly of women's accessories. Company currently has 11 home-based employees.
Requirements: Must be local resident.

DUBRO PRODUCTS, 480 Bonner Rd., Wauconda, IL. 60084
Positions: Hand assembly.
Requirements: Must be local resident. Must obtain a home worker certificate from the Illinois Department of Labor.

EASTER SEAL SOCIETY OF METROPOLITAN CHICAGO, INC., 220 South State Street, Room 312, Chicago, IL 60604.
Positions: This is a not-for-profit program for handicapped Chicago residents. 38 home workers handle small packaging, light assembly, collating, and hand-addressing.
Requirements: Must be handicapped and live in Chicago.
Provisions: Training is provided. Pick up and delivery is provided. Pays piece rates.

FEDERATION OF THE HANDICAPPED, 211 West 14th Street, 2nd Floor, New York, NY 10011.
Positions: The Home Employment Program (HEP) is a workshop program which consists of industrial bench assembly (manual assembly work).
Requirements: All workers must live in New York City and have a disability. Requires evaluation through lengthy interviews and personal counseling before participating.
Provisions: The workshop provides training plus any extra help necessary to overcome any unusual problems an individual might have. Pick up and delivery of supplies and finished work is provided regularly. Pays piece rates. Disability insurance counseling is provided. Number of home workers fluctuates, but over 1000 have participated in the program since the early 60s and there are currently several hundred.

FOUR WORD INDUSTRIES CORPORATION, 9462 Franklin Ave., Franklin Park, IL 60131.
Positions: Hand assemblers insert pins into the backs of metal buttons for this producer of advertising specialties. Currently has 18 home workers and opportunities are decreasing.
Requirements: Must be local resident. Must obtain a home worker certificate from Illinois State Department of Labor.
Provisions: Pays piece rates.

FOXON PACKAGING CORPORATION, 235 West Park St., Providence, RI 02901.
Positions: Home workers assemble string tags for this manufacturer. There are currently about 23 home workers.
Requirements: Must be local resident.

GLASS REFLECTIONS, 2331 Chestnut St., Camp Hill, PA 17011.
Positions: Glass Reflections has been making high quality Tiffany lampshades for twelve years. Home workers tape together the pieces with adhesive tape. No tools required.
Requirements: Must be local resident. Must qualify as Pennsylvania industrial home worker (be either disabled or need to care for invalid family member). Charges a $1.50 pick-up fee.
Provisions: Pays piece rates.

HARPER LEATHER GOODS MANUFACTURING COMPANY, 2133 West Pershing Road, Chicago, IL 60609.
Positions: Light industrial work involved in the manufacture of pet supplies; packaging rawhide "bones", sewing cat and dog toys, and sewing cat collars.
Requirements: Must be local resident. Must obtain home worker certificate from Illinois State Department of Labor.

HYGIENOL COMPANY, INC., 73 Crescent Avenue, New Rochelle, NY 10801.
Positions: Hand assembly involved in the manufacture of powder puffs.
Requirements: Local residents only.
Provisions: Home work force is extremely small now, but at one time (before 1950) there were over 400. Company is considering revitalizing home work program.

INSULFAB PLASTICS, INC., 150 Union Ave., East Rutherford., NJ 07073.
Positions: Hand assembly of name plate badges.
Requirements: Must be local resident.

JACKSON SPRING & MANUFACTURING COMPANY, INC., 2680 American Lane, Elk Grove, IL 60007.
Positions: Packing parts.
Requirements: Must be local resident. Must obtain home worker certificate from Illinois State Department of Labor.
Provisions: Pays piece rates.

JOSEPH'S BROS. EMBROIDERY CORP., 6030 Monroe Place, West New York, NJ 07093.
Positions: Sample mending of embroidery designs.
Requirements: Must be local resident. Experience is required.

LANCASTER COUNTY ASSOCIATION FOR THE BLIND, 244 North Queen St., Lancaster, PA 17603.
Positions: This non-profit organization has both a sheltered workshop and, for those who are homebound, certain hand assembly work can be farmed out to home workers.
Requirements: Must be disabled worker in the Lancaster area.
Provisions: Pays piece rates.

GEO. LAUTERER CORP., 310 W. Washington, Chicago, IL 60096.
Positions: Hand assembly.
Requirements: Must be local resident. Must obtain home worker certificate from Illinois Department of Labor.
Provisions: Pays piece rates.

LENCO ELECTRONICS, INC., 1330 Belden St., McHenry, IL 60050.
Positions: Connecting and soldering wires onto transformers.
Requirements: Must be local resident. Must obtain home worker certificate from Illinois Department of Labor.
Provisions: Provides necessary hand tools. Pays piece rates.

LEWIS SPRING CO., 2652 W. North Ave., Chicago, IL 60697.
Positions: Assembly and packaging.
Requirements: Must be local resident. Must obtain home worker certificate from

Illinois Department of Labor. Currently has 17 home workers.

LIMALDI & ASSOCIATES, 165 Vanderpool Street, Newark, NJ 07114.
Positions: Hand inserting pins into metal buttons. Current number of home workers is 10, but that number fluctuates.
Requirements: Must be local resident.
Provisions: Pick up and delivery of supplies and finished work is provided. Home workers are salaried employees.

LNL, R.D. #3, Bangor, PA 18013.
Positions: Garment sewing.
Requirements: Must be local resident. Must qualify as Pennsylvania industrial home worker (be either disabled or need to care for invalid family member).
Provisions: Pays piece rates.

MAR-DOL, INC., 29 W. Fullerton, Box 91, Addison, IL 60101.
Positions: Hand assembly.
Requirements: Must be local resident. Must obtain home worker certificate from Illinois Department of Labor.
Provisions: Pays piece rates.

MUENTENER EMBROIDERY CO., INC., 6904 Adams St., Guttenberg, NJ 07093.
Positions: Cutting out embroidered emblems.
Requirements: Must be local resident.

MYERS BROTHERS, 481 Paoli Ave., Philadelphia, PA 19128.
Positions: Hand assembly.
Requirements:: Must be local resident. Must qualify as Pennsylvania industrial home worker (be either disabled or need to care for invalid family member).
Provisions: Pays piece rates.

PENT HOUSE SALES CORPORATION, 860 West Central Street, Franklin, MA 02038.
Positions: Hand assembly of shoe parts and accessories. Company currently has 10 home-based employees.
Requirements: Must be local resident.
Provisions: Pays minimum wage.

PHILLIPS MANUFACTURING COMPANY, INC., 190 Emmet Street, Newark, NJ 07114.
Positions: Company manufactures buttons.
Requirements: Home work is only distributed to contractors with valid state permit for redistribution.

PRISM/ODYSSEY, 101 Central St., Millville, MA 01529.
Positions: Jewelry assembly. Company currently has 12 home-based employees.
Requirements: Must be local resident.

PROMOTION SUPPORT SERVICES, 310 3rd St., Rock Island, IL 61201.
Positions: Hand work involved in mailing projects.
Requirements: Must be local resident. Must obtain a home worker certificate from

the Illinois Department of Labor.

R.C. COIL MFG. CO., 490 Mitchell Rd., Glendale Heights, IL 60139.
Positions: Hand packing.
Requirements: Must be local resident. Must obtain a home worker certificate from the Illinois Department of Labor.

REGAL GAMES MANUFACTURING CO., 3714-16 W. Irving Park Rd., Chicago, IL 60618.
Positions: Hand assembly involving insertion of plastic chips in cardboard bingo cards. The company currently has about 8 home workers and opportunities are very limited.
Requirements: Must be local resident. Must obtain home worker certificate from Illinois Department of Labor.
Provisions: Pays piece rates.

RICHLAND SHOE CO., 30 North 3rd St., Womelsdorf, PA 19567.
Positions: Hand assembly.
Requirements: Must be local resident. Must qualify as Pennsylvania industrial home worker (be either disabled or need to care for invalid family member).
Provisions: Pays piece rates.

THE SCREEN PLACE, INC., 90 Dayton Ave., Passaic, NJ 07055.
Positions: Color separation of artwork.
Requirements: Must be local resident. Experience is required.

SCRIPTURE PRESS PUBLICATIONS, 1825 College Avenue, Wheaton, IL 60187.
Positions: Proofreading and packet assembly for religious publisher.
Requirements: Must be local resident. Good English skills required. Must obtain home worker certificate from Illinois State Department of Labor.

SHELTERED EMPLOYMENT SERVICES, INC., 600 N. 5th St., Philadelphia, PA 19123.
Positions: This non-profit agency offers both a sheltered workshop and a homebound work program for disabled workers in Philadelphia. Work consists of hand assembly of small products and some typing.
Requirements: An intake worker will evaluate whether an individual qualifies for the program.
Provisions: Pays piece rates. Training is provided.

STERLING SPRING CORP., 5432 W. 54th St., Chicago, IL 60638.
Positions: Hand assembly and packaging.
Requirements: Must be local resident. Must obtain home worker certificate from Illinois Department of Labor.
Provisions: Pays piece rates.

SUPERIOR SPRING STAMP CO., 5200 N. Otto, Chicago, IL 60656.
Positions: Hand assembly and packaging.
Requirements: Must be local resident. Must obtain home worker certificate form Illinois Department of Labor.
Provisions: Pays piece rates.

SWIBCO, INC., 4820 Venture Rd., Lisle, IL 60532.
Positions: Hand assembly of jewelry onto plastic cards and packaging.
Requirements: Must be local resident of Lisle. Must obtain a home worker certificate from the Illinois Department of Labor.

TELEDYNE ISOTOPES, 50 Van Buren Avenue, Westwood, NJ 07675.
Positions: Two types of work are performed at home. One is the assembly of badge cases and the other is slicing of ultrathin discs.
Requirements: Must be local resident. Prefers referrals.
Provisions: Equipment is provided as necessary.

THREE W MFG. CO., 1016 Springfield Road, Union City, NJ 07083.
Positions: Light assembly work involving carding and boxing of costume jewelry.
Requirements: Must be local resident.

TIFFANY & CO., 801 Jefferson Rd., Parsippany, NJ 07054.
Positions: Pre-packaging and ribboning of gift items.
Requirements: Must be local.

TOMORROW TODAY CORPORATION, P. O. Box 6125, Westfield, MA 01085.
Positions: Hand work consists of tying bows and working with flowers to make decorations. Currently has 76 home workers.
Requirements: Must be local.
Provisions: Pays minimum wage.

UNITED CEREBRAL PALSY ASSOCIATION OF WESTCHESTER COUNTY, INC., 150 Midland Ave., Port Chester, NY 10573
Positions: Hand assembly of various items on subcontract basis. Program is for homebound disabled workers only.
Requirements: All home workers must be approved by the U.S. Dept. of Labor which generally requires a doctor's statement. Local residents only.
Provisions: The screening is tight, but once the program is there, there is a lot of support available. Each participant is assigned a vocational trainer and a counselor that meet with the worker at least once a month after the initial training is completed. Pick up and delivery of supplies and finished work is provided. Any tools and/or equipment necessary for the work are provided. Pays piece rates. Inquiries are welcome from Westchester County and from throughout Connecticut. Some work is opening up in the computer field, too.

WEILER BRUSH CO., INC., One Wildwood Drive, Cresco, PA 18326.
Positions: Hand assembly.
Requirements: Must be local resident. Must qualify as Pennsylvania industrial home worker (be either disabled or need to care for invalid family member).
Provisions: Pays piece rates.

WEST COAST BRUSH COMPANY, 433 Lanzit Ave., Los Angeles, CA 90061.
Positions: Assembly of hand tied stainless steel wire brushes.
Requirements: Must live nearby.
Provisions: Training is provided. Home workers are regular employees and are paid a salary plus basic benefits. There are currently only six home workers and opportunities are nil.

WORKSHOP INDUSTRIES, INC., 400 Clay Ave., Jeannette, PA 15644.
Positions: This is a non-profit organization offering employment opportunities to disabled workers within a 50-mile radius of Jeannette. Work consists of hand assembly of various small products.
Provisions: Training is provided.

YORK SPRING COMPANY, 1551 North La Fox Street, South Elgin, IL 60177.
Positions: Assembly and packaging springs for manufacturer. Home based work force has grown to 51.
Requirements: Must be local resident. Must obtain home worker certificate from Illinois State Department of Labor.
Provisions: Pays piece rates.

OPPORTUNITIES IN SALES

The field of sales has long been a traditional from-home opportunity. Today, most salespeople have offices at home and some even conduct all their business from home.

Sales may be the only true opportunity to earn an executive level income with literally no educational requirements or experience. It is particularly good for women, who often report doubling or tripling their income after leaving other types of jobs. It also allows for a maximum amount of flexibility in terms of time spent and when it is spent.

What does it take to be a good salesperson? Good communication skills are at the top of the list. You must truly enjoy talking to people to make it in sales. You must be careful to listen to them as well. Assertiveness is also important. This does not mean you must be aggressive or go for the "hard sell," but shrinking violets aren't likely to make it in this field. The toughest part of this job is handling rejection. Nobody likes rejection; some people are traumatized by it. But, it goes with the territory. The professional salesperson knows that with each rejection, he/she is one step closer to a successfully-closed sale.

Sales is a profession with its own set of rules, just like any other profession. The job basically consists of prospecting for customers, qualifying the prospect to make sure the potential customer is a viable prospect, making the presentation, overcoming objections, closing the sale, and getting referrals. A good company will teach you all you need to know about each of these steps. You can also find classes in salesmanship for both beginners and advanced students at community colleges and adult learning centers.

Many of the opportunities listed in this section have interesting ways of introducing the product. Home parties are especially fun and easy. Many home parties now seem more like classes than sales pitches with hands-on demonstrations in cooking, baking, needlework, and crafts. If you think you might be interested in a particular company, you can check it out first by hosting your own party. You'll not only be able to check out the company first hand, but you'll earn a bonus gift at the same time.

For those who want to be home all the time, telemarketing is the best bet. It is a marketing method that is mushrooming because it is more efficient and cheaper than face-to-face methods of selling. Telemarketing jobs rarely exceed four hours a day, but the pay can equal a full-time salary for a good communicator. For additional opportunities in telemarketing, look in your local newspaper "help wanted" ads.

ACT II JEWELRY, INC., 818 Thorndale Ave., Bensenville, IL 60106.
Positions: Direct sales of fashion and fine jewelry.

ADE COMMUNICATIONS, 60B South 2nd St., Deer Park, NY 11729.
Positions: Telemarketing or outside sales of electronic equipment (computer terminals, teletypewriters, etc.) to other businesses. Scripts and leads provided. Pays commission. Must live in Nassau or Suffolk area.

ADMAR ENTERPRISES, (202)364-0789.
Positions: Telemarketing, no sales involved. Cold call within your local area exchange to offer free gifts and give location of pick up.
Requirements: Can live anywhere within the greater Washington D.C., Baltimore area. Must be able to speak clearly and be self-assured.
Provisions: All telemarketers are independent contractors and can set own schedules from 9 am to 9 pm, part-time or full-time. Pays base salary from $200 to $600 per week. Company benefits are provided.

ALCAS CUTLERY CORPORATION, 1116 East State Street, P.O. Box 810, Olean, NY 147600-0810.
Positions: Alcas makes cutlery, cookware, and tableware. The products are sold with the aid of mail order catalogs.
Provisions: Catalogs and other supplies are provided. Pays commission.

ALFA METALCRAFT CORPORATION OF AMERICA, 6593 Powers Ave., Suite 17, Jacksonville, FL 32217.
Positions: Direct sales of cookware. Reps can use any direct sales methods. Some reps have incorporated the sales of Alfa cookware into cooking classes in their homes.
Provisions: Pays commission.

ALOE MAGIC, Division of Exalo Tech, 2828 East 55 Place, P.O. Box 20423, Indianapolis, IN 46220.
Positions: Aloe Magic has an extensive line of aloe-based cosmetics and health and skin care products. Reps use a variety of direct sales methods.
Provisions: Pays commission.

ALOETTE COSMETICS, INC., P.O. Box 2346, West Chester, PA 19380.
Positions: Direct sales of skin care cosmetics.

AMERICAN BARTER EXCHANGE, 64 Division Ave., Levittown, NY 11756.
Positions: Telemarketing.
Requirements: Homebased telemarketers are trained to make appointments for outside salespeople to explain company's barter association and benefits. Must be articulate and capable of dealing with business people. Local residents only.
Provisions: Pays base salary plus commission and phone bill.

AMWAY CORPORATION, 7575 East Fulton Road, Ada, MI 49355.
Positions: Amway is well known as the original multilevel organization. There are now five different divisions which include not only products but many services as well such as MTI Long Distance.

ARBONNE INTERNATIONAL, INC., (801) 561-4588.

Positions: Direct sales of European cosmetics and skin care products. Reps build customers bases using any direct sales methods that work for them.
Provisions: Training and ongoing managerial support is provided. Pays commission.

ART FINDS INTERNATIONAL, INC., 5371 Hiatus Road, Sunrise, FL 33351.
Positions: Art Finds International has a line of oil paintings that represent the best art available in the marketplace and the frame line is of the highest quality. They have an inventory of over 150,000 pieces and you can customize your selection for each showing.
Requirements: To become an Art Finds International consultant, there is a one time training fee of $200. This fee covers your comprehensive training course, materials, and all of the necessary paperwork and supplies needed to start your business. Your portfolio of original oil paintings is provided to you on consignment, and a portion of your training fee provides insurance for the oils. You are required to pay $50 in advance. The remaining $150 may be paid from your first month's earnings.
Provisions: The base commission is 20% plus a 4% monthly bonus with personal sales of $4,000 or more. If you were to show twice a week, you could expect to earn $13,000 in commission per year; six shows would yield almost $40,000.

ART & SOUL, INC., 400 W. Sunset Dr., Waukesha, WI 53186.
Positions: Direct sales of personalized products; watercolor and ink cartoon lithographs, magnets, key/bag tags, note pads, frames and designer t-shirts.
Requirements: Although optional, there is a standard business supply kit available for $100. It contains catalogs, advertising brochures, training booklets, personalizing equipment, etc.
Provisions: Prices, and therefore profits, are set by you.

ART TREASURES GUILD, 76 Commercial Way, East Providence, RI 02914.
Positions: Direct sales of fine art replicas. As a consultant you would put together a mobile art gallery to bring fine art into the homes and offices of your clients. The "Art Gallery" designed by Art Treasures Guild is valued at over $3,000 and includes a wide assortment of graphics which represent a broad spectrum of subjects: still lifes, florals, portraits, landscapes, seascapes, hunt scenes and works by Impressionists, Masters and Contemporary artists, frame samples, some complete art replicas, carrying portfolios, display easels and the necessary paper supplies and "tools".
Requirements: Your cost for the Art Gallery is $900 and there are three affordable payment plans available, two of which allows you to start your business for a small down payment of $150, providing you qualify.
Provisions: Consultants earn 28% base profit and the bonus structure increases profits to 33%.

ARTISTIC IMPRESSIONS, INC., 240 Cortland Ave., Lombard, IL 60148.
Positions: Direct sales of art works.

AVACARE, INC., 19501 E. Walnut Dr., City of Industry, CA 91749.
Positions: Direct sales of "natural" cosmetics and skin, hair and healthcare products.
Provisions: Pays commission.

AVON PRODUCTS, INC., 638 Otis Place, N.W., Washington, DC 20010.
Positions: Avon, which is known for door-to-door sales, rarely uses this method anymore. Instead, its huge number of reps uses telemarketing methods to arrange home parties and make appointments for exclusive showings.

Requirements: Reps are required to buy samples, hostess thank-you gifts, and necessary paperwork.
Provisions: Pays commission. Management opportunities are available.

BRUCE BATTY ACCOUNTING SERVICES, 17 Grand Blvd., Scarsdale, NY 10583.
Positions: Telemarketing.
Requirements: Need people with strong telemarketing experience for cold calls. Must have quiet and professional background for making calls to sell accounting services to businesses. Local residents mail resumes.

BEAUTICONTROL, INC., 2101 Midway Road, P.O. Box 345189, Dallas, TX 75234.
Positions: BeautiControl primarily markets a cosmetic line that is tied into the "seasonal" method of color coordination. A secondary line of women's apparel is marketed in the same way. In 1985, the company topped $30 million in gross sales. BeautiControl does not use the party plan method of direct sales, but rather focuses on one-on-one sales. This is accomplished through intensive training, personal development, and corporate support of the consultants, A free color analysis is offered to potential customers; this has proven to be the company's most powerful marketing tool.
Requirements: A one-time investment of $500 is required.
Provisions: Personal earnings are reported in the company's monthly in-house publication, "Achiever", and typically range from $12,000 down to $3,700 per month after being in the company for about two years. It is not unusual for new Consultants to earn $100 to $200 per day.

BEN'S MEATS, 260 Islip Ave., Islip, NY 11751.
Positions: This company sells and delivers customized monthly meat orders. Home-based telemarketers sell the service over the phone. Work is part-time only.
Requirements: Must have some telemarketing experience. Residents of Suffolk County only will be considered.
Provisions: Training is conducted in the office for about two hours. Pays salary plus commissions and bonuses.

BON DEL CORPORATION, 3716 East Main Street, Mesa, AZ 85205.
Positions: Bon Del manufactures household bacteriostatic water treatment units. Independent reps sell the units direct by placing ads in local papers, through telemarketing, and sometimes with company provided leads.
Provisions: Training is provided. Pays commission.

THE BRON-SHOE COMPANY, 1313 Alum Creek Drive, Columbus, OH 43209.
Positions: Direct marketing of baby shoe bronzing services.

BXI INTERNATIONAL, INC., 404 Farmingdale Rd., Babylon, NY 11704.
Positions: Telemarketing for a 30 year old barter association to network businesses. Example: Get a pet food company to sign for a minimum contract of $495 with BXI; you receive 50% in cash or barter on that contract ($495 = $250 yours plus $245 is BXI's). If they give $250 cash plus $250 in pet food trade, you get $125 fro BXI to use on balance of barter trade accumulation. There are 800#'s to call locally and internationally for restaurant use and trip information on such participating barter places as the Caribbean and Mexico. Example: Accumulation trade for a free vacation or just to write a check in participating restaurant for a meal.

CALICO SUBSCRIPTIONS, 800 Charcot Ave., Suite 107, San Jose, CA 95131.
Positions: Telemarketing for periodical subscription renewals.
Requirements: Must be in the Bay area or Silicon Valley.
Provisions: Pays commission only. "Our telemarketers make very good money. We're always looking for good phone people."

CAMEO COUTURES, INC., 9004 Ambassador Row, P.O. Box 47390, Dallas, TX 75234.
Positions: Home party sales of lingerie, cosmetics, and food supplements.
Provisions: Training is provided. Pays commission.

CAMEO PRODUCTS, INC., P.O. Box 590388, Orlando, FL 32859.
Positions: Cameo has been offering quality products and services for over 17 years now. The products are typically craft kits such as needlepunch, fabric painting, bow art, iron-on transfers, etc. Product demonstrators act as craft instructors in a home party style "class". Cameo offers more than just wholesale craft supplies. It entails a complete program of supplies, designs, products, training aids, and sales promotion representatives. Cameo representatives can choose the way they want to demonstrate and sell the products. Many reps sell directly to customers at crafts shows, fairs, open houses, and direct mail. Classes at adult community education centers, retirement centers, schools, and other institutions are also selling avenues.
Provisions: Minimum 25% commission for instructors. Commission plus override for managers.

CHAMBRE COSMETICS, P.O. Box 550369, Dallas, TX 75355.
Positions: Direct sales of cosmetics and food supplements.
Provisions: Pays commission.

CHRYSLER CHEMICAL CO., INC., P.O. Box 335, Hewlet, NY 11557.
Positions: Telephone sales of "Defiance Spray Pen." You will be calling only business establishments (shops, independent stores, etc.) Calls will be made during normal business hours.

CHRISTMAS AROUND THE WORLD, P.O. Box 9999, Kansas City, MO 64134-9999.
Positions: Home party demonstrators and supervisors. Company markets an upscale line of gifts and ornaments. All work is transferred via UPS. No investment requirements of any kind.
Provisions: Full training is provided. Pays commission plus override.

CLUB WATERMASTERS, INC., 5670 W. Cypress St., Suite I, Tampa, FL 33607.
Positions: Direct sales of drinking water systems.

COLLECTORS CORNER, INC., AND AFFILIATES, 5327 W. Minnesota St., Indianapolis, IN 46241.
Positions: Direct sales of oil paintings and limited edition prints.

P.F. COLLIER, INC., Educational Services Division, 135 Community Drive, Great Neck, NY 11021.
Positions: Direct sales of encyclopedias.

CONCEPT NOW COSMETICS, 14000 Anson Street, Santa Fe Springs, CA 90670.
Positions: This 17 year old company has been selling an extensive line of skin care products primarily though party plan sales. Reps operate through the U.S., Mexico, Canada, Puerto Rico, and the Virgin Islands.
Requirements: A start-up kit with $325 requires a $65 investment.
Provisions: No set territories. Training is available and includes tapes, manual, presentation outline and company support. Car allowance is provided along with specified promotions. Pays commission only for reps and override for managers.

CON-STAN INDUSTRIES, INC., 19501 Walnut Dr., City of Industry, CA 91748.
Positions: Direct sales of cosmetics and food supplements.
Provisions: Pays commission.

CONTEMPO FASHIONS, 6100 Broadmoor, Shawnee Mission, KS 66202.
Positions: Direct sales of jewelry and accessories.

COPPERSMITH COMPANY, 410 E. College, P.O. Box 1000, Roswell, NM 88201-7525.
Positions: Coppersmith is a manufacturer of decorative home accessories including tableware and wall decor, all made out of copper. Reps use a variety of means to market the products: home parties, exclusive showings, one-on-one consultations, and catalog sales.
Provisions: Strong company support is provided. Pays commission.

CORNET PRODUCING CORPORATION, 4738 North Harlem, Schiller Park, IL 60141.
Positions: Inside sales of entertainment events to businesses. 20 hours a week.
Requirements: Experience in business-to-business sales is necessary.

COUNTRY HOME COLLECTION, 1719 Hallock-Young Rd., Warren, OH 44481.
Positions: Direct sales of decorative home products.

CREATIVE MEMORIES, 2815 Clearwater Road, St. Cloud, MN 56302.
Positions: Party-plan sales of books, hobby products, photo albums, and photography products.

CREATIVE TREASURES, 6836 Duckling Way, Sacramento, CA 95842.
Positions: Creative Treasures is a home party business that markets quality handcrafts of all kinds. Home party demonstrators and their supervisors are home-based. Items are ordered from a sample that is provided by each crafter.
Requirements: Write a letter of interest.

D.E.L.T.A. INTERNATIONAL, 16910 West 10 Mile Road, Ste. 400, Southfield,MI 48075.
Positions: Direct sales of nutritional supplements.

DELUXE BUILDING MAINTENANCE, 760 Market St., San Francisco, CA 94140.
Positions: Telemarketing. Cold calls only.
Requirements: Experience is required. Must be resident of San Francisco.
Provisions: Pays commission only.

Homeworker Profile: Nancy Maynard

Nancy Maynard's work has changed in ways she never expected since graduating from Berkeley with two degrees. Her work life started in the impersonal corporate world of Xerox.

"I found there was pressure to slow down, to do just what you're supposed to do. There was no encouragement to do more to earn more. Raises were the same for everyone; they came along once a year no matter what. After six years, I asked myself why I should work hard for another $10 a week—especially since I'd get it regardless of my accomplishments."

Shortly before leaving Xerox, Nancy started working with Oriflame, selling their European skin care system. The initial intent was to make a little extra cash. Much to her surprise, she matched her corporate salary within six months. In another six months she became assistant manager and was well on her way to earning her present $40,000 a year salary, plus bonus gifts.

"In direct sales, a person is in control. I can say, 'I need a car. I'll buy it and work an extra four hours a week to pay for it.' She adds, "Of course, I don't need to do that. I've earned a gold Mercedes through Oriflame's incentive bonus plan!"

Nancy believes direct sales is an ideal choice for women who want to combine working and homemaking. It gives them control over their earning power and greater flexibility in their daily schedules.

For Nancy, that means spending time with her husband, who also works at home, and with their five year old daughter. "We both like to take time out of the day when we want to go to the park, have lunch together, or maybe just go for a walk. It allows us to give our daughter a better sense of us as people. What could be better than that?"

DEXI US, INC., 130 W. 42nd St. Bldg. 2900, New York, NY 10036.
Positions: Direct sales of cosmetics.

DIAMITE CORPORATION, 1625 McCandless Dr., Milpitas, CA 95035.
Positions: Now 13 years old, Diamite still offers ground floor opportunities nationwide. Manufacturer of skin care and nutritional products with the latest technology for anti-aging and life extension. Innovative marketing plan through networking part-time or full-time. Product line has 100% customer money back guarantee.
Provisions: Training is provided in the form of literature and videotapes.

DISCOVERY TOYS, INC., 2530 Arnold Dr., Suite 400, Martinez, CA 94553.
Positions: Discovery Toys was started as a home-based business in 1982. The company markets a line of educationally sound toys and accessories through home parties. Home party demonstrators and their supervisors are all home-based.
Requirements: Send letter of interest.
Provisions: Complete training is provided. Pays commission and override. Can live anywhere.

DONCASTER, Box 1159, Rutherfordton, NC 28139.
Positions: Doncaster trains women to be fashion consultants, "Selling the art of dressing well." Fashion Consultants present the Doncaster collection in private showing in their own homes four times a year. These fashions are considered to be investment quality and are designed primarily for career women.
Provisions: Training is provided. Pays commission. Management opportunities are available.

DUDLEY PRODUCTS AND PUBLICATIONS, 1080 Old Greensboro Rd., Kernersville,NC 27284.
Positions: Direct sales of cosmetics using home parties as primary sales method.
Provisions: Training is provided. Pays commission and override for managers.

DUSKIN-CALIFORNIA, INC., 108 E Star of India Lane, Carson, CA 90746.
Positions: Direct sales of household products. Primary focus is on dustcontrol products. Reps use any method of sales they chose.
Provisions: Pays commission.

EAST COAST DRIVING SCHOOL, 842 State Rd., Princeton, NJ 08540.
Positions: Telemarketing.
Requirements: Telephone support needed for evenings and weekends in the Princeton/Trenton area. Script, leads provided.

E.I.E., P.O. Box 764, Stroud, OK 74079.
Positions: Magazine and Biblical video sales. You set your own prices and remit amount from listing. Price mark-ups vary. "We offer a listing of over 1,100 titles. You choose what to sell with no minimums."
Requirements: $5 for kit and listing after registration application has been received. The kit contains complete listing information, occasional samples, promotional materials and business cards.
Provisions: Pays 30% to 60% of retail.

EKCO HOME PRODUCTS CO., 2382 Townsgate Road, Westlake Village, CA 91361.

Positions: Direct sales of cookware and cutlery.

ELECTRIC MOBILITY CORPORATION, Number 1 Mobility Plaza, Sewell, NJ 08080.
Positions: This manufacturer of electric mobility three-wheelers uses a national network of independent reps to demonstrate and sell their products. All reps are home-based, but must travel to demonstrate the products to interested buyers because they are either elderly or handicapped.
Requirements: This is not hard sell; reps must be easy going, caring, efficient and very organized. Apply with resume.
Provisions: Leads are generated through national advertising and are prequalified by telemarketers before being sent to reps. Territories are assigned by zip codes. Commission are about $300 per sale.

ELECTROLUX CORP., 2300 Windy Ridge Parkway, Suite 900 South, Marietta, GA 30067.
Positions: Direct sales of vacuum cleaners, floor polishers, and attachments.

EMMA PAGE JEWELRY, INC., P. O. Box 179, Blairstown, NJ 07825.
Positions: Direct sales of jewelry.

ENCYCLOPAEDIA BRITTANICA, INC., Brittanica Centre, 310 South Michigan Ave, Chicago, IL 60604.
Positions: This is the largest company of its kind in the world. It also has a reputation for having the highest paid direct sales reps of any industry. Britannica is now sold through a variety of means, very little door-to-door effort is used.
Provisions: A two week training session is provided. In most areas, write-in leads are provided. Pays highest commission in the industry, plus override for managers.

ENERGY SAVERS, INC., 101 Ridgeside Ct., Ste. 202, Mt. Airy, MD 21771.
Positions: Direct sales of energy conservation systems.

EQUITY MANAGEMENT SERVICES, INC, 796 Deer Park Ave., N. Babylon, NY 11703.
Positions: Inside telemarketers, outside sales people. This is the home office of a national/international (cargo shippers) collection agency.
Requirements: Company provides training to professional people to call on prospective businesses to sell collection services. Must have clear speaking voice, work in a quiet environment, and be able to speak with professional people. Bilingual a plus. Send resume.
Provisions: You can set your own hours. Receive draw of $5 per hour with escalating scale. First client is additional $20, second client is $25, third is $35, etc. It's possible earn $740 in one week by bringing in ten clients. Debt of $2,000 or more is additional $20 bonus. Company gets 25% and salesperson gets 20% on back end upon completion of collection. Example: $1,000 debt equals $250 to agency and $50 bonus to salesperson. Has telemarketing needs in Manhattan, Upstate New York, Connecticut, Westchester County, Kentucky, and the Springfield area of Massachusetts.

EQUITY RECOVERY CORP., 357 Hempstead Turnpike, W. Hempstead, NY 11552.
Positions: Telemarketers.
Requirements: Need organized individuals with good phone manners for advertising

and collections. Must be honest about leads and calls. Local people send resumes.

FAMILY RECORD PLAN, INC., P.O. Box 605, Woodland Hills, CA 91365.
Positions: Direct marketing of professional and amateur photography products.

FASHION TWO TWENTY, INC., P.O. Box 25220, Cleveland, OH 44202.
Positions: Direct sales of extensive line of quality cosmetics. Reps start by conducting home parties. After building an established clientele, home parties are usually replaced with prearranged personal consultations.
Requirements: There is usually a $15 fee to cover the cost of the manual and data processing. A new rep must also purchase the standard Show-Case kit. New consultants are expected to submit at least $150 retail orders per month.
Provisions: Pays commission. Management opportunities exist.

FINELLE COSMETICS, 137 Marston St., P.O. Box 5200, Lawrence, MA 01842.
Positions: Direct sales of cosmetics and skin care products.

FORYOU, INC., 4235 Main St., Loris, SC 29569.
Positions: Direct sales of cosmetics, self improvement programs, and skin care products. The line is sold mainly through party-plan methods.

G & M MIND GAMES, INC., 2545 Valdina Dr., Beavercreek, OH 45385.
Positions: Sales of Old Testament non-denominational Bible game to churches, stores, and friends.
Provisions: Profit amounts to about $9.00 per game.

GLOBAL PRODUCTS, 1103 South Lafayette, Neosho, MO 64850.
Positions: This crafts company is looking for sub-wholesalers for rack merchandising, wholesaling to retail stores, wagon jobbing, customer retail sales, mall catalog shopping centers, wholesale customer buying clubs, and a home party hostess program
Requirements: The sub-wholesaler program requires a $25 fee for all books and information and a $25 or $50 deposit for display samples, order blanks, etc. The party hostess plan requires a $25 deposit for all books and information and a $100 deposit for party plan samples to start with. Deposits are refundable.

GOLDEN PRIDE, INC., 1501 Northpoint Parkway, Suite 100, West Palm Beach, FL 33407.
Positions: Direct sales of health and beauty aids.

GROLIER INCORPORATED, Sherman Turnpike, Danbury, CT 06816.
Positions: Grolier is best known for publishing Encyclopedia Americana and has expanded into other educational publishing (such as the Disney series and Mr. Light).
Provisions: Training is provided in one-week classroom sessions. No leads, no territories. Sales are direct and usually accomplished by setting appointments by phone in advance of the presentation. Pays commission (about 23%) to reps plus override to managers. Some expenses such as phone and car are reimbursed on an individual arrangement with management.

THE HANOVER SHOE, INC., 118 Carlisle St., Hanover, PA 17331.
Positions: Hanover is over 50 years old and still markets its shoes primarily through

the use of independent reps. Reps sell direct through any method they chose, usually by starting with friends and neighbors and building up an established pool of customers through referrals.
Provisions: A portion of the retail price is returned to the rep.

HEALTH-MOR, INC., 151 E. 22nd St., Lombard, IL 60148.
Positions: Health-Mor is the manufacturer of vacuum cleaners, specifically Filter Queen. Company provides advertising and reps follow up on specific leads.
Provisions: Training is provided. Pays commission.

HEART AND HOME, INC., 76 Commercial Way, East Providence, RI 02314-1006.
Positions: Direct sales of decorative accessories.

HERBALIFE INTERNATIONAL, 9800 La Cienega Blvd., P.O. Box 80210, Los Angeles, CA 90009.
Positions: Direct sales of weight control food products.

HERITAGE CORPORATION OF AMERICA, P.O. Box 401209, Dallas, TX 75240.
Positions: Catalog sales of food supplements.
Requirements: An initial purchase of the products is required.
Provisions: Pays commission.

HIGHLIGHTS EXPRESS, Attn: Business Development Center, P.O. Box 810, Columbus, OH 43216.
Positions: From the people who bring you Highlights for Children magazine comes an exciting new line of fun and educational toys, books, games and videos for ages 2 - 12. Products are sold by Educational Constants like yourself to families like yours as well as preschools, libraries and community organizations.
Requirements: You must be at least age 18 and purchase a Starter Kit of sample products.
Provisions: Hours are flexible. Training and on-going support is provided. Pays commission (25 - 39%), leadership bonus and features monthly produces specials. There are no territories and the home office ships directly to each customer so there is no bagging and tagging of products.

HILLSTAD INTERNATIONAL, 1545 Berger Dr., San Jose, CA 95112.
Positions: Direct sales of nutritional supplements.

HOME INTERIORS & GIFTS, INC., 4550 Spring Valley Road, Dallas, TX 75244.
Positions: Direct sales of pictures, figurines, shelves, foliage, and other home accents. Reps set up exclusive shows that include about 35 pieces of merchandise. After the show, the rep offers individual service and decorating advice to the customers.
Requirements: Reps must order, deliver, and collect.
Provisions: Training is provided in the form of ongoing sales classes, weekly meetings and monthly decorating workshops. The average rep presents about three shows a week and works about 25 hours a week.

HOUSE OF LLOYD, 11901 Grandview Road, Grandview, MO 64030.
Positions: Home party sales reps and supervisors. Product line includes toys and gifts.
Provisions: Training and start-up supplies are provided with no investment. Commission equals approximately $9 an hour. Can live anywhere.

HY CITE CORPORATION, ROYAL PRESTIGE, 340 Coyier Lane, Madison, WI 53713.
Positions: Home party sales of cookware, china, crystal, tableware and stoneware.
Provisions: Training is provided. Pays commission. The company's marketing division provides all of the product literature, sales tools, and field assistance needed. All supplied are training manuals, presentation aids, and videotape and cassette training programs. Reps benefit from national advertising and customer promotion campaigns.

JAFRA COSMETICS, INC., P.O. Box 5026, Westlake Village, CA 91359.
Positions: Jafra makes high quality, "natural" cosmetics and skin care products. Reps sell the products through the party plan and by offering free facials to participants.
Provisions: Pays commission.

JEN DALE, P.O. Box 5604, Charlottesville, VA 22905.
Positions: Direct sales of personal care and vitamins.

KARLA JORDAN KOLLECTIONS, LTD., 3505 N. 124th, Brookfield, WI 53005.
Positions: This company specializes in unique handcrafted jewelry and accessories. Independent sales consultants sell the jewelry in a variety of ways such as personal accessory consultations, in-home presentations, fashion shows, etc. Sales consultants purchase the jewelry andaccessories at wholesale prices direct from the company, hand-picking their own inventory. Opportunities exist anywhere in the U.S.
Provisions: In addition to profiting from sales markups, the company offers special promotional programs and incentives. Commissions are paid to those consultants who develop an organization of reps.

JUST AMERICA, Oak Springs Rd., Rutherfordton, NC 28139.
Positions: Party-plan sales of skin care products.

KIDSWEAR OUTLET, 70 State Highway 10, Whippany, NJ 07981.
Positions: Direct sales of fine children's clothing. This company has been in business for over 45 years and is sold in over 5,000 retail stores.
Requirements: A sample package is available for $250. Send for "A Guide to Selling" if you're interested.

THE KIRBY CORPORATION, 1920 W. 114 St., Cleveland, OH 44102.
Positions: Kirby has been selling its vacuum cleaners door-to-door for many years. Now, reps use telemarketing methods to prearrange demonstrations.
Provisions: Some write-in leads are provided. Pays commissions.

KITCHEN FAIR, 1090 Redmond Rd., P.O. Box 100, Jacksonville, AR 72076.
Positions: Kitchen Fair is a 60 year old maker of cookware, kitchen accessories, and home decorative items. All products are sold in home demonstrations. There is no ordering, packing, or shipping merchandise and no collection by the consultants.
Provisions: Training is provided. Regional advertising is provided by the company and the resulting inquires are passed along to the area consultants. The initial kit is free. Pays commission to consultants and up to 7% override to managers.

L.A.M. ENTERPRISES, 3775 Diane St., Bethpage, NY 11714.
Positions: Telemarketing for Long Island people to work independently, selling subscriptions to Newsday, Daily News, USA Today and other publications. Pays salary

and commission with $600 to $700 a week potential working 4 to 5 hours per day.

L'ESSENCE, P.O. Box 1447, Friendswood, TX 77546.
Positions: Direct sales of perfumes and toiletries.

LITTLE BEAR ENTERPRISES, 3311 S. Saint Lucie Dr., Casselberry, FL 32707.
Positions: Little Bear sells unusual handcrafted home accessories with a country theme through home parties. Customers buy directly from inventory, not catalogs, and the inventory changes constantly to create a demand for additional parties.
Requirements: A minimum investment of $100 is required.
Provisions: A guaranteed return of a minimum $30 base pay for each party plus commissions of 20% are offered.

LONGABERGER MARKETING, INC., 95 Chestnut St., Dresden, OH 43821.
Positions: Longaberger markets maple wood baskets that are handmade in America. Each basket is signed by the weaver. Longaberger consultants sell the baskets though home parties.
Requirements: The initial investment of $300 covers the cost of sample baskets, catalogs, invitations, a handbook, and enough materials to hold several shows.
Provisions: Training is provided not only for sales techniques but for learning how to best decorate and display the baskets. Pays commissions starting at 25% plus overrides for managers. Three levels of management opportunities exist. Managers are provided with special management award baskets, mailings, meetings, training sessions, incentives, and other awards.

LUCKY HEART COSMETICS, INC., 138 Hurling Ave., Memphis, TN 38103.
Positions: Lucky Heart is a line of cosmetics for black women. The products are sold direct by independent distributors in any way they choose.
Requirements: A one-time $10 start-up fee is required.
Provision: Color catalogs, samples and testers are provided. Pays commission plus bonuses. Management opportunities exist.

JOE MARTHA TELEMARKETING, 1615 Republic St., Cincinnati, OH 45210.
Positions: Telemarketing of Catholic publications.
Provisions: Training is provided. Good repeat business. Can be located anywhere in the U.S. Pays good commission.

MARY KAY COSMETICS, INC., 8787 Stemmons Freeway, Dallas, TX 75247.
Positions: Beauty consultants and sales directors. Mary Kay started this cosmetics empire on her kitchen table in 1963. In 1984 there were 151,615 consultants and 4,500 sales directors producing over $300 million in sales. All of these people worked from their homes.
Requirements: An investment of $100 is required to start.
Provisions: Pays commission up to 12%. Offers incentives such as jewelry, furs, cars and trips through special promotions and contests. Consultants can earn over $30,000 annually, generally averaging over $10 an hour after taxes. Directors average over $100,000 a year. Can live anywhere.

MASON SHOE MANUFACTURING COMPANY, 1251 First Avenue, Chippewa Falls, WI 54729.
Positions: Mason is a 35-year-old family business with an extensive line of American

made, quality shoes. All shoes are guaranteed for quality and fit and can be easily exchanged or refunded.
Provisions: Reps are provided with catalogs and all necessary supplies. Incentive bonus plans several times a year. Portion of the retail price is taken out by the rep before placing the order with the company.

MEGATREND TELECOMMUNICATIONS, 1278 Main Street, Suite 127, Watertown, CT 06795.
Positions: Sales of pay phones that operate on both standard phone lines as well as cellular. The cellular payphones allow the user of credit/debit card processing equipment and fax machines over cellular. This would be used by field sales organizations, trade show exhibitors, flea markets, construction companies and tow trucks to name a few. All pay phone systems provide the customer with itemized receipts for phone usage.

METCALFE & ASSOCIATES, 20101 163rd Ave N.E.., Woodinville, WA 98072.
Positions: Distributorships of products manufactured by Quorum International, Inc. The Quorum line of products includes a variety of electrical consumer products.
Requirements: The fee for a distributorship is $45 plus the cost of a demonstration kit.
Provisions: Personal training plus audio and video tapes are provided throughout the United States and Canada.

MICO SEWING SUPPLIES, 110 Crossways Park Dr., Woodbury, NY 11797.
Positions: Telemarketing.
Requirements: Telemarketers sell sewing machine parts to other businesses (industrial parts and machines).
Provisions: Script and leads are provided. Full commission and bonus.

MIRACLE MAID, P.O. Box C-50, Redmond, WA 98052.
Positions: Miracle Maid cookware is sold through pre-arranged product demonstrations in customers' homes.
Provisions: Training is provided. Pays commission.

MORTGAGE RESOURCE, 602 Brentwood Pl., Everett, WA 98203.
Positions: Finding people looking for mortgages and getting paid a finder's fee for your referrals.
Requirements: An investment of under $100 is required.
Provisions: For about 2 hours of work on the telephone, you can expect to get 4 referrals on average. One of those referrals will proceed with the loan which translates into a fee of $200 to $500.

MULTIWAY ASSOCIATES, 633 Lawrence Street P.O. Box 2796, Batesville, AR 72501.
Positions: Multiway sells its line of health products through independent contractors who are free to sell the products in any manner they wish. Although the company has suggested retail prices and the reps deduct the wholesale prices to deduct their commissions, the reps are free to set any prices they want.
Requirements: A one-time fee of $39 is required for a starter kit which includes all necessary instructions, paperwork and samples. No product inventory is required. No set territories.

NATIONAL ASSOCIATION OF BUSINESS LEADERS, 4132 Shoreline Dr., Ste.

J, Earth City, MO 63045.
Positions: NABL is a professional association whose mission is to assist small to medium-sized businesses achieve greater profitability and success by providing resources and benefits that, until now, have been available only to large companies. NABL provides members access to timely management information, business and employee benefits, credit and financing resources, and even a $10,000 NABL charge credit line with the opportunity to become registered and rated by Dun & Bradstreet. As an independent NABL distributor, you'll have the job of signing up new members in your area.

NATIONAL MARKETING SERVICES, 451 E. Carson Plaza Dr., Ste. 205, Carson, CA 90746.
Positions: Work is available for various telemarketing projects; most involve selling tickets to charity events. Projects are available nationally as well as locally.
Requirements: Experience is required.
Provisions: Pays commission which varies with each project, but is typically in the $6 to $15 an hour range. Hours can be part-time or full-time, days or evenings. Scripts are provided.

NATIONAL PARTITIONS & INTERIORS, INC., 340, W. 78th Rd., Hialeah, FL 32707.
Positions: National Partitions is a major manufacturer and exporter of modular in-plant and exterior building systems. The company is looking to expand its domestic and foreign sales and in having foreign firms license the their products.
Provisions: A 5% finder's fee is paid to anyone securing sales and a 10% finder's fee to anyone securing foreign licensing agreements for the company.

NATIONAL SAFETY ASSOCIATES, INC. 4260 E. Raines Road, Memphis, TN 38118.
Positions: Direct sales of water treatment systems. NSA offers a proven program for part-time sales opportunities wherein a person can work 8-12 hours per week and earn up of $10,000 a year.
Requirements: New distributors of NSA products must first be sponsored by someone who is already a distributor. If one cannot be located, then the interested person must attend a regional training class. A schedule will be provided upon request.
Provisions: Training is provided. NSA products are sold through a trial use approach. A customer is given the opportunity to try the product for a few days, and then make the decision whether or not to purchase. Because of this method of selling, NSA recommends that distributors have 4-5 units on hand for this purpose. NSA provides a credit line so that the new distributor has no purchase requirements to get started. Pays commission plus bonuses through the company-sponsored rebate program.

NATURAL IMPRESSIONS CORPORATION, 182 Liberty Street, Painesville, OH 44077.
Positions: Direct sales of jewelry.
Provisions: Pays commission. Catalogs are provided.

NATURE'S SUNSHINE PRODUCTS, INC., 1655 N. Main, P.O. Box 1000, Spanish Fort, UT 84660.
Positions: Direct sales of herbs, vitamins, and personal care products.
Requirements: New distributors must attend a one-week training session at company headquarters at their own expense. Reps are trained to sell the products through network

marketing.
Provisions: Commissions start at 8% and go up to 30%. Managers receive generous override commissions. Participating managers receive health and dental insurance, new car allowance, and a retirement program. Sales aids and incentive programs are provided to everyone.

NATUS CORP., 4550 W. 77th St., #300, Edina, MN 55435.
Positions: Direct sales of haircare, skincare and health and fitness products.

NEO-LIFE COMPANY OF AMERICA, P.O. Box 5012, Fremont, CA 94537.
Positions: Direct sales of household products, vitamins, minerals, and some food products. Multilevel techniques are used.
Requirements: A small investment is required.
Provisions: Pays commission on a sliding scale.

NOEVIR, INC., 1095 S.E. Main St., Irvine, CA 92714.
Positions: Direct sales of cosmetics manufactured by Noevir, all of which are completely natural and herbal. Noevir has over 15,000 operators currently serving the U.S. The company is an affiliate of a larger Japanese company, and also has an office in Canada. Noevir is a wholly-owned subsidiary of Noevir, Co., Ltd., the second largest direct selling company in Japan.
Requirements: The initial investment in Noevir is $30 for registration in addition to the purchase of one starter kit. These kits contain products, training information, and samples for the new operator. The kits, (choice of 2) are $150. There is also an option "C" which is a "build-your-own" kit. The minimum purchase for this kit is $50.
Provisions: Noevir offers a generous compensation package in addition to very high quality products.

NUTRI-METRICS INTERNATIONAL, INC., 12723 166th St., Cerritos, CA 90701.
Provisions: Direct sales of cosmetics, food supplements, and bras.

NUTRITIONAL EXPRESS, Houston, TX.
Positions: Nutritional Express (formerly Consumer Express) offers a wide variety of products including food, cleaning products, cosmetics, and health care. It also offers services such as the Legal Services Plan. Direct distributors are free to market these products and services anyway they wish with no set territories or methods.
Requirements: Pays commission plus bonus plan. This is a multilevel marketing plan so extra bonus plans for enrollments are available, but it is not the primary thrust of the program. Complete training is available.

KENNETH OLSON & ASSOCIATES, 257 Merritt Rd., Los Altos, CA 94022.
Positions: Telemarketers for business-to-business insurance sales.
Requirements: Must be local resident. Prefers experience in business-to-business dealings.
Provisions: Specific training is provided. Leads are also provided. No high pressure selling involved. Part-time hours only. Pays salary plus "substantial" commission.

OMNI CREATIONS, 27815 Lorjen Rd., Canyon Country, CA 91351.
Positions: Direct sales of extensive jewelry line. Reps sell through home parties, fashion shows, wholesale, and any other method they choose. Company is now 11 years old.

Requirements: No investment is required. The company is expanding nationwide, but for now it is mostly operating in New York, New Jersey, California, Illinois, and Florida.
Provisions: There is a start-up program available for anyone interested in management opportunities in states not mentioned above. Work is part-time and reps average $30,000 a year.

ORIFLAME INTERNATIONAL, 76 Treble Cove Road, North Billerica, MA 01862.
Positions: Direct sales reps for European cosmetics line. Oriflame International is a high-quality cosmetic line that has gained a reputation for being "the largest, most prestigious direct sales company in Europe." Company has been expanding throughout the U.S. for about five years. Advisors are trained as skin consultants. Business does not usually consist of door-to-door or party style sales. More often, advisors act as make-up artists and customers come to their home offices by appointment only. Opportunity also for part-time sales leadership positions. Significant "groundfloor" opportunity for Group Directors.
Provisions: Complete training is provided. Commissions are reportedly the highest in the U.S. for a direct sales company.

PAMPERED CHEF, 4600 Normandale, Bloomington, MN 55437.
Positions: Consultants and their supervisors conduct gourmet cooking demonstrations in order to show the Pampered Chef line of kitchen tools.
Provisions: Training is provided. Pays commission plus override for supervisors. Incentive bonuses are offered to everyone including part-timers.

PARENT & CHILD RESOURCE CENTER, INC., P.O. Box 269, Columbus, OH 43215.
Positions: Direct sales of educational publications and magazine.

PARTYLITE GIFTS, Building 16, Cordage Park, Plymouth, MA 02360.
Positions: Home party sales of decorative accessories and giftware for the home.
Provisions: Pays commission plus bonuses. Management opportunities available.

PEABODY ADVERTISING CO., INC., 103 Godwin Ave., Suite 1100, Midland Park, NY 07432.
Positions: Telephone sales. Individuals will sell advertising space for different types of media: bowling centers, college centers, golfcourses, etc. Example: you find a bowling center that wants score cards printed, you now call on local businesses to advertise on these score cards and sell them print space.
Requirements: Need people with outside sales or direct sales experience. Must have good phone voice and be sincere, independent, persistent, and money motivated. Men and women, college students and seniors welcome. Must live on Long Island or any of the five boroughs.
Provisions: Part-time and full-time work available.

PETRA FASHIONS, INC., 335 Cherry Hill Drive, Danvers, MA 01923.
Positions: Direct sales of lingerie and sleepwear. All items are under $30. Petra consultants demonstrate the lingerie collection in private home parties. Consultants test show guests' "romance ratings" and offer fashion advice on garment style and fit. They do not collect money, take inventory or make deliveries. Petra accepts Mastercard and VISA and all show orders are shipped C.O.D. by UPS directly to the party hostess.

Sue Rusch
The Pampered Chef

Sue Rusch left her corporate job over 12 years ago to sell the Pampered Chef line of gourmet kitchen tools through home parties. Today, she is one of only three people at her level of management in the company. Her expertise is in helping others start no matter where they live. She developed video and audio training materials, and she communicates with people by phone, fax, and letter.

The Pampered Chef was actually founded by a working mother who wanted to create an opportunity with a workstyle for today. It is now one of the fastest growing direct selling companies in the nation, doubling in size every year for the last seven years. Sue says there are two reasons for such phenomenal growth: "First, the opportunity is very in sync with what women need and want which is a chance to put family first, but maintain an active career life. Second, the product we offer appeals to everyone, especially busy working women. Our best customer is the busy nine-to-five woman because she is stressed out and she needs help."

Women new to Pampered Chef start out as demonstrators. They go to other people's homes and prepare one or two recipes. The products are shown while they are cooking and they help people discover that gourmet cooking isn't hard and doesn't have to take a lot of time. For that they are paid commission and bonuses.

One of the bonuses is the travel incentive plan which is designed to include everyone, even part-timers. "The company wants everyone to earn it," says Sue. "This year we're getting a family trip to Disneyworld. It would only take three demonstrations a week to earn a trip for a family of five. Thousands of people are expected to make it. We're going to take up most of the Dolphin Hotel!"

Sue says anyone who enjoys being around people will do well in this job. "It's a company that puts respecting somebody working out of their home and making family life a priority. Why clash with corporations when even as a demonstrator, hour for hour, the rate of pay can't even come close?"

Requirements: No investment or experience is necessary. Petra offers a free starter kit of sample garments and paperwork that is valued at more than $500. There are no quotas or sales territories.
Provisions: Petra provides free training, hostess incentives, profit per show in excess of $75, advancement opportunities, overrides, awards, and recognition.

DAVID PHELPS INSURANCE, 7844 Madison Avenue, Suite N111, Fair Oaks, CA 91361.
Positions: Insurance sales for special program offered by National Association of Self Employed (NASE).
Requirements: Must live in Northern California to work for this particular agency.
Provisions: All leads are supplied by the association. Pays commission. Training is provided.

PLANTMINDER, INC., 22582 Shanon Circle, Lake Forest, CA 92630.
Positions: Direct sales of self-watering plant containers. Reps sell the product in a variety of ways, usually starting by placing ads.
Provisions: Pays commission.

POINT OUT PUBLISHING, 26 Homestead St., San Francisco, CA 94114.
Positions: This European publisher of maps and guides uses home-based telemarketers to make appointments for salespeople. Work is not permanent; it comes and goes all the time.
Requirements: Good phone manner and experience is required. San Francisco residents only.
Provisions: Pays $8 an hour.

POLA, U.S.A., INC., 250 East Victoria Avenue, Carson, CA 90746.
Positions: Home party sales of cosmetics.
Requirements: A start-up kit requires an investment.
Provisions: Pays commission.

PRIMA FACEY, 783 Park, Glen Ellyn, IL 60137.
Positions: Image consultants give personal and corporate workshops to men and women on how they can enhance their image. The consultants work on location, which can be in their own home or in someone else's home or office.
Requirements: There is a $500 initial investment to become certified as an image consultant and for the necessary tools to start. This investment can result in annual commissions of $40,000 or more.
Provisions: Training sessions are held throughout the country on a regular basis. Hours are extremely flexible.

PRINCESS HOUSE, INC., 455 Somerset Avenue, North Dighton, MA 02764.
Positions: Home party sales of crystal products.
Provisions: Pays commission plus override for managers. Training is provided.

PRO-AG, INC., 5010 Broadmore St., Maple Plain, MN 55359.
Positions: Direct sales of Impro/NU-AG agricultural products.

PROFESSIONAL ACCOUNTANCY PRACTICE, 14111 Buckner Drive, San Jose, CA 91361.

Positions: Telemarketing of professional services to businesses only.
Requirements: Must be local resident. Experience is required.
Provisions: Specific training is provided. Pays commission weekly.

THE W. T. RAWLEIGH COMPANY, 1501 Northpoint Parkway, Suite 100, W. PalmBeach, FL 33407.
Positions: Direct sales of household products, food, cleaning products, medicine, and pet supplies. Reps use any sales methods they choose.
Provisions: Pays commissions.

REGAL WARE, INC., 1675 Reigle Dr., Kewaskum, WI 53040.
Positions: Direct sales of cookware, usually through home parties.
Provisions: Training is provided. Pays commission.

REMOTE CONTROL, 514 Via de la Valle, Suite 306, Solana Beach, CA 92075.
Positions: Over 50 telemarketers sell the company's software from their home phones.
Requirements: Sales experience and a background working with a computer are required.

RENA-WARE COSMETICS, INC., P.O. Box 97050, Redmond, WA 98073.
Positions: Cookware is sold by independent reps in any manner they choose.
Provisions: Pays commission.

REXAIR, INC., P.O. Box 3610, Troy, MI 48007.
Positions: Direct sales of rainbow vacuum cleaners, AquaMate, and related products.

RICH PLAN CORP., 4981 Commercial Dr., Yorkville, NY 13495.
Positions: Direct sales of food, beverage products, and home appliances.

RUBINO PUBLISHING, INC., (800)749-1333.
Positions: Publishers of business manuals seeks independent contractors to market secured credit cards. Work mostly involves taking incoming phone orders.
Requirements: Manual and instructions costs (one time fee) $59.95.
Provisions: Can live anywhere. Bank processing centers pay regardless of approval.

SALADMASTER, INC., 912 113th St., Arlington, TX 76011.
Positions: Home party sales of cookware and tableware.
Provisions: Training is available. Pays commission plus bonus plan.

SALES PLUS, P.O. Box 28441, Baltimore, MD 21234.
Positions: Part-time telemarketers set appointments from home. Business to business calls only.
Requirements: Must be local resident. Experienced professionals only.

SAMANTHA JEWELS, INC., 162-27 99 Street, P.O. Box 477, Station B, Howard Beach, NY 11414.
Positions: A line of more than 2,000 kinds of jewelry (mostly gold and diamond) are sold direct with the aid of mail order catalogs.
Requirements: A $4 fee for a sales package including the catalog price instructions, sales instructions and paperwork supplies.
Provisions: Pays commission of a minimum 55%.

SAN FRANCISCO CHRONICLE, Circulation Department, 925 Mission, SanFrancisco, CA 94103.
Positions: Telemarketers sell subscriptions. Work is part-time.
Requirements: Some previous telemarketing experience is required.
Provisions: Can live anywhere in Northern California. Training is provided. Some leads are supplied. Pays commission and bonuses.

SCHOOL CALENDAR, P.O. Box 280, Morristown, TN 37815.
Positions: Account executives sell advertising space. Company is a 30 year old publishing firm.
Requirements: Must be bondable.
Provisions: A protected territory is assigned. Training and accounts are provided. Pays commission and bonuses.

SDF PROFESSIONAL COMPUTER SERVICES, 813 S. Evans St., Greenville, NC 27834.
Positions: Sales.
Requirements: Sell computer software and peripherals to businesses within 50 mile radius. Company car or gas allowance.

SHAKLEE CORPORATON, Shaklee Terraces, 444 Market Street, San Francisco, CA 94111.
Positions: Shaklee's line of products includes "natural" cosmetics, health care products, household products, and now some services as well. All of Shaklee's products are sold by independent distributors.
Requirements: Distributors must stock inventory in all basic products which does require a cash investment.
Provisions: Pays commission.

SILKS BY ROSE, 2060 Lincoln Way East, Chambersburg, PA 17201.
Positions: This product line includes handmade silk flowers, ivy, plants, ferns, bonsais, trees, etc. along with a wide selection of baskets, brass planters, prints, collectables, tapestry pillows, napkins, placemats and rugs are of the highest quality, but very well priced. The products are sold mostly through in-home demonstrations that are coordinated

by a hostess. The company currently has about 50 representatives.
Provisions: The "decorator" receives 25% - 30% commission on sales or $75- $100 for about 2 hours effort.

SOCIETY CORPORATION, 1609 Kilgore Ave., Muncie, IN 47304.
Positions: This is a manufacturer of cookware, china and crystal. The product line is sold through independent reps with assigned exclusive territories.

THE SOUTHWESTERN COMPANY, P.O. Box 305140, Nashville, TN 37230.
Positions: Southwestern is a well established publisher of educational books and cassettes. Independent reps sell the products, mostly with the aid of company provided leads. Exclusive territories are assigned and many are taken by long-time reps so there may not be anything available in your area.
Provisions: Pays commission plus bonus plan.

SPEARMAN, P.O. Box 2598, Gardena, CA 90247.
Positions: Direct sales of Essence Perfumes, duplications of designer perfumes.
Requirements: Starter package costs $6 and includes a sample of the product, a master flyer, instructions, etc. Be sure to include your phone number.
Provisions: Pays commission. Shipment of products performed by the company.

SPIRIT PLUS, P. O. Box 305140, Nashville, TN 37230.
Positions: Direct sales of personally designed T-shirts.

STANHOME, INC., 333 Western Avenue, Westfield, MA 01085.
Positions: Direct sales of household cleaning products and personal grooming aids. Reps can used any method for marketing the products.
Provisions: Pays commission.

STEINHAUS AUTO ELECTRIC SERVICE, 3717 2nd Avenue, Sacramento, CA 95816.
Positions: Telemarketers set appointments for alarm systems salespeople.
Requirements: Must live in Sacramento. Experience preferred.
Provisions: Training provided. Pays guaranteed hourly rate.

THE STUART MCGUIRE COMPANY, INC., 115 Brand Road, Salem, VA 24156.
Positions: Direct sales of shoes and clothing for both men and women through the use of catalogs.
Provisions: Catalogs are provided. Pays commission on a sliding scale.

SUBSCRIPTION PLUS, 228-35 Edgewood Avenue, Rosedale, NY 11422.
Positions: Subscription agents for several hundred major consumer magazines.
Provisions: Some training is provided. Can be located anywhere in U.S. Pays commission up to 50%.

SUCCESS MOTIVATION INSTITUTE, INC., P.O. Box 2508, Waco, TX 76702.
Positions: SMI is the world leader in personal and professional development. Their products help businesses and sales organizations improve results.
Requirements: Must fill out application and be accepted by the company. $100 for a sales kit is the only cost.
Provisions: Sales training kit includes a cassette tape, full-color visual, two video

tapes, starter supply of forms, and a "Success Guide".

SUCCESSFUL SOFTWARE, P.O. Box 680636, San Antonio, TX 78268.
Positions: Need independent agents to sell useful, easy-to-use IBM and compatible PC software program titles to local home and leisure markets. Agents can select which title(s) to market.
Requirements: Must sign a non-transferable Agent's Application and Agreement and pay a one-time start-up fee of $50. For application and Agreement, send a long self-addressed, stamped envelope plus $3 to cover handling to the address above. The $3 is deductible from the registration fee.
Provisions: You will receive copies of the software to run and evaluate, order forms, and 50% of retail price.

SUITCASE BOUTIQUE, 12228 Spring Place Court, Maryland Heights, MO 63043.
Positions: Suitcase Boutique is a home party business. Home party demonstrators sell hand crafted items like stuffed animals, wood crafts, toys, soft sculpture, framed pictures, and cross-stitch.
Requirements: Investment is required for start-up kit, but kit will be bought back upon request.
Provisions: Pays commission. Training is provided. Work is part-time; average income for demonstrators is $9,000 a year. Can live anywhere.

THE SUNRIDER CORPORATION, 452 West 1260 North, Orem, UT 84057.
Positions: Direct sales of food products and personal care items using the multilevel techniques.
Requirements: A small investment in inventory is required.
Provisions: Pays commission on a sliding scale plus bonus incentives.

TAMP COMPUTER SYSTEMS, 1732 Remson Ave., Merrick, NY 11566.
Positions: Telemarketing. Telemarket a publication to Fortune 5000 companies. Speak to department managers and offer this $99 publication. You must have a comfort level with speaking to department manager. TAMP provides leads by territories on a national basis; they also offer a script and suggest closes. Pays flexible salary and compensation package.

TECHPROSE, 370 Central Park West, Suite 210, New York, NY 10025.
Positions: This is an unusual company that does electronic marketing for clients using electronic databases, modems, and fax machines to conduct its business. Market researchers and their support staff handle the various telecommunications tasks and prepare reports from their home offices.
Requirements: A solid background in marketing plus experience with electronic networking are required. Send resume.

TELEMARKETING ASSOCIATES, 2924 North River Rd., River Grove, IL 60171.
Positions: Telemarketing in various fund raising projects. Some projects are nationwide so home workers can live anywhere. Most projects, however, are in Illinois only.
Provisions: Training is provided. Pays hourly wage or high commission.
"One of our projects pays $500 and up per week in commission."

TIARA EXCLUSIVES, 717 E St., Dunkirk, IN 47336.

Positions: Home party sales of decorative home accessories mostly consisting of glassware.
Provisions: Training is provided. Pays commission plus override for managers.

TIME-LIFE BOOKS, 777 Duke St., Alexandria, VA 22314.
Positions: Direct sales of educational publications.

TOMORROW'S TREASURES, INC., 111 North Glassboro Road, Woodbury Heights, NJ 08097.
Positions: Direct sales of photo albums, cameras, and other photographic equipment. Reps mostly use direct mail.
Provisions: Pays commission.

TOPHATS AND TAILS, INC., 1265 Sunrise Highway, Bayshore, NY 11706.
Positions: Telemarketing chimney sweep services. Training is available for well spoken individuals in the area. Pays salary and commission and bonuses: $7 per hour, $5 for each spot, and additional bonus for 4 or more in one day.

TOWN & COUNTRY, 5060 Gardenville Road, Pittsburgh, PA 15236.
Positions: Telemarketing for carpet cleaning company.
Requirements: Must live in the greater Pittsburgh area.
Provisions: Training is provided. Each telemarketer is assigned a territory. Pays commission.

TRI-CHEM, INC., One Cape May Street, Harrison, NJ 07029.
Positions: Tri-Chem has manufactured craft products since 1948 and the complete line is now sold in more than 40 countries around the world. The leading product in their line is a liquid embroidery paint. Reps conduct craft classes to show potential customers how to use the products.
Requirements: To become a Tri-Chem instructor, you must hostess an introductory class, book at least 4 more classes for your first two weeks, and pay a small registration fee.
Provisions: Training is provided. Pays commission starting at 25% and going up to 50% with volume. Tri-Chem offers new instructors a consultant kit worth up to $260 and bonus coupons for free products worth up to $234. Bonus programs provide additional earnings, vacation trips plus special seminars and conventions to enhance training. Management opportunities are available.

TRI COUNTY C.U., 2533 Addy Gifford Rd., Addy, WA 99100.
Positions: Telemarketers.
Requirements: This company provides financial consulting services teaching how to increase net value through investments, savings protection, and tax benefits (offers 100% money back guarantee). Needs telemarketers nationally to spearhead in their local areas as front-end people (consultants) to invite business associates to attend a financial seminar. Must solicit and bring to life a registration for this seminar, allowing two to three weeks to set up ten people per location and give part-time support after presentation.
Provisions: Pays salary plus commission plus great pay on follow-ups.

TUPPERWARE HOME PARTIES, P.O. Box 2353, Orlando, FL 32802.
Positions: Direct sales of plastic food storage containers, cookware, and children's toys.

TYNDALE HOUSE PUBLISHERS, INC., 351 Executive Dr., Wheaton, IL 60189.
Positions: Home-based telemarketers.
Requirements: Must be local resident. Experience required.

UNITED CONSUMERS CLUB, 8450 South Broadway, Merrillville, IN 46410.
Positions: This is a consumer group buying system that solicits new members through home parties.

U.S. SAFETY & ENGINEERING CORPORATION, 2365 El Camino Avenue, Sacramento, CA 95821.
Positions: Direct sales of security systems including fire and burglar alarms. Reps have exclusive territories and are free to use any sales methods they choose. Most use telemarketing to set appointments for personal consultations.
Provisions: Pays commission.

UNDERCOVERWEAR, INC., 331 New Boston St., Wilmington, MA 01887.
Positions: Home party sales of clothing, mostly lingerie.
Requirements: Rep is required to host a home party first.
Provisions: Pays commission. Training is provided.

UNION TRIBUNE, 4069 - 30th Street, Suite 9, San Diego, CA 92104-2631.
Positions: Telemarketers sell subscriptions.
Requirements: Must live in the San Diego area. Self-discipline is important.
Provisions: Training is provided. Some leads are supplied. Pays commission plus bonus.

UNITED LABORATORIES OF AMERICA, INC., 515 Congress Ave., Ste. 1708, Austin, TX 78701.
Positions: Direct sales of photo albums, photo enlargements, books and Bibles.
Provisions: Pays commission.

UNITED MARKETING GROUPS, 374 S. Elm Ave., Webster Grove, MO 63119.
Positions: Telemarketers work on a variety of projects throughout the Bay area.
Requirements: Experience is required in some kind of phone work. Must live in the Bay area.
Provisions: Training is provided. Leads are supplied. Pays commission.

USA TODAY, 1000 Wilson Blvd., Circulation Dept., Arlington, VA 22234.
Positions: Telemarketers solicit subscriptions. Work is distributed to home workers on a local basis only through USA Today's distributors. Distributors can be found in the phone book, or you can contact the main office to locate the distributor in your area.

USBORNE BOOKS AT HOME, P.O. Box 470663, Tulsa, OK 74147.
Positions: Usborne's award-winning children's books have been sold worldwide since 1973. The books are all four color, lavishly illustrated, information packed books that children love to read. There is a wide range of subject covering hobbies, science, nature guides and more. Beginning in 1981, Usborne books have been successfully sold through home party plans in Australia, Hong Kong, Singapore, England and now the United States. The home business division sells over 600 Usborne titles with new publications being announced semi-annually. It also offers four methods of selling: home parties,

fund raisers, book fairs, and direct sales. Usborne Books at Home is also a member of the Direct Selling Association.
Provisions: No experience necessary, training materials provided, no territories, no inventory to maintain, and no collections or product delivery. The investment of $69.95 or $159.95 includes all training materials, supplies and the base kit or mini-kit of Usborne books. The start-up kit includes training materials and supplies for only $25.00.

VITA CRAFT CORPORATION, 11100 West 58 Street, Shawnee, KS 66203.
Positions: Home party sales of cookware, china, crystal, tableware and cutlery.
Provisions: Pays commission and bonuses. Training is provided.

VIVA AMERICA MARKETING, 1239 Victoria St., Costa Mesa, CA 92627.
Positions: Direct sales of cleaning products, cosmetics, and nutritional supplements through home parties.

WATER RESOURCES INTERNATIONAL, INC., 2800 East Chambers St., Phoenix, AZ 85040.
Positions: Direct sales of water conditioning and purification systems.

WATKINS INCORPORATED, P.O. Box 5570, Winona, MN 55987.
Positions: Watkins is a well established company that uses independent reps to sell its extensive line of household goods including food, health products, and cleaning items.
Requirements: A small start-up investment is required.
Provisions: Pays commission.

WEBWAY, INC., 2815 Clearwater Road, P.O. Box 767, St. Cloud, MN 56302.
Positions: Direct sales of photo albums.

WELCOME WAGON, Welcome Wagon Bldg., 145 Court Ave., Memphis, TN 38103.
Positions: Welcome Wagon is a personalized advertising service. Individuals in all areas work from home to represent local businesses in the homes of brides-to-be, new parents, and newcomers.
Requirements: Outgoing personality, articulate, past-business or community experience. Car is a necessity.
Provisions: Training is provided. Flexible scheduling, part-time or full-time. Pays commission.

THE WEST BEND CO., Premiere Cookware Division, 400 Washington St., WestBend, WI 53095.
Positions: Direct sales of cookware and electrical appliances. The company started in 1911 and has been a member of the Direct Selling Association since 1927. West Bend has a deep respect for the direct selling industry because of the success of their other company, Tupperware.
Provisions: Training is provided through the use of Zig Ziglar training programs. In addition to commission, reps earn bonuses and can advance to management.

WINNING EDGE, P.O. Box 305140, Nashville, TN 37230.
Positions: Direct sales of home safety products including fire extinguishers, water purifiers, and fire alarms.

WORKSHOPS OF GERALD E. HENN, 1001 Country Way, Warren, OH 44481.

Positions: This is a party-plan direct selling company that markets 19th century decorative products. They manufacture the products in Ohio and take great pride in their quality. The company has nearly tripled in size during the past two years and currently has approximately 2,000 independent contractors that work out of their homes as our sales representatives. Over 90% are working part-time and nearly 100% are female.
Provisions: New people start at a commission rate of 25% and ship products directly to the Hostess.

WORLD BOOK, INC., 510 Merchandise Mart Plaza, Chicago, IL 60654.
Positions: World Book, the encyclopedia publisher, sells its products through the use of direct sales reps.
Provisions: Training is provided. Some leads are provided. Pays commission. Sales kit costs $55. Management opportunities are available

ALPHABETICAL INDEX-ALL COMPANIES

JOB BANK LOCATION INDEX

National and/or Multi-Regional Companies

Job Bank State Index

ALABAMA

ARKANAS

ARIZONA

CALIFORNIA

COLORADO

CONNECTICUT

DISTRICT OF COLUMBIA

DELAWARE

FLORIDA

Resource Guide

Note: the following are selections from THE WHOLE WORK CATALOG. To receive a free copy of the complete catalog, see page 328

HOME BUSINESSES
COMPUTER/INFORMATION RELATED

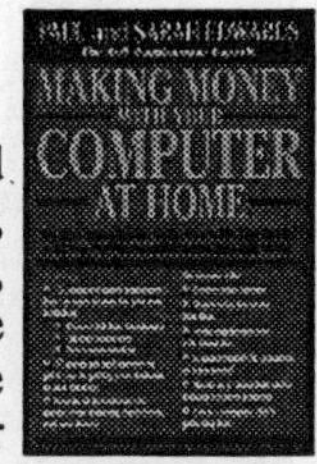

Making Money With Your Computer at Home
Edwards $12.95 **#2757** ©93 pb

This is a terrific idea-generator, profiling 75 different computer-based businesses, including a description of the business, start-up costs, potential earnings, marketing techniques, resources for getting started, and answers to 47 critical questions on how to select, plan and manage your new enterprise. Paul and Sarah Edwards are the authors of the bestselling book "Working From Home," write a monthly column for *Home Office Computing* Magazine, and operate the "Working from Home Forum" on CompuServe. Their insights and broad experience shine through in their writing.

Word Processing Profits at Home: A Complete Business Plan
Peggy Glenn $18.95 **#0115** ©93 pb lg format

The fastest growing segment of the home business boom is data and word processing by computer, according to the U.S. Chamber of Commerce. This comprehensive handbook covers virtually every aspect of running a home-based word processing business. With candor, warmth and humor, Glenn discusses personal considerations, planning, advertising, pricing, equipment, marketing, legal aspects, customer relations, professionalism and much more. Recommended by the Small Business Administration.

How to Make a Whole Lot More Than $1,000,000 Writing, Commissioning, Publishing and Selling "How-To" Information
Lant $39.95 **#1898** ©93 pb

Jeffrey Lant has built a one-person information empire, and he's adamant that anyone with motivation can do the same. This is a hefty volume with an impressive amount of detail on making money from books, booklets, audio cassettes and special reports. Full information is provided both for producing your own material and/or commissioning others to do the writing (while you concentrate on marketing). If you really want to ride the information-age wave—working at home with just your computer, fax machine and creative marketing imagination—you'll love this book.

Make Money Reading Books: How to Start & Operate Your Own Home-Based Freelance Reading Service
Bruce Fife $15.95 **#2735** ©93 pb

A college degree is helpful but not really necessary to break into the freelance reading business, according to Fife. Covers literary services, book reviewing, researching, translating, indexing, manuscript reading, literary representation (becoming a literary agent) and other opportunities. Includes sections on setting up your business, marketing your services (to newspaper, book and magazine publishers, writers, students, businesses, government, non-profit organizations and others), how to become a published author, more.

The Information Broker's Handbook
Rugge $34.95 **#2229** ©96 pb

Information brokering is one of the hottest entrepreneurial fields of the 90s, and this is easily the most comprehensive, authoritative, up-to-date guide to the opportunities available. Starting from scratch, author Sue Rugge grew her own information brokerage company to the $2 million annual sales level, and she covers all the nuts and bolts here. Includes a free disk of business forms, information on all the search and retrieval options available today, details on establishing an office, marketing and selling your services, pricing and billing, etc. *Highly recommended.*

900 Know-How: How to Succeed With Your Own 900 Number Business
Mastin $19.95 **#2574** ©94 pb

This book shows how to start a business selling pre-recorded information—anything from pork belly prices to horoscopes— over the phone to a national market. According to the author, the 900 number industry has grown to $975,000,000 in just a few years and presents tremendous opportunities for anyone wanting to work part-time from home. "offers detailed advice on how to succeed with a 900 number"-*The Midwest Book Review*

The Consultant's Kit: Establishing and Operating Your Successful Consulting Business Lant $34.95 **#0124** ©91 pb

We usually avoid carrying $35 books, but in a very few cases the expense seems justified. This is such a book—brimming with insights, tips and ideas, written by an acknowledged expert who quickly, easily and specifically shows you what works—and what doesn't. How to select a marketable skill, create a diversified service line, find and retain clients, get money each month from retainers, profit from commission contracts, spin off seminars and workshops, get free publicity and basically sell what you know in the most effective manner possible.

Bookkeeping on Your Home-Based PC
Stern $15.95 **#2723** ©93 pb

The phenomenal growth of small businesses in recent years is good news for self-employed bookeepers. Rather than hiring full-time employees, growing numbers of small businesses contract for their bookkeeping tasks, creating excellent opportunities for home-based bookkeepers. Stern shows how to start a thriving bookkeeping business with as little as $2,000 and a computer, gives insider tips and tricks from successful work-at-home bookkeepers, shows how to learn the skills you need, how to find clients, how much to bill for your services and more.

Making Money on the Internet
Glossbrenner $19.95 **#4614** ©95

With a user base of more than 30 million people that is doubling every year, the Net offers tremendous business opportunities. Glossbrenner shows opportunities for using the Net's electronic "storefronts," mailing lists, newsgroups, and World Wide Web "home pages" to sell online, communicate with customers, conduct market research and exploit international opportunities. Also explains how to put a catalog online, find Internet access providers and consultants, and avoid getting "flamed." Good profiles of Internet entrepreneurs.

Owning and Managing a Newsletter Business
Rogak $15.95 **#4710** ©95 pb

In today's information age, newsletter publishers are some of the most successful, enviable entrepreneurs around. The author has published five newsletters over the past 14 years and clearly knows what works. She shares anecdotes and success stories, plus hard-earned insights on scoping out your niche and refining your idea, keeping cash flowing for the highest profits, tricks for ensuring high subscription renewal rates, writing a month-by-month plan to stay on track, much more. Newsletter publishing is a low-cost, potentially high-profit business that you can operate from home, without employees. What could be better?

Making Money Writing Newsletters
Floyd $29.95 **#4686** ©94

If you don't want to publish your own newsletter, how about starting a newsletter writing and designing service? The author started her service with a $3,000 investment and built it into a $250,000 business in 3 years. Floyd gives 16 low-or no-cost ways to find clients, shows how to price your services, gives tips on shopping for wholesale printing and provides sources for renting or borrowing equipment. Includes 39 copy-ready forms to streamline your business. Subtitle: "From moonlighting to full-time work, how to set up & run a newsletter production service." Looks good.

Money Talks: The Complete Guide to Creating a Profitable Workshop or Seminar in Any Field Lant $35.00 **#0165** ©95 pb

"Workshops, seminars and lectures are a superb way of making money," begins Dr. Lant, who gives over 100 presentations a year himself. Creating programs that sell, training yourself to give effective presentations, breaking into the paying markets, identifying sponsors for your programs, mastering the college, trade and professional association markets, creating audio and video teleconferences, and much more. Highly recommended for anyone who knows how to do something that other people need and can use. "This seminar guide is by far the most complete I've seen."—J. L. Kennedy

The Self-Publishing Manual
Poynter $19.95 **#0423** ©93 pb

If you're a writer you should consider self-publishing to make more money, to keep control of your manuscript, to get into print sooner and to make your manuscript a long-term asset. Poynter has self-published some twenty books, including several best sellers. He shares every detail of how he built an enormously successful one-man publishing company. "Expertly organized and chock full of hard facts, helpful hints, and pertinent illustrations."—*The Southeastern Librarian* "...indispensable"—*Self-Publishing Book Review*

Information For Sale
Everett $16.95 **#4142** ©94 pb
If you enjoy doing library research and you're willing to learn to conduct computerized data base searches, information brokering could be a lucrative opportunity for you. Getting the training you need and leasing the necessary equipment requires only a few hundred dollars, and the potential for growth in this field is extremely good. This edition gives specific details on marketing your service, handling copyrights and other legal issues, conducting efficient on-line searches, keeping up with changing technology and setting fees. Interviews with successful information brokers give valuable insights into what this opportunity is really like.

Health Service Businesses on Your Home-Based PC
Benzel $16.95 **#2721** ©93
As medical costs continue to rise, hospitals, insurance companies and private physicians are increasingly interested in cutting expenses by turning administrative functions over to freelancers. This book focuses on the three most profitable health-related home businesses—computerized billing, claims processing, and records transcription services. For each opportunity a solid plan of action is presented, drawing on the real-life experiences of entrepreneurs who have built successful home-based health services. Covers how to attract clients, how to price services, start-up costs, much more.

Legal & Paralegal Services on Your Home-Based PC
Hussey $16.95 **#4124** ©94 pb
Covering a wide range of opportunities in the legal field, Hussey includes opportunities in litigation and other paralegal services, deposition summarizing, court reporting, scoping and a variety of specializations (independent professional law librarian, multimedia/video specialist, mediation service, estate planning and estate administration, etc.). Besides all that, there's information on finding training and experience and helpful profiles/interviews with successful legal services entrepreneurs.

Owning and Managing a Resume Service
Ramsey $15.95 **#4632** ©95 pb
People are increasingly willing to pay for a powerful, persuasive, up-to-date resume that looks and reads professionally-prepared. This is a relatively easy field to enter if you can communicate clearly, and it can be nicely profitable, too. Ramsey covers all the nuts and bolts: the market for resume services, typical business day for a resume service, training

courses and trade associations, income and profit potentials, tools and equipment, start-up considerations, pricing, marketing and advertising, growth, and more.

The Business of Multimedia
Schuyler $16.95 **#4692** ©95 pb

Unless you've been living in a cave for the last several years you're probably aware of the incredible growth in CD-ROM interactive multimedia. This new book shows how to take advantage of the opportunities in this burgeoning field, covering everything the developer needs to know about costs, distribution channels, financing, content acquisition, licensing and more. Includes examples and anecdotes from pioneers in the field and interviews with leading professionals, sample contracts and agreements, listings of multimedia and interactive organizations and more.

Owning & Managing a Desktop Publishing Service
Ramsey $15.95 **#4610** ©95 pb

With an investment of a few thousand dollars for a computer, lazer printer and the right software, anyone can go into business preparing resumes, brochures, letterheads, pamphlets, business cards, newsletters, menus, invitations, personalized mass mailings—even complete books and magazines. Ramsey covers setting up your service, niche marketing, working with clients, setting rates, building repeat business/referral business, and much more. Very up-to-date information.

How to Start and Profit from a Mailing List Service
Allegato $19.95 **#1945** ©91 75 minute audio program
This two-cassette program covers intriguing opportunities for working at home using a personal computer and mailing list software. Katie Allegato of Allegato & Associates explains how to create mailing lists from client-supplied data, monthly update services you can offer on a subscription basis, opportunities for compiling mailing lists on your own, and more. Covers getting started inexpensively, profitable special services you can offer, pricing and discounting techniques, ways to maximize your profits, how much you can expect to earn, and imaginative, offbeat and unusual ways to market mailing lists.

The Independent Paralegal's Handbook
Ralph Warner, attorney $29.95 **#0174** ©94 pb

Updated edition. More and more people are saving money by turning to independent paralegals instead of lawyers to help them prepare routine legal paperwork. This updated guide shows how to open a legal form-typing business, with information on legal areas open to independent paralegals, where to get necessary training, what to name your business, how much to charge, how to market your services, strategies designed to avoid "unauthorized practice of law" charges, and interviews with six important figures in the paralegal movement. The potential for this type of business is simply enormous. An exciting book and an exciting opportunity.

Write the Perfect Book Proposal
Herman $14.95 **#4660** ©93 pb
Written by two literary agents, this book shows how to write a successful non-fiction book proposal that will sell to a major publisher. Herman and Adams show what editors

are looking for, how to position your book so it stands out from the competition, how to write an effective sample chapter, how to get a bigger advance from the publisher, etc. The second part of the book gives detailed information on 10 book proposals that successfully sold to major publishers, showing exactly what was in the proposals that made them irresistable to publishers and how you can use the same tactics.

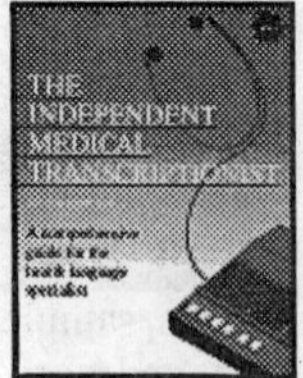

The Independent Medical Transcriptionist
Avila-Weil $32.95 **#4724** ©94 pb
If you're willing to learn to do medical transcription this book can be the key to an outstanding career working for yourself—from a home office if you prefer. Covers breaking into the field the right way, learning to do medical transcription (including home study courses), building a successful medical transcription business, very detailed information on business operations, marketing, financing your business, and much, much more. Includes tables showing standard regional billing rates and hours of daily transcription needed to generate $80,000/year in billings. This edition is new, comprehensive (almost 500 pages) and authoritative. We highly recommend it.

How to Start and Run a Writing & Editing Business
Herman Holtz $17.95 **#2197** ©92 pb
Writing and editing can be a viable business, and part of the trick is simply in knowing enough to position yourself as an editorial consultant. Holtz shows how to turn your writing skills into a steady source of income by servicing a variety of markets—including corporations, profit and nonprofit organizations, and the "vast" government market. Covers getting a full- or part-time writing business off the ground, matching your interests with real opportunities (writing everything from proposals and manuals to catalogs and newsletters), setting up your dream office, more. *Highly recommended.*

How to Make Money Writing Corporate Communications
Collins $12.00 **#4680** ©95 pb
Businesses buy all types of writing from freelancers—everything from book-length corporate histories to annual reports, catalog copy and newsletter material. Collins keeps busy writing for a wide range of major corporations, and in this book she shows how you can, too. How to: define your target companies, zero in on your best contacts, polish your portfolio, negotiate fees with confidence, cultivate client relationships for repeat business, and develop a nice, steady income stream from your writing.

You Can Be a Columnist
Digregorio $13.95 **#2770** ©93 pb
Writing a newspaper or magazine column can lead to fame and, if you become syndicated, a certain amount of fortune. Whether you write advice to the lovelorn, hints for keeping your canary healthy, information on using computers, decorating ideas or bridge instructions, this book can help you to write, market, promote and syndicate a regular column. This can be an ideal way to establish yourself as a writer, and can open doors for you both personally and professionally.

The Resume Pro
Parker $24.95 **#2182** ©93 pb

We know of one woman who spends 15 to 20 hours a week writing resumes for people and makes $1,500 to $2,000 a month for her efforts. With the right know-how, other people can probably do as well—and finally there's a book that provides the right know-how. Yana Parker, author of *The Damn Good Resume Guide* and an acknowledged authority in this field, shows how to create resumes for people with a wide range of skills and experience and covers the nuts and bolts of setting up and operating a resume-writing service. Good book.

The 10 Hottest Consulting Practices: What They Are, How to Get Into Them
Tepper $27.95 **#4620** ©95 hc

Some of these fields are familiar, some fairly obscure—but all are *hot.* Ron Tepper, a well-known consultant, explains which fields are in now and why. Covers opportunities for training consultants, software consultants, compensation specialists, reorganization specialists and others, showing how to launch the practice, make presentations, set fees, write contracts, market your service and more. Numerous interviews with consultants show how these top professionals built their businesses, how they operate and what they advise. Six-figure incomes are surprisingly common among this group. *Highly recommended.*

GREEN OPPORTUNITIES

Profits From Your Backyard Herb Garden
Sturdivant $10.95 **#4636** ©95 pb

New edition. This book,written by a delightful herb and flower grower on an island off the coast of Washington, is for beginning herb growers. It's short, easy to read, and gives good information for starting a small-scale herb business in your backyard. Covers growing, harvesting, packaging, and marketing culinary herbs to local restaurants and supermarkets, starting a backyard potted herb business and more.

Herbs For Sale: Growing and Marketing Herbs, Herbal Products, and Herbal Know-How Sturdivant $14.95 **#4126** ©94 pb

This book, a companion to *Profits From Your Backyard Herb Garden,* covers just about every conceivable herb-related business. The chapter on growing herbs covers profiting from a backyard, greenhouse, or small acreage in culinary herbs, dried flowers, salad greens, potted herbs or gourmet garlic; plus there are chapters on creating an herb farm; making herbal products (medicinal herb teas, herbal extracts, aromatic pillows, body care products, etc.); wildcrafting; teaching about herbs; and other possibilities (herb shops, aromatherapy, etc.).

Flowers For Sale: Growing & Marketing Cut Flowers
Sturdivant $15.95 **#2112** ©92 pb

This book gives an easy, step-by-step plan for starting a flower growing and selling business either in your backyard or on a small acreage. Numerous successful flower businesses are profiled, including Saturday Market flower sellers and one grower who takes in $650,000 on less than an acre of flower production. Hundreds of plant varieties with potential as commercial cut flowers are listed, with seed sources and other information. Covers harvesting, pricing, displaying, selling, business and tax information, collecting flowers and greenery from the wild, and much more.

How to Make Money Growing Plants, Trees & Flowers
Francis Jozwik, Ph.D. $19.95 **#2118** ©92 pb

Dr. Jozwik, who has operated a successful greenhouse and nursery business for over 20 years, shows how to make a significant income growing special ornamental crops in your own backyard. He explains why these ornamentals are in such great demand and gives all the nuts and bolts for getting started without technical expertise or spending a lot of money. Detailed examples show the ins and outs of each type of business with actual economic data for specific operations. Photo illustrations.

Lawn Aeration: Turn Hard Soil Into Cold Cash
Pedrotti $19.95 **#2200** ©92 pb

Lawn aeration is one of those offbeat businesses that nobody's ever heard of—but that can produce a very good income when you know what you're doing. It costs about $6,500 to buy the equipment and supplies, but if you believe the author—and we think he's extremely convincing—you can make $35,000- $50,000 working full time only 8 months of the year. It's also possible to get started with only $500 or so if you rent your equipment. An intriguing opportunity.

Backyard Cash Crops
Wallin $14.95 **#2578** ©89 pb

Subtitled "The Source Book for Growing and Marketing Specialty Plants," this is a guide to earning money growing any of 200 specialty crops including bulbs, culinary herbs, medicinal herbs, ornamentals, sprouts, small fruits, and much more. Covers deciding on the best specialty crop for you, how to sell all you can grow, how to buy wholesale seed and plant starts, where to get free expert advice, and much more. Very nicely illustrated, in-depth information.

Lawn Care & Gardening: a Down-to-Earth Guide to the Business
Rossi $21.95 **#4038** ©94 pb

If you think that opportunities in lawn service businesses are only suitable for neighborhood teenagers, this new book will be a wake-up call. As Rossi clearly shows, lawn and garden services are truly exceptional opportunities for anyone willing to work hard and gradually build a business. All aspects of starting and operating a lawn/garden service are covered in this comprehensive guide, from building a base of satisfied customers to scheduling and managing the workload—to expanding into a highly profitable regional service company. *Highly recommended.*

Secrets to a Successful Greenhouse Business
Taylor $19.95 **#4672** ©94 pb

Based on nearly 20 years experience in growing plants and designing greenhouses, Taylor's book shows how to profit from a wholesale greenhouse business—making up to $20,000 per 30'X96' greenhouse in 90 days. Includes solar greenhouse plans (70° inside/30° outside without heaters), who to sell to (nationwide plant buyers list), when and how to grow the best selling plants, how to profit from hydroponics and organic growing methods, working efficiently so only 7 hours per week are needed to maintain a 96' greenhouse, much more. Impressive book.

Turning Wool Into a Cottage Industry
Simmons $14.95 **#0172** ©91 pb

Simmons has thirty years of experience as a sheepraiser, spinner, weaver, teacher and author, and in this book she shows how a cottage industry involving wool can be the key to the good life. Beginning with raising and managing a flock of sheep or buying wool for resale, here is information on all aspects of home processing and selling raw and washed wool; carding as a cottage industry; the best equipment; business and merchandising tips; ideas for expanding a wool-based income; and descriptions of 18 entrepreneurs who've proved it can be done.

UNIQUE HOME BUSINESS OPPORTUNITIES

Profits in Buying and Renovating Homes
Dworkin $19.75 **#4454** ©90 pb

We personally know people who have basically retired at a very young age as a result of carefully selecting, buying and renovating homes. Women, especially, seem to have a nesting instinct for turning houses into homes and tend to do especially well in this field. This book offers hands-on advice and step-by-step tips for each step involved—from selecting the right property to making the right repairs to selling for top dollar. A substantial, in-depth guide.

How to Write and Sell Greeting Cards, Bumper Stickers, T-Shirts and Other Fun Stuff Wigand $15.95 **#4678** ©92 pb

The "social expression market" covers a wide range of products and is far larger than most people imagine. Wigand shows how to profit from the voracious appetite this market has for new ideas and creative wordsmithing. Covers how greeting card companies work—how they assign writing projects and what they look for in freelancers—plus non-traditional greeting cards, selling your writing, writing for self-expression prouducts, more. Some people make a very good living at this.

From Kitchen to Market: Selling Your Gourmet Food Specialty
Hall $24.95 **#2228** ©92 pb

Hall shows how to become a freelance foodcrafter, taking advantage of America's insatiable hunger for new taste sensations by creating a profitable small-scale food business of your own. Whatever delicacy comes from your kitchen, this unique book shows how to sell it locally, nationally and internationally, with info on start-up costs, pricing, packaging, distribution, etc. "Hall's guide may be the definitive manual in reaching...gourmet store shelves."—*Gourmet News*

How to Earn $15 to $50 an Hour With a Pickup or Van
Lilly $12.95 **#0246** ©87 pb

If you're between careers or just don't want serious commitments for a while, this little guide can show you how to make a decent living with only a battered old truck or van and a willingness to work hard. A side bonus is the treasures you can find while hauling away people's "junk" (the author was paid to haul away a late 19th century oil painting, for example, later appraised at $400). There are some things we don't like about the book--the cover, amateurish layout and slightly inflated price--but overall Lilly covers the topic in a straightforward, honest, very thorough manner.

Creative Cash: How to Sell Your Crafts, Needlework, Designs & Know-how Brabec $14.95 **#0162** ©91 pb lg format

There's a good reason why over 70,000 copies of this book are in print: it is truly outstanding. As *Crafts and Things* Magazine puts it, "A practical (and witty) guide for the would-be entrepreneur that discusses the obvious—and not so obvious—ways of making money from crafts. This may be the best book on making money from crafts that we have ever seen." Informative, thoroughly enjoyable reading, with step-by-step how-to's throughout.

How to Open and Operate a Bed & Breakfast
Stankus $15.95 **#0204** ©92 pb

The most comprehensive book on starting a B & B in your home we've seen, with complete start-up advice, an exclusive "Helping Hands Network" of current hosts from all over the country who are willing to advise newcomers, lots of charts and checklists and a "Should You Become a Bed and Breakfast Host?" quiz. "immensely readable and engaging"—*America's Bed & Breakfast*

How to Open and Operate a Home-Based Secretarial Services Business
Melnik $14.95 **#4138** ©94 pb

Going far beyond typing and data entry, Melnik reveals the many possibilities for generating both work and revenues in this multifaceted business. Drawing from 10+ years of first-hand experience, the author shares time-proven techniques for quickly establishing and operating a home business, including advertising, legal/tax matters, attracting clients, retaining a loyal client base, and pricing services reasonably and profitably.

Writing for Children & Teenagers
Wyndham $14.95 **#0185** ©89 pb

This guide to writing for and selling to the juvenile market will show you how to make time to write, get your story off to a running start, collect characters, spin a plot, build suspense, emotion and atmosphere, organize your book, prepare a professional manuscript submission packet and handle special writing projects such as biographies, mysteries and easy-to-read books. Based on actual, successful experience by the author of more than 50 books.

How to Open and Operate a Home-Based Photography Business
Oberrecht $14.95 **#4450** ©93 pb

Written by a successful home-based photographer, this book shows how to set up and run a thriving photo business—from outfitting your darkroom and finding clients to pricing your services and keeping track of your negatives and transparencies. Oberrecht shows how to estimate your start-up costs, manage your cash flow, deal with contracts and copyrights, schedule work, get paid, and handle the growth of your business.

Marketing Your Invention
Mosley $19.95 **#2758** ©92 pb

Knowing how to market your invention is what separates the successful inventor/entrepreneur from the creative dreamer. Mosley has been involved in hundreds of invention evaluations, counseling sessions with inventors and negotiations with marketers and manufacturers. His book covers protecting the idea, characteristics of a successful new product, invention positioning, finding money for developing the invention, licensing, the business of inventing, much more. Extremely comprehensive.

Sew to Success! How to Make Money in a Home-Based Sewing Business Spike $10.95 **#4624** ©95 pb

Custom sewing is an expanding business, and it can be ideal for those who want or need to work at home. This new book covers starting up, deciding what equipment to buy, marketing, client relations, pricing, bookkeeping, etc., and offers a peek into the lives of successful home-based sewing businesspeople. The author transformed her idea for "earning a little extra money at home" into a thriving dressmaking business and career as a popular international speaker, teacher and columnist for *Sew News*.

How to Make Cash Money at Swap Meets, Flea Markets, etc.
Cooper $14.95 **#1247** ©88 pb

After Jordan Cooper was laid off from his job, he and his wife held a yard sale and then took the leftover items to a local swap meet. In one day, they took in several hundred dollars. He hasn't worked at a regular job since, and sometimes he makes more money in a single weekend than he made in an entire month at his former job. How to start with a minimal investment, select your merchandise, set your prices, advertise, and run a profitable cash business either part-time or full-time.

Painting Contractor: Start and Run a Money-Making Business
Ramsey $19.95 **#4111** ©94 pb

Housepainting—the universal summertime business opportunity for college students—can be turned into a serious and quite lucrative full-time business. The authors cover all the ins and outs of becoming a painting contractor, with information on obtaining financing, structuring your business for the most profit, advertising and marketing your services, estimating jobs and setting prices, hiring and managing employees, maintaining a steady cash flow, and much more. Comprehensive, friendly and up-to-date.

How to Start a Window Cleaning Business
Suval $14.95 **#1392** ©88 pb

Window washers are in high demand, says Suval, and you can expect to make $10 to $25 an hour once you build up speed. It's a skill that's easy to learn, pleasant to do, and has little competition. How to reach potential customers, obtain your equipment, wash windows the professional way, know what to charge, keep business records, and much more. Large format, illustrated, revised third edition.

Cleaning Up for a Living
Aslett $13.95 **#0010** ©91 pb

Aslett, who has built a $12 million commercial cleaning business from scratch, gives step-by-step guidance for would-be cleaning entrepreneurs. He points out that cleaning is a fast growing industry and a relatively easy market to enter, requiring little start-up capital and no specific education . . . but it does take specific know-how to succeed. His book gives all the charts, forms, business rules and information you need to get started. Large format, illustrated, index.

Making $70,000 a Year As a Self-Employed Manufacturer's Representative Silliphant $10.95 **#0266** ©88 pb

For a variety of reasons, more and more companies, both large and small, are turning to the independent representative as a way to effectively sell their products. How to get started and prosper in this lucrative, rapid-growth field. Covers deciding what to sell, negotiating with the manufacturer, choosing travel or non-travel work, planning, locating clients, more.

How to Make $100,000 a Year as a Private Investigator
Pankau $19.95 **#4134** ©93 Photo illustrations.

Maybe Mr. Pankau makes $100K a year, but we doubt that many PI's do, and we hate titles that make exaggerated claims. Still, there <u>are</u> good opportunities in this field. Today's PI has become an information specialist who relies on his phone, computer and fax to locate missing people, find hidden assets, develop trial cases, and analyze the personal and business backgrounds of everyone from credit card applicants to presidential aspirants. A comprehensive, well-executed guide, in spite of its unfortunate title.

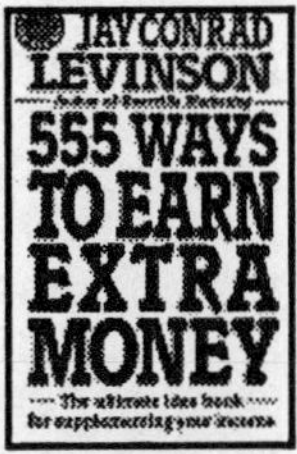

555 Ways to Earn Extra Money
Levinson $14.95 **#0918** ©91 pb

Whether you want to supplement a full-time job with extra earning projects or put together a network of part-time endeavors and give up the nine-to-five altogether, Levinson's book on moonlighting and "Patchwork economics" can help. Includes steps to get started, advertising tactics, suggested company names and unique—even surprising—ways to augment your income. The author is one of our favorites.

The Teaching Marketplace: Make Money With Freelance Teaching, Corporate Trainings, and On the Lecture Circuit Brodsky $14.95 **#1853** ©91

There's a huge, fast-growing market for non-credit education programs because they're fun and a great way to meet new people, in addition to their career advancement aspects. This unusual book shows how to turn almost any experience or personal enthusiasm into such a class—and an enjoyable source of part-time income for you. Covers choosing your topic, attracting students, organizing and selling your classes to schools and corporations—or freelancing on your own, the best times to teach, selecting a class space, keeping records, etc., plus interesting profiles of freelance teachers.

How to Find Your Treasure in a Gift Basket
Perkins $16.95 **#1964** ©91

In the early 80's a few people found they could make a very good living putting together gift baskets for individuals and businesses (who give them to employees or clients). Over the years the popularity of these gifts–and the opportunities for gift basket services–has steadily increased. Perkins shows how to start a home based gift basket service, starting with a minimal investment, and covers how to make beautiful gift baskets (filled with cheese, fruit, candy, wine, and other items), finding customers, popular theme baskets, more.

Multi-Level Money
Lant $19.95 **#4637** ©94 pb

It's not for everyone, but many people do create solid multi-level marketing businesses that generate an impressive income and can grow even when they're away on extended vacations. Dr. Jefferey Lant offers the most comprehensive, realistic approach to developing such a business we've seen—giving detailed, nuts-and-bolts information with a minimum of hype. We understand *The Wall Street Journal* predicts some 50-60% of all goods and services in the U.S. will be sold through multilevel/network methods by the year 2000.

How to Become a Successful Weekend Entrepreneur
Basye $10.95 **#2754** ©93 pb

Subtitled "Secrets of Making an Extra $100 or More Each Week Using Your Spare Time," Basye offers over 100 ideas to turn your weekends into prime income-producing time—without assuming the stress of a second job working for someone else. Includes special money-making sections for moms, teens, computer whizzes and retirees.

The Game Inventor's Handbook
Peek $18.95 **#1936** ©93 pb
Huge sums of money are spent on games every year, and this is the first book written on the creating, developing, manufacturing and marketing of games. Peek–who has designed, developed and/or marketed more than 150 games–gives detailed information for anyone wanting to produce the next *Monopoly* or *Trivial Pursuit.* Covers selling your game to publishers, self-publishing, more.

How to Start and Operate a Mail-Order Business
Dr. Julian Simon $39.95 **#0874** ©93 hc
Mail order is growing almost five times as fast as retail, and this book provides everything you need to know to get a mail-order business off to a good start and then keep it running smoothly, efficiently and profitably. We've seen dozens of books on the subject and don't think any of them seriously compete with Simon's, which is the one we regularly refer to in our own office. A professor of economics and marketing at the U. of Illinois, Simon has started, successfully operated, and profitably sold his own mail-order business. The fifth edition includes a chapter on personal computers and lists 500 products that sell successfully by mail. "You can learn more from this volume than in a month of listening to the experts."—*Direct Mail Briefs* "Crammed with solid, workable advice...in logical sequence and with concrete examples..."—*Specialty Salesman*

Complete Direct Marketing Sourcebook
Kremer $19.95 **#1347** ©92 hc
Somebody had a good idea here–a book which brings together all the forms, sample letters, charts, formulas and procedures you need to run a streamlined, efficient mail-order operation. Some of the forms are masters, ready for you to copy and use; others only require that you add your letterhead at the top before copying. If you're going into the mail-order business this "swipe file" can greatly simplify your life.

Massage: A Career at Your Fingertips
Ashley $19.95 **#2580** ©95 pb

New edition. "...covers everything the massage therapist needs to know: education and certification, marketing, taxes, insurance, office management, and so forth. In addition, it provides extensive resources, including a directory of schools and licensing laws for all 50 states.... Schools offering advanced coursework in the different massage specialties are listed, as are suppliers, professional associations, and newsletters....An invaluable guide."–*Library Journal*

How to Open and Operate a Home-Based Catering Business
Vivaldo $14.95 **#4448** ©93 pb
The author, a successful home-based caterer, shows exactly what it takes to start from scratch, line up business, set prices, estimate quantities, write proposals, stand out from the crowd, cope with surprises, throw successful parties, and stay profitable once you're in business. Includes budget worksheets, equipment checklists, sample catering contracts, sample menu themes, commonsense measures for safe food handling, "the 12 questions new caterers most often ask," and much more.

GENERAL SELF-EMPLOYMENT

Small Time Operator: How to Start Your Own Small Business, Keep Your Books, Pay Your Taxes, and Stay out of Trouble!
Kamoroff $16.95 **#0882** ©95 pb

With a quarter of a million copies in print, this is the most popular small business guidebook in the United States. It's not hard to understand why—in a pleasant, upbeat way it's highly informative, nicely designed and extremely well written. It provides all the income and expenditure ledgers you'll need for your first year, along with clear step-by-step instructions for using them, and the examples given are both interesting and helpful. "The best of the genre...a remarkable step-by-step manual that is a delight to read. All the nitty-gritty of business is here." *—Library Journal*

Free Money For Small Businesses and Entrepreneurs
Blum $14.95 **#0614** ©95 pb

This is a guide to the agencies, foundations, and other organizations that offer outright grants to qualified new and existing small businesses. All totaled, this money tops $2 *billion,* and it's available for a wide range of uses—from start-up capital to research grants. Categorized by type of business, each of the more than 300 listings supplies the name and address of the grant source along with amounts available and special requirements. Includes details on how to apply as well as where to apply.

The Small Business Test
Ingram $8.95 **#1910** ©90 pb large format

Why do some small businesses succeed–often beyond anyone's wildest dreams–when so many others fail? Based on a detailed analysis of almost 100 small businesses, from bakeries to ad agencies–and from your own evaluation of your knowledge, experience, product and other factors– **The Small Business Test** gives you your actual chances for success in your new business. It's also interesting and fun to take. Includes advice on finding unique markets, calculating your business plan, getting the most from suppliers, preventing legal problems and more.

How to License Your Million Dollar Idea Reese
$14.95 **#4670** ©93 pb

This is great—a book that shows you how to make money from new product or service ideas without going into business for yourself or risking your own financial resources. Reese makes a nice living by dreaming up product ideas and licensing them, and he shows how to come up with commercially-viable ideas, package the ideas so they are saleable, make presentations to appropriate companies, and negotiate licensing agreements giving you a percentage of future profits—all told with the kind of insights gained only from extensive first-hand experience. Includes sample patent forms, licensing agreements, disclosure statements, etc., plus examples that are fascinating to read.

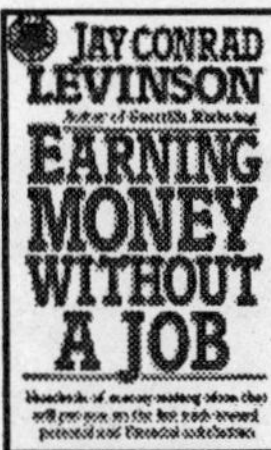

Earning Money Without a Job
Jay Conrad Levinson $9.95 **#0108** ©91 pb

Hundreds of money-making ideas—some obvious, some surprising—all within the realm of immediate opportunity. Hardly any require much capital, and most can be done out of your home. This is an exceptionally well-written book that's a pleasure to read. "The real answer to being your own boss is many small jobs. This book is the best guide available."—*The Next Whole Earth Catalog*

Working Solo Sourcebook: Essential Resources for Independent Entrepreneurs Lonier $14.95 **#4642** ©94 pb

This isn't another "how-to" book. Instead, it's a graphic-based guide to more than 1,200 important resources for entrepreneurs, providing fast, easy access to information needed by anyone in business. Lonier provides detailed listings, a graphic-based locator system, and extensive indexes on books, tapes and videos on a wide range of business topics, innovative programs for entrepreneurial training, government agencies serving small business needs, relevant associations, conferences, technology resources, supplies and services and much more.

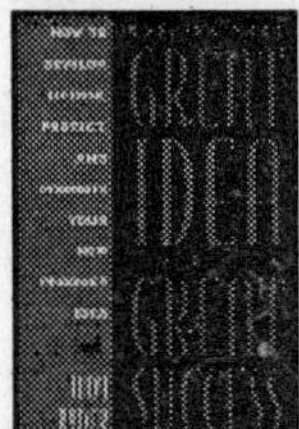

Turning Your Great Idea Into a Great Success
Ryder $14.95 **#4622** ©95 pb

One in every 18 Americans has invented a product or service, but to fully capitalize on a good idea requires knowing how to develop, license, protect and promote it. Ryder gives an eye-opening survey of the product idea market and reveals how to determine your product's chances of making it, how to protect your idea, choosing between manufacturing and licensing, avoiding distribution pitfalls, understanding effective promotion, and knowing when it's wise to seek help. Includes the experiences of dozens of entrepreneurs plus indispensable advice from patent attorneys, marketing executives, venture capitalists, media people and others.

Running a One-Person Business
Whitmyer $14.00 **#0300** ©94

New edition. Previously thought of only as a stunted version of a small business, one-person businesses are now a permanent—and rapidly growing—part of our new economy. The authors convey their excitement about this infinitely-versatile business form, presenting the idea that business can be a lifestyle and a statement of who you are and what you value. This book is a comprehensive guide to forming these unique enterprises, especially small businesses run from the home or professional office.

How to Start a Business Without Quitting Your Job
Holland $9.95 **#2222** ©92 pb

Keeping your job while you get a business up and running on the side makes sense—a whole lot of sense, as you will see in this guide to "the moonlight juggling act." Covers how to choose the right startup business, budget time wisely, and make sure neither job suffers, with firsthand accounts of successful moonlighters and the types of businesses that work for them. Includes chapters on financing, liability, involving your family, and deciding when (or if) to quit your job.

The Complete Work-at-Home Companion
Holtz $14.95 **#5046** ©94 pb

Working at home can be extremely efficient and enjoyable—if you know the ins and outs of making the most of a home office. Henry Holtz has long been one of our favorite authors, and this comprehensive guide covers best office design ideas, marketing your product or service, setting your prices, using lawyers and accountants, overcoming distractions, incorporating, zoning considerations, getting the most from computer and other home office equipment, and much more. An interesting, well written book.

Becoming Self-Employed
Elliott $9.95 **#4146** ©94 pb

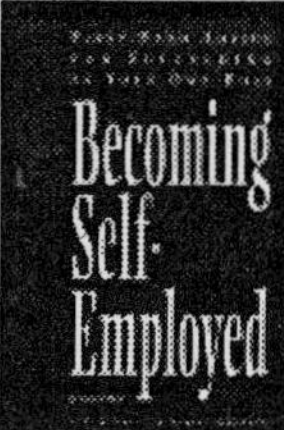

New edition. Talking candidly about what's really involved in self-employment, the 20 people interviewed in this book make it clear that ordinary people can succeed in small but successful businesses. Most important, it's clear these people love their work—whether it's running a country inn, operating a restaurant, writing, baking, organizing canoe trips or running an art gallery. In their own words they tell what they did right, what they did wrong, why they went out on their own and what their plans are for the future. There's not a dull page in this extremely well-written book.

Franchise Opportunities Handbook
Ludden $16.95 **#4698** ©95 pb

Did you know that the average earnings for franchise owners is over $120,000 per year? It's true, and it's also true that franchising accounts for more than 20,000 new businesses every year. This new guide covers an incredible range of opportunities (some 1,500 in all), with full details on each opportunity, explanations of what franchising is and what it can offer you, information on how to evaluate and select a franchise that's right for you, and much more. The total number of franchises has doubled since 1985, and there's no end in sight.

Guerilla Financing: Alternative Techniques to Finance Any Small Business Blechman $11.95 **#2779** ©91 pb

If you can get the full amount of money you need to get your business started on a sound financial basis, you'll be much less vulnerable to failure than most small business start-ups. Even if you've been turned down by your bank, run out of collateral, established poor credit, or are completely out of cash, the nontraditional techniques described in this book can help. The authors excel at outlining fresh and innovative "alternative" sources of money available to anyone with a winning idea or business.

On The Air: How to Get on Radio And TV Talk Shows and What to Do When You Get There Parinello $12.95 **#4608** ©91 pb

It's easier than you think to get on the air to promote your product or service, because some 20,000 guests are needed to appear on the more than 1,000 talk shows that fill the airwaves each week. Written by a veteran talk show host, this book shows what hosts really look for in selecting guests, how to prepare for your interview, what to expect on the air, how to use one successful interview to get many more invitations, and how to maximize the impact of your interviews on your business success.

OTHER TOPICS

How to Survive Without a Salary
Long $12.95 **#1845** ©92 pb

Some people decide that the benefits of a steady income come at too high a price. For them, a life of voluntary simplicity can be a richer, more rewarding alternative. Long's book is a guide to the practicalities of such a life, as well as a manifesto for the freedom such a life can bring. How to analyze your true needs, find alternatives to buying, avoid consumer traps, make a casual income, and get along beautifully with less. Subtitled "Learning to Live the Conserver Lifestyle."

Part-Time Travel Agent
Monaghan $24.95 **#4092** ©94 pb

This new, 400-page book shows how to open a home-based travel agency, avoiding the high start-up costs of traditional travel agencies. You can make money booking airlines (access computerized airline reservation systems for just $15 a month), tours, cruises, hotels and car rentals. Not only that, you can get free trips from tour operators eager for your business, and even earn your own frequent flyer miles on <u>other</u> people's travel. A detailed guide to the many opportunities created by recent changes in the travel marketplace. *Highly recommended.*

Freedom Road
Hough $16.95 **#4718** ©91 pb

The author chucked a house, two cars, and a high-paying, high-status job for the freedom of life on the road in an RV. He shows how you can reduce your expenses to where you can support yourself with minimal income (earned from hobby businesses or casual, occasional work), live a comfortable, healthy lifestyle while seeing the country, and have an abundance of time to enjoy your family and friends. Covers beautiful places where you can live for free, earning money, living cheap, choosing the right RV, much more. "(These) distinctive observations and good ideas will appeal to independent-minded individuals seeking a simpler way of living."—*Booklist*

The Credit Repair Kit
Ventura $19.95 **#4090** ©93 pb

Used properly, credit is a tool which can help you launch a business, achieve your goals in life, take advantage of opportunities you would otherwise miss, and be prepared for financial emergencies. Ventura, an attorney specializing in credit issues, gives you all the information you need to be fully in control of your credit. Recommended for those who need to repair their bad credit, those who have no credit history, and anyone with financial goals or dreams they want to achieve.

College Degrees You Can Earn From Home NCC with Judith Frey
$14.95 **#4438** ©95 pb

It's entirely possible to earn a legitimate college degree, from an accredited school, through home study. It can take as little as three to six months and can cost less than $1,000. The problem is that most colleges that offer such programs never advertise—and you don't want anything to do with many of those that do advertise. This new guide covers 100+ accredited colleges that offer degrees through written correspondence, on-line computer instruction, cable TV, video tapes and more. Subtitle: "How to get a first-class degree without attending class."

The Tightwad Gazette: Promoting Thrift as a Viable Lifestyle
Dacyczyn $11.99 **#2573** ©92 pb

It's entirely possible to live cheaply with style and have fun in the process. This collection of the best ideas from Dacyczyn's renegade newsletter shows how to slash your food bills in half, save money on health insurance, save hundreds on utility bills, plus strategies for yard sales, the best tightwad tips from readers around the country and "Lifestyles of the frugal and obscure." We like the layout and homey illustrations, but mainly we like Dacyczyn's cheeky, spirited writing and unique ideas.

The Rummager's Handbook
McClurg $12.95 **#4650** ©95 pb

Collecting and selling secondhand merchandise is an entertaining, productive, environmentally responsible activity for many people, and—as McClurg clearly shows—it can be surprisingly profitable as well. How to bargain easily, effectively and politely with various types of sellers; evaluate the age and worth of everything from collectible glassware to electrical appliances; clean and resore a wide range of goods; and cash in by selling your treasures for top dollar. An interesting, attractively illustrated guide. Subtitle: Finding, Buying, Cleaning, Fixing, Using and Selling Secondhand Treasures

The Haggler's Handbook: One Hour to Negotiating Power
Koren $12.95 **#4152** ©91 hc
The premise of **The Haggler's Handbook** is simple—since you must negotiate each day of your life, you might as well be good at it. Koren offers some 130 tips, tactics and strategies that work whether you're in a rug bazaar, a car showroom, a corporate boardroom or your teenager's disaster-zone bedroom. The book is designed for quick reading, fast reference and maximum usefulness. Each tactic is coded by a graphic symbol indicating whether it is best suited for cooperative, cutthroat, or in-between negotiations. Highly useful, reader-friendly information.

Wishcraft: How to Get What You *Really* Want
Sher $9.95 **#1240** ©79 pb
First published in 1979, this is one of those rare books that tends to dramatically change people's lives. "The most irreverent and refreshing self-help manual now on the market...Feisty, funny, and down-to-earth, this book is bound to benefit all those who sense they may have temporarily lost track of their true goals." *—New Age Magazine*

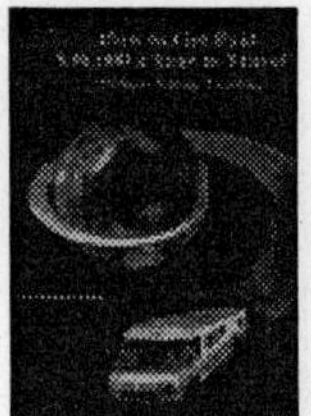

How to Get Paid $30,000 a Year to Travel
Chilton $24.95 **#4626** ©95 pb

You can make $30-$52,000 a year delivering brand new recreational vehicles, limousines, and other specialty vehicles to dealerships around the country (unlike passenger cars, which are delivered by truck). Ordinarily you can use your regular driver's license, you can work full-time, part-time, on vacations, or on weekends—and you can set your own hours. Most companies fly you back home from your trips at *their* expense (but you get to keep the frequent flyer miles). A great opportunity for retired people, couples and others wanting to see the country and be paid for it, all fully detailed in this comprehensive, up-to-date guide.

The 10 Best Opportunities for Starting a Home Business Today New Careers Center/Glenn
$14.95 **#2710** ©93 pb

This is an exceptionally well-written guide that combines start-up information with interesting first-person success stories. A full chapter is devoted to each of the ten best opportunities, and there's a chapter covering considerations common to all. Interesting and informative reading. *Highly recommended.*

I Could Do Anything If Only I Knew What It Was
Sher $11.95 **#4465** ©94 pb

This book—by the author of the bestselling Wishcraft—acknowledges that many of the most competent people can't get what they want *because they just don't know what they want.* Sher notes that everyone's life is filled with clues; everything a person does, or doesn't do, has a good reason behind it. With wisdom and reassurance, she helps peel away the layers, revealing the true hopes and aspirations underlying these clues. Chapters include What Are You Supposed to Be Doing?, Nothing Ever Really Interests Me, I Want Too Many Things—I'm All Over the Map, I've Lost My Big Dream—There's Nothing Left, more.

Free Money When You're Unemployed
Blum $16.95 **#2865** ©96

Blum compiles information on some 1,000 sources of foundation funds available for the millions of Americans now unemployed. These funds—for everything from grocery bills to mortgage payments—are available from foundations and are outright grants rather than loans. Includes contact information, eligibility requirements, etc., including special programs for retirees and those needing aid following a divorce or death of a spouse. According to the author, much of this information has never before been made available to the general public.

ORDERING INFORMATION

(Please see reverse of this page for the order form)

Catalog Requests. We include a copy of "The Whole Work Catalog" with every outgoing order. If you only want to request a catalog, you may do so by calling us at (303) 447-1087 weekdays from 8-5, Mountain Standard Time, or you can drop us a note or fax.

Mastercard/Visa orders may be phoned/faxed in to the number above. $20 minimum on credit card orders, please.

Fax. Our 24-hour fax line is (303) 447-8684.

Our guarantee. We want you to be happy with everything you order from us. If you aren't satisfied with any purchase, please return it to us in new condition any time within **one full year** for a quick and courteous refund. Your satisfaction is our foremost concern.

Delivery. Your order will be shipped promptly, normally within 48 hours, by Bookpost (Special 4th Class Mail). Please allow up to three weeks for delivery, depending on where you live. For faster delivery, we recommend UPS (48 contiguous states). Add $.50 for each item ordered. UPS cannot deliver to a P.O. Box–street address required.

Foreign Shipping Charges. Canadian orders please add 15% of total to basic shipping. All other orders require a U.S. zip code.

Purchase orders: We accept purchase orders from libraries, schools and nonprofit/government agencies. Our Federal I.D.# is 84-1067001. Shipping/handling for invoiced orders is 7% of the merchandise total ($4.50 minimum). Call for our special "institutional" catalog.

The Work-at-Home Sourcebook
Arden $19.95 **#0996** ©94 pb 6th Edition

Please use the order form (reverse of this page) to order additional copies of this book.

ORDER FORM

THE NEW CAREERS CENTER

1515 - 23rd Street, P.O. Box 339-CS, Boulder CO 80306

Name ____________________

Street /apt. no. ____________________

City/State/Zip ____________________

Daytime phone no. ____________________

(in case we need to contact you about your order)

Item No.	Title	Total Price	

Need more room? Just attach another sheet of paper.

Please see reverse page for ordering informating.

Merchandise total		
Colo. residents add 3% tax		
Shipping (except foreign)	4	50
UPS delivery		
TOTAL (U.S. funds only)		

Method of Payment (Sorry, no C.O.D.'s)

☐ Payment enclosed: check or money order for the total amount of ______

☐ Visa ☐ MasterCard Acct. No. ____________________

Credit Card Expiration Date: ______________

Note: $20 minimum on credit card orders, please

X ____________________

Cardholder's signature (required on all credit card orders)